Accountability of Peace Support Operations

International Humanitarian Law Series

VOLUME 9

The International Humanitarian Law Series is a series of monographs and edited volumes which aims to promote scholarly analysis and discussion of both the theory and practice of the international legal regulation of armed conflict.

The series explores substantive issues of International Humanitarian Law including,

- protection for victims of armed conflict and regulation of the means and methods of warfare
- questions of application of the various legal regimes for the conduct of armed conflict
- issues relating to the implementation of International Humanitarian Law obligations
- national and international approaches to the enforcement of the law and
- the interactions between International Humanitarian Law and other related areas of international law such as Human Rights, Refugee Law, Arms Control and Disarmament Law, and International Criminal Law.

The titles in this series are listed at the end of this volume.

Accountability of Peace Support Operations

by

Marten Zwanenburg

MARTINUS NIJHOFF PUBLISHERS
LEIDEN • BOSTON

A C.I.P. Catalogue record for this book is available from the Library of Congress.

Printed on acid-free paper.

ISBN 90 04 14350 5

Koninklijke Brill NV incorporates the imprints Brill Academic Publishers, Martinus Nijhoff Publishers and VSP.

http://www.brill.nl

Typeset by *jules guldenmund layout & text*, The Hague.

Printed and bound in The Netherlands.

Table of contents

Acknowledgements

This book was originally written as a doctoral thesis at the Faculty of Law of Leiden University. It was revised and finalyzed in its current form in August 2004.
There are many people who played a part in various stages of the project, and it is only possible here to mention a few of them. I am grateful first to my supervisor Professor Dr. Horst Fischer for his suggestions and guidance. Professors Nico Schrijver and Niels Blokker were invaluable in commenting on drafts of the book. Bruce Oswald, LL.M., gave useful advice for the purpose of revising the text. I am indebted to Nick Hansen, LL.M., for helping to correct my English. In the personal field, my parents have been a source of continuous warm support both practically and emotionally. Last, but by no means least, I am grateful to my wife Iris for her love and understanding throughout the project.

This book was finalized after I started working as an international lawyer for the Ministry of Defence of the Netherlands. It was written in a personal capacity, and nothing in it should be seen as necessarily reflecting the views of the Netherlands government. Having said this, advising on questions of peace support operations and international humanitarian law on a daily basis has impressed on me the utility as well as the limitations of applying academic research in practice. In practice legal doctrine is not always enough to base solutions on, and the comment made many years ago by Sir Hersch Lauterpacht continues to apply: "If international law is, in some ways, at the vanishing point of law, the law of war is perhaps even more conspicuously, at the vanishing point of international law". I hope this book will make a modest contribution to the field and help to bring it a little closer from the vanishing point.

Leiden

M.C.Z.

Introduction

1 Introduction

In recent years a host of new peace support operations has been established by the United Nations (UN) or by other international actors. In the first half of 2004 alone, the UN established operations in Côte d'Ivoire, Haiti and Burundi, and declared its readiness to establish an operation in Sudan. Many of the operations concerned have been given a comprehensive mandate for the use of force under Chapter VII of the UN Charter. Even in cases where a mandate under Chapter VII is lacking, current doctrine calls for a robust posture.

This situation makes that peace support operations frequently operate in an environment where they may become involved in the use of force. In such an environment the question of the applicability of international humanitarian law, and accountability for breaches of that law, becomes acute. The question of the circumstances in which international humanitarian law applies to peace support operations, if any, has been studied for some time. This has not led to clear answers from a legal perspective, however. Moreover, the question of accountability for breaches of international humanitarian law has largely been neglected.

In recent years a number of important developments have taken place which relate to the application of international humanitarian law to peace support operations. One of these is the promulgation of the Bulletin on Observance of International Humanitarian Law by United Nations Forces by the UN Secretary-General.[1] Another is the entry into force of the Convention on the Safety of United Nations and Associated Personnel.[2]

Also, the question of international accountability has been put high on the international community's agenda. Responsibility for the conduct of peace support operations is an important reference point for the work of the UN International Law Commission's (ILC) work on the responsibility of international organizations.

The above calls for a re-examination of peace support operations and international humanitarian law. This book undertakes that re-examination.

2 Research objective and research questions

This study examines the scope and content of responsibility and accountability for breaches of international humanitarian law by peace support operations. It is concerned with the responsibility and accountability of states and international organiza-

1 Secretary-General's Bulletin, Observance by United Nations Forces of International Humanitarian Law of 6 August 1999, UN Doc. ST/SGB/1999/13.

2 Convention on the Safety of United Nations and Associated Personnel, 9 December 1994, 34 ILM (1995) 482.

tions, not of individuals. This is why it does not include a discussion of the International Criminal Court (ICC), which potentially has an important role to play in preventing and punishing breaches of international humanitarian law by and against peace support operations. However, the ICC is only concerned with individual criminal responsibility.

The central question can be broken down into three main questions. First, to which legal entity must the conduct of a peace support operation be attributed? Principles for the attribution of conduct to states are set out in international humanitarian law instruments and in the ILC's Draft Articles on State Responsibility,[3] but the principles for the attribution of conduct to international organizations are much less developed. It is also necessary to examine whether conduct that is attributable to an international organization can also be attributed to one or more states.

Secondly, what is the scope of international humanitarian law rules which are binding on states and international organizations, that take part in peace support operations? To which international humanitarian law treaties a state is party can be established without much effort. The scope of customary international law rules of international humanitarian law which are binding on states is less clear, although the publication of a useful study by the International Committee of the Red Cross (ICRC) on customary international law is expected. International organizations, however, are not parties to international humanitarian law treaties, and whether and to what extent customary international law and general principles of law apply to them is controversial. One also has to consider the consequences of the special role and nature of the United Nations Security Council. Does this special role exempt the Council, and peace support operations established by it, from the application of international humanitarian law?

Finally, who is entitled to invoke responsibility and accountability for breaches of international humanitarian law by peace support operations, and which mechanisms are available to invoke them? International responsibility and its invocation are traditionally conceived as a relationship between states. International organizations have now joined this group, although the precise conditions under which this has occurred are not yet clear. Individuals could traditionally not invoke international responsibility. Their state of nationality could make a claim on their behalf on the basis of diplomatic protection, but such a claim was based on the state's own interest and not that of the individual. This paradigm has come under pressure from human rights law, which grants individuals rights and, in certain cases, the capacity to invoke international responsibility for breach of those rights. In the light of claims that international humanitarian law also grants rights to individuals, an examination of the possibilities for individuals to invoke responsibility for a breach of those rights by a peace support operation is in order. Such an examination is also justified by the present attention, in legal and international relations scholarship, for the accountability of international organizations, as illustrated by the work of the International Law Association (ILA) committee on this topic. In the work on accountability of international organizations

3 Report of the International Law Commission on the work of its fifty-third session, 23 April – 1 June and 2 July – 10 August 2001, UN Doc. A/56/10, at 43.

there is a strong focus on the accountability toward individuals who are harmed or potentially harmed by activities of international organizations. Although it is difficult to outline the precise legal framework in which accountability operates, it is certain that it has important consequences for international organizations, including for their international responsibility as a component of accountability.

The purpose of this study is to contribute to an understanding of the role of international humanitarian law in peace support operations. It is intended in the first place as a contribution to the academic debate. A deliberate attempt has also been made, however, in particular through making proposals for the establishment of mechanisms to invoke responsibility and accountability in Chapter 6, to make a practical contribution to the protection of persons in time of armed conflict or occupation.

3 Methodology and materials

A primary focus of this study is to discuss and analyze the present state of public international law as it applies to peace support operations and international humanitarian law. This is commonly referred to as the *lex lata*. In comparison with other fields of law, establishing the law as it is in international law presents particular difficulties. As Rosenne argues, this is due to: the substance of the material; its widely diffused, interdisciplinary and unsystematic presentation; the broad variety of primary source-materials to be examined; the many languages in which they are written; the relative inaccessibility of much of this material; and, above all, the essential characteristics of public international law.[4] This study is based on a wide variety of materials. These include in the first instance those referred to in Article 38 of the Statute of the International Court of Justice (ICJ) to be applied by the Court in settling disputes. The list in the article should be regarded as pointing toward the materials where the answer in terms of public international law can be found.[5]

Other materials, not mentioned in Article 38 but nevertheless commonly regarded as valid legal materials have also been used. This category includes in particular resolutions of international organizations.

This study makes relatively extensive reference to legal literature and to the deliberations of private bodies devoted to the study of international law. The latter include in particular the work of the Institut de Droit International (IDI) and the ILA. These materials are part of the "teachings of the most highly qualified publicists" mentioned in Article 38 of the Statute of the ICJ, even though that article refers to them only as subsidiary materials. Because there are relatively few 'primary' materials such as treaties or state practice in the areas of international law that are the subject of this study, such as the law of the responsibility of international organizations, the teachings of publicists take on greater importance than they would if more 'primary' sources existed. This kind of material is particularly open to the criticism that it reflects national or personal prejudices. This criticism however applies to any interpretation of the law,

4 S. Rosenne, Practice and Methods of International Law 1 (1984).

5 *Id.*, at 18.

which is done in the light of ideals and ethico-legal principles which are at its basis and within its sociological context.[6]

The latter applies in particular to the part of this study which is devoted to the law as it ought to be, or *lex ferenda*. This study argues that the proposals that are made will have certain salutary practical results. At the same time, the proposals are reflective of the author's policy preferences.

4 Object of study

The object of this study is the conduct of peace support operations. In particular, this study focuses on peace support operations under the command and control of the UN and the North Atlantic Treaty Organization (NATO). Other international organizations have also undertaken peace support operations or are making preparations for undertaking them. The Economic Community of West African States (ECOWAS) for example has carried out peace support operations in Liberia and Sierra Leone, and in December 2002 decided to deploy an operation in Ivory Coast.[7] The European Union (EU) is likely to play an important role in the deployment of peace support operations in the future. The 1999 Cologne European Council decided that the Council should have the ability to take decisions on the full range of conflict prevention and crisis management tasks, referred to as the 'Petersberg tasks', defined in the Maastricht Treaty. To this end, it decided that the Union must have the capacity for autonomous action, backed up by credible military forces, the means to decide to use them, and a readiness to do so, in order to respond to international crises. This decision set in motion a process that has led to the deployment by the European Union of an international civil police force in Bosnia Herzegovina in January 2003, the deployment of an EU operation in the Former Yugoslav Republic of Macedonia, and a decision to take over the lead of the peace support operation in Bosnia Herzegovina from NATO.[8]

Despite the role of these other organizations, this study is limited to UN and NATO peace support operations, because these two organizations presently appear to dominate the scene in respect of peace support operations and it is likely that they will continue to play an important role in the future. These two organizations have proven military structures, whereas the EU, for example, does not at present. Peace support operations by African organizations are limited by financial constraints.

More specifically than the conduct of UN and NATO peace support operations in general, the object of study is conduct of peace support operations that allegedly involves breaches of international humanitarian law. It may be noted that this is not a hypothetical possibility, as illustrated by the following examples.

The UN Security Council established the United Nations Operation in the Congo (ONUC) in July 1960 to provide the government of the Republic of the Congo with

6 See H.J. Morgenthau, *Positivism, Functionalism, and International Law*, 34 American Journal of International Law 260 (1940), in particular at 269.

7 D. Ba, *Region Pledges Ivory Coast Force, Urges UN Action*, Reuters, 18 December 2002.

8 Council Joint Action on the European Union Military Operation in Bosnia and Herzegovina, OJ L 252 of 28 July 2004, at 10.

such military assistance as might be necessary until, through that government's efforts with UN technical assistance, the national security forces might be able, in the opinion of the government, to fully realize their tasks. The initial mandate of ONUC was to ensure the withdrawal of Belgian forces from the Republic of the Congo, to assist the government in maintaining law and order and to provide technical assistance. The function of ONUC was subsequently modified to include maintaining the territorial integrity and political independence of the Congo, preventing the occurrence of civil war and securing the removal from the Congo of all foreign military, paramilitary and advisory personnel not under UN command, and all mercenaries. The operation was mainly involved in preventing the armed secession of the Katanga province. In the course of carrying out this mandate the force became involved in hostilities with Katangese forces and foreign mercenaries. These operations gave rise to accusations by governments and non-governmental organizations of breaches of international humanitarian law by the UN troops. In particular, the Belgian government complained to the UN about the death of several Belgian civilians, killed by UN forces in the course of the operations, and it urged the UN Secretary-General to:

> issue immediate instructions that United Nations troops should scrupulously respect the obligations of the Geneva Convention and take all necessary measures to safeguard the lives and property of the civilian population, as unfortunately does not appear to be the case at present.[9]

The Belgian government made the following specific charges:

(1) On several occasions, civilians could not be removed from areas of military operations, despite urgent requests; in particular, the urgent representations of the delegate of the International Red Cross for the evacuation of persons trapped in the new hospital met with no response.
(2) Hospitals have been hit, not by isolated shells, but by mortar fire apparently aimed at them, resulting in the wounding of hospital staff and in heavy damage and leading to protests by M. Olivet, delegate of the International Red Cross.
(3) Civilians not taking part in any military operation have been wounded or even killed in their homes by mortar and machine-gun fire.

The United Nations Operation in Somalia (UNOSOM I) was established by the UN Security Council in April 1992 to monitor a cease-fire in Mogadishu, the capital of Somalia, between parties to the civil war in that country, and to provide protection and security for UN personnel, equipment and supplies at the seaports and airports in Mogadishu and escort deliveries of humanitarian supplies from there to distribution centers in the city and its immediate environs. After the situation in the country deteriorated, the Security Council in December 1992 authorized member states to form a Unified Task Force (UNITAF) to establish a safe environment for the delivery of humanitarian assistance. UNITAF, led by the United States, was not under UN command and control and was much more robust than UNOSOM I. It worked in

---

9 Quoted in F. Seyersted, United Nations Forces in the Law of Peace and War 194 (1966).

coordination with UNOSOM I to secure major population centers and ensure that humanitarian assistance was delivered and distributed. In March 1993 the Security Council established UNOSOM II to take over from UNITAF. This operation was given a strong mandate which allowed it to use force to achieve certain objectives. UNOSOM II became involved in a number of violent incidents with local forces, in which force members were killed. In February 1994, after several violent incidents and attacks on UN soldiers, the Security Council revised UNOSOM II's mandate to exclude the use of coercive methods. UNOSOM II was withdrawn in early March 1995. A number of non-governmental organizations have accused UNOSOM of breaches of international humanitarian law. The non-governmental organization African Rights issued a report in 1993 detailing alleged breaches of international humanitarian law.[10] The report includes allegations of an attack on a hospital, the shooting of unarmed persons taking part in demonstrations, other killings of unarmed persons in unwarranted circumstances, illegal detentions, demolition of property and forced relocations of persons. Amnesty International published a report in 1994 on peacekeeping and human rights in which it expressed its concern about the conduct of UN troops in Somalia and in which it stated that "some of the civilians killed by UN or US troops seem to have been victims of the use of lethal force in breach of human rights and International Humanitarian Law obligations".[11] Belgian, Italian and Canadian personnel have been prosecuted in their home countries for abuses of the civilian population during the operations in Somalia.

The UN Security Council authorized the establishment of the Kosovo Force (KFOR) led by NATO, after the air campaign against the Federal Republic of Yugoslavia (FRY) had been suspended on 10 June 1999 and after the conclusion of a Military Technical Agreement between NATO and the Federal Republic of Yugoslavia on 9 June, which provided for the withdrawal of Yugoslav forces from Kosovo and the deployment of a peace support operation. The operation's mandate includes the tasks of maintaining and where necessary enforcing a cease-fire, establishing a secure environment in which refugees and displaced persons can return home in safety and the international civil presence can operate, a transitional administration can be established, and humanitarian aid can be delivered. The operation was also mandated to ensure public safety and order until the international civil presence established by the UN could take responsibility for this task. The force has not become involved in hostilities like ONUC and UNOSOM, but non-governmental organizations, human rights monitoring bodies and the Organization for Security and Cooperation in Europe (OSCE) have criticized conduct by the Kosovo Force, in particular conduct relating to law enforcement. This conduct includes the shooting of a man, claimed by KFOR to be a sniper, in Mitrovica in February 2000, and the subsequent detention of several persons, allegedly under inhumane conditions.[12] The Special Representative of the United Nations Commission on Human Rights on the

---

10 African Rights, Somalia: Human Rights Abuses by the United Nations Forces (1993).

11 Amnesty International, Peace-keeping and Human Rights 13 (1994).

12 Amnesty International, Setting the Standard? UNMIK and KFOR's Response to the Violence in Mitrovica (2000).

situation of human rights in the former Yugoslavia has expressed his concern about military detentions by KFOR.[13] If, as it arguably does, the law of occupation is applicable in Kosovo,[14] international humanitarian law is the relevant law to determine whether this conduct is legal.

5 Outline of the study

This study is divided into three parts. The first part is concerned with the attribution of conduct of peace support operations. Second, the scope of applicability of rules of international humanitarian law in peace support operations is examined. The third and final part contains an analysis of the existing possibilities for invoking responsibility and accountability of peace support operations for breaches of international humanitarian law, complemented by proposals for improving the means for invoking responsibility and accountability.

Part I starts with a discussion in Chapter 1 of the content of the expression 'peace support operation' as it is used in this study. This requires a historical overview of the creation and the evolution of such operations, from the United Nations Emergency Force (UNEF) established in 1956 to the variety of operations presently deployed by the UN and NATO. Such an overview is necessary to understand the distinctions between the many existing 'peace' terms, and to define the object of study. Special legal and operational characteristics of peace support operations are identified. These characteristics are essential as the basis for an examination of the attribution of the conduct of peace support operations in Chapter 2. A theory on the attribution of conduct of peace support operations to the international organization establishing the operation, troop contributing states and the member states of the organization is presented, based on an analysis of elements of the law of state responsibility and the emerging law of the responsibility of international organizations as mainly demonstrated through state and organization practice as well as the work of the ILC.

Part II in Chapter 3 deals with the question of the scope of application of international humanitarian law to peace support operations. This requires a discussion of the extent to which the UN and NATO are bound by general international law, and the consequences of the special position of the UN Security Council in this respect. It also requires an examination of the threshold of application of international humani-

13 Report of the Special Representative of the Commission on Human Rights on the situation of human rights in Bosnia and Herzegovina and the Federal Republic of Yugoslavia, Jose Cutileiro of 8 January 2002, UN Doc. E/CN.4/2002/41, at 23-24, para. 86-91. See also OSCE Department of Human Rights and Rule of Law, Kosovo: A Review of the Criminal Justice System 1 September 2000 - 28 February 2001 (2001).

14 J. Cerone, *Minding the Gap: Outlining KFOR Accountability in Post-Conflict Kosovo*, 12 European Journal of International Law 469 (2001), at 484-485; T. Irmscher, *The Legal Framework for the Activities of the United Nations Interim Administration Mission in Kosovo: The Charter, Human Rights, and the Law of Occupation*, 44 German Yearbook of International Law 353 (2001); but see J. Burger, *International Humanitarian Law and the Kosovo Crisis: Lessons Learned or to Be Learned*, 82 International Review of the Red Cross 129 (2000).

tarian law; that is, when a peace support operation can be considered to be a party to an armed conflict or in occupation of a territory, triggering the application of international humanitarian law. Chapter 4 addresses the legal consequences of responsibility and accountability for violations of international humanitarian law, based on a discussion of the law of state responsibility and responsibility of international organizations and the practice in peace support operations.

Part III focuses on the practical implementation of responsibility and accountability, particularly the possibilities for the invocation of these concepts. Chapter 5 provides an overview of the existing mechanisms for invoking responsibility and accountability. The chapter focuses in particular on the mechanisms that are at the disposal of individuals. The idea underlying this approach is that since international humanitarian law grants rights to individuals, there should also be a mechanism for individuals to obtain redress when these rights are violated. The chapter concludes that present mechanisms are not effective. Consequently, Chapter 6 proposes the modification of existing mechanisms and the establishment of new mechanisms to improve the legal position of individuals that are injured by breaches of international humanitarian law by peace support operations. The chapter includes an exploration of the ombudsperson concept, which is the basis for a proposal to establish an international humanitarian law ombudsman in peace support operations.

Part IV recapitulates the main findings of this study and its conclusions.

Table of Abbreviations

ACTORD	Activation Order
AFNORTH	Allied Forces North
AOI	Arab Organization for Industrialization
AOR	Area of Responsibility
AU	African Union
AUC	Autodefensas Unidas de Colombia
CEMAC	Communauté Économique et Monétaire de l'Afrique Centrale
CINCSOUTH	Commander in Chief Allied Forces, Southern Europe
DRC	Democratic Republic of the Congo
ECHR	European Court of Human Rights
ECOWAS	Economic Community of West African States
EPIL	Encyclopedia of Public International Law
ESDP	European Security and Defence Policy
EU	European Union
FARC	Fuerzas Armadas Revolucionarias de Colombia
FC	Force Commander
FRY	Federal Republic of Yugoslavia
FYROM	Former Yugoslav Republic of Macedonia
ICC	International Criminal Court
ICCPR	International Covenant on Civil and Political Rights
ICJ	International Court of Justice
ICRC	International Committee of the Red Cross
ICTR	International Criminal Tribunal for Rwanda
ICTY	International Criminal Tribunal for the former Yugoslavia
IDI	Institut de Droit International
IFC	International Finance Corporation
IFOR	Implementation Force
ILA	International Law Association
ILC	International Law Commission
INTERFET	International Force for East Timor
ISAF	International Security Assistance Force
ITC	International Tin Council
KFOR	Kosovo Force
MIGA	Multilateral Investment Guarantee Agency
MINURSO	Mission des Nations Unies pour l'Organisation d'un Référendum au Sahara
MONUC	Mission de l'Organisation des Nations Unies en République Démocratique du Congo
MRT	Moldovan Republic of Transdniestria
NAC	North Atlantic Council
NATO	North Atlantic Treaty Organization

OAS	Organization of American States
OAU	Organization of African Unity
OJ	Official Journal of the European Union
ONUC	Opération des Nations Unies au Congo
OPLAN	Operation Plan
OSCE	Organization for Security and Cooperation in Europe
PLO	Palestine Liberation Organization
PSO	Peace Support Operation
ROE	Rules of Engagement
SACEUR	Supreme Allied Commander, Europe
SFOR	Stabilization Force
SHAPE	Supreme Headquarters Allied Powers Europe
SNA	Somali National Alliance
SOFA	Status of Forces Agreement
SRSG	Special Representative of the Secretary-General
TOA	Transfer of Authority
UN	United Nations
UNAMIR	United Nations Assistance Mission for Rwanda
UNAMSIL	United Nations Mission in Sierra Leone
UNEF	United Nations Emergency Force
UNFICYP	United Nations Force in Cyprus
UNIFIL	United Nations Interim Force in Lebanon
UNITAF	Unified Task Force
UNJY	United Nations Juridical Yearbook
UNMEE	United Nations Mission in Ethiopia and Eritrea
UNMIK	United Nations Mission in Kosovo
UNOSOM	United Nations Operation in Somalia
UNPROFOR	United Nations Protection Force
UNTSO	United Nations Truce Supervision Organization
USC	United Somali Congress

1

Definition and Characteristics of Peace Support Operations

1.1 Introduction

Since the subject matter of this study is 'peace support operations' it seems necessary to give a definition of this term. Also, because the characteristics of peace support operations have important consequences for the attribution of responsibility for their conduct it seems necessary to describe these characteristics in some detail. These, the definition of peace support operations and a description of their characteristics, are the purposes of this chapter.

Giving a definition of peace operations is however not easy. Different operations which are all referred to as 'peace support operations' by the UN, NATO or writers can differ widely in the field. The Panel on United Nations Peace Operations in its 2000 report, often referred to as the 'Brahimi report' in reference to the chairman of the Panel, states that: "United Nations peace operations entail three principal activities: conflict prevention and peacemaking; peacekeeping; and peace building."[1] But officials of the UN, NATO, doctrinal publications of different national armed forces and writers use other terms to describe the same operations and distinguish between different subcategories. The Special Committee on Peacekeeping Operations established by the UN General Assembly in 1965, with a mandate of a comprehensive review of the whole question of peacekeeping operations in all their aspects, has tried to develop guidelines for further peace operations. The Committee produced 'Draft Articles of Guidelines for United Nations Peacekeeping Operations under the Authority of the Security Council and in Accordance with the Charter of the United Nations' in 1974. The most recent version of the draft was published in 1977 but it has not been adopted in final version.[2]

Absence of a clear definition is at least in part a consequence of the way in which peace support operations have developed. The terms 'peace operations', 'peace support operations' or 'peacekeeping' do not appear in the UN Charter. The concept was invented as an improvised and practical response to the failure of the United Nations Charter system of collective security. Ryan states that "peacekeeping began as an unplanned response to a particular set of problems at a particular time."[3] It has continued to develop

1 Report of the Panel on United Nations Peace Operations of 21 August 2000, UN Doc. A/55/305, S/2000/809, para. 10.

2 Report of the Special Committee on Peace-Keeping Operations, eleventh report of the working group of 2 December 1977, UN Doc. A/32/394.Ann.2, Appendix 1.

3 S. Ryan, *United Nations Peace-keeping: A Matter of Principles?*, in T. Woodhouse & O. Ramsbotham (Eds.), Peacekeeping and Conflict Resolution 27 (2000).

since its initiation as the UN has tried to manage conflicts changing in nature. Definitions are influenced to a large extent by historical events, so that a historical account is necessary to properly understand the context and connotations of a definition.

It must be pointed out that the absence of express reference to the concept of peace support operations from the UN Charter has led to debates on their constitutional basis in the Charter. Until the 1990s peace operations were considered to fall between Chapters VI and VII of the UN Charter,[4] although writers tried to find more specific answers.[5] Clearly such a conclusion is no longer appropriate for operations in the 1990s that were established on the basis of Chapter VII.[6] In any case the constitutional basis of peace operations as such is not directly relevant to the questions that this study is concerned with and will therefore be left out of the discussion.

1.2 Initiation of peace support operations under UN command

The official view in the UN is that the United Nations Truce Supervision Organization (UNTSO) was the first UN peace support operation.[7] After the General Assembly had adopted a partition plan for Palestine in 1947, fighting broke out. It intensified when Jewish leaders proclaimed the state of Israel. The Security Council called for a cease-fire which was accepted by the parties in question. Because of the Cold War the United States and the Soviet Union were not willing to let the other intervene. UNTSO was established by the Security Council as a neutral third party to supervise the observance of the cessation of hostilities.[8] It consisted of unarmed military observers acting with the consent of the parties in question.

The United Nations Emergency Force (UNEF) was instrumental in the development of the concept of peace support operations.[9] On 26 July 1956 Egyptian President Gamal Nasser nationalized the Suez Canal area. Israel in response attacked Egypt, followed by a British-French ultimatum to both parties to end the hostilities within twelve hours or face intervention by them. On 3 November, British and French paratroopers

---

4 It is difficult to subsume all these various operations under any one clause of the Charter. It is clear that they fall short of the provisions of Chapter VII described above, which deal with enforcement. At the same time they go beyond purely diplomatic means or those described in Chapter VI of the Charter. As former Secretary-General Dag Hammerskjöld put it, peace-keeping might be put in a new Chapter 'Six and a Half'. United Nations, The Blue Helmets: A Review of United Nations Peacekeeping 5 (1990).

5 See *e.g.* J. Halderman, *Legal Basis for United Nations Armed Forces*, 56 American Journal of International Law 971 (1962); D. Ciobanu, *The Power of the Security Council to Organize Peace-Keeping Operations*, in A. Cassese (Ed.), United Nations Peace-Keeping: Legal Essays 15 (1978).

6 See N. White, *The UN Charter and Peacekeeping Forces: Constitutional Issues*, in M. Pugh (Ed.), The UN, Peace and Force 43 (1997).

7 United Nations, The Blue Helmets: A Review of United Nations Peacekeeping 4 (1996).

8 Security Council Resolution 50 of 29 May 1948, UN Doc. S/RES/50 (1948).

9 For an account of the establishment of UNEF see M. Fröhlich, *Keeping Track of UN Peace-keeping – Suez, Srebrenica, Rwanda and the Brahimi Report*, 5 Max Planck Yearbook of United Nations Law 185 (2001), at 192-211. See also R. Higgins, United Nations Peacekeeping: Documents and Commentary: 1, the Middle East (1969).

commenced their invasion of Egypt. Between these dates there was much diplomatic action that focused on the General Assembly because of the threat of the British or French veto in the Security Council. In these circumstances a proposal by Canadian Foreign Minister Lester Pearson for an international force with a mandate to keep the peace found more and more support. On 3 November the General Assembly adopted a resolution requesting the Secretary-General to submit a plan for setting up, with the consent of the nations concerned, an emergency force to secure and supervise the cessation of hostilities.[10] On 4 November Secretary-General Dag Hammarskjöld presented an interim report and on 6 November a final report that laid down principles for the force which until now are quoted as authoritative principles for peace support operations .[11] These principles included that the chief officer of the force should be appointed by the United Nations, and that he should be responsible ultimately to the General Assembly and the Security Council. His authority should be so defined as to make him fully independent of any one nation. Another principle was that since the force resulted from General Assembly action according to the Uniting for Peace Resolution, the force could not use powers under Chapter VII of the United Nations Charter, which could only be invoked by the Security Council. The legal basis of the force's presence rested on the consent of the parties concerned. Hammarskjöld stated that the force was limited in its operations "to the extent that consent of the parties concerned is required under generally recognized international law."[12] On the basis of these principles General Assembly Resolution 1001 established UNEF.[13] Because it was the first armed peace operation that could use force in self-defense, the operation was a major departure from the past practice of sending only a few unarmed observers.

UN Secretary-General Dag Hammarskjöld insisted on specific principles for the force because he was convinced that the force should set a precedent for future operations. He prepared two reports on the experience derived from the establishment and operation of the force.[14] In the second report he stated that in:

> the following paragraphs, certain principles and rules are laid down in the light of the experience gathered in the past years, which, if they were to meet with the approval of the General Assembly, would provide a continuing basis on which useful contacts might be established with interested Governments, with the aim of being prepared for any requests which might arise from future decisions by the Assembly on a force or similar arrangement to deal with a specific case.[15]

The three main principles identified were consent of the host state to the presence of the force; impartiality of the force and non-intervention in the state's domestic affairs; and the non-use of force except in self-defense. Some writers add the exclusion of the

---

10 General Assembly Resolution 998 of 4 November 1956, UN Doc. A/RES/998 (ES-I).

11 UN Doc. A/3289 of 4 November 1956 and UN Doc. A/3302 of 6 November 1956.

12 UN Doc. A/3302 of 6 November 1956, para. 9.

13 General Assembly Resolution 1001 of 7 November 1956, UN Doc. A/RES/1001 (ES-I).

14 UN Doc. A/3694 of 9 October 1957 and UN Doc. A/3943 of 9 October 1958.

15 UN Doc. A/3943 of 9 October 1958.

permanent members of the Security Council from participating, and UN control over the force, to the list.[16]

1.3 Development of the concept of peace support operations

The principles established by UNEF were the model for peace support operations in the next decades. Until the withdrawal of the force in 1967, after Egypt withdrew its consent, seven other peace operations were established in what could be called an 'assertive period' of peace operations. The withdrawal of UNEF called into question the effectiveness of peace operations, causing no new operations to be created until 1973 in a dormant period. After 1973 there was a resurgent period in which three new operations were established including a second United Nations Emergency Force (UNEF II) in Egypt to supervise the cessation of hostilities between Israel and Egypt after the Yom Kippur war.[17] Between 1978 and 1988 there was again a period in which no new operations were established.

Some of these operations established between 1956 and 1988 consisted of observers who did not carry arms and whose task was to monitor the situation in a particular area and report to the organization, similar to UNTSO. Other operations consisted of armed military forces with a broader mandate, similar to UNEF. Together, these two kinds of operations were called 'peace-keeping operations' by the UN. A 1990 UN monograph on peace operations stated:

> United Nations peace-keeping operations can be divided into broad categories: observer missions, which consist largely of officers who are almost invariably unarmed; and peace-keeping forces, which consist of lightly armed infantry units, with the necessary logistic support elements.[18]

These categories are not watertight. For example, unarmed observers may assist an armed operation. All the operations established until 1988 to a large extent were based on the principles developed in UNEF reviewed above.

Consent of the host state is a principle that necessarily arises out of the character of peace operations – at least until 1988 – as operations not established under Chapter VII of the UN Charter. They are bound by Article 2 (7) of the Charter, which provides that nothing shall authorize the UN to intervene in matters which are essentially within the domestic jurisdiction of any state. Except when the Security Council decides to send a force under Chapter VII, the initial consent of the host state to the entry of the force is legally required. Such consent has to be continuous. Once it is withdrawn the operation can no longer stay in the country. This was illustrated by the withdrawal of UNEF after the Egyptian government formally asked for the force to

16 M. Goulding, *The Evolution of United Nations Peacekeeping*, 69 International Affairs 451 (1993); D. Brown, *The Role of the United Nations in Peacekeeping and Truce-monitoring: What are the Applicable Norms*, 27 Revue Belge de Droit International 559 (1994).

17 Security Council Resolution 340 of 25 October 1973, UN Doc. S/RES/340.

18 United Nations, *supra* note 4, at 8.

be withdrawn from its territory on 18 May 1967.[19] In a report on the withdrawal of UNEF, Secretary-General U Thant stated in relation to the General Assembly resolutions on the force that it:

> was thus a basic legal principle arising from the nature of the Force, and clearly understood by all concerned, that the consent of Egypt was a prerequisite to the stationing of UNEF on Egyptian territory, and it was a practical necessity as well in acquiring contingents for the Force.[20]

In interstate conflict it is clear that the consent of the governments concerned is required. In intra-state conflict, however, the question is whether the consent of other, non-state actors, is required. In contrast to host-state consent, consent of non-state actors is not legally necessary. This is illustrated for example by the establishment of United Nations Interim Force in Lebanon (UNIFIL). In the relevant resolution the Security Council refers only to the request from the government of Lebanon to establish such a force, even though the government did not control a large part of its territory.[21] Similarly, the Security Council has continued to extend the mandate of the United Nations Force in Cyprus (UNFICYP) referring to the consent of the government of Cyprus even though a large part of the island is controlled by another administration supported by Turkey.[22] In practice the UN has always tried to gain the consent of relevant actors other than the host state as a matter of practical necessity. A peace support operation is not able to function without the co-operation of the parties on the ground. This practical necessity in certain cases also results in reference to non-state actors in enabling resolutions. The preamble to Security Council Resolution 872 establishing the United Nations Assistance Mission in Rwanda (UNAMIR), for example, stressed the urgency of the deployment of an international force "as underlined both by the Government of the Republic of Rwanda and by the Rwandese Patriotic Front."[23]

Impartiality is the requirement that a force is not to advance the interests of one party against those of another.[24] Hammarskjöld, in his final report on the establishment of the Emergency Force, stated that the UN did not intend to "influence the military balance in the conflict and, thereby, the political balance affecting efforts to settle the conflict."[25] The principle of impartiality is related to the character of peace

19 See *e.g.* N. Elaraby, *United Nations Peacekeeping by Consent: A Case Study of the Withdrawal of the United Nations Emergency Force*, in J. Norton Moore (Ed.), The Arab-Israeli Conflict, Volume II: Readings 620 (1974).

20 UN Doc. A/6730/Add.3 of 26 June 1967, para. 70.

21 Security Council Resolution 425 of 19 March 1978, UN Doc. S/RES/425.

22 See *e.g.* Security Council Resolution 1416 of 13 June 2002, UN Doc. S/RES/1416.

23 Security Council Resolution 872 of 5 October 1993, UN Doc. S/RES/872.

24 See S. Vohra, *Impartiality in United Nations Peace-Keeping*, 9 Leiden Journal of International Law 63 (1996).

25 UN Doc. A/3302 of 6 November 1956, para. 8.

operations as a holding action, an attempt to create a peaceful environment in which the parties themselves can resolve their disputes peacefully.

The requirement of the non-use of force except in self-defense is related to the requirement of consent. In principle a peace support operation has the co-operation of the host state and does not need to resort to force. The co-operation of the parties should guarantee that problems are resolved through negotiation. The only exception is the use of force in self-defense. Such use of force cannot be excluded because it is an inherent right. According to a memorandum of the United Nations Office of Legal Affairs "the use of force in self-defense is an inherent right of United Nations forces exercised to preserve a collective and individual defense."[26] The concept of self-defense in peace support operations evolved over time.[27] Hammarskjöld wrote in his report on UNEF that the:

> rule is applied that men engaged in the operation may never take the initiative in the use of armed force, but are entitled to respond with force to an attack with arms, including attempts to use force to make them withdraw from positions which they occupy under orders from the Commander, acting under the authority of the Assembly and within the scope of its resolutions. The basic element involved is clearly the prohibition against any initiative in the use of armed force.[28]

In the case of UNFICYP the definition of 'self-defense' was expanded. The Secretary-General in an *aide-mémoire* repeated the rule that troops were not to take the initiative in the use of armed force but also stated that they could use force in self-defense where:

> specific arrangements accepted by both communities have been or ... are about to be violated, thus risking a recurrence of fighting or endangering law and order ... [or where there were] attempts by force to prevent them from carrying out their responsibilities as ordered by their commanders.[29]

In the case of the second United Nations Emergency Force (UNEF II), self-defense was redefined as including "resistance to attempts by forceful means to prevent it from discharging its duties under the mandate of the Security Council."[30] This definition may be regarded as covering all subsequent UN peace operations.

These definitions of self-defense by the Secretary-General are broad guidelines which require interpretation, as described for example in a case study on UNIFIL.[31]

---

26 UNJY 1993, at 372.

27 K. Cox, *Beyond Self-defense: United Nations Peacekeeping Operations & the Use of Force*, 27 Denver Journal of International Law & Policy 239 (1999).

28 UN Doc. A/3943 of 8 October 1958, para. 179.

29 UN Doc. S/5653 (1964), para. 17 (c)-18 (c).

30 UN Doc. S/11052/Rev.1 of 12 October 1973, para. 4 (a).

31 R. Murphy, *UN Peacekeeping in Lebanon and the Use of Force*, 6 International Peacekeeping 38 (1999).

Definitions by the Secretary-General are political statements which are not appropriate for use by the members of a peace operation in the field. Rules of Engagement (ROE) express the military consequences of these political guidelines.[32] United States military doctrine states that in:

> peace operations, ROE define when and how force may be used. ROE may reflect the law of armed conflict and operational considerations but are principally concerned with restraints on the use of force. ROE are also the primary means by which commanders convey legal, political, diplomatic, and military guidance to the military force.[33]

In UN peace operations ROE are developed and issued by the UN although troop-contributing states may be involved in their development.[34] Each operation has rules of engagement which apply to all contingents, but in translations of these rules for individual contingents by their governments further restrictions may be imposed. Sometimes commanders interpret rules in a way that conflicts with the interpretation by other commanders.[35]

A definition of 'peacekeeping operations' by the UN in 1990 reflects these principles which developed in the practice of peace support operations described above:

> As the United Nations practice has evolved over the years, a peacekeeping operation has come to be defined as an operation involving military personnel, but without enforcement powers, undertaken by the United Nations to help maintain or restore international peace and security in areas of conflict. These operations are voluntary and are based on consent and co-operation. While they involve the use of military personnel, they achieve their objectives not by force of arms, thus contrasting them with the 'enforcement action' of the United Nations under Article 42.[36]

1.4 New developments in peace support operations after 1988

In 1990, however, the classical model of peace support operations was already changing. The deployment of the United Nations Transition Assistance Group (UNTAG) in Namibia in 1989 marked the first of a new type of peace operations.[37] These opera-

32 See *e.g.* A. Paphiti, *Rules of Engagement within Multinational Land Operations*, 89 Militair Rechtelijk Tijdschrift 1 (1996).

33 United States Field Manual 100-23, Peace Operations, Chapter 3.

34 As expressed for example by the government of the Netherlands in a letter to parliament relating to the United Nations Mission in Ethiopia and Eritrea. Bijlagen Handelingen II 2000-01, 22 831, nr. 10, at 17.

35 See *e.g.* B. Janssens, *Les Règles d'Engagement pendant les Opérations des Nations Unies en Somalie*, 35 Military Law and Law of War Review 209 (1996).

36 United Nations, *supra* note 4, at 4.

37 See *e.g.* N.J. Schrijver, *Introducing Second Generation Peace-keeping: the case of Namibia*, 6 African Journal of International and Comparative Law 1 (1994).

tions were deployed as part of a negotiated political settlement and the responsibilities of peacekeepers included a range of new tasks such as disarmament, resettlement of refugees, police training and supervision and election monitoring. Such operations were referred to as 'complex', 'multifunctional' or 'second-generation' operations to distinguish them from first generation operations the principal function of which was limited to separation of the parties.[38] United Nations Secretary-General Boutros-Ghali wrote in a 1992 article that it:

> is now almost always the case that operations undertaken by the United Nations must include civilian police, electoral personnel, human rights experts, information specialists, and a significant number of political advisory staff.
> U.N. operations may now involve nothing less than the reconstruction of an entire society and state. This requires a comprehensive approach, over an extended period.[39]

In this period East-West relations improved and there was an unprecedented level of political will on the part of most of its members, most significantly the five permanent members, to address a broad range of conflicts leading to the establishment of five new operations in 1988-1989 alone.[40] This optimism was reflected in the Secretary-General's 1992 Agenda for Peace, a strategy document for United Nations action in preventive diplomacy, peacemaking and peacekeeping.[41] Two proposed departures from previous practice in An Agenda for Peace were critical. First, the document defined peacekeeping as the "deployment of a United Nations presence in the field, *hitherto* with the consent of all the parties concerned."[42] Here was a clear signal that the UN might, in some instances, seek to deploy operations without consent of the parties to the conflict. Second, the document proposed the utilization of 'peace-enforcement units' in cases where the UN is called upon to send forces to restore and maintain a cease-fire and this task exceeds the mission of peace-keeping forces and the expectations of peace-keeping force contributors. Such peace-enforcement units would be warranted under Article 40 of the UN Charter.

These proposals demonstrated a willingness to depart from the established principles of peace operations. In the same 1992 article referred to above, the Secretary-General wrote:

---

38 See *e.g.* R. Lee, *United Nations Peacekeeping: Developments and Prospects*, 28 Cornell International Law Journal 619 (1995); M. Griffin, *Retrenchment, Reform and Regionalization: Trends in UN Peace Support Operations*, 6 International Peacekeeping 1 (1999), at 2.

39 B. Boutros-Ghali, *Beyond Peacekeeping*, 25 New York University Journal of International Law and Politics 113 (1992), at 115.

40 D. Malone & K. Wermester, *The Changing Nature of UN Peacekeeping*, 7 International Peacekeeping 37 (2000), at 39.

41 UN Doc. S/24111 of 17 June 1992, reproduced in 31 ILM 953 (1992). See specifically paragraph 3 for the optimism in United Nations action.

42 *Id.*, para. 20 (emphasis added).

> And when the established rules of engagement for peacekeeping operations are no longer sufficient, U.N. forces may need authorization to demonstrate a resolve to use force. If this is not effective, the situation may call for wider rules of engagement so that U.N. peacekeepers may react to force and, in some cases, use force to forestall an escalation in violence.
> Between Chapter VI and Chapter VII lie cases which are sui generis and where earlier certainties about actions with or without the parties' agreement may need to be re-examined with each new approach.[43]

These ideas played an important role in the establishment and management of UN operations in the former Yugoslavia and in Somalia, established in the wake of An Agenda for Peace. These operations were given the power to use force under Chapter VII of the UN Charter for specific purposes other than self-defense, a radical departure from the established principle of the minimal use of force.[44] Some writers referred to these operations as 'third-generation peacekeeping' because of this departure from established doctrine. The United Nations Protection Force (UNPROFOR) was established in February 1992 with a mandate to demilitarize three 'United Nations Protected Areas', monitor police activities and assist in the return of displaced persons to the protected areas.[45] When the conflict in the former Yugoslavia spread to Bosnia Herzegovina, the mandate of the operation came to include a number of activities in Bosnia Herzegovina, including ensuring the security of Sarajevo airport and the protection of the delivery of humanitarian assistance.[46] The mandate was expanded several times, *inter alia* with the task of deterring attacks against towns designated as 'safe areas' in Resolution 824. Resolution 776 authorized UNPROFOR to use force to secure the delivery of humanitarian assistance under Chapter VII. Resolution 836 authorized it to use force to deter attacks against the 'safe areas', to monitor the cease-fire, to promote the withdrawal of military and paramilitary units other than those of the government of the Republic of Bosnia Herzegovina and to occupy some key points on the ground under Chapter VII. It is well-known that this did not have the desired effect and that air strikes by NATO, authorized under Security Council Resolutions 770 and 836, forced the parties to accept the Dayton Peace Agreements in 1995.

The Security Council established the second United Nations Operation in Somalia (UNOSOM II) in March 1993 to take over from the United States-led Unified Task Force (UNITAF). The Secretary-General recommended a broad mandate for the force and the endowment of enforcement powers under Chapter VII of the UN Charter.[47] He was especially concerned that the task of disarming the parties

43 B. Boutros-Ghali, *supra* note 39, at 120.

44 See *e.g.* C. Gray, *Host-state Consent and United Nations Peacekeeping in Yugoslavia*, 7 Duke Journal of Comparative & International Law 241 (1996).

45 Security Council Resolution 743 of 21 February 1992, UN Doc. S/RES/743.

46 Security Council Resolution 758 of 8 June 1992, UN Doc. S/RES/758.

47 UN Doc. S/25354 of 3 March 1993, para. 56-68.

should be enforceable.[48] The Security Council adopted the recommendations of the Secretary-General in Resolution 814. The resolution gave the force a broad mandate, including monitoring the cessation of hostilities, protecting personnel, installations and equipment of the UN, its agencies and non-governmental organizations, assisting in the repatriation of refugees and disarming factions, and gave the force enforcement powers under Chapter VII to accomplish its mandate.[49] Over time, hostility toward the operation developed among factions in Somalia, and in particular the faction led by Mohamed Aidid. On 5 June 1993 the force was ambushed when it tried to inspect a weapons storage site of Mr. Aidid's faction. Eighteen Pakistani peacekeepers were killed. The next day the Security Council adopted Resolution 837, which reaffirmed that "the Secretary-General is authorized under Resolution 814 (1993) to take all necessary measures against all those responsible for the armed attacks."[50] Lalande explains that the:

> reaction of the UN to the attack against its forces sparked a guerrilla-type war in Mogadishu, with UNOSOM II becoming a new warring party in the civil war, which was contrary to its mandate to restore law and order in the country.[51]

On 3 October 1993, United States Rangers which remained under United States command and who were deployed to assist the United Nations force, launched an operation in south Mogadishu aimed at capturing a number of key aides of Mr. Aidid who were suspected of complicity in the 5 June attack. During the course of the operation, two United States helicopters were shot down by Somali militiamen using automatic weapons and rocket-propelled grenades. In the fight that followed eighteen Rangers and one Malaysian member of the UN operation were killed. Following the events of 3 October 1993, President Clinton announced the intention of the United States to withdraw its forces from Somalia by 31 March 1994. This led other governments to do the same and ultimately led to the withdrawal of the UN Operation in the beginning of 1995.

UN operations in the former Yugoslavia and Somalia not only were authorized to use more force than previous operations, they also departed from the principle of consent. Kofi Annan – then Under-Secretary-General for Peacekeeping Operations – wrote in 1994 that "the need for consent of the parties was overridden by humanitarian concerns."[52] The weakening of the principle of consent was related to a change in the type of conflicts confronting the UN, from primarily interstate to much more

48 *Id.*, para. 63.

49 Security Council Resolution 814 of 26 March 1993, UN Doc. S/RES/814.

50 Security Council Resolution 837 of 6 June 1993, UN Doc. S/RES/837, para. 5.

51 S. Lalande, *Somalia: Major Issues for Future UN Peacekeeping*, in D. Warner (Ed.), New Dimensions of Peacekeeping 69 (1995), at 92.

52 K. Annan, *Peace-keeping in Situations of Civil War*, 26 New York University Journal of International Law & Politics 623 (1994), at 624. See also O. Corten & P. Klein, *Action Humanitaire et Chapitre VII: La Redéfinition du Mandat et des Moyens d'Action des Forces des Nations Unies*, 39 Annuaire Français de Droit International 105 (1993).

complex intrastate conflicts in which only some of the parties may give their consent or in which factions that give consent may not have full control over their areas. At the same time the principle of consent was not totally abandoned, as illustrated by the withdrawal of UNPROFOR from Croatia when that state withdrew its consent for the operation.[53] UNOSOM II also to a certain extent relied on consent. Other factions than the one led by Mr. Aidid continued to co-operate with the operation.[54]

The operations in the former Yugoslavia and Somalia were generally considered unsuccessful.[55] The UN was also criticized for standing by while genocide took place in Rwanda in 1994 while a UN peace support operation was deployed there.[56] This perception of United Nations failure led to a rethinking of peace support operations symbolized by a famous 1994 article by Adam Roberts entitled "The Crisis in UN Peacekeeping."[57] Within the UN this rethinking led to a retrenchment. The euphoria which accompanied the end of the Cold War and the accompanying expectation that the Security Council would finally take center stage in the maintenance of international peace and security as the drafters of the Charter intended, an expectation which was reflected in An Agenda for Peace, did not last. It was felt that the UN should return to the principles of traditional peacekeeping: consent, impartiality and the non-use of force except in self-defense. Departure from these principles was regarded as the cause of the problems with the operations in the former Yugoslavia and Somalia.[58] Peacekeeping and enforcement should be clearly distinguished.[59]

In 1995, the Secretary-General presented a supplement to An Agenda for Peace which reflected these ideas. The Secretary-General stated that UN peacekeeping operations should respect the principles of consent, impartiality and the non-use of force except in self-defense.[60] According to the Secretary-General this was illustrated by the operations in the former Yugoslavia and Somalia. In both cases, existing peacekeeping operations were given additional mandates which required the use of force and therefore could not be combined with existing mandates requiring the consent of the parties, impartiality and the non-use of force. It was also not possible for them to

53 C. Gray, *supra* note 44, at 265-269.

54 See also G. McDonald, Peace Enforcement: Mapping the 'Middle Ground' in Peace Operations, dissertation University of Geneva 2001 (unpublished), UNOSOM II, Consent.

55 M. Bothe, United Nations Forces, EPIL 1107 (1992), at 1113; C. Crocker, *The Lessons of Somalia: Not Everything Went Wrong*, 74 Foreign Affairs 2 (1995).

56 See *e.g.* M. Boot, *Paving the Road to Hell: The Failure of U.N. Peacekeeping*, 79 Foreign Affairs 143 (2000); M. Barnett, Eyewitness to a Genocide: The United Nations and Rwanda (2002).

57 A. Roberts, *The Crisis in UN Peacekeeping*, 36 Survival 93 (1994).

58 See *e.g.* S. Tharoor, *The Changing Face of Peace-keeping and Peace-enforcement*, 19 Fordham International Law Journal 408 (1995); R. Higgins, *Second-Generation Peacekeeping*, 89 ASIL Proc. 275 (1995).

59 M. Berdal, *The Security Council, Peacekeeping and Internal Conflict after the Cold War*, 7 Duke Journal of Comparative & International Law 71 (1996).

60 B. Boutros-Ghali, UN Doc. S/1995/1 of 3 January 1995, para. 33.

be executed without much stronger military capabilities than had been made available. Peacekeeping and enforcement did not mix well because the:

> logic of peace-keeping flows from political and military premises that are quite distinct from those of enforcement; and the dynamics of the latter are incompatible with the political process that peace-keeping is intended to facilitate. To blur the distinction between the two can undermine the viability of the peace-keeping operation and endanger its personnel.[61]

The Secretary-General also stated that neither the Security Council nor the Secretary-General at present had the capacity to deploy, direct, command and control operations for the purpose of enforcement action, except perhaps on a very limited scale.[62] He instead emphasized increased reliance on states and regional organizations as a possible approach in enforcement actions, but also in peacekeeping. Co-operation between regional organizations and the UN could take a number of forms including operational support and co-deployment. This new approach of a more important role for regional organizations has been followed ever since.[63] In 1999 Kofi Annan wrote:

> In recent years, the Secretariat has seen a wide-ranging consideration of the ways in which regional actors can enhance their participation in United Nations work for peace. In view of certain practical and political limitations, such partnerships cannot be considered a panacea to the problems facing peacekeeping. However, they have, in certain situations and under the right conditions, proved crucial to advancing peace.[64]

1.5 Regional organizations and peace support operations, in particular the North Atlantic Treaty Organization

Chapter VIII of the UN Charter provides explicitly for a role for 'regional arrangements or agencies' in the maintenance of international peace and security. Article 52 essentially legitimizes the existence of regional arrangements or agencies. Article 53 provides that the Security Council may utilize them for enforcement action where appropriate.

In the last decades, regional organizations have played an important role in respect of peace support operations. Whether these activities fall within Chapter VIII of the UN Charter depends mainly on the interpretation of the terms 'regional

61 *Id.*, para. 35.

62 *Id.*, para. 77.

63 See e.g. E. Berman, *The Security Council's Increasing Reliance on Burden-Sharing: Collaboration or Abrogation?*, 5 International Peacekeeping 1 (1998); J. Morris & H. McCoubrey, *Regional Peacekeeping in the Post-Cold War Era*, 6 International Peacekeeping 129 (1999).

64 Report of the Secretary-General on the Implementation of the Recommendations of the Special Committee on Peacekeeping Operations of 23 February 1999, UN Doc. A/AC.121/43, para. 81.

arrangements or agencies' and 'enforcement action' in Articles 52-53. A discussion of these questions falls outside the scope of this book, because they mainly go to the legal basis for peace support operations and do not appear to have a direct impact on the issues of accountability addressed below.

It may be noted, however, that the UN appears to interpret the term 'regional arrangement or agency' extensively. In 'An Agenda for Peace' the UN Secretary-General stated:

> The Charter deliberately provides no precise definition of regional arrangements and agencies, thus allowing useful flexibility for undertakings by a group of States to deal with a matter appropriate for regional action which also could contribute to the maintenance of international peace and security. Such associations or entities could include treaty-based organizations, whether created before or after the founding of the United Nations, regional organizations for mutual security and defence, organizations for general regional development or for cooperation on a particular economic topic or function, and groups created to deal with a specific political, economic or social issue of current concern.[65]

It may also be noted that of the peace support operations mentioned below, only the deployment by the Economic Community of Western African States (ECOWAS) was explicitly authorized by the Security Council under Chapter VIII of the UN Charter.[66]

The following is a non-exhaustive list of examples of regional or sub regional organizations which have carried out peace support operations in the past or which are carrying out such operations in the present.[67]

In Latin America, the Organization of American States (OAS) has played a role in the maintenance of regional security. One example is the case of the intervention in the Dominican Republic in 1965. In that year the United States deployed a force to the Dominican Republic which it labelled a 'peacekeeping force'. The United States sought retroactive OAS authorization for this force. In response the OAS adopted a resolution establishing the 'Inter-American Armed Force in the Dominican Republic'. This intervention was highly controversial and led to extensive debates in the Security Council.[68]

---

65 *Supra* note 41, para 61. See also G. Wilson, *UN Authorized Enforcement: Regional Organizations versus 'Coalitions of the Willing'*, 10 International Peacekeeping 89 (2003), at 96. See also *e.g.* the press release of the Ministry of Foreign Affairs of the Russian Federation of 1 March 2004 on the adoption of Security Council Resolution 1529 which refers to "political control by the Security Council over the peacekeeping efforts of international and regional organizations, as well as groups of interested states in accordance with the provisions of Chapter VIII of the UN Charter."

66 Security Council Resolution 1464 of 4 February 2003, UN Doc. S/RES/1464, para. 9.

67 See generally H. McCoubrey & J. Morris, Regional Peacekeeping in the Post-Cold War Era (2000).

68 See A.F. Lowenthal, The Dominican Intervention (1972); C.G. Fenwick, *The Dominican Republic: Intervention or Collective Self-Defense*, 60 American Journal of International Law 64 (1966).

In Africa, there are a number of organizations which have deployed peace support operations. The Organization of African Unity (OAU) established a peace support operation in Chad in 1979 with a mandate to ensure the defense and security of the country whilst awaiting the integration of government forces. The force, which operated from 1980 to 1982, encountered great difficulties and failed in the realization of its objectives.[69] Following this failure, the OAU in 1995 established a mechanism for conflict prevention, management and resolution which was a significant improvement on previous practice and structures. After the establishment of the mechanism the OAU deployed small missions in Rwanda (1990-1993), Burundi (1993-1996), the Comoros (1997-1999) and the Democratic Republic of the Congo (DRC, 1999-2000).[70] When in 2002 the OAU was replaced by the African Union (AU), foreign ministers agreed on the need to set up a robust stand-by peace force.[71] In April 2003 the AU deployed its first peace support operation in Burundi. The operation's mandate was to supervise ceasefire accords between the Burundi government and three Hutu opposition groups.[72] The AU mission was replaced by a UN peace support operation in June 2004.[73]

The Economic Community of West African States (ECOWAS) has fielded operations in Liberia (1990-1999), Sierra Leone (1997-2000)[74] and Guinea-Bissau (1998-1999). In 2003 ECOWAS established yet another peace support operation in Liberia in anticipation of a United Nations operation, and deployed peacekeepers in Côte d'Ivoire.[75]

The Central African Monetary and Economic Community (CEMAC) deployed a peace support operation in the Central African Republic in 2003. Despite a coup in March 2003 which toppled President Patassé, the force remained in the country with a redefined mandate.[76]

In Europe, the European Union (EU) is ambitious in respect of peace support. The development of the European Security and Defence Policy (ESDP) and the role of the so-called 'Petersberg tasks' will not be described in detail. This development could be said to have started at the 1999 Helsinki European Council where the Heads of State and Government decided to proceed toward the practical implementation of

69 See G. Naldi, *Peace-keeping Attempts by the Organisation of African Unity*, 34 International & Comparative Law Quarterly 593 (1985).

70 E. Berman & K. Sams, *Regional Peacekeeping in Africa*, 3 Conflict Trends 50 (2001).

71 See *African Ministers Agree on Robust Peacekeeping Force*, Agence France Presse, 1 July 2002.

72 *African Union ready to deploy Burundi peacekeeping force: South Africa*, Agence France Presse, 18 February 2003.

73 C. Lynch, *UN Approves Peacekeeping Force for Burundi*, The Washington Post, 22 May 2004, at A15.

74 See M. Gasiokwu, *ECOWAS Intervention in Liberia and Sierra Leone: A New Dimension in Regional Security Systems*, 24 Polish Yearbook of International Law 157 (2001).

75 See K. Vick, *Troops Land in Liberia: West African Forces Begin International Mission*, The Washington Post, 5 August 2003.

76 See *Central African leaders seek to keep peacekeeping force in CAR*, Agence France Presse, 21 March 2003.

the security ambitions of the Amsterdam Treaty and the Cologne European Council Declaration. In particular, the Helsinki Council agreed that the EU should be able in 2003 to deploy within 60 days and sustain for at least one year military forces of up to 50,000-60,000 persons capable of the full range of Petersberg tasks.[77] These tasks are humanitarian and rescue tasks, peacekeeping tasks and combat-force tasks in crisis management, including peacemaking. In April 2003 the European Rapid Reaction Force was declared operational.[78] In September 2003, the EU and the UN issued a Joint Declaration on UN-EU Cooperation in Crisis Management, which welcomed the existing cooperation in this field between the two organizations and which provides a basis for the further strengthening of practical cooperation.

In January 2003 the EU launched a peace support operation, named Operation Concordia, in the Former Yugoslav Republic of Macedonia (FYROM) as a follow-on to the NATO operation there. On 27 January 2003 the Council adopted a Joint Action for this purpose.[79] This was the first military operation of the EU. In July 2003, at the request of the Macedonian government, the operation's mandate was extended until 15 December 2003. In December 2003 it was replaced by an EU police monitoring mission (EUPOL 'Proxima') at the request of the Macedonian government.[80] In June 2003 the EU decided to take on a more challenging task in establishing a peace support operation in the DRC, named 'Operation Artemis' and comprising 1400 troops.[81] This is the first EU operation outside the European continent. The operation was authorized by the United Nations Security Council in Resolution 1484, which also set out the force's mandate. The operation, which ended in September 2003, was generally seen as a success. On 12 July 2004 the EU decided to deploy a peace support operation to Bosnia Herzegovina in December 2004 to take over from SFOR.[82] The EU operation is named 'Operation Althea'. The EU decision followed the adoption of UN Security Council Resolution 1551 on 9 July 2004, in which the Security Council welcomed the EU's intention to launch an EU mission in Bosnia Herzegovina, including a military component.[83]

The above demonstrates that there are various regional or sub regional organizations with the ambition to play an important role in the peace support 'business'. At present these organizations have their limitations, however. In the case of African

77 Presidency Conclusions of the European Council Meeting In Helsinki, 10 and 11 December 1999, Doc. SN300/1/99, para. 28.

78 Declaration on the Operational Capability of the Common European Security and Defence Policy, Annex II to the Presidency Conclusions of the European Council Meeting In Laeken, 14 and 15 December 2001, Doc. SN300/1/01REV1.

79 Council Joint Action 2003/92/CFSP of 27 January 2003 on the European Union military operation in the Former Yugoslav Republic of Macedonia.

80 Council Joint Action 2003/681/CFSP of 29 September 2003 on the European Union Police Mission in the Former Yugoslav Republic of Macedonia (EUPOL 'Proxima').

81 Council Joint Action 2003/423/CFSP of 5 June 2003 on the European Union military operation in the Democratic Republic of Congo.

82 Council Joint Action on the European Union Military Operation in Bosnia and Herzegovina, OJ L 252 of 28 July 2004, at 10.

83 Security Council Resolution 1551 of 9 July 2004, UN Doc. S/RES/1551, para. 9.

organizations, for example, these are mostly financial: most African countries are not capable of undertaking peace support operations without substantial external assistance. In the case of the EU, its military structures have not yet been proven, especially in operations where it cannot make use of NATO assets.[84] For this reason NATO is, at least under the present circumstances, the most important regional actor in the field of peace support operations.

While the UN was experiencing difficulties with peacekeeping in the early 1990s, NATO was looking for a new role. It was established in 1949 as a collective defensive organization mainly to defend Western Europe and the United States against the Eastern Bloc. After the Cold War it needed a new role. This new role has been defined more and more as including peace support operations.[85] In 1992, the organization's foreign ministers declared that the organization was prepared to support, on a case by case basis, peacekeeping activities under the responsibility of Conference for Security and Co-operation in Europe.[86] This was followed six months later by a similar declaration concerning UN operations.[87] In NATO's 1999 Strategic Concept, the organization states:

> In pursuit of its policy of preserving peace, preventing war, and enhancing security and stability and as set out in the fundamental security tasks, NATO will seek, in cooperation with other organisations, to prevent conflict, or, should a crisis arise, to contribute to its effective management, consistent with international law, including through the possibility of conducting non-Article 5 crisis response operations. The Alliance's preparedness to carry out such operations supports the broader objective of reinforcing and extending stability and often involves the participation of NATO's Partners. NATO recalls its offer, made in Brussels in 1994, to support on a case-by-case basis in accordance with its own procedures, peacekeeping and other operations under the authority of the UN Security Council or the responsibility of the OSCE, including by making available Alliance resources and expertise.[88]

---

84 The EU and NATO in March 2003 agreed on a number of arrangements between them which are referred to as the 'Berlin Plus agreements'. These essentially make possible the use of NATO facilities for EU crisis response operations, including through assured EU access to NATO planning capabilities able to contribute to military planning for EU-led operations and the presumption of availability to the EU of pre-identified NATO capabilities and common assets for use in EU-led operations. See M. Reichard, *Some Legal Issues Concerning the EU-NATO Berlin Plus Agreements*, 73 Nordic Journal of International Law 37 (2004).

85 See D. Lightburn, *NATO and the Challenge of Multifunctional Peacekeeping*, 44 NATO Review 10 (1996); D. Boothby, Background paper, Report of an International Peace Academy Seminar on UN/NATO Relationship, New York, 11 June 1999.

86 Final Communiqué of the Ministerial Meeting of the North Atlantic Council, 4 June 1992, para. 11.

87 Final Communiqué of the Ministerial Meeting of the North Atlantic Council, 17 December 1992, para. 4.

88 Strategic Concept 1999, para. 31.

In the former Yugoslavia the organization initially used limited coercion in support of the UN Operation by providing air support. In 1995, greater use of air power and the emplacement of a Rapid Reaction Force by the organization, authorized by the Security Council under Chapter VII of the UN Charter, followed.

The 1995 Dayton Peace Agreements provided for the replacement of the UN Operation in the former Yugoslavia by a NATO-led Implementation Force (IFOR) to help ensure compliance with the agreements. The Security Council authorized the force in Resolution 1031 in which it noted the consent of the parties to the multinational implementation force.[89] Nevertheless, the Council, acting under Chapter VII of the UN Charter, authorized the force to take all necessary measures to effect the implementation and to ensure compliance with its mandate.[90] In 1996 the force was replaced with the NATO-led Stabilization Force (SFOR) with essentially the same mandate.

After Operation Allied Force, the intervention by the organization in Kosovo in early 1999, the Security Council authorized a NATO-led Kosovo Force (KFOR). The Federal Republic of Yugoslavia gave its consent for the force in a Military-Technical Agreement between that state and the commander of the Kosovo Force on 9 June 1999.[91]

Under Chapter VII of the UN Charter, the Security Council authorized the establishment of the force in Resolution 1244 with all necessary means to fulfill its responsibilities.[92] The mandate of the force is essentially to facilitate the conditions under which a United Nations-led transitional administration (UNMIK) can operate.[93]

On 11 August 2003, NATO assumed command of the International Security Assistance Force (ISAF) in Afghanistan.[94]

It may be pointed out that since the early 1990s, the Security Council has not only authorized regional organizations, but also individual states or groups of states to use force.[95] The expression 'coalition of the able and willing' is often used to describe such a group of states. In some cases such an operation falls within the definition of 'peace support operations' used in this study. An example is the Australian-led International

89 Security Council Resolution 1031 of 15 December 1995, UN Doc. S/RES/1031, para. 13.

90 *Id.*, para. 15. White states that even while IFOR is performing a basic peacekeeping function, the threat of enforcement action if the peace is broken, combined with its greater military capacity, makes it a much more capable military operation than UNPROFOR. N. White, *supra* note 6.

91 Military Technical Agreement between the International Security Force (KFOR) and the Governments of the Federal Republic of Yugoslavia and the Republic of Serbia of 9 June 1999, reproduced in 38 ILM 1217 (1999).

92 Security Council Resolution 1244 of 10 June 1999, UN Doc. S/RES/1244, para. 7.

93 See M. Guillaume, *Le Cadre Juridique de l'Action de la KFOR au Kosovo*, in C. Tomuschat (Ed.), Kosovo and the International Community 243 (2002), at 248-252.

94 NATO press release (2003)091 of 8 August 2003.

95 See *e.g.* L.N. Blokker, Is the Authorization Authorized? Powers and Practice of the UN Security Council to Authorize the Use of Force by 'Coalitions of the Able and Willing', 11 European Journal of International Law 541 (2000).

Force in East Timor (INTERFET) from September 1999 until February 2000,[96] and another the initial phase of ISAF. Before NATO took command of ISAF, it was led by different so-called 'lead nations'. Since this study focuses on peace support operations under the command and control of the UN and NATO, these operations carried out by individual states or *ad hoc* groups of states are not discussed, although they do raise interesting questions of accountability.[97]

1.6 Upsurge in United Nations peace support operations and Brahimi Report

During the early days of this development of peace support activities by regional organizations in general and NATO in particular, there was a decline in UN peace support operations influenced by budget crises and the sense that the UN cannot undertake extensive enforcement operations. The new policy of the United States toward peace operations in the 1995 Presidential Decision Directive on Reforming Multilateral Peace Operations (PDD-25) was also an important element in this development.[98] This document, the Clinton administration's policy on reforming multilateral peace operations, set strict limits on United States political support for the establishment of, and military participation in, United Nations-led peace support operations.

Since 1998 however, there has again been an upsurge in United Nations-led operations. These include operations based on the principles of first-generation peacekeeping. The United Nations Mission in Ethiopia and Eritrea (UNMEE) for example is an operation without enforcement powers with the main task of supervising a cessation of hostilities with the consent of the parties.[99] Other operations, including the United Nations Mission in Sierra Leone (UNAMSIL)[100] and the United Nations Mission in the Democratic Republic of the Congo (MONUC),[101] have multifunctional mandates and limited enforcement powers under Chapter VII of the United Nations Charter. Finally, the United Nations has established transitional administrations in Kosovo and East Timor which do not have a military element but rely for their security on operations led by *ad hoc* coalitions of states or a regional organization. These administrations have taken over unprecedented responsibility for governance of

96 See *e.g.* Ryan, *The Strong Lead-nation Model in an ad hoc Coalition of the Willing: Operation Stabilise in East Timor*, 9 International Peacekeeping 23 (2002).

97 See *e.g.* D. Sarooshi, The U.N. and the Development of Collective Security: The Delegation by the Security Council of its Chapter VII Powers (1999).

98 See D. Scheffer, *Problems and Prospects for UN Peacekeeping*, 89 ASIL Proc. 285 (1995).

99 Security Council Resolution 1320 of 15 September 2000, UN Doc. S/RES/1320.

100 Security Council Resolution 1270 of 22 October 1999, UN Doc. S/RES/1270. UNAMSIL's enforcement powers are limited to action to ensure the security and freedom of movement of its personnel and, within its capabilities and areas of deployment, to afford protection to civilians under imminent threat of physical violence, taking into account the responsibilities of the Government of Sierra Leone and ECOMOG.

101 Security Council Resolution 1291 of 24 February 2000, UN Doc. S/RES/1291. MONUC's enforcement powers are limited to actions to protect United Nations and co-located JMC personnel, facilities, installations and equipment, ensure the security and freedom of movement of its personnel, and protect civilians under imminent threat of physical violence.

the territories in question.[102] Guéhenno, United Nations Under-Secretary-General for Peacekeeping Operations, states that there are several reasons for this upsurge:

> First, we learned during the 1996-98 period of retrenchment that regional and sub regional initiatives were confronted with the same challenges which had previously stymied UN peacekeeping operations. It means little which organization is leading the operation if the parties on the ground simply are not committed to peace. Second, we learned that, in certain circumstances, regional or sub regional organizations are not appropriate to take on the task, because one or more of their members may actually be parties to the conflict. Third, we were reminded of the importance of the universal legitimacy that only the UN can offer, and which some parties to a conflict will consider as the only acceptable form of international involvement. And, fourth, we had to come to terms with the fact that few regional or sub regional arrangements have the necessary capacity to do the job.[103]

In 2000 the Panel on United Nations Peace Operations presented its report.[104] This report was commissioned by the Secretary-General to evaluate the whole range of UN activities in the area of peace and security and to make recommendations for change. In relation to peace support operations, the panel stated that the consent of the local parties, impartiality and use of force only in self-defense should remain the bedrock principles of peacekeeping. Yet these criteria were modified or at least restricted in their practical application.[105] In particular, the panel recommended giving peacekeeping operations robust rules of engagement, making forces "able to pose a credible deterrent threat, in contrast to the symbolic and non-threatening presence that characterizes traditional peacekeeping."[106] Although the panel distinguished peacekeeping from enforcement action, this brings peacekeeping close to the concept of 'peace enforcement' of the mid-1990s.[107] This, a muscular from of peacekeeping,[108] also seems

---

102 M. Matheson, *United Nations Governance of Postconflict Societies*, 95 American Journal of International Law 76 (2001); C. Stahn, *The United Nations Transitional Administrations in Kosovo and East Timor: A First Analysis*, 5 Max Planck Yearbook of United Nations Law 105 (2001).

103 J.M. Guéhenno, *On the Challenges and Achievements of Reforming UN Peace Operations*, 9 International Peacekeeping 69 (2002), at 71.

104 *Supra* note 1.

105 H. Spieker, *Changing "Peacekeeping" in the New Millennium? – The Recommendations of the Panel on United Nations Peace Operations of August 2000*, 6 International Peacekeeping 144 (2000), at 147.

106 *Supra* note 1, para. 51.

107 See also Fröhlich, *supra* note 9, at 227.

108 White states that:

> The Brahimi report attempts to tread the tightrope between peacekeeping and enforcement with a little more care than the Secretary General did in 1992. However, the report still seems to be based on the untested assumption that peacekeepers can somehow act in a more muscular fashion without over-stepping the line between peacekeeping and enforcement.

to be a concept supported by the Secretary-General. In 2000 he was quoted as saying that the organization should abandon outdated concepts of neutral peacekeeping and replace them with a more muscular form of peace enforcement.[109]

1.7 Definition of peace support operations

Until 1988 it was relatively clear what the term 'peace support operation', or 'peacekeeping' as the preferred term at that time, referred to, as can be readily understood from the description above. After 1988, a wide variety of terms emerged to describe and distinguish between new types of operations. Writers used the terms 'peace enforcement', 'wider peacekeeping', 'aggravated peacekeeping', 'robust peacekeeping', 'muscular peacekeeping', 'peace support operations' and others, but they did not agree on their meaning. The UN itself has changed its use of terms over time. In 'An Agenda for Peace', the Secretary-General distinguished between the concept of peacemaking, which included peace-enforcement units, and peacekeeping. In the 1995 supplement to 'An Agenda for Peace', the concept of 'peace enforcement' did not return. Instead, the Secretary-General distinguished between preventive diplomacy and peacemaking (without the enforcement element), peacekeeping, post-conflict peace-building and enforcement action. The Brahimi report uses the term 'peace operations', divided into conflict prevention and peacemaking, peacekeeping and peace building.

The present study uses the term 'peace support operation' (PSO) to describe the category of military operations which are intended to be the subject of study in subsequent chapters. It conforms to the use of the term 'peace support operation' by NATO. This is appropriate because NATO is one of the two organizations addressed in this book. NATO has done extensive doctrinal work on the different categories of military operations. As a result it has developed the following definition of 'peace support operations' (PSO):

> PSO are multifunctional operations, conducted impartially, normally in support of an internationally recognised organisation such as the UN or Organisation for Security and Cooperation in Europe (OSCE), involving military forces and diplomatic and humanitarian agencies. PSO are designed to achieve a long-term political settlement or other specified conditions. They include Peacekeeping and Peace Enforcement as well as conflict prevention, peacemaking, peacebuilding and humanitarian relief.[110]

The term includes 'classic' peace support operations which display the characteristics of consent of the host state, impartiality and the non-use of force except in self-defense. This kind of operation would fall within the category of 'peacekeeping operation', which in NATO doctrine is a subcategory of 'peace support operation' and is defined as follows:

N. White, *Commentary on the Report of the Panel on United Nations Peace Operations (The Brahimi report)*, 6 Journal of Conflict and Security Law 127 (2001), at 130.

109 C. McGreal, *Africans Urge UN to Toughen Mandate*, The Guardian, 30 May 2000.

110 AJP-3.4.1, Peace Support Operations, July 2001, para. 0202.

> PK operations are generally undertaken in accordance with the principles of Chapter VI of the UN Charter in order to monitor and facilitate the implementation of a peace agreement. A loss of consent and a non-compliant party may limit the freedom of action of the PK force and even threaten the continuation of the mission. Thus, the requirement to remain impartial, limit the use of force to self-defence, and maintain and promote consent would guide the conduct of PK.[111]

Also included in 'peace support operation' for the purpose of this book is 'peace enforcement'. The NATO definition of 'peace enforcement' (PE) is as follows:

> PE operations normally take place under the principles of Chapter VII of the UN Charter. They are coercive in nature and conducted when the consent of all Parties to the conflict has not been achieved or might be uncertain. They are designed to maintain or re-establish peace or enforce the terms specified in the mandate. In the conduct of PE, the link between military and political objectives must be extremely close. It is important to emphasise that the aim of the PE operation will not be the defeat or destruction of an enemy, but rather to compel, coerce and persuade the parties to comply with a particular course of action. The provision of adequate military forces to establish a coercive combat capability is critical to any decision to deploy Alliance forces on a PSO.[112]

NATO doctrine provides that peace support operations, including peace enforcement operations, are neither in support of, nor against a particular party, but rather are conducted in an impartial and even-handed manner. As a consequence, 'peace support operations' must be distinguished from 'enforcement action or war', which are not impartial. Examples of the latter are the military operations in Korea in the early 1950s and the NATO military operation in the Federal Republic of Yugoslavia (FRY) in 1999.

The definition of 'peace support operation' for the purposes of this book thus includes operations which hold the middle ground between 'traditional peacekeeping' on the one hand, and 'enforcement action' on the other hand. Such a middle ground is recognized in the military doctrine of many armed forces. An important example is United States military doctrine. United States Joint Publication 3-07.3 distinguishes between two types of 'peace operations': 'peacekeeping operations' and 'peace enforcement operations'.[113] The definition of the former draws on the characteristics of 'traditional' peace support operations conducted by the United Nations, *i.e.* consent, impartiality and the non-use of force except in self-defense. The latter are defined as "the application of military force or the threat of its use, normally pursuant to international authorization, to compel compliance with resolutions or sanctions designed

---

111 *Id.*, para. 0216.

112 *Id.*, para. 0217.

113 Joint Publication 3-07.3, Joint Tactics, Techniques, and Procedures for Peace Operations, 12 February 1999.

to maintain or restore peace and order."[114] Peace enforcement operations are distinguished from 'wars' In war, an aggressor is defined and military victory is sought. The goal of peace enforcement, on the other hand, is to enforce the provisions of a mandate designed to maintain or restore peace and order. Peace enforcement operations use force or the threat of force to coerce or compel compliance with resolutions or sanctions.[115] Other states' military doctrine also recognizes such a middle ground. Dutch Army doctrine recognizes 'peacekeeping operations' and 'peace enforcement operations' as subcategories of 'peace support operations'.[116] The difference between the two is that the former is present and conducts operations in the host state with the consent of the parties, while there is no such consent in the case of the latter.[117] Impartiality is a characteristic of all peace support operations. An important element of impartiality is even-handedness, defined as a fair and consistent application of rules and sanctions.[118] Impartiality is what distinguishes a 'peace enforcement operation' from 'war'.[119]

For the purposes of this book, the principal difference between 'enforcement' and robust peace support operations is that the latter are impartial.[120] The UK manual on Peace Support Operations, which builds on NATO doctrine, explains that the distinction between coercive peace support operations and 'enforcement action or war' will be determined in an examination of the mandate and desired end-state. A peace support operation mandate will not designate an enemy, neither will it relate to military victory, whereas a military enforcement operation will attempt to change the correlation of local forces and impose a solution by military action.[121]

The term 'peace support operation' as defined for the purposes of this book attempts to provide more clarity than UN 'doctrine'. In the *Certain Expenses* Advisory Opinion, the International Court of Justice distinguished peacekeeping from 'coercive or enforcement action'. 'Coercive or enforcement action' was such action as was solely within the province of the Security Council. In respect of ONUC the Court held that:

> It can be said that the operations of ONUC did not include a use of armed force against a State which the Security Council, under Article 39, determined to have committed an act of aggression or to have breached the peace. The armed forces

114 *Id.*, at I-7.

115 *Id.*, at III-1.

116 Landmachtdoctrinepublicatie III, Vredesoperaties (Army Doctrine Publication III, Peace Operations), 1999.

117 *Id.*, at 81.

118 *Id.*, at 105.

119 *Id.*, at 61, 81.

120 See for the same distinction F. Hampson, *States' Military Operations Authorized by the United Nations and International Humanitarian Law*, in L. Condorelli, A.M. La Rosa & S. Scherrer (Eds.), The United Nations and International Humanitarian Law 371 (1996), at 376-379.

121 Joint Warfare Publication 3-50, Peace Support Operations, para. 303.

> which were utilised in the Congo were not authorised to take military action against any State. The operation did not involve 'preventive or enforcement measures' against any State under Chapter VII and therefore did not constitute 'action' as that term is used in Article 11.[122]

The ICJ thus appears to have defined 'enforcement action' as military action under Chapter VII of the UN Charter. It emphasized that such action has to be against a state.[123] It is unclear how the ICJ would have characterized military action under Chapter VII of the UN Charter against a non-state entity.

The UN appears to distinguish between 'enforcement' and 'peacekeeping'. The Brahimi report makes this distinction, and states that "Where enforcement action is required, it has consistently been entrusted to coalitions of willing States, with the authorization of the Security Council, acting under Chapter VII of the Charter."[124]

'Peacekeeping operations' appear to include operations established by the UN without reference to Chapter VII of the Charter, as well as operations with enforcement powers under Chapter VII. This is also reflected in recent reports on the work of the organization submitted by the UN Secretary-General to the General Assembly. For example, the report of the Secretary-General on the Work of the Organization for 2003 reports on UNMEE as well as on MONUC and UNAMSIL under the heading 'peacekeeping and peacebuilding'.[125] In contrast to the *Certain Expenses* Advisory Opinion, military action against non-state entities by states authorized under Chapter VII of the UN Charter appears to be regarded as 'enforcement action'.

Apart from impartiality, consent also plays a role in peace support operations and the distinction with 'enforcement'. Because peace support operations are designed to create a secure environment in which civilian agencies can rebuild the infrastructure necessary to create a self-sustaining peace, and self-sustaining peace requires the co-operation and consent of the parties and the local population, the promotion of consent is fundamental to achieving the political end-state in all peace support operations.[126] In other words, a peace support operation will attempt to maintain consent if it exists, and will attempt to promote consent where it does not.

Having selected a term to define the subject of this study, it is important to stress the need for flexibility. In practice there are so many different military operations that some of them defy ready classification. This is precisely why NATO is constantly revising its doctrine. For example, in 2003 an effort was initiated to update the doctrine concerning 'Peace Enforcement'.

---

122 Certain Expenses of the United Nations (Article 17, paragraph 2 of the Charter), Advisory Opinion of 20 July 1962, 1962 ICJ Reports 151, at 176-177.

123 A. Orakhelashvili, *The Legal Basis of United Nations Peace-keeping Operations*, 43 Virginia Journal of International Law 485 (2003).

124 *Supra* note 1, para. 53.

125 Report of the Secretary-General on the Work of the Organisation of 28 August 2003, UN Doc. A/58/1.

126 *Supra* note 110, para. 0310.

This study is limited to peace support operations by the UN and NATO for several reasons. First, peace support operations by international and regional organizations in particular raise questions of the applicability of international humanitarian law, *inter alia* because only states are parties to international humanitarian law treaties. Responsibility for internationally wrongful acts also raises specific questions in relation to international organizations, while the principles of state responsibility are relatively clear.[127]

Secondly, the two organizations in question are presently important organizations in the maintenance of international peace and security. A central role for the UN is guaranteed by the UN Charter, in particular Chapter VII which gives the Security Council a monopoly of the authorization of the use of force except in case of self-defense. NATO's military capability, unmatched by any other regional organization, guarantees its important role in peace support operations. Indeed, in 1993 Kofi Annan stated that with "its existing military structure, resources and political weight, NATO has a lot to contribute to the concept of peacekeeping, particularly in its more muscular form." [128]

'Coalitions of the able and willing' fall outside the scope of this study. This term refers to operations which are carried out by an individual state or an *ad hoc* group of states on the basis of a Security Council authorization under Chapter VII of the UN Charter.[129]

1.8 Legal status of peace support operations

1.8.1 The importance of legal status for this study

Peace support operations involve several international actors, in particular the international organization which establishes the operation, the states which contribute troops to the operation and the host state. The UN does not have armed forces of its own and relies on member states to contribute troops to a specific operation. NATO peace support operations also consist of national contingents contributed by member and non-member states. The relationship between the different international actors – in other words, the legal status of peace support operations – is an important element to determine the responsible entity for conduct of an operation and possible breaches of international humanitarian law. Command and control relationships in particular are important. Attribution of conduct in international law is based to a large extent on the concept of control or authority.[130] In military terms, the possession of control or

127 See also Hampson, *supra* note 120.

128 K. Annan, *UN Peacekeeping Operations and Cooperation with NATO*, 41 NATO Review 3 (1993).

129 See *e.g.* Wilson, *supra* note 65.

130 See *e.g.* P. Klein, La Responsabilité des Organisations Internationales dans les Ordres Juridiques Internes et en Droit des Gens 378 (1998); M. Perez Gonzalez, *Les Organisations Internationales et le Droit de la Responsabilité*, 92 Revue Générale de Droit International Public 63 (1988), at 83.

authority is expressed by the term 'command and control'. Command in NATO terms for example means the "authority vested in an individual of the armed forces for the direction, coordination, and control of military forces."[131] For this reason the regulation of command is of crucial importance.[132] The UN Secretary-General reaffirmed the relationship between command and control and responsibility in 1996:

> The international responsibility of the United Nations for combat-related activities of United Nations forces is premised on the assumption that the operation in question is under the exclusive command and control of the United Nations.[133]

1.8.2 Legal status of United Nations peace support operations

In the absence of a pre-determined legal framework for UN peace support operations, setting up a new operation requires *ad hoc* measures. A number of instruments are adopted or concluded to regulate the legal status of each specific operation.[134] Over time the content of these instruments has developed into a more or less uniform pattern. A peace support operation is established by a Security Council or General Assembly resolution which defines the mandate of the operation, the so-called 'enabling resolution'. The resolution usually makes reference to a more detailed plan prepared by the Secretary-General. Peace support operations are composed of national contingents contributed by member states. The Secretary-General is responsible for finding the necessary participants through informal consultations. He consults primarily with the Security Council about offers he receives. If the Council gives its consent, the agreement on the supply of troops is recorded in an exchange of letters between the Secretary-General and the government in question.

The composition of a peace support operation of military personnel belonging to states requires detailed regulation of their legal status.[135] In this regard the Secretary-General stated in his second report on UNEF that a "problem of first instance, therefore, was that of harmonizing the international character of the Force with the fact of its being composed of national contingents."[136]

Conditions under which a contingent will be contributed are agreed on between the UN and each participating state. In some cases these are informal written or even oral agreements but in other cases they are formalized.[137] The Secretary-General has

131 NATO Glossary of terms and Definitions, AAP-6 (V), 2003, at 2-C-8.

132 See *e.g.* K. Wellens, Remedies against International Organisations 100 (2002).

133 UN Doc. A/51/389 of 20 September 1996, para. 17.

134 EPIL 1110 (1992).

135 P. Dewast, *Quelques Aspects du Statut des "Casques Bleus"*, 81 Revue Générale de Droit International Public 1007 (1977), at 1030.

136 UN Doc. A/3943 of 9 October 1958, para. 127.

137 See *e.g.* Agreement between the United Nations and India concerning the service with the United Nations Emergency Force of 14 August 1957, UNTS 3968 (1957); Agreement between the United Nations and Denmark concerning service with the United Nations Peace-Keeping force in Cyprus of 21 February 1966, UNTS 8108 (1966).

developed a draft model agreement based on established practice and drawing extensively on previous participating state agreements. The model is intended to serve as a basis for drafting individual agreements.[138]

A participating state agreement refers to the Status of Forces Agreement (SOFA) concluded between the UN and the host state, which defines the relation between the force and the host state.[139] In principle such an agreement is concluded for every peace support operation. In practice a SOFA is not always concluded or is concluded after a certain period.[140] An agreement was not concluded in the case of the United Nations Operation in Somalia, for example, because there was no government with which to negotiate an agreement. In the United Nations Mission in Western Sahara (MINURSO) there was no agreement with Morocco until a year after the force deployed. Until 1990 the legal situation was very unclear in the absence of an agreement. In 1990 the Secretary-General prepared a model SOFA based on established practice.[141] In 1992 the General Assembly recommended that pending the conclusion of a SOFA, the model would apply provisionally.[142] This arrangement was applied for example in the United Nations Mission in Ethiopia and Eritrea until the UN and Ethiopia signed an agreement on 23 March 2001.[143]

This raises the question whether the provisions of the UN Model SOFA are an expression of customary international law. Suy states that in the absence of a SOFA between the UN and the host state concerned, it is generally accepted that principles laid down in previous agreements constitute general principles of law that are applicable.[144] If this refers to the specific provisions of previous SOFAs which have been reproduced in the Model SOFA, the conclusion is contestable. There appears to be no state practice to support such a conclusion. In this context it is interesting that in the first years following the General Assembly's recommendation in 1992, enabling resolutions of peace support operations "noted" or "recalled" that the Model SOFA *should* apply provisionally until a SOFA was concluded with the host state.[145] In more recent resolutions the Security Council has proceeded to note that the Model SOFA *shall* apply provisionally.[146] It is

138 Model Agreement between the United Nations and Member States Contributing Personnel and Equipment to United Nations Peace-keeping Operations of 23 May 1991, UN Doc. A/46/185.

139 *Id.*, para. 4.

140 J-M. Thouvenin, *Le Statut des Forces de Maintien de la Paix des Nations Unies*, 3 International Law Forum 105 (2001), at 106.

141 Model Status-of-Forces-Agreement for Peace-keeping Operations of 9 October 1990, UN Doc. A/45/594.

142 General Assembly Resolution 52/12 B of 9 January 1998, UN Doc. A/RES/52/12 B, para. 7.

143 Bijlagen Handelingen TK, 2000-01, 22831, 15.

144 E. Suy, *Legal Aspects of UN Peace-keeping Operations*, 35 Netherlands International Law Review 318 (1988), at 320. See also EPIL 1115 (1992).

145 See *e.g.* Security Council Resolution 1118 of 27 March 1998, UN Doc. S/RES/1118, para. 19; Security Council Resolution 1320 of 15 September 2000, UN Doc. S/RES/1320, para. 6.

146 See *e.g.* Security Council Resolution 1509 of 19 September 2003, UN Doc. S/RES/1509, para. 7; Security Council Resolution 1528 of 27 February 2004, UN Doc. S/RES/1528, para. 9; Security Council Resolution 1445 of 22 May 2004, UN Doc. S/RES/1445, para. 10.

unknown if all the host states concerned had agreed to such application before the resolutions were adopted. If not, it appears that the Security Council has imposed the provisional application of the Model SOFA. Such imposition would be superfluous if the model constituted customary international law.

Forces contributed to a UN operation are incorporated into the organization.[147] The participating state agreement, together with the 'Transfer of Authority' (TOA), integrates the contingent into the organizational apparatus of the UN. The troop contributing state gives its contingent instructions to serve the UN.[148] The operations are subsidiary organs of the main organ by which they have been established. Operations established by the General Assembly are subsidiary organs under Article 22 of the UN Charter and operations established by the Security Council are subsidiary organs under Article 29. Their legal personality is identified with that of the UN. The personnel of the force remain in their national service but are for the period of their assignment international personnel. This is the model that was used for UNEF and that has been used ever since. [149] The Secretary-General in his report on UNEF called this arrangement an "effective marriage of national military service with international function."[150] The International Court of Justice in the *Certain Expenses* case affirmed that ONUC was a subsidiary organ of the Security Council. It stated in relation to ONUC that:

> The Charter does not forbid the Security Council to act through instruments of its choice: under Article 29 it 'may establish such organs as it deems necessary for the performance of its functions'.[151]

The Model Participating State Agreement refers to the status agreement to affirm the international nature of the operation as a subsidiary organ of the UN.[152] It also states that the functions of the operation are exclusively international in character and that the personnel made available by the participating state shall regulate their conduct with the interests of the UN only in view.[153] This is the same language as used in previous agreements with individual participating states.[154]

---

147 N. Quoc Dinh, P. Daillier & A. Pellet, Droit International Public 969 (1999).

148 M. Bothe, Streitkräfte internationaler Organisationen: Zugleich ein Beitrag zu völkerrechtlichen Grundfragen der Anwesenheit fremder Truppen 44 (1968).

149 For a description of the status under international law of the Emergency Force see G. Rosner, The United Nations Emergency Force 142-157 (1963).

150 UN Doc. A/3943 of 9 October 1958, para. 128.

151 Certain Expenses of the United Nations (Article 17, paragraph 2 of the Charter), Advisory Opinion of 20 July 1962, 1962 ICJ Reports 151, at 176.

152 UN Doc. A/46/185 of 23 May 1991, para 4.

153 *Id.*, para. 9.

154 See *e.g.* Agreement between the United Nations and Denmark concerning service with the United Nations Emergency Force of 16 July 1957, UNTS 3959 (1957); Agreement between the United Nations and Canada concerning service with the United Nations Peace-keeping Force in Cyprus of 21 February 1966, UNTS 8107 (1966).

While assigned to a peace support operation, military personnel of national contingents comprise an integral part thereof.[155] The UN has the power to take decisions concerning operational activities and activities concerning third parties. The Secretary-General has full authority over the deployment, organization, conduct and direction of the operation, including the personnel made available by the participating states, in close coordination with the Security Council. Seyersted states that the "substantive (legislative and administrative) jurisdiction in operational matters – and this is the most important – is vested in the Organization."[156] The participating states however retain a number of powers over the troops they contribute. These powers are limited to administrative authority, including promotion and pay. Participating states also retain criminal jurisdiction over the troops they contribute. This is necessary to the extent that the United Nations has no law enforcement and judicial organs of its own. It is also politically necessary because participating states require it as a condition for contributing troops. The Secretary-General affirmed in his 1958 report on UNEF that the policy of exclusive jurisdiction of the participating state "obviously, makes easier the decision of States to contribute troops from their armed forces."[157]

The peace support operation's status as a subsidiary organ of the Security Council or General Assembly gives it privileges and immunities related to those of the UN.[158] It also results in exclusive UN authority to protect the rights of the operation and its personnel.[159]

1.8.3 Military command and control over United Nations peace support operations

In the field, military command over a peace support operation is exercised on behalf of the Secretary-General by the Force Commander (FC) who is usually appointed by the Secretary-General.[160] He is responsible only to the Secretary-General and, through the chain of command, exercises command over contingents. Since the inclusion in peace support operations of large civilian elements, the practice has been to appoint

155 See Legal Status of Members of the National Military Contingents Serving in United Nations Peacekeeping Operations, 1996 UNJY 450. The status of military personnel in the United Nations Operation in the former Yugoslavia has also been analyzed by the International Criminal Tribunal for the former Yugoslavia in the context of the question who has to give permission for them to testify. The Appeals Chamber has held in this regard that an officer "is present in the former Yugoslavia as a member of an international armed force responsible for maintaining or enforcing peace and not qua member of the national military structure." *Prosecutor* v. *Tihomir Blaskič*, Judgement on the Request of the Republic of Croatia for Review of the Decision of Trial Chamber II of 18 July 1997, Case No. IT-95-14-AR108 bis, A. Ch., 2 October 1997.

156 F. Seyersted, United Nations Forces in the Law of Peace and War 97 (1966).

157 UN Doc. A/3943 of 9 October 1958, para. 136.

158 UN Doc. A/45/594 of 9 October 1990, para. 15.

159 Seyersted, *supra* note 156, at 112-117.

160 H. McCoubrey & N. White, The Blue Helmets: Legal Regulation of United Nations Military Operations 142 (1996). See also R. Murphy, *Legal Framework of UN Forces and Issues of Command and Control of Canadian and Irish Forces*, 4 Journal of Armed Conflict Law 41 (1999).

a Special Representative of the Secretary-General (SRSG) who has authority over the civilian as well as military elements. The Special Representative, or in his absence the Force Commander, is the Head of Mission. According to the model participating state agreement, the authority of the Secretary-General in the field "shall be exercised by the Head of Mission, who shall be responsible to the Secretary-General."[161] In practice, the division of responsibilities between the SRSG and the FC is arranged in an internal document.[162]

The level of command and control conferred on the UN is not easy to express in definite terms. The UN does not have agreed terms to designate levels of command and control such as NATO has.[163] In principle the level of command conferred on the UN FC is set out in the participating state agreement and/or Transfer of Authority (TOA) and may vary. The TOA is the action by a state that brings military personnel under the command of the international commander. The use of terms in the TOA is connected to, and varies with, national use of terms.

The German government for example referred to UN command over German troops in the United Nations Operation in the former Yugoslavia as 'operational control',[164] a term with a distinct meaning in NATO terminology. The Dutch gov-

---

161 UN Doc. A/46/185, para. 7.

162 See *e.g.* in relation to the United Nations Mission in Ethiopia and Eritrea Bijlagen Handelingen II, 2000-01, 22831, 10, para. 12.

163 The North Atlantic Treaty Organization distinguishes the following levels of command and control in the NATO Glossary of Terms and Definitions, AAP-6, 2004:

Full command

The military authority and responsibility of a superior officer to issue orders to subordinates. It covers every aspect of military operations and exists only within national services.

Operational Command (OPCOM)

The authority granted to a commander to assign missions or tasks to subordinate commanders, to deploy units, to reassign forces, and to retain or delegate operational and/or tactical control as may be deemed necessary. It does not of itself include responsibility for administration or logistics. May also be used to denote the forces assigned to a commander.

Operational control (OPCON)

The authority delegated to a commander to direct forces assigned so that the commander may accomplish specific missions or tasks which are usually limited by function, time, or location; to deploy units concerned, and to retain or assign tactical control of those units. It does not include authority to assign separate employment of components of the units concerned. Neither does it, of itself, include administrative or logistic control.

Tactical command (TACOM)

The authority delegated to a commander to assign tasks to forces under his command for the accomplishment of the mission assigned by higher authority.

Tactical control (TACON)

The detailed and, usually, local direction and control of movements or manoeuvres necessary to accomplish missions or tasks assigned.

164 Bulletin 32 of 23 April 1993, cited in BverGE 90, 286, at 311.

ernment referred to UN command over Dutch troops in the same operation as 'operational command',[165] although there is no clear indication that the Dutch government granted different powers over its contingent than the German government over its contingent. It is certain that participating states always retain full command, in other words the authority to withdraw the troops.

The Secretary-General presented a report in 1994 in relation to command and control over UN peace support operations. This report states that:

> In general, United Nations command is not full command and is closer in meaning to the generally recognized military concept of "operational command". It involves the full authority to issue operational directives within the limits of (1) a specific mandate of the Security Council; (2) an agreed period of time, with the stipulation that an earlier withdrawal requires adequate prior notification; and (3) a specific geographical range (the mission area as a whole).[166]

According to the Secretary-General, it is clearly impermissible for contingent commanders to be instructed by national authorities to depart from UN policies, or to refuse to carry out orders.[167]

Illustrative of the confusion in this area is that only a year after the presentation of the Secretary-General's report, the Special Committee on Peacekeeping Operations stated that "the authority of the UN Force Commander is based on the concept of operational control."[168]

In practice, the actual level of UN command, whatever the term used, depends to a certain extent on political factors. It is a compromise between the desire for unity of command and legitimate interests of the participating states.[169] This compromise can for example be institutionalized by appointing officers from participating states to the staff of an operation.[170]

Of much greater concern is that in certain cases participating states do not respect more or less formal agreements relating to command and control. There are reports of cases in which commanders of national contingents countermanded orders of a UN commander or where national authorities bypassed the chain of command. The Secretary-General for example states that during the United Nations Operation in Somalia, while some contingents were ostensibly part of the operation, they were

165 Handelingen II 1994-95, p. 5987.

166 UN Doc. A/49/681 of 21 November 1994, para. 6.

167 *Id.*, para. 7.

168 Report of the Special Committee on Peace-keeping Operations of 22 June 1995, UN Doc. A/50/230, para. 53. The Committee also states that "it would be useful for the Department of Peacekeeping Operations, in co-operation with member States, to reach an agreed definition of the different kinds of command relationships applicable to peacekeeping operations.", para. 54.

169 Interview with a senior official in the United Nations Department of Peacekeeping Operations of 18 September 2002.

170 See *e.g.* S. Gordon, *Icarus Rising and Falling: The Evolution of UN Command and Control Structures*, in D. Gordon & F. Toase (Eds.), Aspects of Peacekeeping 19 (2001).

in fact consulting first with their national capitals.[171] Similar problems occurred in the United Nations Operation in the former Yugoslavia. There are reports that then President Chirac of France bypassed UN commanders on several occasions. United Nations commander Rose gives a number of other examples in his account of the operation.[172] A continuing question is whether or not the Dutch government directly gave orders to the Dutch contingent in Srebrenica in 1995, which the government denies.[173] There were reports in September 2000 that the Nigerian contingent in the United Nations Mission in Sierra Leone ignored orders from the Indian Force Commander.[174] In general, as these examples illustrate, intervention by national authorities is more frequent in a volatile environment.

1.8.4 Legal status of North Atlantic Treaty Organization peace support operations

In the case of NATO peace support operations the legal status of each individual operation is specified in several instruments. These operations have differed in legal basis, scale and other respects, but proven structures, procedures and command and control arrangements in the organization have developed.

Operations by the organization have included two smaller-scale operations in the former Yugoslav Republic of Macedonia (FYROM) at the request of the government. The first, Operation Essential Harvest, had a mandate to collect arms and ammunition voluntarily turned over by ethnic Albanian insurgents, and thereby help to build confidence in the broader peace process. The second, Operation Amber Fox, had the mandate to contribute to the protection of international monitors from the EU and the OSCE overseeing the implementation of a peace plan.[175]

The organization also deployed an operation in Albania (April-September 1999), Operation Allied Harbour later renamed Operation Joint Guardian, at the request of the Albanian government to assist the government in resolving a refugee crisis. Two other NATO-led operations were deployed in the context of the Kosovo crisis. Operation Eagle Eye (30 October 1998 – 24 March 1999) consisted of verification flights over Kosovo in support of the Kosovo Verification Mission conducted by the OSCE. The legal basis for the operation was the Kosovo Verification Mission Agreement signed by the government of the Federal Republic of Yugoslavia, and Security Council Resolution 1199.[176] In the same context the organization deployed

---

171 United Nations, The United Nations and Somalia 1992-1996 86 (1996). See also L. Ahlquist (Ed.), Co-operation, Command and Control in UN Peace-keeping Operations (1996).

172 M. Rose, Fighting for Peace 85, 116 (1998).

173 Bijlagen Handelingen II 1996-97, 22181, 181.

174 C. McGreal, *Nigerian Peace Force Accused of Sabotage*, the Guardian 14 September 2000.

175 See for a detailed discussion of the legal status of these operations P. Dreist, *Die Task Force Harvest und die Task Force Fox – Beiträge zur Stabilisierung Makedoniens*, 8 Humanitäres Völkerrecht – Informationsschriften 4 (2002).

176 Letter dated 22 October 1998 from the Chargé d'Affaires a.i. of the Mission of the United States of America to the United Nations of 23 October 1998, UN Doc. S/1998/991; Security Council Resolution 1199 of 23 September 1998, UN Doc. S/RES/1199.

a contingency force (Operation Determined Guarantor) in the former Yugoslav Republic of Macedonia, with the consent of the government, with a mandate to assist in the extraction of the Kosovo Verification Mission if necessary.

By far the most important NATO peace support operations in terms of scale, mandate, powers and potential for internationally wrongful acts, however, are the Implementation Force (IFOR, later Stabilization Force (SFOR)) in Bosnia-Herzegovina and Croatia, and the Kosovo Force (KFOR) in Kosovo. In addition, on 11 August 2003 NATO assumed command of the International Security Assistance Force (ISAF) in Afghanistan. The legal basis for ISAF is found in Annex 1 to the 'Bonn Agreement', which was concluded on 5 December 2001 at a meeting which brought together UN officials, representatives of various Afghan political groups and factions and representatives of states and international organizations. The Security Council subsequently authorized the establishment of ISAF under Chapter VII of the UN Charter as envisaged in the Bonn Agreement, to assist the Afghan Interim Government in the maintenance of security in Kabul and its surrounding areas.[177]

1.8.5 *Legal status of IFOR and SFOR*

IFOR had its origin in Annex 1A (Agreement on the Military Aspects of the Peace Settlement) to the Dayton Peace Agreements. Article 1, paragraph 1, subparagraph a of the agreement states that:

> The United Nations Security Council is invited to adopt a resolution by which it will authorize Member States or regional organizations and arrangements to establish a multinational military Implementation Force (hereinafter "IFOR"). The Parties understand and agree that this Implementation Force may be composed of ground, air and maritime units from NATO and non-NATO nations.

Subparagraph b of paragraph 1 describes that:

> It is understood and agreed that NATO may establish such a force, which will operate under the authority and subject to the direction and political control of the North Atlantic Council ('NAC') through the NATO chain of command.

Status of Forces Agreements concerning the force were signed between NATO on the one hand, and Bosnia Herzegovina, Croatia and the Federal Republic of Yugoslavia on the other hand, and attached to Annex 1A as appendices. The Status of Forces Agreements were complemented with Technical Arrangements. A Technical Arrangement was concluded between Croatia and the North Atlantic Treaty Organization on behalf of IFOR. Another Technical Arrangement was concluded between Bosnia Herzegovina and IFOR itself.

The Security Council Resolution referred to in the agreement was adopted as Resolution 1031. It authorized member states acting through or in cooperation with

---

177 Security Council Resolution 1386 of 20 December 2001, UN Doc. S/RES/1386.

the organization referred to in Annex 1A of the Peace Agreement to establish a multinational implementation force under unified command and control in order to fulfill the role specified in Annex 1A and Annex 2 of the peace agreement.[178]

Participating state agreements between NATO and its members concerning service with the force were not concluded. Conditions of service for contingents from non-member states were agreed in correspondence between the governments in question and the organization.[179]

Some writers state that IFOR was not a subsidiary organ of NATO. [180] Others even state that the organization was "merely providing Command, Control, Communication and Intelligence (C^3I) infrastructure and co-ordination between United Nations Member States contributing to IFOR without thereby affecting the legal status of their contribution.".[181] According to this view, although Annex 1A of the peace agreement provides that IFOR will be established by NATO, Security Council Resolution 1031 only authorized *member states* to establish a force, albeit "through or in cooperation with the organization referred to in Annex 1A of the Peace Agreement." Therefore the organization itself would not be entitled to establish a force under the resolution. Figà-Talamanca states that:

> Aside from political considerations, however, NATO involvement is restricted to the co-ordination of United Nations Member States for the establishment of IFOR under unified command and control. The fact that members of NATO are choosing to provide their troops and equipment under the NATO insigniae should not be confused with an intervention of NATO as an Alliance.[182]

This description does not seem a reflection of the organization's actual role in IFOR. Operational planning was conducted by the organization's organs leading to Operational Plan (OPLAN) 10405. The North Atlantic Council (NAC), an organization organ, adopted the operational plan and authorized a NATO commander to command the operation. This commander used an organization procedure called an activation order (ACTORD) to authorize troops under his control to move into active duty. Reports on Implementation and Stabilization Force operations to the Security Council have been submitted by the Secretary-General of NATO and not by member states.[183] This does not point to the establishment of the operation by member states

178 Security Council Resolution 1031 of 15 December 1995, UN Doc. S/RES/1031, para. 14.

179 UN Doc. S/1996/49 of 23 January 1996, para. 4.

180 M. Donner, *Völkerrechtliche und Verfassungsrechtliche Aspekte der Militärischen Abischerung der Friedensvereinbarung von Dayton*, 10 Humanitäres Völkerrecht 63 (1997), at 67; M. Bothe, *Peacekeeping and International Humanitarian Law: Friends or Foes?*, 3 International Peacekeeping 91 (1996), at 93.

181 N. Figà-Talamanca, *The Role of NATO in the Peace Agreement for Bosnia and Herzegovina*, 7 European Journal of International Law 164 (1996).

182 *Id.*

183 See *e.g.* UN Doc. S/1996/49 of 23 January 1996; UN Doc. S/1996/1066 of 24 December 1996, and UN Doc. S/1997/81 of 27 January 1997.

using the organization merely as a facilitating instrument. Lüder argues that SFOR is not a subsidiary organ of NATO because participating states have merely conferred operational control.[184] On this basis, it is argued, the commander could not enforce his orders against the national contingent. Lüder does not make clear how the situation is different from UN peace support operations, in which the German government has also conferred operational control[185] but which are nevertheless subordinate organs of the Security Council or the General Assembly.[186] Regular political consultation with non-NATO member contributors takes place at the level of the NAC and at the deputy level, but there are also regular political meetings with troop contributing states in UN operations. In 1996, the Security Council adopted procedures for consultations which are to be held as a matter of course between members of the Council, troop-contributing countries and the Secretariat.[187] In 2001, the Security Council adopted detailed provisions on format, procedures and documentation of meetings with troop-contributing countries.[188] An important role of NATO in IFOR does not necessarily mean that the operation is a subsidiary organ of the organization. The 1949 Washington Treaty provides that the North Atlantic Council "shall set up such subsidiary bodies as may be necessary", but there is no definition of the term 'subsidiary body' or 'subsidiary organ' in the organization or in international law. The term subsidiary organ is also used in the United Nations, *inter alia* for peace support operations. A UN document defines a subsidiary organ as:

> one which is established by or under the authority of a principal organ of the United Nations, in accordance with Article 7, paragraph 2, of the Charter, by resolution of the appropriate body.... Most subsidiary organs have in common their establishment by parent bodies which presumably may change their terms of reference and composition, issue policy directives to them, receive their reports and accept or reject their recommendations. Generally speaking, a subsidiary organ may be abolished or modified by action of the parent body.[189]

184 S. Lüder, *Die Völkerrechtliche Verantwortlichkeit der Nordatlantikvertrags-Organisation bei Militärische Absicherung der Friedensvereinbarung van Dayton*, 43 Neue Zeitschrift für Wehrrecht 107 (2001), at 116.

185 See para. 1.8.3.

186 See also the statement by the Netherlands government that:

> In de praktijk draagt Nederland aan deze "Major NATO Commanders" en aan lagere commandanten zoals commandant SFOR, evenals aan VN-commandanten zoals de Force Commander van UNMEE, Operational Control over.
>
> (In practice the Netherlands transfers Operational Control to these "Major NATO Commanders" and to subordinate commanders such as Commander SFOR, as well as to UN Commanders such as the UNMEE Commander) Translation by the author.

Bijlagen Handelingen II 2000-01, 26454, 18.

187 UN Doc. S/PRST/1996/13 of 28 March 1996.

188 Security Council Resolution 1353 of 13 June 2001, UN Doc. S/RES/1353.

189 Summary of internal Secretariat studies of constitutional questions relating to agencies within the framework of the United Nations: this document was subsequently proposed to the General Assembly, UN Doc. A/C1/758, paras 1-2, cited in D. Sarooshi, *supra* note 97.

According to this definition, *mutatis mutandis*, IFOR meets the requirements for a subsidiary organ of NATO. It is established by the NAC, a principal organ of the organization, and it is under the authority and control of that principal organ.

1.8.6 Military command over the Implementation Force and Stabilization Force

The Supreme Commander Allied Forces Europe (SACEUR), one of the two major NATO commanders, was directed by the NAC to assume operational command and control over the operation. He delegated his command to a subordinate NATO commander, the Commander-in-Chief Allied Forces Southern Europe (CINCSOUTH), as the commander of IFOR.[190] Participating states conferred operation control, as defined in NATO terminology, to the IFOR commander. A separate command and control arrangement was concluded in relation to the Russian contingent. Command relationships in SFOR are essentially the same as in IFOR. A NATO commander exercises operational control over national contingents.[191]

1.8.7 Legal status of the Kosovo Force

The first reference to an international security presence in Kosovo is in a statement adopted by G-8 Foreign Ministers on 6 May 1999. This statement was adopted during the NATO air campaign in the Federal Republic of Yugoslavia and concerned general principles on the political solution to the Kosovo crisis agreed on by the G-8. The peace plan presented to the leadership of the Federal Republic of Yugoslavia by the President of Finland, Martti Ahtisaari, representing the European Union, and Viktor Chernomyrdin, Special Representative of the President of the Russian Federation, and adopted by the Parliaments of the Federal Republic of Yugoslavia and Serbia on 3 June 1999, provided for an international security presence under UN auspices with substantial NATO participation under unified command and control.[192]

On 9 June a Military Technical Agreement was signed between the International Security Force and the governments of the Federal Republic of Yugoslavia and the Republic of Serbia. Article 1 of the Agreement states:

> The Parties to this Agreement reaffirm the document presented by President Ahtisaari to President Milosevic and approved by the Serb Parliament and the Federal Government on June 3, 1999, to include deployment in Kosovo under UN auspices of effective international civil and security presences. The Parties further

---

190 Bijlagen Handelingen II 1995-96, 22181, 137.

191 Bijlagen Handelingen II 1996-97, 22181, 174.

192 Letter Dated 7 June 1999 From the Permanent Representative of Germany to the United Nations Addressed to the President of the Security Council, UN Doc. S/1999/649 (1999) (Agreement on the principles (peace plan) to move towards a resolution of the Kosovo crisis presented to the leadership of the Federal Republic of Yugoslavia by the President of Finland, Martti Ahtisaari, representing the European Union, and Viktor Chernomyrdin, Special Representative of the President of the Russian Federation, 3 June 1999), paras. 3-4.

> note that the UN Security Council is prepared to adopt a resolution, which has been introduced, regarding these presences.
>
> The State Governmental authorities of the Federal Republic of Yugoslavia and the Republic of Serbia understand and agree that the international security force ("KFOR") will deploy following the adoption of the UNSCR referred to in paragraph 1 and operate without hindrance within Kosovo and with the authority to take all necessary action to establish and maintain a secure environment for all citizens of Kosovo and otherwise carry out its mission. They further agree to comply with all of the obligations of this Agreement and to facilitate the deployment and operation of this force.[193]

The resolution referred to in the Agreement was adopted the next day as Security Council Resolution 1244. The Security Council, acting under Chapter VII of the UN Charter, authorized member states and relevant international organizations to establish the international security presence in Kosovo.[194]

The Military Technical Agreement provides that the parties will agree on a Status of Forces Agreement as soon as possible.[195] Such an agreement for the Kosovo Force was drafted by NATO.[196] Negotiations were not started with the Federal Republic of Yugoslavia, however, because the international community and member states wanted to politically isolate the regime in Belgrade and therefore did not want to conclude international agreements with it. Concluding an agreement would also have impinged on the competence of the UN-led civilian mission.[197]

Instead of in a bilateral agreement, the legal status of the force, or at least those aspects thereof commonly governed by a SOFA, were regulated unilaterally. The commander of KFOR promulgated an 'Interim Status of Forces policy' in 1999. The document stated that the legal basis for such a policy was the provision in the Military Technical Agreement that authorizes the commander to do all that he judges necessary and proper to protect the international security force.[198] This policy was replaced by a common declaration by the Kosovo Force and the United Nations Mission in Kosovo signed on 17 August 2000 and issued the next day as Regulation 2000/47 by the SRSG as the legislating power in Kosovo. The regulation provides *inter alia* for privileges and immunities of the civil and security presences. In contrast to UN peace support operations, requests for waiver of jurisdiction are referred to the respective commander of

193 Military Technical Agreement Between the International Security Force ("KFOR") and the Governments of the Federal Republic of Yugoslavia and the Republic of Serbia, reproduced in 38 ILM 1217, Article 1, paras. 1-2.

194 Security Council Resolution 1244 of 10 June 1999, UN Doc. S/RES/1999, para. 7.

195 *Supra* note 193, Annex 2, para. 3.

196 P. Dreist, *Rechtliche Aspekte des KFOR-Einsatzes*, 43 Neue Zeitschrift für Wehrrecht 1 (2001), at 4.

197 M. Guillaume, *supra* note 93, at 253.

198 KFOR Interim Status of Forces Policy, copy on file with the author.

the national element. The regulation also provides that Kosovo Force personnel shall be subject to the exclusive jurisdiction of their respective sending states.

Operational planning for the Kosovo Force was done within NATO. The NAC approved the Operational Plan (OPLAN) on 9 June 1999 after consultations with non-member participating states.[199]

The above-mentioned considerations relating to IFOR as possibly a subsidiary organ of the NAC also apply to the Kosovo Force. The force was established by the NAC, a principal organ of the organization, and it is under the authority and control of that principal organ. In addition and in contrast to IFOR, Security Council Resolution 1244 authorized member states and relevant international organizations, instead of member states acting through an organization, to establish the international security presence in Kosovo.[200]

1.8.8 Military command and control over the Kosovo Force

As in the case of IFOR and SFOR, military command of KFOR was initially conferred on the Supreme Allied Commander Europe (SACEUR), who delegated his command to another NATO command, Commander in Chief Allied Forces, Southern Europe (CINCSOUTH). SACEUR was responsible to the NAC.[201] The KFOR Commander was appointed by NATO and responsible to CINCSOUTH. Participating states conferred operational control over national contingents to the KFOR Commander.[202]

A special agreement concerning command and control was concluded concerning command and control over Russian troops, similar to the agreement concerning command and control over Russian troops in IFOR.[203] Multinational command did not extend to administrative control over national contingents or to personnel management.

Some writers refer to the existence of a so-called 'red card procedure', which would give each contingent the right to not take orders if they contradict their national policy.[204] It may be noted however that generally, there is no formalized procedure for such refusal of orders.[205] Troop contributing states often send a national representative

---

199 Bijlagen Handelingen II 1998-99, 22181, 284.

200 Security Council Resolution 1244 of 10 June 1999, UN Doc. S/RES/1244, para. 7.

201 In March 2001 the Minister for Foreign and Commonwealth Affairs of the United Kingdom stated that the "commander of KFOR is appointed by NATO and is accountable to NATO", Hansard HC, 27 March 2001, col. 824.

202 See *e.g.* Bijlagen Handelingen II, 2000-01, 22181, 331; Hansard HC, 7 February 2002, col. 1084W.

203 Agreement on Russian Participation in KFOR, News Release No. 301-99, Office of Assistant Secretary of Defense, 18 June 1999.

204 See *e.g.* J. Cerone, *Minding the Gap: Outlining KFOR Accountability in Post-Conflict Kosovo*, 12 European Journal of International Law 469 (2001), at 486.

205 White uses the term red card to describe the case in which a UN contingent commander ignores the orders of the UN commander on instruction from his national capital. White, *supra* note 108, at 136.

to the mission area. This representative is called the 'Senior National Representative' (SNR). The SNR may combine his national role with a staff function in the peace support operation. The SNR formally has no authority concerning the operations of the national contingent, although he does coordinate with the international commander when important changes occur concerning the tasks, execution of the mandate, the Rules of Engagement (ROE), the Area of Responsibility (AOR) or the composition of the force. Formally, however, concerns of the SNR should be relayed to the capital of the troop contributing nation who should then take them up with NATO through diplomatic channels.. In specific circumstances, troop contributing states may agree with the international commander to formally deploy a 'red card holder'. The specific circumstances generally relate to the sensitivity of the means deployed, for example attack helicopters or fighter planes. The red card holder is a national representative of the troop contributing state. In contrast to the SNR, the red card holder has formal authority to reject specific missions given to the national contingent by the international commander.

1.8.9 Legal status of ISAF

The situation of NATO in relation to ISAF appears to be much the same as in relation to SFOR and KFOR. The NAC decision of 16 April 2003 to continue and enhance NATO support to ISAF included agreement to assume strategic command, control and coordination exercised by SACEUR, as well as the exercise of political direction and coordination by the NAC. On 11 August 2003 NATO took over command of ISAF. Prior to that date command over the force was exercised by consecutive 'lead nations', the first of which was the United Kingdom. Operational planning for the operation is performed by planning staff at the NATO Supreme Headquarters of the Allied Powers in Europe (SHAPE), who have developed several OPLANs for ISAF. The NATO Secretary-General reports on the activities of ISAF to the UN.[206]

1.8.10 Military command and control over ISAF

Initially ISAF was under the command of subsequent 'lead nations'. During this period the operation was a 'coalition of the able and willing' composed of an *ad hoc* group of states. Under NATO command after 11 August 2003, the North Atlantic Council provides political direction to ISAF, in consultation with non-NATO ISAF troop contributing nations. Military command was conferred to SACEUR, who delegated it to Commander, Allied Forces North (AFNORTH), a subordinate NATO commander. AFNORTH acts as the operational-level Joint Force Command headquarters between SACEUR and Commander ISAF, who is appointed by NATO. NATO provides a composite headquarters to form the permanent core of the ISAF headquarters. Troop contributing states conferred operational control over national contingents to the ISAF Commander. ISAF also provides an example of a 'red card holder'. In March 2003 the Netherlands contributed six AH-64 helicopters to ISAF.

206 See *e.g.* UN Doc. S/2003/503 of 28 April 2003; UN Doc. S/2003/970 of 8 October 2003.

A 'red card holder' monitors the application of the Rules of Engagement and the tactical missions assigned to the helicopter pilots.[207]

1.9 Conclusion

It may seem unnecessary to give an account of the evolution of peace support operations to arrive at a definition of the term 'peace support operation'. This chapter however demonstrates that the operations which are referred to in common usage as 'peace support operations' vary widely. The UN initiated the first peace support operation as a pragmatic response to a problem that could not be addressed through the procedures envisaged by the drafters of the UN Charter. The *ad hoc* way in which the first operation was established became characteristic of all subsequent peace support operations. One author notes that the concept "reflects the crisis management approach of the Organisation's work concerning international peace and security."[208] Peace support operations have evolved in response to new political environments and they will continue to evolve. The proposals in the Brahimi Report will probably to a certain extent plot the course for further evolution. A definition of peace support operations can only be properly understood taking account of this continuing development, which makes it very difficult to strictly separate different kinds of operations.

The definition of 'peace support operations' used in this study is in line with NATO doctrine. It encompasses certain non-coercive as well as coercive operations. Importantly, the element of impartiality distinguishes peace support operations from 'enforcement' or war.

This study is limited to peace support operations led by the UN and by NATO for two main reasons: first, because these organizations are presently important actors in the maintenance of international peace and security, and second, because peace support operations led by international organizations raise particular questions of applicable law and accountability.

These questions arise from the involvement of international organizations on the one hand, and the relationship between these organizations and states on the other hand. Neither the UN nor NATO has a standing army for peace support operations. The UN depends on voluntary contributions of troops by member states to deploy an operation because the agreements provided for in Article 43 of the Charter, which would have made troops available to the organization on its call, were never concluded. NATO also depends on voluntary contributions in the case of peace support or non-Article 5 operations. This requires regulation of the competences of the international organization in question and the troop contributing states.

The relationship between the international organization in question and the troop contributing states requires regulation for each individual peace support operation because of the *ad hoc* character of such operations. The result of this regulation may vary, because it depends to a large extent on the specific situation in which an

207 Bijlagen Handelingen II, 2003-04, 27925, 11.

208 N. White, Keeping the Peace: The United Nations and the Maintenance of International Peace and Security 184 (1993).

operation is established, but certain procedural as well as substantive patterns may be discerned. Procedurally, the legal status of national contingents in peace support operations is generally regulated in participating states agreements and in a Status of Forces Agreement, although in certain cases it may not be necessary or possible to conclude one or more of these agreements. In NATO operations, a distinction is made between member states, whose relationship with the organization is already defined to a large extent, and non-member states.

Substantively, the troop contributing states confer certain decision-making powers over their contingent to the international organization in question while retaining certain others, in particular criminal jurisdiction. A certain level of military command is conferred from the states to a multinational commander, although in practice the formal agreement concerning transfer of authority is not respected in all cases. The result of these arrangements is that the national contingents are to a certain extent integrated into the organization in question while retaining their national identity. This is generally accepted in respect of national contingents in UN peace support operations which are recognized as part of a subsidiary organ of the UN principal organ which established the operation, but it also seems to be the case for national contingents in NATO peace support operations whose legal status seems to resemble that of UN operations to a degree which is not generally recognized.

The legal status of peace support operations, in other words the relationship between the international persons involved, is the key to determine the applicable law and questions of accountability in the following chapters. These chapters will make clear that the complex character of the legal status and its *ad hoc* development are reflected in questions of applicable law, and in particular, questions of accountability. The *bricolage institutionnel* in the establishment of peace support operations must have its repercussions on the legal issues involved.[209]

209 See J.M. Sorel, *La Responsabilité des Nations Unies dans les Opérations de Maintien de la Paix*, 3 International Law Forum 127 (2001), at 138.

2

Attribution of Conduct of Peace Support Operations

2.1 Introduction

International responsibility requires the breach of an obligation under international law which is attributable to a legal person. This chapter discusses the element of attribution, that is to which entity the conduct of peace support operations is attributable. The second element, the breach of an international obligation, is discussed in the next chapter.

As noted above, this study focuses on peace support operations under the command and control of the UN and those under the command and control of NATO. As a consequence, this chapter is principally concerned with those two types of peace support operations. Nevertheless, it is inevitable that certain general assertions are made, in particular in connection with the responsibility of international organizations.

Different actors are involved in the establishment, deployment and functioning of a peace support operation. In particular, these are the international organization concerned, its member states, troop contributing states as well as the host state. It is largely this multiplicity of actors and the intricate relationship between them which makes the question of attribution of conduct of a peace support operation so complex. Another reason for the complexity of attribution of conduct of peace support operations is that it is connected with questions of state responsibility as well as the responsibility of international organizations. State responsibility on the one hand is governed by a relatively developed set of principles. The ILC adopted a set of draft articles on state responsibility in 2001 after many years of work on the topic. Many of these articles are considered by states to be a codification of customary international law. Principles of the responsibility of international organizations on the other hand are very much underdeveloped. Until quite recently it was unclear whether an international organization can incur responsibility and if so, on what basis.

2.2 The basis of state responsibility

In doctrine and practice, state responsibility is regarded as a consequence of the breach or non-performance of an international obligation by the state. International responsibility is the term which describes the new legal relations to which the non-performance of an international obligation gives rise. Such non-performance automatically leads to a new legal relationship, or as Special Rapporteur García Amador wrote in his first report on the topic for the ILC "international responsibility, of whatever specific type, is invariably the consequence of the breach or non-performance of an international obligation."[1] A classical statement of the principle is by Judge Huber in the *British Claims in the Spanish Zone of Morocco* case that responsibility is "the necessary corollary of rights. All international rights entail international responsibility."[2] More recently the International Court of Justice stated in the *Gabčikovo-Nagymaros* case that:

> It is moreover well established that, when a State has committed an internationally wrongful act, its international responsibility is likely to be involved whatever the nature of the obligation it has failed to respect.[3]

Article 1 of the ILC draft articles on state responsibility restates this basic principle, and Article 2 specifies the conditions required to establish the existence of an internationally wrongful act of the state:

> **Article 1**
> **Responsibility of a State for its internationally wrongful acts**
>
> Every internationally wrongful act of a State entails the international responsibility of that State.
>
> **Article 2**
> **Elements of an internationally wrongful act of a State**
>
> There is an internationally wrongful act of a State when conduct consisting of an action or omission:
> (a) Is attributable to the State under international law; and
> (b) Constitutes a breach of an international obligation of the State.

Among other things, the above demonstrates that state responsibility is closely connected to the concept of international legal personality. The existence of an international obligation of the state is a requirement for state responsibility. A state is capable of having international obligations under international law because it has international legal personality.[4]

---

1 F.V. García Amador, First Report on State Responsibility, YBILC 1956, Vol. II (Part I) 173, at 184, para. 58.

2 UNRIAA vol. II, 615 (1925), at 641.

3 Gabčikovo-Nagymaros Project (*Hungary* v. *Slovakia*), 1997 ICJ Reports 7, at 38, para. 47. For other judicial statements of the principle see Report of the International Law Commission on the work of its fifty-third session, 23 April - 1 June and 2 July - 10 August 2001 (A/56/10), at 63-65, paras. 2-3.

4 See García Amador, *supra* note 1, at 185, para. 64: "Responsibility is a consequence of the breach or non-observance of an international obligation. Its imputability therefore necessarily depends upon who is or are the subject or subjects of that obligation. International doctrine and practice have developed in accordance with a conception of international law in which the State is the only subject capable of possessing or assuming international obligations."

2.3 The basis of the responsibility of international organizations

The connection between the possession of international rights and obligations and international responsibility is also the basis for the recognition in theory of the responsibility of international organizations. This basis is widely accepted by writers.

For example, Eagleton asserts: "A state, or other international legal person, may be held responsible only to the extent that it has rights and duties which it is free to exercise",[5] and Sands and Klein contend that from:

> a theoretical point of view, the fact that international organisations may be held accountable for the consequences of their illegal or wrongful acts is widely accepted. Liability is thus generally presented as the logical corollary of the powers and rights conferred upon international organisations.[6]

In the specific case of the UN, the International Court of Justice's Advisory Opinion in the *Reparations for Injuries Suffered in the Service of the United Nations* case is considered to confirm the link between international legal personality and international responsibility. In this Advisory Opinion the Court established a connection between the international legal personality of the organization and the capacity to maintain its rights by bringing international claims or, in other words, its 'passive' international responsibility.[7] Although the Court did not discuss the question of the 'active' international responsibility of the UN, *i.e.* its capacity for being responsible, recognition of such responsibility is implicit because the passive and active sides of responsibility are inseparable.[8]

---

5 C. Eagleton, International Organization and the Law of Responsibility, 76 Recueil des Cours (1950-I), 386.

6 P. Sands & P. Klein, Bowett's Law of International Institutions 513 (2001), para. 15-087; see also P. Reuter, *Sur Quelques Limites du Droit des Organisations Internationales*, in E. Diez, J. Monnier, J. Müller, H. Reimann and L. Wildhaber (Eds.), Festschrift für Rudolf Bindschedler, Botschafter, Professor Dr. Iur. Zum 65. Geburtstag 8. Juli 1980, 491 (1980), at 505; M.H. Arsanjani, *Claims against International Organizations: Quis custodiet ipsos custodes*, 7 The Yale Journal of World Public Order 131 (1981), at 132; M. Perez-Gonzalez, *Les Organisations Internationales et le Droit de la Responsabilité*, 92 Revue Générale de Droit International Public 63 (1988), at 64; P. de Visscher, Rapport définitif, Les Conditions d'application des Lois de la Guerre aux Opérations Militaires des Nations Unies, Annuaire IDI 54-I (1971) 116.

7 "*the Court has come to the conclusion that the Organization is an international person.* That is not the same as saying that it is a State, which it certainly is not, or that its legal personality and rights and duties are the same as those of a State. Still less it is the same thing as saying that it is 'a super-State', whatever that expression may mean. It does not even imply that all its rights and duties must be upon the international plane, any more than all the rights and duties of a State must be upon that plane. *What it does mean is that it is a subject of international law and capable of possessing international rights and duties, and that it has capacity to maintain its rights by bringing international claims.*" Reparations for Injuries Suffered in the Service of the United Nations, Advisory Opinion of 11 April 1949, 1949 ICJ Reports 174, at 179 (emphasis added).

8 See B. Amrallah, *The International Responsibility of the U.N. for the Activities Carried out by U.N. Peacekeeping Forces*, 32 Revue Egyptienne de Droit International 57 (1976), at 60-61.

The capacity of international organizations for international responsibility is also recognized in the work of the ILC. The first report on the topic of state responsibility submitted to the ILC by Special Rapporteur García Amador in 1956 covered international responsibility in general. The report recognized that the appearance of new subjects on the international stage, including international organizations, could not remain without consequences for international responsibility.[9] One of these consequences was that international organizations could be held responsible. One of the 'bases of discussion' at the end of the report, in which the Special Rapporteur presented a summary of his research and some of his conclusions, stated that:

> Basis of discussion No. II
> The active subjects of international responsibility
>
> (1) International responsibility being the consequence of the breach or non-observance of an international obligation, its imputability depends on who is the direct subject of the obligation.
> (2) Accordingly, the following may be active subjects of international responsibility:
> ...
> (c) International organizations, in respect of acts or omissions of their organs so far as the duty to make reparation for the injury caused is concerned.[10]

This basis of discussion was not taken up for discussion by the Commission, however. The Commission adopted the recommendation made by the Special Rapporteur that, at that stage, codification should be confined to the law on the responsibility of states for damage caused to the person or property of aliens. In 1963, the Commission reconsidered its approach to the topic of state responsibility and decided to focus on "the definition of the general rules governing the international responsibility of the State." International responsibility of international organizations was still not covered. In its work on state responsibility the Commission consciously tried to avoid the topic

9 "In contemporary international law, in which full recognition had been given to the existence of other subjects of international responsibility, traditional theory and practice must be reconsidered in order to adapt them to the new state of affairs." García Amador, 370th meeting, YBILC 1956 , at 229, para. 26.

10 See García Amador, *supra* note 1, at 219-220. Also: "A brief reference will be made to the cases in which responsibility is imputable to international organizations; in a sense, these cases do not present complications and difficulties as to other subjects of international law. In the first place, the international personality of these organizations, particularly of some of them, is no longer in doubt, especially so far as their rights and their capacity to exercise them are concerned, as will be seen in the next chapter. Nor can there be any doubt concerning their duties, for some of these are explicitly prescribed in their constitutions or rules and regulations. Accordingly, it cannot be denied that the non-performance of those obligations, like the breach or non-observance of any other international obligation, necessarily involves them in responsibility. In some respects, it is even possible to establish a definite analogy with the responsibility imputable to the State.", *Id.*, at 189, para. 83.

of the responsibility of international organizations. An example of such efforts is the statement in the commentary to draft article 13 adopted on first reading that:

> In studying the questions which arise in the context of this article, care must be taken not to go beyond the scope of the draft under consideration which, as already stated, is limited in respect of international responsibility to the responsibility of States, and does not deal with questions relating to the responsibility of subjects of international law other than States.[11]

In 1998, Special Rapporteur Crawford stated that some of the draft articles adopted on first reading by the Commission raised awkward issues with regard to the responsibility of international organizations. He proposed the adoption of a savings clause in the draft articles reserving any question of the responsibility under international law of an international organization or of any state for the acts of an international organization.[12] Acting on this recommendation the Commission adopted draft article 57, which states:

> These articles are without prejudice to any question of the responsibility under international law of an international organization, or of any State for the conduct of an international organization.

Despite all these efforts by the Commission to avoid mention of the responsibility of international organizations, discussions on state responsibility sometimes led to statements concerning the responsibility of international organizations. Such statements were made in connection with a draft article concerning the attribution to the state of the conduct of organs placed at its disposal by another state or by an international organization (draft article 9), and in connection with a draft article concerning the attribution to the state of conduct of organs of an international organization (draft article 13). These statements recognized the possibility of an international organization being responsible under international law,[13] although many of them also reaffirmed that the Commission did not have to define the rules on the possible responsibility of international organizations in the context of the draft articles on state responsibility.[14]

The commentary to draft article 57 of the draft articles on state responsibility also recognizes that international organizations can be responsible. The commentary states that:

---

11 YBILC 1975, Vol II, at 89-90.

12 J. Crawford, First Report on State Responsibility, Addendum of 22 July 1998, UN Doc. A/CN.4/490/Add.5, at 29, para. 234 and at 37, para. 262.

13 See *e.g.* YBILC 1974, Vol I, at 47, para. 39; YBILC 1975, Vol. I, at 45, para. 29, at 46, para. 35, at 47, paras. 5-6, at 60, para. 42.

14 See *e.g.* YBILC 1975, Vol. I, at 57, para 17, Bilge: "he considered that article 12 should not attempt to define the responsibility of international organizations."

> Such an organization possesses separate legal personality under international law, and is responsible for its own acts, i.e. for acts which are carried out by the organization through its own organs or officials.[15]

The clearest recognition by the ILC that international organizations can be responsible is that in 2002, pursuant to a request by the General Assembly,[16] the Commission included the topic of the responsibility of international organizations in its program of work. The ILC decided to establish a working group on responsibility of international organizations to be chaired by Mr. Giorgio Gaja. The commission also appointed Mr. Gaja as Special Rapporteur for the topic of responsibility of international organizations. In 2003 the Special Rapporteur submitted his first report on responsibility of international organizations to the ILC. The report starts with an overview of earlier work of the ILC on the topic. This work consists of the remarks made by the ILC in the process of compiling the draft articles on state responsibility as reviewed above. In this respect the report concludes as follows:

> While the draft articles adopted on second reading have left all the specific questions open, the Commission's work on State responsibility cannot fail to affect the new study. It would be unreasonable for the Commission to take a different approach on issues relating to international organizations that are parallel to those concerning States, unless there are specific reasons for doing so. This is not meant to state a presumption that the issues are to be regarded as similar and would lead to analogous solutions. The intention only is to suggest that, should the study concerning particular issues relating to international organizations produce results that do not differ from those reached by the Commission in its analysis of State responsibility, the model of the draft articles on State responsibility should be followed both in the general outline and in the wording of the text.[17]

This paragraph suggests that the effect of the draft articles on state responsibility on the drafting of the law of responsibility of international organizations is limited to the placement of particular articles. The suggestion appears to fail to recognize the fundamental correspondence between the two topics which is the result of the connection between legal personality and international responsibility. The latter connection is discussed in more detail below.

The report continues with a discussion of the scope of the study. This concerns the definition of 'international organization' for the purposes of the draft articles on responsibility of international organizations. The point of departure for this definition is that responsibility under international law may arise only for a subject of interna-

15 Report of the International Law Commission on the work of its fifty-third session, 23 April – 1 June and 2 July – 10 August 2001 (A/56/10), at 361, para. 2.

16 General Assembly Resolution 56/82 of 18 January 2002, UN Doc. A/RES/56/82, para. 8.

17 G. Gaja, First Report on Responsibility of International Organizations of 26 March 2003, UN Doc. A/CN.4/532, para. 11.

tional law.[18] The report espouses the so-called 'objective theory' of international legal personality. According to this theory, the characterization of an organization as a subject of international law appears as a question of fact.[19] The report proposes a number of elements for a definition of 'international organization'. These are the intergovernmental character of the organization, the exercise of normative, executive or judicial functions by the organization, and that the organization may be considered as a separate entity from its members. The report states that the question of the responsibility of a state either because it has contributed to the organization's unlawful act or else because it is a member of the organization should be included in the scope of the study, but:

> without prejudice to the way in which these questions should be answered. Even if the present study were to conclude that States are never responsible for the conduct of the organizations of which they are members, the scope of the present draft articles would not be accurately stated unless it was made clear that it includes those questions that were left out of the draft articles on State responsibility because of their relation to issues concerning responsibility of international organizations.[20]

The report states that the general principles of state responsibility also apply to international organizations, without giving substantive supporting arguments for this proposition.[21] This lack of argument is striking in view of the suggestion in another part of the report that principles from the draft articles on state responsibility can only be transposed to the draft articles on the responsibility of international organizations after careful study.[22] The report concludes with text proposals for three draft articles.

The Special Rapporteur's report was discussed by the ILC during its 2003 session. The most passionately debated issue was the definition of 'international organization' for the purposes of the draft articles. Specifically, there was much criticism of the Special Rapporteur's proposal to include the exercise of certain governmental functions as an element of the definition. Several members of the Commission either maintained that the expression 'certain governmental functions' was inaccurate because it equated international organizations to states,[23] or that the expression was too vague,[24] or that it unjustifiably excluded certain organizations, for example those devoted to scientific research.[25] On the other hand, several members of the Commission stressed that the possession of international legal personality should be

18 *Id.*, para. 15.

19 See para. 2.4.

20 *Supra* note 17, para. 33.

21 *Id.*, paras. 35-37.

22 See this para. above.

23 See *e.g.* Chee, UN Doc. A/CN.4/SR.2754, at 17; Galicki, UN Doc. A/CN.4/SR.2755, at 9; Escarameia, UN Doc. A/CN.4/SR.2755, at 10.

24 See *e.g.* Momtaz, UN Doc. A/CN.4/SR.2754, at 17; Candioti, UN Doc. A/CN.4/SR.2755, at 25.

25 See *e.g.* Koskeniemmi, UN Doc. A/CN.4/SR.2754, at 4.

an element of the definition.[26] It was pointed out that international legal personality is a prerequisite of international responsibility. One member of the Commission for example stated that:

> As a first step, it was important to establish that the organization possesses international personality, because that was what invested it with duties or obligations a breach of which might entail international responsibility.[27]

Another member of the Commission suggested that the Special Rapporteur might consider the viability of linking the issue of definition to the notion of legal personality by indicating the most relevant criteria pertaining to such personality.[28] This illustrates that members of the Commission felt that international legal personality is central to the notion of international responsibility.[29]

Draft article 1 on the scope of the draft articles, which the Special Rapporteur proposed in his first report, stated that the draft articles: "also apply to the question of the international responsibility of a State for the conduct of an international organization."[30] In the passage relating to this proposal in the Special Rapporteur's first report, specific mention is made of "conduct which, unlike that of international organizations acting as State organs, is to be attributed to an organization."[31] This leaves open both the possibility that a state is responsible for conduct attributable to an international organization that is in breach of an obligation of the organization itself, as well as the possibility that the state is responsible for conduct attributable to the organization that is in breach of an international obligation of that state.

The report continues to state that the responsibility of a state may arise "either because it has contributed to the organization's unlawful act or else because it is a member of the organization."[32] This appears to discard the possibility that the draft articles deal with the possibility that a state is responsible for an act that is attributable to an international organization which breaches an obligation of that state. The text of the report does not indicate whether this was the intention of the Special Rapporteur. During the ILC's 2003 deliberations on the responsibility of international organizations, none of the members referred to the possibility of state responsibility for conduct that is attributable to an international organization and that breaches an obligation of the state. Several members held that the draft articles on state responsibility already covered the question of the responsibility of a state for the conduct of an international organization. In so far as they were referring to Part One, Chapter II, of the draft arti-

26 See Pellet, UN Doc. A/CN.4/SR.2753, at 13; Sepúlveda, UN Doc. A/CN.4/SR.2754, at 14; Momtaz, UN Doc. A/CN.4/SR.2754, at 17; Galicki, UN Doc. A/CN.4/SR.2755, at 9; Candioti, UN Doc. A/CN.4/SR.2755, at 25.

27 Addo, UN Doc. A/CN.4/SR.2755, at 11.

28 Comissario Afonso, UN Doc. A/CN.4/SR.2755, at 21.

29 See also para. 2.5.1.

30 Gaja, *supra* note 17, para. 34.

31 *Id.*, para. 33.

32 Gaja, *supra* note 17, para. 33.

cles on state responsibility, it is strictly speaking not correct to say that this is a question of state responsibility for conduct of an international organization. Rather, this Chapter covers state responsibility for conduct of a state in the context of an international organization. The example given by one member of the Commission,[33] where an international organization enters into an agreement on privileges and immunities with a state and responsibility is thereby incurred by that state, is a case in point. In that case the state is responsible for having entered into the agreement, instead of for the conduct of the organization.[34]

A small number of members of the Commission questioned the inclusion of a reference to state responsibility for the conduct of an international organization in the first draft article.[35] They considered that to include a reference to such responsibility essentially required that its existence be demonstrated. Neither the Special Rapporteur nor the rest of the Commission appear to have shared this point of view. They appear to want not to exclude this question from the scope of the draft articles at this point, while reserving an analysis of whether and to what extent such responsibility actually exists for a later stage in the Commission's study.[36]

A noteworthy feature of the deliberations was the statement by one member of the Commission that although state responsibility might be incurred through the conduct of an international organization, this would come within the scope of the draft articles on the responsibility of states, and it was odd to refer to such problems in the first article on the responsibility of international organizations.[37] As the Special Rapporteur pointed out, however, the question of the international responsibility of states for the conduct of international organizations had been left out of the draft articles on state responsibility.[38] It would be odd if the question was not addressed in the draft articles on state responsibility because of its link to international organizations, and not addressed in the draft articles on the responsibility of international organizations because of its link to states.

At the ILC session in 2003 the draft articles proposed by the Special Rapporteur were referred to the ILC Drafting Committee. The Drafting Committee adopted the draft articles with certain amendments as follows:

---

33 Sreenivasa Rao, UN Doc. A/CN.4/SR.2755, p. 24. See also Kamto, UN Doc. A/CN.4/SR.2755, at 6; Yamada, UN Doc. A/CN.4/SR.2754, at 10.

34 The example bears a striking resemblance to the facts in the *Waite & Kennedy* v. *Germany* and *Beer & Regan* v. *Germany* cases before the European Court of Human Rights. In these cases the granting of immunity by Germany to the European Space Agency was at issue. *Waite & Kennedy* v. *Germany*, (1999) 30 EHHR 261; *Beer & Regan* v. *Germany* (1999) 33 EHHR 54.

35 Pellet, UN Doc. A/CN.4/SR.2753, at 8; Candioti, UN Doc. A/CN.4/SR.2755, at 25.

36 See *e.g.* Gaja, UN Doc. A/CN.4/SR.2756, at 6.

37 Koskeniemmi, UN Doc. A/CN.4/SR.2754, at 3.

38 Gaja, UN Doc. A/CN.4/SR.2755, at 27.

Article 1
Scope of the present draft articles

1 The present draft articles apply to the international responsibility of an international organization for an act that is wrongful under international law.
2 The present draft articles also apply to the international responsibility of a State for the international wrongful act of an international organization.

Article 2
Use of terms

For the purposes of the present draft articles, the term "international organization" refers to an organization established by a treaty or other instrument governed by international law and possessing its own international legal personality. International organizations may include as members, in addition to States, other entities.

Article 3
General principles

1 Every internationally wrongful act of an international organization entails the international responsibility of the international organization.
2 There is an internationally wrongful act of an international organization when conduct consisting of an action or omission:

(a) Is attributable to the international organization under international law; and
(b) Constitutes a breach of an international obligation of that international organization.[39]

In 2004 Gaja submitted a second report on responsibility of international organizations.[40] The report addressed the rules of attribution of conduct to international organizations. The approach to drafting these rules, which is in line with the approach of the first report, was set out as follows:

> The need for coherency in the Commission's work requires that a change, in respect of international organizations, in the approach and even the wording of what has been said with regard to States needs to find justification in differences concerning the relevant practice or objective distinctions in nature.[41]

---

39 Responsibility of international organizations, Titles and texts of the draft articles 1,2 and 3 adopted by the Drafting Committee, UN Doc. A/CN.4/L.632 of 4 June 2003.

40 G. Gaja, Second Report on Responsibility of International Organizations of 2 April 2004, UN Doc. A/CN.4/541.

41 *Id.*, at 3, para. 5.

The content of the report is analyzed below.

2.4 Accountability and international responsibility

Attention for the responsibility of international organizations is fueled *inter alia* by an increasing concern for accountability of international organizations. Similar to certain other popular expressions such as 'global governance'[42] the vagueness of accountability is part of its attractiveness. Reinisch states that accountability can mean many different things to different people.[43]

Black's law dictionary definition of accountability is "state of being responsible or answerable." A slightly more specific description is that "those who exercise power on behalf of others can be held accountable if that power is misused or abused."[44] This description however is still very general, and it has been noted that: "Accountability itself is such a complex concept, with many different definitions in different contexts and according to different political theories, that it makes little sense to address it apart from specific factual situations."[45]

Concern for the accountability of international organizations developed as a consequence of the proliferation of international organizations and the expanding scope of the activities of international organizations.[46] The contemporary practice of many international organizations reflects an important role being played in many fields of activity, including the maintenance of international peace and security. To enable organizations to play this role, states have increasingly conferred powers upon them. In the field of international peace and security for example, UN member states have given the organization the power to decide whether there is a threat to the peace, breach of the peace or act of aggression and more importantly, the power to decide on the use of force. More generally, the increasing powers of international organizations have led to calls for increased accountability, because accountability is considered a desirable, if not necessary, corollary of power. In a more specific sense a consequence of the increase in activities and powers of international organizations is that international organizations have come to operate much closer to, and have a direct impact on the lives of, individuals. Peace support operations are a good example because these operations by definition are in the field and in direct contact with the population of the host state. The decisions of international organizations used to affect individuals

42 See *e.g.* A. Franceschet, *Justice and International Organization: Two Models of Global Governance*, 8 Global Governance 19 (2002); L. Finkelstein, *What is Global Governance?*, 1 Global Governance 367 (1995); M. Hewson & T. Sinclair (Eds.), Approaches to Global Governance Theory (1999); Commission on Global Governance, Our Global Neighbourhood: Report of the Commission on Global Governance (1995).

43 A. Reinisch, *Governance Without Accountability?*, 44 German Yearbook of International Law 270 (2002), at 273.

44 A.M. Slaughter, *The Accountability of Government Networks*, 8 Indiana Journal of Global Legal Studies 347 (2001), at 349.

45 *Id.*, at 360.

46 See *e.g. The Accountability of International Organizations to Non-State Actors*, 92 ASIL Proc. 359 (1998).

almost exclusively through the intermediation of their sovereign.[47] This sovereign was in most cases accountable to the individuals under its sovereignty through the democratic political process or through other means. Hey states that international law, however, does not reflect the notion that if international organizations, in fact, exercise public policy competences, the exercise of those competences should be subject to the controls and rules applicable to the exercise of governmental powers in national societies and that states, by attributing public policy competences to international organizations, thus arguably may circumvent the procedures which, at the national level, otherwise may be available for controlling the exercise of such competences.[48] This development has led to an increasing call for accountability of international organizations.[49] It also helps to explain why the call for accountability is strongest in cases where international organizations take on complex peacemaking operations.[50] In these cases, and in particular in the case of transitional administration, an international operation acts as a state. Grossman and Bradlow state that those:

> Cases in which the international community has been willing to undertake complex peacemaking operations, involving the assumption of certain governmental functions, raise important considerations of responsibility and accountability. The peacekeepers relate to the general population within the country in much the same way that governmental actors relate to the population within a country. This suggests that the international community, in defining the mandate and in the execution of these operations, needs to ensure that the international peacekeepers perform their responsibilities to these private actors to the same extent and in a comparable manner to what would be expected of a national government.[51]

The increasing attention that the issue of the accountability of international organizations has received from the international legal community is demonstrated by the establishment by the ILA of a committee to study the topic. The point of departure of the committee is the one discussed above, *i.e.* that accountability is linked to the authority and power of an international organization and that "power entails accountability, that is the duty to account for its exercise."[52] The committee has developed a set of recommended rules and practices aimed at making accountability operational by

---

47 See P. Stephan, *Legitimacy, Accountability, Authority, and Freedom in the New Global Order*, 70 University of Colorado Law Review 1555 (1999).

48 E. Hey, *The World Bank Inspection Panel: Towards the Recognition of a New Legally Relevant Relationship in International Law*, 2 Hofstra Law & Policy Symposium 61 (1997), at 64-65.

49 See *e.g.* A. Reinisch, *Securing the Accountability of International Organizations*, 7 Global Governance 131 (2001).

50 See *e.g.* R. Wilde, *Accountability and International Actors in Bosnia and Herzegovina, Kosovo and East Timor*, 7 ILSA Journal of International & Comparative Law 455 (2001).

51 C. Grossman & D. Bradlow, *Are We Being Propelled Towards a People-Centered Transnational Legal Order?*, 9 American University Journal of International Law & Policy 1 (1993), at 21.

52 Committee on Accountability of International Organisations, Third Report 2 (2002).

inter alia fostering the effectiveness and appropriateness of the use of power and sanctioning the abuse or derailment of power.[53] It has not given a definition of accountability, other than a description of the components of accountability. Nevertheless, the description of components gives a reasonably clear idea of the concept. Accountability of and towards international organizations is described as comprising three interrelated and mutually supportive components:

1. the extent to which international organizations, in the fulfillment of their responsibilities as established in their constituent instruments, are and should be subject to or exercising forms of internal and external scrutiny and monitoring, irrespective of potential and subsequent liability and/or responsibility;
2. tortious liability for injurious consequences arising out of acts or omissions not involving a breach of any rule or norm of international and/or institutional law; (e.g. environmental damage as a result of lawful nuclear or space activities);
3. responsibility arising out of acts or omissions which do constitute a breach of a rule or norm of international and/or institutional law (e.g. violations of human rights or humanitarian law, breach of contract, gross negligence, or as far as institutional law is concerned acts of organs *ultra vires* or violating the law of employment relations).[54]

The broadest contours of accountability in this description, *i.e.* monitoring and scrutiny, imply certain elements which make such monitoring and scrutiny possible, such as transparency – including access to information – responsiveness and reporting. These and other implications have been elaborated by the committee in draft 'recommended rules and practices'.[55] Unlike international responsibility, which is by definition legal, accountability of international organizations can present itself in different forms: legal, political, administrative or financial.[56] This is an important point because it makes clear that accountability is broader than international responsibility, in the sense of responsibility for internationally wrongful acts in the ILC's project on the responsibility of international organizations. Accountability encompasses political, administrative, and various informal, non-legal mechanisms by which an entity or an individual may be answerable for something. This also means that the yardstick of accountability of international organizations is not limited to international obligations binding on those organizations.

The concept of accountability may apply differently to different entities. In every case, however, the main questions to make the concept operational are what the yardstick of accountability should be, who can raise accountability and how accountability can be implemented. In the context of peace support operations these questions can be answered as follows. First, this study is concerned with the application of international humanitarian law and as a consequence the relevant yardstick is international

53 *Id.*

54 Committee on Accountability of International Organisations, First Report 17 (1998).

55 *Supra* note 53.

56 *Supra* note 54, at 16.

humanitarian law. Secondly, traditionally the only relevant relationship in international organizations is the one between the organization and its member states. There is sometimes a tendency to think of accountability of international organizations principally in relation to member states. This focus leads to concern for, *inter alia*, voting rights of member states and the possibilities of judicial review of organs of international organizations.[57] Accountability is increasingly considered from the perspective of individuals instead of states, however. The activities of international organizations have a direct impact on the lives of individuals. If all affected parties should be able to hold those who make and implement policies that affect them accountable for their actions, and if the scope of those who can raise accountability is determined by "who is actually affected by the decisions that have been taken and the consequences thereof",[58] than this must include individuals. The claim by individuals to accountability is reinforced by the increasing recognition that they have a legal personality of their own, and that as a consequence there is a legally relevant direct relationship between them and international organizations. The United Nations Department of Peacekeeping Operations (DPKO) also takes this people-centered perspective in its evaluation of the United Nations Operation in Somalia where it writes under the heading 'accountability' that:

> For the United Nations to successfully promote respect for human rights and good governance in collapsed states, as well as gain some measure of credibility, it must demonstrate a commitment to the principles of accountability and transparency in its own work. In UNOSOM, no independent oversight existed which could serve as an ombudsman to consider grievances registered by the local population against the United Nations.[59]

Finally, there are many instruments to implement accountability. Responsibility is usually implemented by adjudicative means. Accountability in a broader sense can also be achieved through various quasi-judicial or even political or administrative means.

2.5 International legal personality of the United Nations and the North Atlantic Treaty Organization

As noted above, the capacity to have rights and obligations under international law is critical to the possibility of being held responsible for an internationally wrongful

57 For an article discussing accountability from this perspective see N. White, *Accountability and Democracy Within the United Nations: A Legal Perspective*, 13 International Relations 1 (1997).

58 Grossman & Bradlow, *supra* note 51, at 24.

59 The Comprehensive Report on Lessons Learned from United Nations Operation in Somalia (UNOSOM), para. 57.

act.[60] The status of being capable of bearing legal rights and duties under international law is defined as having international legal personality.[61]

States by definition have international legal personality. The possession of legal personality, in other words the capacity to enter into relations at the international level, is necessary evidence of statehood.[62] This is expressed in article 1 of the 1933 Montevideo Convention on the Rights and Duties of States that refers to "the state as a person of international law."[63]

Not all international organizations on the other hand have international legal personality. It is therefore necessary to determine whether the international organizations that this study focuses on, the United Nations and the North Atlantic Treaty Organization, are international legal persons.

Doctrine has developed two main theories on the bestowal of international legal personality on international organizations. The first is the theory of objective international personality. According to this theory international law bestows legal personality when an organization meets certain criteria, irrespective of the will of the member states. It is not the provisions of the constitution or the intention of its framers which establish the international personality of an international organization, but the objective fact of its existence.[64] This theory appears to be making a comeback in the literature,[65] although it is not unproblematic. It does not seem to be supported by the *Reparations for Injuries* case in which the ICJ in several passages referred to the

---

60 See also International Law Association, *supra* note 54, at 21; C.F. Amerasinghe, Principles of the Institutional Law of International Organizations 239 (1996): "Once the existence of international personality for international organizations is conceded, it is not difficult to infer that, just as organizations can demand responsibility of other international persons because they have rights at international law, so they can also be held responsible to other international persons because they have obligations at international law."

61 "*the Court has come to the conclusion that the Organization is an international person*. That is not the same as saying that it is a State, which it certainly is not, or that its legal personality and rights and duties are the same as those of a State. Still less it is the same thing as saying that it is 'a super-State', whatever that expression may mean. It does not even imply that all its rights and duties must be upon the international plane, any more than all the rights and duties of a State must be upon that plane. *What it does mean is that it is a subject of international law and capable of possessing international rights and duties, and that it has capacity to maintain its rights by bringing international claims.*" Reparations for Injuries Suffered in the Service of the United Nations, Advisory Opinion of 11 April 1949, 1949 ICJ Reports 174, at 179 (emphasis added); see also B. Cheng, *Introduction to Subjects of International Law*, in M. Bedjaoui (Ed.), International Law: Achievements and Prospects 23 (1991), at 25.

62 See D. Raič, Statehood and the Law of Self-Determination 23 (2002).

63 Convention on the Rights and Duties of States (Montevideo Convention), 26 December 1933, 165 L.N.T.S. 19, 28 American Journal of International Law (Supplement) 75 (1934).

64 F. Seyersted, *Objective International Personality of Intergovernmental Organizations*, 34 Nordisk Tidsskrift for International Ret 1 (1964), at 39-40.

65 See *e.g.* N.D. White, The Law of International Organisations 29 (1996); I. Brownlie, Principles of Public International Law 679-680 (1998); C. Brölmann, *A Flat Earth? International Organizations in the System of International Law*, 70 Nordic Journal of International Law 319 (2001), at 325.

intention of the member states. It is also at pains to explain the ability of non-member states to withhold recognition of the personality of the organization.

The second, subjective, theory maintains that organizations have international legal personality because this status is given to them by member states. Member states can do so expressly or implicitly. In the latter case personality can be derived from the functions and rights and duties of the organization. If the member states would not have wished the organization to have international legal personality, they would not have given it these attributes. This theory is supported by the *Reparations for Injuries* case.[66] It may be noted that the practical effects of the objective theory of international personality and of the subjective theory, *i.e.* that the intention of the member states can be derived from functions, rights and obligations, are very similar. The ICJ determined in its Advisory Opinion in the *Reparations for Injuries Suffered in the Service of the United Nations* case that the UN has international legal personality. It stated that:

> In the opinion of the Court, the Organization was intended to exercise and enjoy, and is in fact exercising and enjoying, functions and rights which can only be explained on the basis of the possession of a large measure of international personality and capacity to operate upon an international plane. It is at present the supreme type of international organization, and it could not carry out the intentions of its founders if it was devoid of international personality. It must be acknowledged that its Members, by entrusting certain functions to it, with the attendant duties and responsibilities, have clothed it with the competence required to enable those functions to be effectively discharged. Accordingly, the Court has come to the conclusion that the Organization is an international person.[67]

The international legal personality of the UN has subsequently been confirmed on numerous occasions in law and practice.

There is no similar international judicial authority with regard to the international legal personality of NATO. The constitutive instrument of the organization does not expressly provide that it has legal personality in international law. Explicit recognition is not the only way in which international legal personality is conferred on international organizations.

Application of the objective as well as application of the subjective theory of international legal personality leads to the conclusion that NATO is an international legal person.[68] The organization is a permanent association of states established by the 1949 North Atlantic Treaty with the lawful object of collective self-defense. It is

66 H. Schermers & N. Blokker, International Institutional Law 989 (2003); P. Sands & P. Klein, *supra* note 6, at 472.

67 *Supra* note 61, at 178-179.

68 See also A. Pellet, *L'Imputabilité d'Éventuels Actes Illicites Responsabilité de l'OTAN ou des États Membres*, in C. Tomuschat (Ed.), Kosovo and the International Community 193 (2002), at 198; E. Stein & D. Carreau, *Law and Peaceful Change in a Subsystem: "Withdrawal" of France from the North Atlantic Treaty Organization*, 62 American Journal of International Law 577 (1968), at 602.

equipped with organs, the most important of which is the North Atlantic Council. The functions of the organization are distinct from those of the member states. The most recent statement of these functions is in section 10 of the 1999 Strategic Concept of the organization.[69] The organization exercises powers on the international plane, notably treaty-making power. Article 25 of the 1951 Ottawa treaty on the status of the organization for example provides that the North Atlantic Council acting on behalf of the organization may conclude supplementary agreements with member states. The organization also concludes international agreements on other issues with member states[70] and with non-member states.[71] There is also state practice supporting legal personality of the organization. In the *Banković* case before the European Court of Human Rights (ECHR) the French government argued that a bombardment during Operation Allied Force was not imputable to its member states but to NATO as an organization with an international legal personality separate from that of the respondent states. The challenge of the admissibility of the case by all the respondent states on the ground that the ECHR would be determining the rights and obligations of NATO itself also points in this direction.[72] This challenge assumes that NATO itself has rights and obligations under international law, which can only be the case if the organization has international legal personality. Trial Chambers of the International Criminal Tribunal for the former Yugoslavia (ICTY) have also treated NATO as an international legal person separate from its member states. Trial Chamber I in the *Todorović* case ordered the NAC to disclose to the defense copies of documents and the identity of certain individuals in connection with the arrest of the accused.[73] The order was based on article 29 of the ICTY Statute which provides that states shall cooperate with the Tribunal. The Trial Chamber stated that:

---

69 The Alliance's Strategic Concept approved by the Heads of State and Government participating in the meeting of the North Atlantic Council in Washington D.C. on 23-24 April 1999, para. 10.

70 *E.g.* Briefwisseling tussen de Regering van het Koninkrijk der Nederlanden en de Noord-Atlantische Verdragsorganisatie houdende een overeenkomst inzake the functioneren in Nederland van het NATO Airborne Early Warning and Control Programme Management Agency (NAPMA), 's Gravenhage/Brussel, 31 augustus en 11 september 1979, Trb. 1979 159.

71 *E.g.* Agreement Between the Republic of Bosnia and Herzegovina and the North Atlantic Treaty Organization Concerning the Status of NATO and its Personnel, Appendix B to Annex 1A to the General Framework Agreement for Peace in Bosnia and Herzegovina, 35 ILM 75 (1996).

72 *Vlastimir and Borka Banković, Živana Stojanović, Mirjana Stoimenovski, Dragana Joksimović and Dragan Suković* v. *Belgium, the Czech Republic, Denmark, France, Germany, Greece, Hungary, Iceland, Italy, Luxembourg, the Netherlands, Norway, Poland, Portugal, Spain, Turkey and the United Kingdom*, Decision of 12 December 2001 (Appl. No. 52207/99), at 9, para. 31. See para. 5.6.4.

73 *Prosecutor* v. *Blagoje Simić, Milan Simić, Miroslav Tadić, Stevan Todorović and Simo Zarić*, Decision on Motion for Judicial Assistance to be Provided by SFOR and Others, Case No. IT-95-9-PT, Tr. Ch. I, 18 October 2000. This statement was espoused by Trial Chamber II in *Prosecutor* v. *Dragan Nikolić*, Decision on Defence Motion Challenging the Exercise of Jurisdiction by the Tribunal, Case No. IT-94-2-PT, Tr. Ch. II, 9 October 2002, para. 49.

> A purposive construction of the Statute yields the conclusion that such an order should be as applicable to collective enterprises of States as it is to individual States; Article 29 should, therefore, be read as conferring on the International Tribunal a power to require an international organization or its competent organ such as SFOR to cooperate with it in the achievement of its fundamental objective of prosecution of persons responsible for serious violations of international humanitarian law, by providing the several modes of assistance set out therein.[74]

In the *Legality of the Use of Force* cases before the ICJ several of the respondent states explicitly mentioned that NATO is an international legal person during the hearings held in April 2004. Portugal drew attention to NATO's development since its establishment, in particular the institutionalization of the organization.[75] It maintained that "NATO is an international organisation in the strict sense, with its own international legal personality."[76] France referred to the criteria for international legal personality identified in the *Reparations for Injuries* case. It submitted that under these criteria NATO possesses international legal personality.[77] The applicant accepted NATO's international legal personality. However, it maintained that this personality is "limited" on the basis of NATO's founding instrument and other NATO documents.[78]

2.6 State responsibility and attribution

A state is only responsible for conduct which is attributable to the state. A state as an abstract legal entity cannot in reality act. Imputability is the legal fiction which assimilates the actions or omissions of persons to the state itself. The attribution of conduct to the state as a subject of international law is based on criteria determined by international law and not on the mere recognition of a link of factual causality.[79]

The ILC specified conditions under which conduct is attributed to the state in Chapter II of Part One of the draft articles on state responsibility. The ones which appear most relevant for the present purposes are the following:

> **Article 4**
> **Conduct of organs of a State**
>
> 1 The conduct of any State organ shall be considered an act of that State under international law, whether the organ exercises legislative, executive, judicial or any other functions, whatever position it holds in the organization of the State,

74 *Id.*, para. 48.
75 CR 2004/18 of 22 April 2004, para. 4.3.
76 CR 2004/9 (translation) of 19 April 2004, para. 4.3.
77 CR 2004/12 of 20 April 2004, para. 51.
78 CR 2004/23 of 23 April 2004, para. 8.
79 Report of the International Law Commission on the work of its fifty-third session, *supra* note 3, at 81, para. 4

and whatever its character as an organ of the central government or of a territorial unit of the State.

2 An organ includes any person or entity which has that status in accordance with the internal law of the State.

Article 6
Conduct of organs placed at the disposal of a State by another State

The conduct of an organ placed at the disposal of a State by another State shall be considered an act of the former under international law if the organ is acting in the exercise of elements of the governmental authority of the State at whose disposal it is placed.

Article 7
Excess of authority or contravention of instructions

The conduct of an organ of a State or of a person or entity empowered to exercise elements of the governmental authority shall be considered an act of the State under international law if the organ, person or entity acts in that capacity, even if it exceeds its authority or contravenes instructions.

Article 8
Conduct directed or controlled by a State

The conduct of a person or group of persons shall be considered an act of a State under international law if the person or group of persons is in fact acting on the instructions of, or under the direction or control of, that State in carrying out the conduct.

2.7 Responsibility of international organizations and attribution

2.7.1 Attribution to the organization

An international organization is an abstract person and rules are necessary to impute the conduct of individuals to it. These rules have not yet been codified. As mentioned above, the ILC has started its study of the responsibility of international organizations only recently.

In the absence of codification, the principles of attribution to international organizations are determined by customary international law. The identification of customary rules requires state practice, however, and in connection with the responsibility of international organizations state practice is limited. Questions of the responsibility of international organizations are often resolved without explicit reference to legal grounds.[80] The body of international case law on the topic is also very limited. The ICJ has addressed the attribution of conduct to an international organization in one case,

80 Reuter, *supra* note 6, at 497.

and that was in an *obiter dictum*. In its advisory opinion on the *Difference relating to immunity from legal process of a Special Rapporteur of the Commission on Human Rights* the Court stated that:

> the question of immunity from legal process is distinct from the issue of compensation for any damages incurred as a result of acts performed by the United Nations or by its agents acting in their official capacity.
> The United Nations may be required to bear responsibility for the damage arising from such acts.[81]

In the absence of any considerable practice in respect of the responsibility of international organizations commentators generally maintain that the principles of the law of state responsibility apply by analogy to international organizations.[82]

This is logical in view of the connection between legal personality and international responsibility. The legal personality of states and international organizations, in the sense of the capacity to possess rights and obligations under international law, is the same. Only the scope of the legal personality, the actual rights and obligations that the legal person possesses, is different because of the functional character of international organizations. One of the main functions of the institution of international responsibility is the defense of the legal order against breaches by a subject of that legal order. This legal order is affected in the same way by the breach of an obligation by an international organization as by a breach by a state. This is summed up well by one author:

> The steadily growing participation of international organizations in international relations calls for a closer scrutiny of the question of legality of the acts of international organizations, understood as the proper fulfillment of their statutory functions with due respect to the rights of other subjects of international intercourse. The institution which serves to evaluate, under universal international law, the actions of a given subject and the possible consequences of a violation of an obligation is international responsibility, whose source constitutes the internationally wrongful act. The fundamental role of international responsibility ensuring the proper functioning of the international legal order can be played effectively only when the rules governing responsibility in that order apply to all subjects.[83]

---

81 Difference Relating to Immunity from Legal Process of a Special Rapporteur of the Commission on Human Rights, 1999 ICJ Reports 62, para. 66.

82 See *e.g.* P. Klein, La Responsabilité des Organisations Internationales dans les Ordres Juridiques Internes et en Droit des Gens 376 (1998); I. Scobbie, *International Responsibility*, in R.J. Dupuy (Ed.), Manuel sur les Organisations Internationales 886 (1998), at 887; Jimenez de Aréchaga, *International Responsibility*, in M. Sørensen (Ed.), Manual of Public International Law 532 (1968), at 595, M. Perez Gonzalez, *supra* note 6, at 81, M. Hirsch, The Responsibility of International Organizations Toward Third Parties: Some Basic Principles (1995).

83 E. Butkiewicz, *The Premisses of International Responsibility of Inter-Governmental Organizations*, 11 Polish Yearbook of International Law 117 (1981-82).

International organizations could develop separate principles applying to their responsibility and different from the principles of state responsibility. The development of such a separate regime has taken place in respect of the privileges and immunities of international organizations, for instance. The practice of international organizations does not demonstrate that a separate regime has developed in respect of international responsibility.[84] This circumstance is in itself an argument for applying the principles of state responsibility. It is necessary that there are principles applicable to the responsibility of international organizations.[85] Without the application of the principles of state responsibility a legal vacuum would open up, because there no other responsibility regime has been developed.

The legal basis for this application is the customary international law status of the core of the legal regime of state responsibility. Customary international law applies in principle to international organizations.[86] When an international organization arrives on the international scene it is bound by the general international law that is applicable on that scene. It is in a similar position as a newly independent state, which is in principle bound by customary international law. In the case of the latter however it has been argued that it should be able to choose whether to be bound by a customary international rule because it has not been able to object to that rule during the period it was created. This argument is not applicable to international organizations, because these are established by states that have been able to object and that would otherwise be able to indirectly free themselves from the rule.[87]

As was noted above, Gaja in his second report to the ILC on the responsibility of international organizations took principles of attribution in state responsibility as a starting point for the formulation of principles of attribution of conduct to international organizations, while taking into account that where necessary the rules must be adapted. In other words, they must be applied *mutatis mutandis*.[88]

The report first discussed the "general rule on attribution of conduct to an international organization", which corresponds to article 4 of the ILC draft articles on state responsibility. It noted that the ICJ has held that conduct of the UN includes, apart from that of its principal and subsidiary organs, conduct of its 'agents'.[89] This rule, the report submitted, applies more generally to international organizations.[90] The term 'agent' is intended to refer not only to officials but also to other persons acting for the international organization on the basis of functions conferred by the organization. It underlines that what matters for the purpose of attribution is the existence of a link between the international organization and the person or entity which acts or

84 C. Pitschas, Die völkerrechtliche Verantwortlichkeit der Europäischen Gemeinschaft und ihrer Mitgliedstaaten: Zugleich ein beitrag zu den völkerrechtlichen Kompetenzen der Europäischen Gemeinschaft 43 (2001).

85 Reuter, *supra* note 6, at 491.

86 Schermers & Blokker, *supra* note 66, at 834. See also para. 3.5

87 Pitschas, *supra* note 84, at 44.

88 See also Perez Gonzalez, *supra* note 6, at 67.

89 *Supra* note 40, at 8, para. 15.

90 *Id.*, at 10, para. 18.

omits, and not whether that person or entity has an official status. The report proposed to refer to the "rules of the organization" in order to establish the existence of the link between an organ or agent and an international organization. This term is taken from the Vienna Convention on the Law of Treaties between States and International Organizations. However, the report proposed to modify the definition given of the term in the Vienna Convention. On this basis the report proposed a draft article on the general rule of attribution.

The report then analyzed the attribution of conduct of organs placed at the disposal of an international organization by a state or another international organization. It noted that most of the practice in this context relates to peacekeeping forces and reproduced some of this practice, including a number of the statements discussed below. It noted that on the one hand peacekeeping forces are regarded as subsidiary organs of the UN, but on the other hand the fact that troop contributing states retain control over disciplinary matters and have exclusive jurisdiction in criminal affairs should be taken into account. Thus the national contingent is not fully placed at the disposal of the UN and this may have consequences with regard to attribution of conduct. According to Gaja:

> It would be going too far to consider that the existence of disciplinary power and criminal jurisdiction on the part of the contributing State totally excludes forces being considered to be placed at the disposal of the United Nations. As has been held by several scholars, the decisive question in relation to attribution of a given conduct appears to be who had effective control over the conduct in question.[91]

The report underlined that attribution of conduct should be based on a factual criterion of control. Although a contingent might officially have been placed under the command of a UN force commander, it would be difficult to attribute its conduct to the UN if he was not in effective control. What matters is not exclusive control, which for instance the UN never has over national contingents, but the extent of effective control. This would also leave the way open for dual attribution of certain conduct.

With regard to infringements of international humanitarian law, the report stated that:

> the United Nations Secretary-General referred to "concurrent responsibility" of the United Nations and the contributing State, without clarifying the basis of responsibility. This would depend on the circumstances of the infringement. One may have to conclude for joint attribution of the same conduct; however, one could also consider that the infringing acts are attributed to either the State or the United Nations, while omission, if any, of the required preventive measures is attributed to the other subject.[92]

---

91 Gaja, *supra* note 40, para. 40.

92 *Id.*, para. 42.

The report proposed a draft article on the attribution of conduct of organs placed at the disposal of an international organization by a state or another international organization.

The report also addressed the question of the attribution of *ultra vires* conduct of an international organization. This could be either conduct beyond the powers conferred on the organization or conduct exceeding the powers of a specific organ. It proposed that such conduct be attributed to the organization, because the need to protect third parties requires an extension of the attribution of conduct for the same reason that underpins the validity of treaties concluded by an international organization notwithstanding minor infringements of rules concerning competence to conclude treaties. It was noted that as with state organs, for responsibility to arise there needs to be some connection between the entity's or person's official duties and the conduct in question. It asserted that with regard to the attribution of *ultra vires* conduct, the rule which applies to states is also applicable to international organizations. It proposed a draft article based on article 7 of the draft articles on state responsibility with minor changes.

Finally, the report discussed the attribution of conduct acknowledged and adopted by an international organization as its own as well as other cases of attribution of conduct to an international organization and proposed a draft article concerning the former. With regard to other cases of attribution of conduct it noted that these seemed to be of limited interest with regard to international organizations.

The ILC considered the report during four meetings, after which it referred the draft articles proposed by the Special Rapporteur to the Drafting Committee. On 4 June 2004 it adopted draft articles 4 to 7 on first reading as revised by the Drafting Committee.

These draft articles read as follows:

Article 4
General rule on attribution of conduct to an international organization

1. The conduct of an organ or agent of an international organization in the performance of functions of that organ or agent shall be considered as an act of that organization under international law whatever position the organ or agent holds in respect of the organization.
2. For the purposes of paragraph 1, the term "agent" includes officials and other persons or entities through whom the organization acts.
3. Rules of the organization shall apply to the determination of the functions of its organs and agents.
4. For the purpose of the present draft article, "rules of the organization" means, in particular: the constituent instruments; decisions, resolutions and other acts taken by the organization in accordance with those instruments; and established practice of the organization.

Article 5
Conduct of organs or agents placed at the disposal of an international organization by a State or another international organization

The conduct of an organ of a State or an organ or agent of an international organization that is placed at the disposal of another international organization shall be considered under international law an act of the latter organization if the organization exercises effective control over that conduct.

Article 6
Excess of authority or contravention of instructions

The conduct of an organ or agent of an international organization shall be considered an act of that organization under international law if the organ or agent acts in that capacity, even though the conduct exceeds the authority of that organ or agent or contravenes instructions.

Article 7
Conduct acknowledged and adopted by an international organization

Conduct which is not attributable to an international organization under the preceding draft articles shall nevertheless be considered an act of that international organization under international law if and to the extent that the organization acknowledges and adopts the conduct in question as its own.

Draft article 4 adopted by the ILC, in contrast to the draft article proposed by the Special Rapporteur, explicitly refers to an 'agent' of an international organization. It also provides a definition of that term. The commentary explains that this definition gives the term 'agent' a wide meaning which also covers those persons which in the draft articles on state responsibility are covered by articles 5 and 8. Article 5 concerns conduct of persons or entities exercising elements of governmental authority and article 8 concerns persons or groups of persons acting in fact on the instructions, or the direction or control, of a state.

It may be noted that the ILC appears to give a different meaning to the term 'agent' than it did in the context of state responsibility. France commented in 1998 on what is now article 4 of the draft articles on state responsibility that the term 'State organ' was too restrictive and that it would be better to use the expression 'any State organ or agent'."[93] It appears that France considered that the term 'agent' referred to a single individual making up part of the organization of the state. The ILC however considered that an 'agent' would seem to denote a person acting on behalf of the state but not belonging to the state proper.[94] In other words, it considered that the term

93 Comments and observations received from Governments, 25 March 1998, UN Doc. A/CN.4/488, at 36.

94 See commentary to article 5 of the 1996 draft articles, YBILC 1973, Vol II, at 193, para. 13.

'agent' did not include state officials. The ILC now appears to have abandoned this point of view in the context of the responsibility of international organizations.

Draft article 5 as adopted by the ILC on first reading takes a similar approach as article 6 of the draft articles on state responsibility. However, it makes more explicit that the criterion for attribution of conduct of an organ or agent which is placed at the disposal of an international organization is the factual control which is exercised over the specific conduct taken by the organ or agent. With regard to peacekeeping operations, the commentary states that:

> While it is understandable that, for the sake of efficiency of military operations, the United Nations insists on claiming exclusive command and control over peacekeeping forces, attribution of conduct should also in this regard be based on a factual criterion.[95]

The wording of draft article 6 closely follows that of article 7 on state responsibility. The commentary states that the key element for attribution in both articles is the requirement that the organ or agent acts "in that capacity". This indicates that only conduct of organs purportedly or apparently carrying out their official functions is attributable to the international organization, and not the private conduct of individuals who happen to be organs or agents of the organization. The commentary underlines that *ultra vires* conduct of an organ or agent is attributable to the organization when that conduct is linked with the organ's or agent's official functions.

Below, state practice concerning the attribution of conduct of UN and NATO peace support operations is examined in the light of these draft articles.

2.7.2 Grounds for attribution to member states of conduct of the organization

Some writers state that the responsibility of an international organization for conduct of the organization does not exclude the responsibility of member states for that same conduct. A common concern for the writers in question is that states cannot absolve themselves of their responsibility by establishing or joining an international organization. The treaty establishing an international organization does not bind third parties and consequently it cannot as such limit the responsibility of member states towards third parties, they argue.

For some of these writers member state responsibility takes the form of responsibility for conduct of the organization which breaches an international obligation of the member state. Lawson states that if the conduct of an international organization is a *prima facie* breach of obligations of the member states, the conduct must be attributed to the member states so that it can be established whether there has been an actual breach. If the conduct breaches an obligation which binds the member states as well as the international organization, the conduct must be attributed to the organization. In this situation the member states may be co-responsible for the internationally

95 Draft Report of the ILC on the Work of its Fifty-sixth Session of 6 July 2004, UN Doc. A/CN.4/L.654/Add.1, at 16, para. 8.

wrongful act of the organization, based on the constituent document, the obligation breached or legitimate expectations of third parties.[96]

For other writers member state responsibility takes the form of responsibility for conduct of the organization which breaches an international obligation of the organization.[97] In other words, not only the conduct, but the entire internationally wrongful act of the international organization, is attributed to the member states. These writers disagree on the principles to determine whether member states are responsible in a specific situation for the internationally wrongful act of the organization. Herdegen for example suggests principles on elements of attribution and responsibility that will directly serve as a basis for the liability of the member states only if the primary obligation incurred by the international organization itself flows from international law. The principles he suggests are "based on the founding act as well as on the remaining influence and control of the founders – without entailing a strictly accessory and full liability of all members for obligations incurred by the organization."[98] Pescatore states that the member states of the European Communities are subsidiarily responsible for the conduct of the Communities because of their influence on the Communities and because the member states can modify the treaties establishing the Communities.[99]

The common concern of most of these writers is that unsuspecting third parties should not be victimized by states that transfer their activities to international organizations. Consequently, these writers state that member states are not responsible if third parties have been put on notice that the member states have limited their responsibility for the conduct of the organization. Most of them agree that this is the case if there is an express clause in the constituent instrument of the organization limiting member states' responsibility. They disagree, however, on whether it is possible for member states to limit their responsibility for conduct of the organization without an express clause to that effect.

---

96 R. Lawson, Het EVRM en de Europese Gemeenschappen: Bouwstenen voor een Aansprakelijkheidsregime van Internationale Organisaties 281-283 (1999).

97 See *e.g.* W. Meng, *Internationale Organisationen im völkerrechtlichen Deliktsrecht*, 45 Zeitschrift für ausländisches öffentliches Recht und Völkerrecht 324 (1985); R. Sadurska & C. Chinkin, *The Collapse of the International Tin Council: A Case of State Responsibility?* 30 Virginia Journal of International Law 845 (1989); H. Schermers, Liability of International Organizations, 1 Leiden Journal of International Law 3 (1988), I. Seidl-Hohenveldern, *Piercing the Corporate Veil of International Organizations: The International Tin Council Case in the English Court of Appeals*, 32 German Yearbook of International Law 43 (1980). Note that the latter author has adjusted his point of view to defend a much more limited theory of member state responsibility, I. Seidl-Hohenveldern, *Liability of Member States for Acts or Omissions of an International Organization*, in S. Schlemmer-Schulte & K-Y. Tung (Eds.), Liber Amicorum Ibrahim F.I. Shihata: International Finance and Development Law 727 (2001).

98 M. Herdegen, *The Insolvency of International Organizations and the Legal Position of Creditors: Some Observations in the Light of the International Tin Council Crisis*, 35 Netherlands International Law Review 135 (1988).

99 P. Pescatore, *Les Relations Extérieures des Communautés Européennes*, 103 Recueil des Cours (1966-II), at 224.

Judicial decisions concerning member state responsibility were made in cases concerning the International Tin Council and in cases concerning the Arab Organization for Industrialization (the *Westland* case).

2.7.3 The Westland *case*

The *Westland* case originated in the winding up of the Arab Organization for Industrialization.[100] The organization was established in 1975 by the United Arab Emirates, Saudi Arabia, Qatar and the Arab Republic of Egypt with the object of developing an arms industry for the benefit of the four states. The constituent instrument set up a higher committee composed of ministers delegated by the four states. In 1978 the organization concluded an agreement with Westland helicopters called the 'Shareholders' Agreement' to create a joint stock company named the Arab British Helicopter company. After the Arab Republic of Egypt recognized Israel in 1979, the other three member states of the organization announced that they were putting an end to the existence of the organization and set up a liquidation committee. Westland then filed a request for arbitration claiming damages against the organization, the four member states and the Arab British Helicopter company.

Egypt expressed reservations about the jurisdiction of the arbitral tribunal over the four states because the arbitration was based on an arbitration clause in the shareholders agreement to which the four states were not parties. The Tribunal decided to restrict the initial proceedings to the question of jurisdiction. It held that the question whether the four states were bound by the arbitration clause was exactly the same as the substantive law question whether the four states were bound in general by the obligation contracted by the organization.

The Tribunal found that the organization was an international legal person. However, the attribution of legal personality to the organization did not exclude the possible liability of the member states. The Tribunal based this conclusion on general principles of law and on good faith. It explained that the notion that excludes cumulative liability of a legal person and of the individuals which constitute it is nowhere accepted or given effect without limitation and gave several examples from domestic company law in Switzerland, Germanic law and France. The Tribunal stated that:

> These observations show that the designation of an organization as "legal person" and the attribution of an independent existence do not provide any basis for a conclusion as to whether or not those who compose it are bound by obligations undertaken by it. One must therefore disregard any question relating to the personality of the AOI. The possible liability of the four States must be determined by directly examining the founding documents of the AOI in relation to this problem.[101]

---

100 International Chamber of Commerce, Court of Arbitration, 5 March 1984, Westland Helicopters Ltd. and Arab Industrialization Organization, United Arab Emirates, Kingdom of Saudi Arabia, State of Quatar, Arab Republic of Egypt and Arab British Helicopters Company, 80 ILR 610 (1989).

101 *Id.*, at 612.

The founding documents of the organization did not stipulate anything on the question of the responsibility of the member states. The Tribunal stated that:

> In the absence of any provision expressly or impliedly excluding the liability of the four States, this liability subsists since, as a general rule, those who engage in transactions of an economic nature are deemed liable for the obligations which flow therefrom. In default by the four States of formal exclusion of their liability, third parties which have contracted with the AOI could legitimately count on their liability. This rule flows from general principles of law and from good faith.[102]

The Tribunal considered that its foregoing arguments were all the more true because the member states of the Arab Organization for Industrialization effectively controlled the actions of the organization, so that "in reality, in the circumstances of this case, the AOI is one with the States".[103]

The Tribunal concluded that the four states were bound by the arbitration clause because the obligations under substantive law cannot be dissociated from those that exist on the procedural level.

Egypt appealed against the arbitral award before the Court of Justice of Geneva. It maintained that the Tribunal had no jurisdiction over it because Egypt had not signed the arbitration agreement. The Court agreed with this point of view and annulled the award under appeal to the extent that the Arbitral Tribunal declared itself competent in respect of Egypt.[104] It considered that in the absence of an arbitration agreement which Egypt had signed, it was for the other party to rebut the presumption that it had not accepted the jurisdiction of the Tribunal. The Court concluded that Westland did not succeed in this task, taking into account that the AOI had a separate legal personality from the founding states.

Westland appealed against the decision of the Court of Justice of Geneva before the Federal Supreme Court of Switzerland. The Federal Supreme Court rejected the appeal.[105] Like the Arbitral Tribunal, it addressed both the question of member states being bound by substantive obligations entered into by the AOI as well as the question of jurisdiction. It held that the AOI was an organism under public international law and:

> The personality accorded to the AOI, as well as the autonomy conferred on it at the legal, financial and procedural level ... are the obvious and unequivocable signs of the total legal independence of the Organization in relation to the founding States. This autonomy rules out the possibility of the contracts it concluded with third parties,

---

102 *Id.*, at 613.

103 *Id.*, at 614.

104 *Arab Organization for Industrialization and Others* v. *Westland Helicopters*, Court of Justice of Geneva, 23 October 1987, reproduced in 80 ILR 622.

105 *Westland Helicopters* v. *Arab Organization for Industrialization and Others*, Federal Supreme Court, Switzerland, 19 July 1988, reproduced in 80 ILR 652.

> and more particularly the arbitration clauses to which it subscribes, being regarded as acts undertaken by a delegate or an organ engaging the founding States.[106]

This conclusion was not affected even in the case of an entity which is closely dependent on the state which partly finances, supervises, controls and imposes on it very detailed rules of conduct.[107] This approach has been criticized as being formal and legalistic.[108]

2.7.4 The International Tin Council *cases*

Other judicial decisions in connection with the question of the responsibility of member states for the debts of an international organization resulted from the collapse of the International Tin Council in 1985. The International Tin Council was an international organization established to prevent excessive fluctuations in the price of tin and to secure an adequate supply of tin at fair prices to the consumers and remunerative to the producers. The organization was founded by the Sixth International Tin Agreement (ITA 6). Twenty-three states and the European Economic Community (EEC) were parties to the agreement. A headquarters agreement between the organization and the United Kingdom gave the organization legal personality under United Kingdom law. The headquarters agreement was implemented in the United Kingdom by an Order in Council that provided that the organization had "the legal capacities of a body corporate". Neither the International Tin Agreement nor the headquarters agreement contained an express clause limiting the responsibility of the member states.

When the organization announced that it could not pay its debts, creditors started legal proceedings in United Kingdom courts against the members of the organization to recover the organization's debts. The creditors claimed, *inter alia*, that if the organization had legal personality or a degree of legal personality, then this was analogous to that of bodies in the nature of quasi-partnerships well known in civil law systems, where both the entity and the members are liable to creditors, or the members are in any event liable for the debts of the entity. The proceedings were unsuccessful for the creditors. The High Court decided that the International Tin Council was a legal person under domestic law. Under the applicable domestic law its members were not liable to third parties on the basis of their membership. The Court of Appeal and the House of Lords dismissed appeals against the High Court judgments.

Most of the judges decided the claim primarily in accordance with domestic law instead of international law. Some of the judges also discussed whether there is a rule of member states responsibility under international law, but only when they were of the opinion that domestic law did not include sufficient rules to adjudicate the case. Judge Staughton in a High Court judgment stated that "it is open to question

106 *Id.*, at 658.

107 *Id.*, at 659.

108 Sadurska & Chinkin, *supra* note 97, at 876.

whether in international law a legal personality necessarily excludes direct liability of the members of association to its creditors."[109]

Judge Kerr in the Court of Appeal judgment was prepared to accept that under international law, member states can be liable secondarily for the obligations of an international organization, stating that "on the available material the better view may well be that the characteristics of an international organization are those of a 'mixed' entity rather than that of a body corporate."[110] Such member state responsibility could however not be enforced under domestic law.

Judge Nourse also decided that there was a rule of secondary responsibility of member states under international law which could not be enforced under United Kingdom law. He based the existence of a rule in international law on the intention of the members of the organization to be held responsible which he deduced from the provisions of the International Tin Agreement and on the 'extensive participation and control' in the affairs of the organization by the members. Judge Nourse also referred to certain circumstances of this particular case.[111]

Judge Gibson, however, stated that in the absence of any express or implied term or rule of law imposing liability on the member states such responsibility could not be assumed, but that members did have an obligation to indemnify the organization. Lord Templeman in the House of Lords stated that if there had existed a rule of international law that imposed on members the obligation to discharge the debts of the organization, such obligation could not be enforced by the domestic courts.[112] Lord Oliver of the House of Lords stated that the authorities to which the House of Lords was referred "totally failed to establish any generally accepted rule of the nature contended for."[113] In his view, a rule of member state responsibility was not certain and accepted generally by the body of civilized nations.

2.7.5 *Arguments* de lege ferenda *and the Institut de Droit International*

The practice in the *Westland* and *International Tin Council* cases is not conclusive on the question of the existence of a customary rule of member state responsibility

---

109 *J.H. Rayner (Mincing Lane) Ltd.* v. *Department of Trade and Industry*, High Court, Queen's Bench Division, 24 June 1987, reproduced in 77 ILR 55 (1985), at 77.

110 *Maclaine Watson* v. *Department of Trade and Industry* and *J.H. Rayner (Mincing Lane) Ltd.* v. *Department of Trade and Industry and others*, Court of Appeal, 27 April 1989, reproduced in 80 ILR 49 (1989), at 108.

111 (1) the obligations arise out of an activity as mundane as that of buying and selling tin on the London Metal Exchange; (2) it must have been apparent to the members that in periods of world over production it might prove impossible to finance the necessary purchases wholly out of funds in the hands of the ITC; (3) anyone who sold tin under such conditions would be entitled to assume that if the manager did not have funds at his disposal the members had instructed him to buy without them; and (4) the members did not, as they easily could have done, expressly exclude or limit their liability for the obligations of the ITC.

112 *Maclaine Watson* v. *Department of Trade and Industry* and *J.H Rayner (Mincing Lane) Ltd.* v. *Department of Trade and Industry and others*, House of Lords, 26 October 1989, [1989] 3 All ER 523.

113 *Id.*

because of the widely divergent reasoning of the judges in question and because the cases were decided primarily in accordance with domestic law.[114]

In the absence of a rule of customary international law commentators examine whether there is a general principle of law that emerges from domestic corporate laws. The question is whether domestic systems generally exclude or limit the responsibility of the constituent parts of corporations with a separate legal personality. Many writers conclude that a single principle does not exist in domestic laws.[115] Most domestic systems include limited liability companies as well as mixed entities that do not exclude the liability of the members.

Another problem is that the parallel between international organizations and domestic corporations is tenuous. Important differences exist between domestic corporations and international corporations such as the Arab British Helicopter company and the differences are even greater between domestic corporations and organizations such as the UN and NATO.

Many writers invoke policy arguments in the absence of a clear rule of customary international law or general principle of law. At this point a discussion of member state responsibility becomes *de lege ferenda* rather than *de lege lata*. Amerasinghe for example discusses "conceptual considerations".[116] Expressly or implicitly, the policy factors which carry the most weight for these authors include the following. One is the value of protecting unsuspecting third parties in their relations with an international organization. Hirsch explains that exemption of member states from responsibility:

> would lead in many cases to situations in which the injured party would have no remedy for the harm inflicted upon it. Such might be the case when the organization does not agree to provide a remedy (as in the Westland Case) or when the organization does not have sufficient resources to meet its obligations (as happened in the International Tin Council Case). Justice and efficiency militate against a principle according to which those who benefit from the operations of the organization do not

---

114 C. Amerasinghe, *Liability to Third Parties of Member States of International Organizations: Practice, Principle and Judicial Precedent*, 85 American Journal of International Law 259 (1991), at 273; Meng, *supra* note 97, at 332; M. Hirsch, *supra* note 82, at 127-128. But see Sands & Klein, *supra* note 6, at 524:

> It is clear from these judicial precedents – the conclusions of which were confirmed by the Institute of International Law in its 1995 resolution – that the organisations themselves are the only subjects that may be held liable for the consequences of their wrongful acts, to the exclusion of their members.

115 Schermers, *supra* note 97, at 9; I. Seidl-Hohenveldern, *supra* note 97, at 46-47; Lawson, *supra* note 96, at 27. Hirsch identifies a general principle of member states responsibility that is incompatible with his own statement that a "general principle of law cannot be deduced from such a fundamental divergence of principles as those applying in domestic legal systems", Hirsch, *supra* note 82, at 129-136.

116 Amerasinghe, *supra* note 114. Another example is Meng, who states that for the solution of future cases of damage that are not governed by treaty only commonplaces of argumentation ("argumentationstopoi") can be found. Meng, *supra* note 97, at 332.

> provide any remedy for the loss caused by the organization, when the latter is unable or unwilling to provide adequate remedy.[117]

The other policy factor in question is the possibility that member states will interfere unduly in the affairs of the independent organization. If member states are responsible for the conduct of an international organization they may attempt to control the daily life of the organization in such a way as to make it impossible for the organization to operate as an independent entity.

Many of the considerations discussed above were expressed by members of the Institut de Droit International (IDI) when the institute considered the question of the legal consequences for member states of the non-fulfillment by international organizations of their obligations toward third parties. Rapporteur Higgins prepared a preliminary, provisional and final report.[118] In 1995 the IDI discussed the final report and adopted a resolution on the topic.[119]

The focus was the legal consequences for states, in international law, for the non-fulfillment by international organizations of the obligations of those organizations toward third parties. The IDI did not discuss the responsibility of member states for violation of obligations of the member states by the conduct of an international organization. The majority of the members of the IDI took for granted that an international organization with legal personality is responsible for its obligations because "liability follows personality".[120] It did not follow, however, that separate personality is necessarily determinative of whether member states have a concurrent or residual liability.

The IDI decided to divide its work and its resolution on the topic into a section on the contemporary state of the law and a section on recommendations for future practice. In other words, it distinguished between *lex lata* and *lex ferenda*. The IDI accepted that the contemporary state of the law allows member states to exclude or limit their responsibility expressly or implicitly in the rules of the international organization. Rapporteur Higgins examined *inter alia* case law, writings and state practice in connection with cases where the rules of the organization did not provide a solution. She concluded that:

> by reference to the accepted sources of international law, there is no norm which stipulates that member states bear a legal liability to third parties for the non-fulfillment by international organizations of their obligations to third parties.[121]

This conclusion raised a series of further questions. Does the absence of a specific norm determining state liability mean that there is no liability? Or is the correct posi-

117 Hirsch, *supra* note 82, at 150.

118 Preliminary exposé and draft questionnaire, Annuaire IDI 66-I (1995) 249, Provisional report Annuaire IDI 66-I (1995) 373, Final report, Annuaire IDI 66-I (1995) 461.

119 Annuaire IDI 66-II (1995) 233.

120 *Id.*, at 244.

121 Annuaire IDI 66-I (1995) 415, para. 113.

tion that, unless states can be shown to have excluded or limited their liability, the liability must be presumed to exist? The members disagreed on the correct answer. Rapporteur Higgins and the majority held that member state liability was not to be presumed. A minority held the contrary view that in principle there is member state liability.

In her final report, the rapporteur stated that all agreed that in determining the metaphysical question of presumption of liability one key issue was the analysis of relevant policy considerations:

> Confrères Schermers, Vukas, Salmon and Waelbroeck thought that protection of innocent third parties, and other factors, pointed in the direction of liability. Mr Seidl-Hohenveldern came to accept the argument, expressed by the Rapporteur in her Initial Report, that state liability would inevitably lead to encroachments upon the independence of international organizations.[122]

This statement implies that policy considerations which properly belong to the *lex ferenda* seem to also have played a role in the institute's assessment of the *lex lata*.

The IDI adopted a resolution on the topic in 1995. Article 6 of the resolution states:

> a) Save as specified in article 5, there is no general rule of international law whereby States members are, due solely to their membership, liable concurrently or subsidiarily, for the obligations of an international organization of which they are members.

The article seems to provide that there is a presumption that member states are not liable, but that impression was disputed by several members of the IDI. Waelbroeck for example stated that:

> It had been agreed that the Resolution would say that international law was unclear or that there was no general rule of international law saying that member States were liable. He acknowledged that he now realized that Members were interpreting the Resolution in the sense that, since there was no general rule stating that member States were liable, it meant that they would not be liable. He stressed that this was a fundamental ambiguity in the present situation.[123]

Article 5 of the resolution also qualifies any presumption that member states are not liable:

---

122 *Id.*, at 462.

123 Annuaire IDI 66-II (1996), at 277. See also the statement by Henkin at 274: "Mr Henkin suggested that the Rapporteur's point that there was no rule either way be made clearer in the draft".

a) The question of liability of the members of an international organization for its obligations is determined by reference to the Rules of the organization.
b) In particular circumstances, members of an international organization may be liable for its obligations in accordance with a relevant general principle of international law, such as acquiescence or the abuse of rights.

In conclusion, the case law, writings and state practice do not conclusively demonstrate either the existence or the absence of a rule of international law that member states are responsible for the conduct of an international organization. State practice in respect of peace support operations examined below may help to clarify the issue.

2.8 *Lex specialis* in International Humanitarian Law

2.8.1 *Absolute responsibility*

Article 55 of the ILC draft articles on state responsibility states that the draft articles do not apply where and to the extent that the conditions for the existence of an internationally wrongful act or the content or implementation of the international responsibility of a state are governed by special rules of international law.[124] Draft article 55 reflects the maxim *lex specialis derogat legi generali*.[125]

A number of treaty provisions in international humanitarian law are *lex specialis* in connection with attribution of internationally wrongful acts.

Article 3 of the 1907 Hague Convention (IV) respecting the Laws and Customs of War on Land,[126] to which the Hague Regulations concerning the Laws and Customs of War on Land are annexed, states:

Article 3

A belligerent party which violates the provisions of the said Regulations shall, if the case demands, be liable to pay compensation. It shall be responsible for all acts committed by persons forming part of its armed forces.

Conduct by the armed forces is attributable to the state on the basis of article 4 and article 7 of the draft articles on state responsibility because armed forces are an organ of the state. For an act of a state organ to be considered as an act of that state under international law, the draft requires that the organ was acting in that capacity. Cases where officials acted in their capacity as such, albeit unlawfully or contrary to instruc-

124 See Commissie van Advies inzake Volkenrechtelijke Vraagstukken, Aansprakelijkheid voor Onrechtmatige Daden Tijdens VN Vredesoperaties, Advies No. 13, 14 February 2002, at 17.

125 Report of the International Law Commission on the work of its fifty-third session, *supra* note 3, at 356, para. 2.

126 Hague Convention (IV) respecting the Laws and Customs of War on Land and its annex: Regulations concerning the Laws and Customs of War on Land, 18 October 1907, 3 Martens Nouveau Recueil (ser. 3) 504.

tions, must be distinguished from cases where the conduct is so removed from the scope of official functions that it should be assimilated to that of private individuals, not attributable to the state. The draft articles do not attribute the private conduct of individuals to the state, even if the individual happens to be an organ or agent of the state.

Article 3 of Hague Convention (IV) is broader than these principles because it provides that even private acts of members of the armed forces are attributable to the state if those acts violate the Hague Regulations.[127] The principle expressed in the article is a principle of absolute responsibility, in the sense that all the conduct by armed forces which violates the provisions of the Hague Regulations is attributable to the state.[128] The German delegate who introduced the proposal for the article explained:

> Nous pensons donc que la responsabilité pour tout acte illicite, commis en contravention du Règlement par les personnes faisant parties de la force armée, doit incomber aux Gouvernements dont elles relèvent.[129]

The 1949 Geneva Conventions do not contain an article on attribution of conduct. A common article on liability of the contracting states with regard to grave breaches states:

> No High Contracting Party shall be allowed to absolve itself or any other High Contracting Party of any liability incurred by itself or by another High Contracting Party in respect of breaches referred to in the preceding Article.

The article does not explain when a contracting party incurs liability. In other words, it does not specify the applicable principles of attribution. Some writers state that the principle in Article 3 of Hague Convention (IV), that all conduct by members of the armed forces of a state is attributable to that state, applies to all violations of international humanitarian law including violations of the 1949 Geneva Conventions.[130] The Red Cross commentary to Article 131 of the third Geneva Convention states that the article "should be compared with Article 3 of the Fourth Hague Convention of

127 F. Kalshoven, *State Responsibility for Warlike Acts of the Armed Forces: From Article 3 of the Hague Convention IV of 1907 to Article 91 of Additional Protocol I of 1977 and Beyond*, 40 International & Comparative Law Quarterly 827 (1991), at 837 and M. Sassòli, *State Responsibility for Violations of International Humanitarian Law*, 84 International Review of the Red Cross 401 (2002), at 406.

128 See R. Bierzanek, *The Responsibility of States in Armed Conflicts*, 11 Polish Yearbook of International Law 93 (1981-1982), at 97; L. Condorelli, *Imputation à l'Etat d'un Fait Internationalement Illicite*, 189 Hague Recueil (1984-VI), at 145-149.

129 Deuxième Conférence internationale de la Paix, La Haye 15 juin – 18 octobre 1907, Actes et Documents (Actes), Vol. III, at 145.

130 Condorelli, *supra* note 128, at 146; E. Castren, The Present Law of War and Neutrality 490 (1954).

1907, which states the same principle."[131] Military manuals also apply the principle of Article 3 to all violations of international humanitarian law.[132]

Article 91 of Additional Protocol I to the 1949 Geneva Conventions explicitly applies the principle in article 3 of Hague Convention (IV) to the Geneva Conventions and the Protocol. The article states:

> A Party to the conflict which violates the provisions of the Conventions or of this Protocol shall, if the case demands, be liable to pay compensation. It shall be responsible for all acts committed by persons forming part of its armed forces.

The article is the result of a proposal by Vietnam at the 1977 diplomatic conference. The proposal was designed to restate the principle in Article 3 of Hague Convention (IV) and the principle of non-exoneration of responsibility in the 1949 Geneva Conventions.[133] The original text of the proposal was changed in a working group, which deleted a paragraph reproducing article 148 of Geneva Convention IV and also deleted a reference to grave breaches.[134]

The first Committee of the Conference adopted the article without further discussion.[135] Statements in this committee demonstrate that Article 91 was intended to have the same meaning as Article 3 of Hague Convention (IV).[136]

2.8.2 Responsibility toward individuals

Article 3 of Hague Convention (IV) was discussed above as a provision concerning inter-state responsibility. Some writers argue that the article is not only *lex specialis* because it provides for absolute state responsibility, but also because it established state responsibility toward individuals. Kalshoven states that:

> the records of the conference that adopted the text, i.e. the Second Hague Peace Conference 1907, provide convincing evidence that the delegates sought not so much to lay down a rule relating to the international responsibility of one State vis-à-vis another, as one relating to a State's liability to compensate the losses of individual persons incurred as a consequence of their direct (and harmful) contact with its armed forces.[137]

---

131 J. Pictet (Ed.). Commentary: Geneva Convention III Relative to the Treatment of Prisoners of War 630 (1960).

132 See *e.g.* the German Manual Humanitarian Law in Armed Conflicts, 1992, para. 1214.

133 Official Records of the Diplomatic Conference on the Reaffirmation and Development of International Humanitarian Law Applicable in Armed Conflicts, Geneva (1974-1977) (Official Records), Vol. 9, at 355 (CDDH/I/SR.67, paras. 67, Mr. Van Luu).

134 *Id.*, Vol. 10, at 215 (CDDH/I/338/Rev.1/Add.1).

135 *Id.*, Vol. 9, at 397 (CDDH/I/SR.70).

136 *Id.*, at 415 (CDDH/I/SR.71, para 5) and 416 (CDDH/I/SR.71, para. 9).

137 Kalshoven, *supra* note 127.

On the one hand, the article was drafted at a time when states were generally regarded as the only subjects of international law, and consequently as the only entities capable of having rights under international law. This establishes a presumption against the idea that the drafters of Article 3 wished to create responsibility toward individuals. Writers have generally interpreted Article 3 as creating responsibility toward other states. Freeman for instance states that the responsibility is not one which flows directly to any injured individual, but, consistently with orthodox concepts, it runs directly to the state of the person injured.[138] The ILC also considered Article 3 in the context of responsibility between states in the commentary to article 10 of the 1996 draft articles on state responsibility.[139]

On the other hand, the *travaux préparatoires* of Article 3 contain a number of statements which seem to refer to the rights of individual persons. In his introduction of the proposal that ended up as Article 3 the German delegate, Major-General von Gündell, stated that the proposal's importance lay in cases where the Hague Regulations were breached without the fault of the government. If in such a case:

> les personnes lésées par suite d'une contravention au Règlement, ne pouvaient demander réparation au Gouvernement, et qu'elles fussent obligées à se retourner contre l'officier ou le soldat coupable, elles seraient, dans la majorité des cas, destituées de la faculté d'obtenir l'indemnisation qui leur est due.[140]

The initial proposal distinguished between nationals of the enemy and nationals of neutral states. One part of the proposal required a belligerent party to compensate neutral persons as soon as possible for all acts committed by members of its armed forces. The other part provided that if the victims of the violation were persons belonging to the adverse party, the compensation would be settled at the conclusion of peace. The end result of Article 3 is based on the first part of the proposal, as a consequence of strong objections by several delegations to the distinction between neutral and enemy nationals. This distinction led the President of the sub-commission drafting the article to state that "il y a là droit et obligation, mais aucun droit n'est stipulé pour le préjudice causé 'à des personnes de la Partie adverse'."[141] In his report to the Second Commission of the Conference the President was clearer. He stated in respect of enemy nationals that "on ne leur reconnaît donc aucun droit."[142] It could be argued that this leads to the conclusion that a right was granted to neutral nationals. However, other statements from the *travaux préparatoires* suggest that this was not the case. A statement by one delegation for example suggests that this delegation considered Article 3 as relating to inter-state responsibility, by referring to the settlement

138 A. Freeman, *Responsibility of States for Unlawful Acts of their Armed Forces*, 88 Recueil des Cours (1955-II), at 333. See also A. Waltzog, Recht der Landkriegführung 11 (1942).

139 YBILC 1975, vol. II, at 69, para. 26.

140 Deuxième Conférence Internationale de la Paix, Actes et Documents, Vol III, at 145 (1907).

141 *Id.*, at 144.

142 *Id.*, at 28.

of cases by the states concerned.[143] The German delegate responded to this statement that he could not have defended the proposition better himself, suggesting that this was also what the sponsor of the proposal had in mind.[144] Indeed, the conferral of rights on individuals must be distinguished from the conferral of a right to invoke a breach of those rights in their own name. As the Permanent Court of International Justice pointed out "it is scarcely necessary to point out that the capacity to possess civil rights does not necessarily imply the capacity to exercise those rights oneself."[145]

In conformity with this interpretation, in a great majority of cases in which individual claimants have based their claim on Article 3, courts have held that this article did not create an individual right of action, *i.e.* a secondary right, without stating that it did not create a primary right.[146]

2.9 State practice of attribution of conduct of United Nations peace support operations

2.9.1 Lump sums in the Congo

During the United Nations Operation in the Congo a number of Belgian, Greek, Italian, Luxemburg and Swiss nationals lodged claims for damage to persons and property with the United Nations. The governments of these individuals then exercised diplomatic protection by espousing the claims. The UN negotiated agreements with the governments on compensation in the form of lump sums. The governments distributed the lump sums between the individual claimants. The Secretary-General stated in the agreements with the governments that the organization:

> would not evade responsibility where it was established that United Nations agents had in fact caused unjustifiable damage to innocent parties. It is pointed out that, under these principles, the United Nations does not assume liability for damage to persons or property which resulted solely from military operations or which, although caused by third parties, has given rise to claims against the United Nations.[147]

143 "Le règlement des indemnités dues à des neutres pourra, le plus souvent, avoir lieu sans retard, par la simple raison que l'Etat belligérant responsable est en paix avec leur pays et continue avec ce dernier des relations pacifiques qui permettront *aux deux Etats* de liquider aisément et sans délai tous les cas venant à se présenter. La même facilité ou possibilité n'existe pas entre les belligérants, par le fait même de la guerre, et, bien que le droit à une indemnité naisse en faveur de leurs ressortisants respectifs aussi bien qu'en faveur de neutres, le règlement des indemnités, *entre belligérants*, ne pourra guère être arrêté et effectué qu'à la conclusion de la Paix." Deuxième Conférence internationale de la Paix, La Haye 15 juin – 18 octobre 1907, Actes et Documents (Actes), Vol. III, at 147 (emphasis added).

144 *Id.*

145 Appeal from a Judgment of the Hungaro-Czechoslovak Mixed Arbitral Tribunal (the Peter Pazmany case), PCIJ Series A/B, No. 61, at 231.

146 See *e.g.* Goldstar (Panama) S.A. v. United States, 967 F.2d 965 (4th Cir. 1992). See also the cases referred to in para. 5.5.2.

147 Agreement between the United Nations and Belgium relating to the settlement of claims filed against the United Nations in the Congo by Belgian nationals of 20 February 1965,

The Soviet Union protested against the compensation provided by the organization. It was of the opinion that Belgium had forfeited its moral or legal basis for making claims against the organization either on its own behalf or on behalf of its citizens, because it had committed aggression against the Republic of the Congo.[148] The Secretary-General replied to the Soviet note that:

> It has always been the policy of the United Nations, acting through the Secretary-General, to compensate individuals who have suffered damages for which the Organization was legally liable. This policy is in keeping with generally recognized legal principles and with the Convention on Privileges and Immunities of the United Nations. In addition, in regard to the United Nations activities in the Congo, it is reinforced by the principles set forth in the international conventions concerning the protection of the life and property of the civilian population during hostilities as well as by considerations of equity and humanity which the United Nations cannot ignore. Accordingly, the claims submitted were investigated by the competent services of ONUC and at United Nations Headquarters in order to collect all the data relevant to determining the responsibility of the Organization. Claims of damage which were found to be solely due to military operations or military necessity were excluded. Also expressly excluded were claims for damage found to have been caused by persons other than United Nations personnel.[149]

2.9.2 Claims settlement procedures

The UN has established procedures for handling third-party claims of a private law character against peace support operations. These procedures concern claims by the government of the host state as well as nationals of the host state. SOFAs provide that claims of a private law character shall be settled by a standing claims commission established for that purpose. The provision used in earlier agreements was reproduced in Article 51 of the Model SOFA:

> Any dispute or claim of a private law character to which the United Nations peacekeeping operation or any member thereof is a party and over which the courts of [host country/territory] do not have jurisdiction because of any provision of the

---

535 UNTS 199 (Spaak-U Thant Agreement). See also Exchange of letters constituting an agreement relating to the settlement of claims filed against the United Nations in the Congo by Swiss nationals of 3 January 1966, 564 UNTS 193; Exchange of letters constituting an agreement relating to the settlement of claims filed against the United Nations in the Congo by Greek nationals of 20 January 1966, 565 UNTS 3; Exchange of letters constituting an agreement relating to the settlement of claims filed against the United Nations in the Congo by Luxembourg nationals of 28 December 1966, 585 UNTS 147; Exchange of letters constituting an agreement relating to the settlement of claims filed against the United Nations in the Congo by Italian nationals of 18 January 1967, 588 UNTS 197.

148 Letter of 2 August 1965 from the Acting Permanent Representative of the USSR addressed to the Secretary-General, UN Doc. S/6589.

149 *Id.*

> present Agreement, shall be settled by a standing claims commission to be established for that purpose. One member of the commission shall be appointed by the Secretary-General of the United Nations, one member by the Government and a chairman jointly by the Secretary-General and the Government.[150]

The model SOFA provides that any appeal which the UN or the host state agree to allow from the award of the claims commission shall, unless otherwise agreed by the parties, be submitted to an arbitral tribunal. The decisions of the claims commission and the arbitral tribunal shall be binding on both parties.

However, to date, third-party claims of a private law nature have been settled without resort to the establishment of standing claims commissions. Instead, it has been the practice, with respect to most past and present UN operations, for a local claims review board established in the mission on the basis of authority delegated by the Controller to examine, approve or recommend settlement of third-party claims for personal injury or death and for property loss or damage that are attributable to acts performed in connection with official duties by civilian or military members of the mission. When the claims review board approves a settlement amount within its delegated financial authority, the relevant administrative office of the peacekeeping mission, normally the claims unit, proceeds to offer such a settlement amount to the claimant. In the vast majority of cases, the offer is accepted by the claimant and payment is made.

UN claims review boards do not accept claims in connection with acts of members of peace support operations committed while off duty. In a 1986 memorandum the UN Office of Legal Affairs stated that UN policy in regard to off-duty acts of the members of peacekeeping forces is that the organization has no legal or financial liability for death, injury or damage resulting from such acts. The memorandum states that:

> A soldier may be considered 'off duty' not only when he is 'on leave' but also when he is not acting in an official or operational capacity while either inside or outside the area of operations. In this regard, we wish to point out that there have been such off-duty determinations made with respect to previous incidents involving soldiers acting in a non-official capacity in the area of operations. We consider the primary factor in determining an 'off-duty' situation to be whether the member of a peace-keeping mission was acting in a non-official/non-operational capacity when the incident

150 See also Report of the Secretary-General on arrangements concerning the status of the United Nations Emergency Force in Egypt of 8 February 1957, UN Doc. A/3526; Exchange of Letters Constituting an Agreement between the United Nations and the Government of the Republic of Cyprus concerning the Status of the United Nations Peace-Keeping Force in Cyprus, 492 UNTS 58, article 38; Agreement between the United Nations and the Republic of South Africa concerning the Status of the United Nations Transition Assistance Group in Namibia (South West Africa), UN Doc. S/20412/Add.1 of 16 March 1989, article 57; Agreement between the United Nations and the Government of the Republic of Rwanda on the Status of the United Nations Assistance Mission for Rwanda, 5 November 1993, UNJY 1993, at 102, Art. 50.

> occurred and not whether he/she was in military or civilian attire at the time of the incident or whether the incident occurred inside or outside the area of operations.[151]

The Secretary-General submitted a report in 1995 which discussed the scope of UN liability for activities of UN forces.[152] The report was written pursuant to a request by the Advisory Committee on Administrative and Budgetary Questions (ACABQ) to study the procedures for settling third-party claims.[153] The report states that:

> The international liability of the United Nations for the activities of United Nations forces is an attribute of its international legal personality and its capacity to bear international rights and obligations. It is also a reflection of the principle of State responsibility – widely accepted to be applicable to international organizations – that damage caused in breach of an international obligation and which is attributable to the State (or to the Organization), entails the international responsibility of the State (or of the Organization) and its liability in compensation.
> In recognition of its international responsibility for the activities of its forces, the United Nations has, since the inception of peacekeeping operations, assumed its liability for damage caused by members of its forces in the performance of their duties. In conformity with section 29 of the Convention on the Privileges and Immunities of the United Nations, it has undertaken in paragraph 51 of the model status-of-forces agreement (see A/45/594) to settle by means of a standing claims commission claims resulting from damage caused by members of the force in the performance of their official duties and which for reasons of immunity of the Organization and its Members could not have been submitted to local courts.
> The undertaking to settle disputes of a private law nature submitted against it and the practice of actual settlement of such third-party claims – although not necessarily according to the procedure provided for under the status-of-forces agreement – evidence the recognition on the part of the United Nations that liability for damage caused by members of United Nations forces is attributable to the Organization.[154]

151 UNJY 1986, 300.

152 Report of the Secretary-General on the Financing of the United Nations Protection Force, the United Nations Confidence Restoration Operation in Croatia, the United Nations Preventive Deployment Force and the United Nations Peace Forces headquarters; Administrative and budgetary aspects of the financing of the United Nations peacekeeping operations: financing of the United Nations peacekeeping operations of 20 September 1996, UN Doc. A/51/389.

153 Advisory Committee on Administrative and Budgetary Questions, Report on the Financing of the United Nations Protection Force (UNPROFOR), the United Nations Confidence Restoration Operation in Croatia (UNCRO), the United Nations Preventive Deployment Force (UNPREDEP), the United Nations Peace Forces headquarters (UNPF), the United Nations Mission in Bosnia and Herzegovina (UNMIBH) and the United Nations Transitional Administration in Eastern Slavonia, Baranja and Western Sirmium (UNTAES), UN Doc. A/50/903/Add.1.

154 *Supra* note 152, paras. 6-8.

The report distinguished between the responsibility of the organization for the ordinary operation of a force and for combat-related activities. The responsibility of the UN for combat-related activities is determined by the principles and rules of international humanitarian law. The report discussed the principles of attribution of conduct by peace support operations which violates international humanitarian law on the basis of command and control:

> The international responsibility of the United Nations for combat-related activities of United Nations forces is premised on the assumption that the operation in question is under the exclusive command and control of the United Nations. Where a Chapter VII-authorized operation is conducted under national command and control, international responsibility for the activities of the force is vested in the State or States conducting the operation. The determination of responsibility becomes particularly difficult, however, in cases where a State or States provide the United Nations with forces in support of a United Nations operation but not necessarily as an integral part thereof, and where operational command and control is unified or coordinated. This was the case in Somalia where the Quick Reaction Force and the US Rangers were provided in support of the United Nations Operation in Somalia (UNOSOM II), and this was also the case in the former Yugoslavia where the Rapid Reaction Force was provided in support of the United Nations Protection Force (UNPROFOR).
> In joint operations, international responsibility for the conduct of the troops lies where operational command and control is vested according to the arrangements establishing the modalities of cooperation between the State or States providing the troops and the United Nations. In the absence of formal arrangements between the United Nations and the State or States providing troops, responsibility would be determined in each and every case according to the degree of effective control exercised by either party in the conduct of the operation.
> The principle that in coordinated operations liability for combat-related damage in violation of international humanitarian law is vested in the entity in effective command and control of the operation or the specific action reflects a well-established principle of international responsibility While it would be desirable to make provisions for the attributability of responsibility in the arrangements with the State or States providing troops, absent such arrangements, claims for damage caused by auxiliary troops should be submitted to their Governments for processing and settlement. This, in fact, was the procedure followed in the case of UNOSOM II and the forces made available in support of the United Nations operation.[155]

The Secretary-General also suggested that the General Assembly consider the concurrent responsibility of the state of nationality of the member of a peace support operation that violates international humanitarian law:

> Given the exclusive criminal jurisdiction of the State of nationality and its obligation to ensure respect for international humanitarian law by members of its force, the

155 *Id.*, paras. 17-19.

> General Assembly may wish to consider recognizing the concurrent responsibility of the State of nationality for violations of international humanitarian law by members of its national contingent and its responsibility in compensation.[156]

When the Fifth Committee of the General Assembly discussed the Secretary-General's report it did not consider this suggestion,[157] nor does it seem to have been taken up in other organs.

2.9.3 National case law

In *N.K.* v. *Austria* the superior provincial court of Vienna decided that Austria was not responsible for damage to the property of a member of the Austrian contingent in the peace support operation in the Golan Heights.[158] The plaintiff sought compensation from the state alleging that Austria was liable for the negligent act of another Austrian soldier in the same contingent that caused the damage. The court of first instance dismissed the action on the ground that, at the time in question, the negligent soldier had been acting as an organ of the UN and not of Austria. The superior provincial court dismissed the appeal on the basis of Austrian law, which accepts the so-called 'organ theory'. According to this theory, in determining which legal entity is liable under the Austrian state liability law, what is decisive is not whose organ (from the organizational standpoint) the person alleged to have caused the damage actually was, but rather in whose name and for whom (from the functional standpoint) that person was acting at the moment when the act occurred. The court, taking this theory as the starting point, decided that the negligent soldier was not acting as an organ of the state. It discussed the agreement between the UN and Austria concerning the contribution of troops and the annexed regulations, which stated that members of the force, whilst remaining in the service of their national state, become, during the period of their assignment to the force, international personnel under the authority of the UN and that through the chain of command, they are subject to the instructions of the commander appointed. The court concluded that:

> Starting from the premise that the order at issue in this case was given by the "Commander", albeit indirectly through a "senior authority", to a "member of the United Nations Forces in Cyprus" under his command (cf. Point 5c of the Regulations), this Court concurs with the view of the court of first instance that the Lance-Corporal, according to the organtheorie explained above, was acting as an organ of the United Nations and not of the Republic of Austria when he caused the damage at issue. The defendant is therefore not capable of being sued.[159]

---

156 *Id.*, para. 44.

157 See UN Doc. A/C.5/51/SR.14 of 25 October 1996.

158 Austria, Superior Provincial Court (Oberlandesgericht) of Vienna, *N.K.* v. *Austria*, 26 February 1979, reproduced in 77 ILR 470.

159 *Id.*, at 474.

In *Nissan* v. *Attorney-General* the tenant of a hotel in Nicosia, Cyprus, claimed compensation from the United Kingdom for damage resulting from the occupation and possession of the hotel by, *inter alia*, British members of the United Nations Force in Cyprus after 27 March 1964. The defendant claimed that the members of the force were temporarily servants of the commander and that his master was in turn the UN, who were to be treated as equivalent to an independent sovereign state.

The case concerned a number of preliminary questions, including whether the defense by the government that the acts of the soldiers were acts of the UN and not of the government disclosed a 'good defense' in law to the claim of compensation. According to the government:

> The British forces operating in the Republic of Cyprus from and after Mar. 17, 1964, were contingents of the United Nations force aforesaid. In the premises no action lies against the Crown in respect of any of the actions of the said forces.[160]

It was made clear by the government that the last sentence of this paragraph covered three separate contentions, one of which was that the force and its British soldiers were agents of the UN. Judge Stephenson relied on the agreements between the UN and Cyprus, and the organization and the United Kingdom, to decide whether the force occupied the hotel as agents of the state or of the UN. He stated that:

> The British troops derived their authority to occupy the hotel no longer from her Majesty but from the United Nations, and occupied it as agents of the United Nations exclusively. From that date, until they were withdrawn from service with the United Nations force, it no longer rested with the British government to say whether they stayed in the hotel or left, and the only authority which their own commander had so long as they remained members of the force to order them in or out of the hotel or any other premises required for their accommodation or the fulfillment of their functions was derived from the commander of the force and through him from the United Nations.[161]

The court of appeal dismissed Nissan's appeal concerning the decision of Judge Stephenson that the government was not responsible for the British members of the UN force. The court decided that once the British forces became part of the United Nations force, the responsibility for their acts fell on the UN. Lord Denning stated that:

> They were under the command of the United Nations commander. They flew the United Nations flag. They wore the berets and arm-flashes to denote that they were

160 *Nissan* v. *Attorney-General*, Queen's Bench Division, 17 February 1967, [1967] 2 All ER 200, at 208.

161 *Id.*, at 220.

> no longer the soldiers of the Queen, but the soldiers of the United Nations. They were acting as agents for the United Nations, which is a sovereign body corporate.[162]

The government appealed the order of the court of appeal. The House of Lords decided that Nissan did have an action against the government. Lord Pearce stated that:

> All the judgments, however, took the view that during the second period the British troops no longer occupied the hotel in the Queen's name but in the name of the United Nations. I do not think so. The United Nations is not a superstate nor even a sovereign state. It is a unique legal person or corporation. It is based on the sovereignty of its respective members. But it is not a principal carrying out its policy through states acting as its agents. It is an instrument of collective policy which it enforces by using the sovereignty of its members. In carrying out the policies each member still retains its own sovereignty, just as any sovereign state, acting under its treaty obligations to another state, would normally still retain its sovereignty.
> This view of the matter is strongly reinforced by the relevant letters and regulations. They show that the commander of the United Nations force is head in the chain of command and is answerable to the United Nations. The functions of the force as a whole are international. But its individual component forces have their own national duty and discipline and remain in their national service.[163]

In *Manderlier* v. *Belgium* the plaintiff claimed compensation from the UN and the Belgian government for damage suffered from acts of the Ethiopian contingent in ONUC. The court of first instance[164] and the court of appeals[165] declared the claims against the UN inadmissible because the organization enjoyed immunity from jurisdiction. The judgment of the court of first instance does not make clear the precise basis for the plaintiff's claim against the Belgian government. The plaintiff seems to have based his claim against the state on the alleged failure of the state to exercise effective diplomatic protection.[166] It is not clear whether the plaintiff also considered

---

162 *Nissan* v. *Attorney-General*, Court of Appeal, Civil Division, 29 June 1967, [1967] All ER 1238, at 1244.

163 *Attorney-General* v. *Nissan*, House of Lords, 11 February 1969, [1969] All ER 629, at 647.

164 *Manderlier* v. *United Nations and Belgium*, Court of first instance of Brussels, 11 May 1966, 81 Journal des Tribunaux No. 4553 (1966), 721, 45 ILR 446.

165 *Manderlier* v. *United Nations and Belgium*, Court of appeals of Brussels, 15 September 1969, 69 ILR 139.

166 The court of appeals stated that:

> The appellant alleges that the respondent failed to fulfill its obligation of protection in a satisfactory manner. He accuses the respondent, in particular, of not having applied to the International Court of Justice. He alleges that this failure constitutes fault engaging its responsibility. In his submissions he also accuses the respondent of not honouring its formal undertaking to defend individually the rights of each victim and in particular the appellant.

Manderlier v. *United Nations and Belgium*, *supra* note 165, at 144.

that the conduct of the members of the peace support operation could be attributed to Belgium. In any event the court of first instance did discuss this possibility:

> Whereas the facts of which the plaintiff complains have taken place abroad and they have been committed by foreigners; and that the second defendant, the Belgian state, is a third party in relation to these facts, and its organs have not committed them; that it could not have prevented them by itself;[167]

2.9.4 International Law Commission

It was noted above that despite the efforts by the ILC not to discuss the topic of the responsibility of international organizations in the course of its work on state responsibility, discussions on the latter topic did in fact lead to statements concerning the responsibility of international organizations. Some of these statements concerned attribution of conduct to international organizations, and attribution of conduct of peace support operations in particular.

In his third report on state responsibility Special Rapporteur Ago pointed out that the principle that the conduct of an organ of one state placed at the disposal of another state must be attributed to the second state (draft article 6 of the 2001 draft articles on state responsibility), was confirmed by the practice concerning acts or omissions of organs placed at the disposal of international organizations by states.[168] He discussed the practice during the operations undertaken in Korea in 1950 on behalf of the UN by armed forces of the United States and other countries, as well as the payment of lump sums by the UN in connection with ONUC. He stated that:

> Here, too, the decisive criterion for determining responsibility in such cases is the actual circumstances in which the acts or omissions concerned have been committed. In cases where State organs have been placed at the disposal of an organization on a purely formal basis and they have continued in fact to act under the sole control and in accordance with the instructions of the State to which they belong, it is that State and not the organization which has been held responsible for their acts. On the other hand, in cases where the organs have really been placed under the sole authority of an organization by the State to which they belong and have acted in accordance with instructions genuinely emanating from the organization, the organization itself has accepted its responsibility and borne the financial consequences; and – this is an interesting point – none of the member States has ever raised any objections.[169]

---

167 *Manderlier* v. *United Nations and Belgium*, *supra* note 164, at 723. Translation by the author. The original states:

> Attendu que les faits dont le demandeur se plaint se sont passés à l'étranger où ils ont été commis par des étrangers; que le second défendeur, l'Etat belge, est à leur égard un tiers, dont les organes ne les ont point commis; qu'il n'aurait pu de sa seule initiative les empêcher;

168 YBILC 1971 Vol. II (Part One), at 272.

169 *Id.*

Members of the ILC also discussed the attribution of conduct to an international organization in connection with a draft article which excluded the attribution of conduct of an organ of an international organization by reason only of the fact that such conduct has taken place in the territory of that state. Several members indicated that the conduct of an organ of an international organization acting in that capacity should be attributed to the organization. El-Erian stated:

> In practice, the conduct of an organ of an international organization performing a function of a State should not raise legal difficulties, since the organ would have been accepted by the State. An international organization which had the capacity to enter into a contract or treaty with a State in which its organ was to operate, would clearly be responsible for the acts of that organ.[170]

Ushakov also accepted that the conduct of an organ of an international organization should be attributed to the organization, but he left the door open to attribution to a state as well:

> With regard to the conduct of an organ of an international organization, when the armed forces of an international organization acted in that capacity in the territory of a State, it was open to question whether it was only the international organization that acted, or whether the act should not also be attributed to the States whose contingents composed the armed forces of the organization. In that case, too, there might perhaps be a joint act by the international organization and the States which had provided contingents.[171]

In its work on the responsibility of international organizations attribution of conduct is an important element. Gaja's second report to the ILC addressing attribution of conduct and the ILC debates pursuant to that report were analyzed above. It may be noted that much of the state practice referred to above was referred to in the part of the report concerning the attribution of conduct of organs placed at the disposal of an international organization by a state or another organization. It may be recalled that the report and draft article 5 adopted on first reading by the ILC make attribution of conduct dependent on the factual control which is exercized over the specific conduct taken by the organ or agent placed at the receiving organization's disposal.

170 YBILC 1975 Vol. I, at 46, para. 35. See also Reuter, at 45, para. 29.

171 *Id.*, at 47, para. 5.

2.10 Analysis of state practice in connection with United Nations peace support operations

2.10.1 Application of the principle in article 6 of the draft articles on state responsibility

State practice in connection with UN peace support operations demonstrates that the UN and states accept that, in certain circumstances, conduct of the operations which violates international humanitarian law is attributable to the international organization.

The clearest example is the payment of lump sums by the UN in connection with violations of international humanitarian law by the UN operation in the Congo. In these cases the organization acknowledged that it was responsible where it was established that UN agents had in fact caused unjustifiable damage to innocent parties.

Some writers discuss the procedures for the settlement of third-party claims developed by the UN to demonstrate that the conduct of peace support operations is attributed to the UN. Scobbie for example refers to paragraph 51 of the model UN SOFA, which provides that claims of a private law character arising from a peace-keeping operation shall be settled by a claims commission, as proof of international responsibility of the UN.[172]

Cases decided by claims commissions and local claims review boards however are not examples of attribution of conduct to the UN on the basis of international law, because these bodies do not apply international law but the private law of torts. The procedures established by the UN in this regard should be considered as local remedies which must be exhausted before a claim can be made under international law. Simmonds states that:

> When the injuries are to persons and their property, a rule akin to the rule of exhaustion of local remedies would apply so that the Government would take up the claim against the UN only when there had been, via the UN's own procedures for settlement of claims, a 'denial of justice'.[173]

The proper role of claims settlement procedures is placed in perspective by the statement of the UN Secretary-General that these procedures are in conformity with section 29 of the Convention on the Privileges and Immunities of the United Nations. In other words, these procedures were established because the immunity of the UN prevents claims from being adjudicated by local courts. Claims settlement procedures were established to prevent such an *a priori* denial of justice.

The principles of attribution used by claims review boards do indirectly demonstrate the applicable principles under international law because claims settlement procedures were established by the UN "in recognition of its international responsi-

172 I. Scobbie, *International Responsibility*, in R.J. Dupuy (Ed.), Manual on International Organizations 886 (1998), at 889.

173 R. Simmonds, Legal Problems Arising from the United Nations Military Operations in the Congo 238 (1968). See also B. Amrallah, *supra* note 8, at 76.

bility for the activities of its forces."[174] The claims review boards provide a remedy in private law in cases where the UN could be held responsible under international law. The 1995 report of the Secretary-General was an express acceptance of the international responsibility of the UN for violations of international humanitarian law by peace support operations under the exclusive command and control of the UN. The Secretary-General's report states that the attribution to the UN of combat-related activities is premised on the assumption that the operation in question is under the exclusive command and control of the organization. In joint operations command and control can be vested according to the arrangements between the state or states providing the troops and the UN. In the absence of formal arrangements responsibility would be determined in each and every case according to the degree of effective control exercised by either party in the conduct of the operation.

The same principle of attribution was used by the Austrian court in the *NK* v. *Austria* case, as well as by the United Kingdom High Court and Court of Appeal in the *Nissan* case. The Austrian court for example primarily inquired "whose instructions the commander of a unit sent abroad is subject to." The relevant arrangements between Austria and the UN demonstrated that the commander was subject to the instructions of the UN. Therefore the conduct of a member of the unit was not attributable to Austria.

However, international law was not deemed to be the applicable law in these domestic cases. The Austrian court for example decided the case on the basis of the '*Organtheory*' developed in Austrian administrative law. Domestic case law cannot be used to prove the existence of a principle of attribution under international law.[175]

State practice, as placed in context in the Secretary-General's report, demonstrates the application of the principle in article 6 of the draft articles on state responsibility to the UN. Draft article 6 is concerned with the conduct of organs placed at the disposal of a state by another state. The situation of contingents in peace support operations is that of organs placed at the disposal of the UN by troop contributing states. The ILC's commentary to draft article 6 states that the:

> notion of an organ placed at the disposal of the receiving State is a specialized one, implying that the organ is acting with the consent, under the authority of and for the purposes of the receiving State. Not only must the organ be appointed to perform functions entrusted to it by the beneficiary State, the organ must also act in conjunction with the machinery of that State and under its exclusive direction and control, rather than on instructions from the sending State.[176]

---

174 Report of the Secretary-General, *supra* note 152, para. 7. This is illustrated by the Secretary-General's discussion of the principles of attribution of conduct of peace support operations that violates international humanitarian law without distinguishing between settlement of claims by claims review boards or through lump sum settlement under international law in paras. 17-19. See also Gaja, *supra* note 40, at 18, para. 36.

175 For example M. Bothe, Streitkräfte Internationaler Organisationen: Zugleich ein beitrag zu völkerrechtlichen Grundfragen der Anwesendheit fremder Truppen 54 (1968); Hirsch, *supra* note 82, at 73-76.

176 *Supra* note 3, at 95, para. 2.

The parallel with the principle of attribution applied to the conduct of peace support operations is obvious, *inter alia* because the principle in draft article 6 is based in part on state practice in connection with peace support operations. When Special Rapporteur Ago proposed the principle in draft article 6 to the ILC in 1971, he stated that the validity of the principle was undoubtedly provided by the practice concerning acts or omissions of organs placed at the disposal of international organizations by states, in particular the practice in connection with the UN operation in the Congo.[177]

Draft article 5 on the responsibility of international organizations, adopted on first reading by the ILC in 2004, takes up the principle in article 6 of the draft articles on state responsibility. Draft article 5 is based to a large extent on state practice concerning UN peace support operations. The commentary states that the situation which the article deals with "occurs for instance in the case of military contingents that a State places at the disposal of the United Nations for a peacekeeping operation."[178] The commentary takes the following statement by the UN Secretary-General to sum up UN practice relating to peacekeeping forces:

> As a subsidiary organ of the United Nations, an act of a peacekeeping force is, in principle, imputable to the Organization, and if committed in violation of an international obligation entails the international responsibility of the Organization and its liability in compensation.[179]

This statement implies that a provision on direction and control in an agreement between the sending state and the UN can play a role in the attribution of conduct of the organ in question. If the agreement provides that the organ is under the orders of the receiving organization, there is a presumption that conduct of the organ is attributable to that organization. The presumption can be based on the clauses in agreements between troop contributing states and the UN concerning command and control over peace support operations. Command and control relate to the nature of the authority exercised by military commanders over the forces assigned to them and as such it is an indication of who gives instructions in the sense of draft article 5. Troop contributing states transfer a level of command and control to the UN which involves the full authority to issue operational directives within the limits of a specific mandate, an agreed period of time and a specific geographical range. Giving such military command and control over an organ is the equivalent of placing the organ at the disposal of an international organization in the sense of draft article 5.

For the contingent to be placed at the disposal of the organization it must be established that the organ was not acting on the instructions or under the direction and control of the sending state. It is not necessary that the sending state gave express instructions. Hirsch states:

177 YBILC 1971, Vol. II (Part One), at 272, para. 210.

178 *Supra* note 95, at 11, para. 1.

179 Draft Report of the International Law Commission on the work of its fifty-sixth session, *supra* note 95, at 13, para. 5.

> Each individual case must be examined as to whether the specific legal act was performed under the control of the organization or the sending state. If a member of such a force performs an act under the direction of its national government, that government will be the proper addressee of any claim arising from that act; this conclusion will not be altered even in cases where the contingent to which that member belongs is generally under the operational control of the organization.[180]

Support for such an interpretation can be found in the drafting history of article 6 of the draft articles on state responsibility. The ILC's commentary on article 9 of the draft articles adopted on first reading, and containing the principle now in draft article 6, states that the article excludes:

> those situations in which the organs of a State or of an international organization perform functions appertaining to another State in the territory of that other State and with its consent, but nevertheless act under the authority, direction and control of the sending State or organization.

One of the cases mentioned in the commentary adopted on second reading to draft article 6 is *Drozd and Janousek* v. *France and Spain*, in which the European Court of Human Rights held that French and Spanish judges were placed at the disposal of Andorra because "their judgments are not subject to supervision by the authorities of France and Spain."[181] Writers who apply the principle to peace support operations also do not require express instructions.[182]

An example in which conduct would be attributable to the troop contributing state is the hypothetical situation that the Netherlands contingent of UNPROFOR in Srebrenica received instructions from its government concerning the attitude it must take toward the transfer of the local population by Bosnian Serb forces. If such were the case, the conduct of the contingent would be attributable to the government, even though the agreement between the Netherlands and the UN concerning the participation of Dutch troops in the operation specified that the UN was in command.[183] In the case at hand the government has denied that it gave instructions to the contingent.[184]

State practice does not provide examples of the attribution of the conduct of peace support operations to states on the basis of their membership of the UN. On the other hand, state practice does not provide evidence of a conviction that member state responsibility is excluded. At the most it justifies the conclusion that member state responsibility is secondary: in other words, that a claim must be addressed to the UN

180 Hirsch, *supra* note 82, at 64-65. See also Amrallah, *supra* note 8, at 65.

181 *Drozd and Janousek* v. *France and Spain*, E.C.H.R. Series A, No. 240 (1992), para. 96.

182 Klein, *supra* note 82, at 380-381; Hirsch, *supra* note 82, at 64; Amrallah, *supra* note 8, at 66.

183 See R. Siekmann, *The Fall of Srebrenica and the Attitude of Dutchbat from an International Legal Perspective*, 1 Yearbook of International Humanitarian Law 301 (1998).

184 Aanhangsel Handelingen II 1996/97, nr. 181.

before it is addressed to member states. The governments which exercised diplomatic protection of their nationals in connection with ONUC first directed their claims at the UN, and because negotiations with the organization were successful, the question of secondary responsibility did not arise.[185] In this sense state practice is disappointing because it does not give guidance on the practical existence or lack thereof of the theories of member state responsibility. The application of draft article 6 of the draft articles to peace support operations does not *a priori* exclude a secondary responsibility of member states in cases in which it leads to attribution of conduct to the UN.

State practice does not provide examples of the attribution of the conduct of peace support operations to troop contributing states. Here too, there is on the other hand no evidence of a conviction that troop contributing state responsibility is excluded. In certain circumstances the attribution of conduct of members of a peace support operation to a troop contributing state would be entirely consistent with principles of state responsibility developed by the ILC and international courts. This is also Gaja's point of view, who would "leave the way open for dual attribution of certain conducts."[186]

Condorelli states that the application of the principle in article 6 of the draft articles on state responsibility to peace support operations is appropriate.[187] Application of the principle, he argues, leads to the conclusion that conduct of a national contingent is attributable to the UN as well as to the state contributing the contingent in question. Condorelli bases attribution of the conduct of a national contingent to the troop contributing state in question on the state's supposed authority, direction and control over the contingent and on his submission that the contingent is acting in the exercise of elements of the governmental authority of the state.

As a general proposition Condorelli's argument is correct, but his application of the principle to UN peace support operations is not. Article 6 of the ILC draft articles accepts that there is a presumption of attribution to the receiving state (or international organization) if the organ in question is placed under its orders in an agreement. This presumption is established in agreements between troop contributing states and the UN, which provide that during the period of their assignment the personnel made available by the troop contributing state shall be under the command of the UN and that accordingly, the Secretary-General shall have full authority over the deployment, organization, conduct and direction of the operation, including the personnel. The presumption can be rebutted if it is established that the organ acted under the direction and control of the sending state, the clearest example of which would be specific instructions. The mere provision in agreements between the UN and troop contributing states that national administrative matters remain the responsibility of the government of the troop contributing state, or that the orders of the inter-

185 State practice supports only half of Brownlie's statement that there is no "presumption in law that the United Nations bears either an exclusive or a primary responsibility for the tortious acts of such forces", I. Brownlie, Principles of Public International Law 686 (1998).

186 Gaja, *supra* note 40, at 23, para. 48.

187 L. Condorelli, *Le Statut des Forces de l'ONU et le Droit International Humanitaire*, *78* Rivista di Diritto Internazionale 881 (1995).

national commander are received by the contingent through the national operational commander of the contingent, do not establish such a situation.[188] Condorelli mainly bases his argument on the appointment of so-called 'contingent commanders' by troop contributing states, by which he appears to refer to the SNR.[189] It seems, however, that he misconstrues the role of such commanders in according them much more authority than they actually have. It may be recalled that attribution of conduct of contingents is not excluded but can only be based on a strict application of the criterion of control exercised over the contingents in the circumstances in which the conduct was committed.[190]

Another case is that in which a state or states provide the UN with forces in support of a UN operation but not as an integral part thereof, such as in the case of the Quick Reaction Force in Somalia. The Terms of Reference Agreement between the United States and the UN provided that the Quick Reaction Force was under the operational control of United States Central Command (USCINCCENT).[191] Tactical control could be delegated from USCINCCENT to the commander of US forces in Somalia, who was also deputy commander of the UN operation. In a case in which tactical control had been delegated there would not be a clear presumption of attribution because the Commander of US forces in Somalia was by agreement under the command of USCINCCENT as well as the UNOSOM force commander. To establish responsibility it would have to be established whether conduct of the Quick Reaction Force was on the instructions or under the direction and control of the sending state or the United Nations. Situations could also arise where the Quick Reaction Force acted on the joint instructions of the UN and the United States. In this case the conduct in question would be attributable to both.

The presumption that the conduct of troops which are an integral part of a peace support operation is attributable to the UN, is rebutted if it is established that the troops were acting in fact on behalf of a troop contributing state. As the Secretary-General states, the responsibility of the UN for combat-related activities of UN forces is premised on the assumption that the operation in question is under the exclusive command and control of the UN, implying that such an assumption can be rebutted.

The IDI discussed the situations in which this is the case when it studied the conditions of application of humanitarian rules of armed conflict to hostilities in which United Nations forces may be engaged in 1971. Rapporteur Paul de Visscher submitted both a preliminary and a final report and the IDI adopted a resolution after discussion of final report.[192] De Visscher stated in his reports that responsibility is based on control:

188 Cf. *mutatis mutandis* in national law the court in *NK* v. *Austria*.

189 See para. 1.8.8.

190 Klein, *supra* note 82, at 380.

191 Terms of Reference for US Forces Somalia, United Nations Operation Somalia, Annex A to United States Army Field Manual 100-23, Peace Operations, <www.adtdl.army.mil/cgi-bin/adtdl.dll/fm/100-23/fm100_7.htm> .

192 Preliminary Report, Annuaire IDI 54-I (1971) 45; Final Report, Annuaire IDI 54-I (1971) 116; Resolution, Annuaire IDI 54-II (1971) 449.

> in case men or objects the conduct or presence of which is at the origin of an internationally wrongful act are *prima facie* susceptible of attachment to two distinct legal persons, responsibility must in principle be imputed to the person who exercised preponderant or exclusive control over the conduct in question.[193]

De Visscher maintained that state practice in connection with peace support operations demonstrated that in the opinion of the UN, troop contributing states and host states, effective but not exclusive control by the organization over the activities of national contingents could and should justify exclusive responsibility of the organization.[194] De Visscher also stated that the principle of exclusive responsibility of the UN for activities of contingents under its control was supported by a logical interpretation of the legal personality and objectives of the organization.

In the discussions following the presentation of de Visscher's final report, a majority of the members of the IDI supported the principle that the conduct of armed units under the control of the UN is attributable exclusively to the organization, but it was difficult to agree on the words to describe the control in question.[195] De Visscher proposed the words '*haute direction*'. He explained that this expressed that tactical control of operations was not enough control to base attribution on. '*Haute direction*' was based on a bundle of elements, including the status of personnel and the way the commander was appointed. Ago objected that this term suggested that there existed two kinds of control: formal control and effective control, and proposed to replace '*haute*' with '*effective*'. He explained that conduct is not attributable to the UN in case a state controls the operation; the applicable criterion is real control and the source of instructions given to the UN force. Ago's less abstract criterion based on real control instead of agreements that may or may not be respected in practice seems to adequately reflect state practice.

Although the resolution adopted by the IDI uses the words '*haute direction*', it is not clear whether the institut also adopted de Visscher's interpretation of the expression. Rolin for example stated that the words '*haute direction*' were intended to express that real control was decisive for the purpose of attributing conduct.[196]

Only two members of the IDI stated that the conduct of a peace support operation was attributable to troop contributing states even in case the UN exercized control over the operation in question. Koretsky stated that the troops remained those of the troop contributing states, so that the conception of the rapporteur concerning

193 Preliminary Report, Annuaire IDI 54-I (1971) 45, at 48-49. Translation by the author. Original text:

> Dans ces conditions, lorsque les hommes ou les choses dont l'activité ou la présence sont à l'origine d'un dommage internationalement illicite sont, prima facie, susceptibles de rattachement à deux personnes juridiques distinctes, la responsabilité devra, en principe, être imputée à celle d'entre elles qui, quant à l'acte dommageable consideré, exerçait à leur égard le contrôle prépondérant ou exclusif.

194 *Id.*, at 50.

195 See Annuaire IDI 54-II (1971), 183-192 and 209-216.

196 "En utilisant le mot 'haute', on a voulu montrer que c'était la direction réelle qui importait", *Id.*, at 188.

the problem of responsibility of the UN had to be revised. Wengler referred to the judgment of the House of Lords in *Nissan* v. *United Kingdom*. In his view, it would be regrettable to exclude or limit the responsibility of states towards victims. Such a limitation could lead officers of national contingents to no longer check the legality of orders from the UN, which would be nefarious.[197]

2.10.2 Ultra vires *acts*

Article 7 of the ILC draft articles on state responsibility is concerned with responsibility of states for conduct of an organ of a state or of a person empowered to exercise elements of the governmental authority in excess of authority or contravention of instructions, also referred to as *ultra vires* acts of state organs or entities. The draft article essentially precludes a state from invoking the internal distribution of competences between state organs. The ILC commentary notes that the state cannot take refuge behind the notion that, according to the provisions of its internal law or to instructions which may have been given to its organs or agents, their conduct ought not to have occurred or ought to have taken a different form. This is so even where the organ or entity in question has overtly committed unlawful acts under the cover of its official status. Though the state is responsible for conduct of organs purportedly or apparently carrying out their official functions, it is not responsible for private acts or omissions of individuals who happen to be organs or agents of the state. In practice, it can be difficult to distinguish between official conduct and private conduct. The same difficulty obtains in the field of state immunity, because a state can only have immunity for conduct that can be attributed to it.[198]

It may be noted that the ILC commentary refers to Article 91 of Additional Protocol I as confirming the principle in draft article 7. Article 91, however, is much broader than draft article 7, because it not only makes the state responsible for acts of its armed forces acting with apparent authority but also for acts of members of its armed forces committed in a private capacity.[199]

Because draft article 7 is concerned with the internal distribution of competences, the kind of conduct it governs could be referred to as 'internal' *ultra vires* conduct. In international organizations, there is also the possibility of conduct that could be referred to as 'external' *ultra vires* conduct. This is conduct that is in excess of the competences of the international organization itself. In contrast to the competences of states, those of international organizations are limited to the competences explicitly or implicitly conferred on the organization by its member states. Although article 7 of the ILC draft articles cannot be applied directly, the UN employs a test which is based on the same distinction made in that draft article in the case of peace support operations.

---

197 *Id.*, at 214.

198 See J. Salmon, *Immunités et Actes de la Fonction*, 38 Annuaire Français de Droit International 314 (1992).

199 See para. 2.6.1.

The UN Office of Legal Affairs in a 1986 memorandum explained that the UN does not consider itself responsible for 'off-duty acts' of the members of peace-keeping forces. The primary factor in determining that there is an 'off-duty' situation is:

> whether the member of a peace-keeping mission was acting in a non-official/non-operational capacity when the incident occurred and not whether he/she was in military or civilian attire at the time of the incident or whether the incident occurred inside or outside the area of operations.[200]

Moreover, the Office stated that a member of the operation on a state of alert may none the less assume an off-duty status "if he/she acts in an individual capacity, not attributable to the performance of official duties, during that designated 'state-of-alert' period."[201] These passages make a similar distinction between acts committed in an individual capacity and acts committed in an official capacity, the latter including not only acts committed under real authority but also under apparent authority.[202]

This interpretation is supported by state practice. On the one hand, the responsibility of the UN does not seem to have been invoked in the case of an off-duty member of UNIFIL who was accused of smuggling explosives into Israel for use by the PLO.[203] On the other hand, the UN does seem to have accepted its responsibility in cases where civilians were killed by members of UNEF and ONUC and where no official function or superior order required the member to fire and where the responsible soldier was therefore prosecuted in his home country for his conduct.[204] The UN also accepted responsibility for conduct committed under apparent authority of the organization by Belgian members of UNOSOM.[205]

This practice demonstrates that the principle in Article 3 of the Hague Convention (IV) of 1907 and Article 91 of Additional Protocol I, that a state is responsible for all the conduct of its armed forces on or off duty, is not applied to peace support operations.

This approach would seem to be the most accurate, because the principle is based on the structure of the armed forces, including the chain of command and the disciplinary power of the commander. The structure of armed forces provides better opportunities to prevent violations of international law than the structure of other state organs.[206] In peace support operations these opportunities are not reproduced because the UN commander is in command but does not have disciplinary powers in the same sense as national commanders. The head of mission of a peace support operation has general responsibility for the good order and discipline of the operation, but respon-

200 UNJY 1986, at 300.
201 *Id.*
202 But see Klein, *supra* note 82, at 390.
203 UNJY 1979, at 233.
204 Simmonds, *supra* note 173, at 233.
205 See para. 4.5.4.
206 See for example Condorelli, *supra* note 128, at 148.

sibility for disciplinary action with respect to military personnel made available by a troop contributing state rests with an officer designated by the government of the state for that purpose.

Draft article 6 adopted by the ILC on first reading in 2004, concerning attribution of conduct exceeding authority or contravening instructions to international organizations, takes the same approach as above. The wording of the article closely follows that of article 7 on state responsibility. The commentary states that:

> The key element for attribution both in article 7 on State responsibility and in the present article is the requirement that the organ or agent acts "in that capacity". This wording is intended to convey the need for a close link between the ultra vires conduct and the organ's or agent's functions.[207]

2.10.3 Common Article 1 of the 1949 Geneva Conventions and Additional Protocol I: A due diligence obligation of the state in respect of conduct of an organization

In case a troop contributing state does not effectively control members of a peace support operation it is still the case that the state has transferred powers over part of its armed forces to an international organization. The transfer itself is attributable to the state and can possibly breach an obligation of the state under international law. One such obligation could possibly be based on the duty in common Article 1 of the 1949 Geneva Conventions to "ensure respect for the present Convention in all circumstances."

In 1961, in connection with ONUC, the ICRC addressed a memorandum to states parties to the 1949 Geneva Conventions concerning the application of the conventions by military contingents placed at the disposal of the UN. The Red Cross implied in the memorandum that common Article 1 requires troop contributing states to ensure that the peace support operation respect humanitarian law:

> the International Committee would like to remind governments that could provide contingents for a United Nations emergency force that in common article 1 of the four Geneva Conventions, the High Contracting Parties have undertaken not only to respect, but also to ensure respect for the provisions of those conventions. The Committee therefore expresses the hope that they will if necessary use their influence to ensure that the provisions of humanitarian law are applied by all contingents as well as by the unified command.[208]

---

207 *Supra* note 95, at 18, para. 4.

208 Translation by the author. Original text: "le Comité international se permet de rappeler aux Etats qui pourraient fournir des contingents à une Force d'urgence des Nations Unies qu'aux termes de l'article Ier commun aux quatre Conventions de Genève, les Hautes Parties contractantes se sont engagées non seulement à respecter, mais encore à 'faire respecter' les dispositions de ces Conventions. Il exprime donc l'espoir qu'ils voudront bien, chacun, en cas de besoin, user de leur influence pour que les dispositions du droit humanitaire soient appliquées par l'ensemble des contingents engagés, comme par le commandement unifié.", reproduced in 43 International Review of the Red Cross 592 (1961).

The reasoning in the memorandum is based on an interpretation by the ICRC of common Article 1 in which the duty to 'ensure respect' obliges states parties to the Geneva Conventions to ensure that other states, and international organizations, respect humanitarian law. For the ICRC 'to ensure respect' means that states, whether engaged in conflict or not, must take steps to ensure that the rules are respected by all. Arguably, a state's transfer of powers over part of its armed forces to an international organization without adequate guarantees that the organization will respect humanitarian law breaches such an obligation.

Despite arguments that such an interpretation of common Article 1 was not the one originally envisaged by the drafters,[209] recent state practice supports the position that states currently interpret common Article 1 as imposing obligations with respect to violations of the Geneva Conventions by other states. The International Court of Justice decided on the basis of the obligation to ensure respect for humanitarian law that the United States was under "an obligation not to encourage persons or groups engaged in the conflict in Nicaragua to act in violation of the provisions of common Article 3 to the four 1949 Geneva Conventions."[210] Common Article 1 was the legal basis for convening a conference of states parties to the fourth Geneva Convention on measures to enforce the Convention in the Occupied Palestinian Territory in 1999 and the resumption of the conference in December 2001. General Assembly resolution ES-10/6 states that the General Assembly:

> Reiterates its recommendation that the High Contracting Parties to the Fourth Geneva Convention convene a conference on measures to enforce the Convention in the Occupied Palestinian Territory, including Jerusalem, and to ensure respect thereof in accordance with common article 1, and further recommends that the High Contracting Parties convene the said conference on 15 July 1999 at the United Nations Office at Geneva.[211]

The Conference took place on 15 July 1999, but was adjourned taking into consideration the prospect of a resumption of the peace process. On 5 December 2001 the Conference was reconvened and issued a Declaration reflecting the common understanding of the participants. The Declaration states *inter alia* that:

---

209 F. Kalshoven, *The Undertaking to Respect and Ensure Respect in all Circumstances: From Tiny Seed to Ripening Fruit*, 2 Yearbook of International Humanitarian Law 3 (1999).

210 Military and Paramilitary Activities in and against Nicaragua (*Nicaragua* v. *United States of America*), Judgment, 1986 ICJ Reports 14, para. 220.

211 General Assembly Resolution ES-10/6 of 9 February 1999, UN Doc. A/RES/ES-10/6, para. 6. See also the statement by the permanent representative of Pakistan in the resumed tenth emergency session of the General Assembly:

> In Article 1 of the Convention, "The High Contracting Parties undertake to respect and to ensure respect for the present Convention in all circumstances". Therefore, it is our collective responsibility to ensure compliance by Israel to the provisions of the Geneva Convention of 1949.

<http://www.un.int/pakistan/12990205.htm>.

> The participating High Contracting Parties welcome and encourage the initiatives by States Parties, both individually and collectively, according to Art. 1 of the Convention and aimed at ensuring the respect of the Convention, and they underline the need for the Parties, to follow up on the implementation of the present Declaration.[212]

There are also other indications that the obligation in common Article 1 is now interpreted as referring to third states.[213] For example, the UN Conference on Human Rights in 1968 adopted a resolution which noted that states have a responsibility to take steps to ensure the respect of these humanitarian rules in all circumstances by other states, even if they are not themselves directly involved in an armed conflict.[214] The General Assembly, in its Resolution 57/125 of 24 February 2003, called upon all High Contracting Parties to Geneva Convention (IV) "in accordance with article 1 common to the four Geneva Conventions, to continue to exert all efforts to ensure respect for its provisions by Israel" in the Occupied Territories.[215] This interpretation of common Article 1 was also reaffirmed by participants, including state representatives, at regional seminars on 'Improving Compliance with International Humanitarian Law' organized by the ICRC in 2003. The report of these seminars states that by virtue of common Article 1, third states are bound by a legal obligation to neither encourage a party to an armed conflict to violate international humanitarian law nor take action that would assist in such violations.[216] In other words, this is a negative obligation, *i.e.* an obligation to refrain from doing something. The report goes on to state that:

> Seminar participants also acknowledged a positive obligation on States not involved in an armed conflict to take action – unilaterally or collectively – against States who are violating international humanitarian law, in particular to intervene with States over which they might have some influence to stop the violations. All participants affirmed that this entails at minimum a moral responsibility and that States have the right to take such action, with the majority of participants agreeing that this constitutes a legal obligation under common Article 1. This is not to be construed as an obligation to reach a specific result, but rather an 'obligation of means' on States to

212 Declaration of the Conference of High Contracting Parties to the Fourth Geneva Convention, 5 December 2001, para. 17.

213 See also U. Palwankar, *Measures Available to States for Fulfilling their Obligation to Ensure Respect for International Humanitarian Law*, 76 International Review of the Red Cross 9 (1994), and J. Pictet (Ed.), Commentary: IV Geneva Convention Relative to the Protection of Civilian Persons in Time of War 16 (1958).

214 Resolution XXIII of the International Conference on Human Rights, Tehran, 1968, preambular para. 9.

215 General Assembly Resolution 57/125 of 24 February 2003, UN Doc. A/RES/57/125, para. 3. Adopted with 155 in favor, 6 opposed and 3 abstentions.

216 International Committee of the Red Cross, International Humanitarian Law and the Challenges of Contemporary Armed Conflicts, Background document for the 28th International Conference of the Red Cross and Red Crescent, 03/IC/09 (2003), at 48.

> take all appropriate measures possible, in an attempt to end international humanitarian law violations.[217]

The Secretary-General's proposal to the General Assembly to consider recognizing the concurrent responsibility of the state of nationality for violations of international humanitarian law by members of its national contingent in a peace support operation given "the exclusive criminal jurisdiction of the State of nationality and its obligation to ensure respect for international humanitarian law of its force" also seems to be based on such an interpretation of common Article 1. It must be pointed out, however, that the IDI has not been willing to affirm the existence of a positive obligation, rather than a right, under common Article 1. In its resolution on 'The Application of International Humanitarian Law and Fundamental Human Rights, in Armed Conflicts in which Non-State Entities are Parties', the IDI merely states that:

> Without prejudice to the functions and powers which the Charter attributes to organs of the United Nations, in case of systematic and massive violations of humanitarian law or fundamental human rights, States, acting individually or collectively, are entitled to take diplomatic, economic and other measures towards any party to the armed conflict which has violated its obligations, provided such measures are permitted under international law.[218]

On the other hand, the *travaux préparatoires* of the resolution reveal that several members held that common Article 1 imposes a positive obligation.[219]

The ICJ in its Advisory Opinion on *Legal Consequences of the Construction of a Wall in the Occupied Palestinian Territory* held by thirteen votes to two that common Article 1 imposes a positive obligation. It stated that:

> The Court would also emphasize that Article 1 of the Fourth Geneva Convention, a provision common to the four Geneva Conventions, provides that "The High Contracting Parties undertake to respect and to ensure respect for the present Convention in all circumstances." It follows from the provision that every State party to that Convention, whether or not it is a party to a specific conflict, is under an obligation to ensure that the requirements of the instruments in question are complied with.[220]

The Court failed to clarify the scope of the obligation.

---

217 *Id.*, at 49.

218 Institut de Droit International, The Application of International Humanitarian Law and Fundamental Human Rights, in Armed Conflicts in which Non-State Entities are Parties, Annuaire IDI 65-II (1999), at 387, para. VII.

219 See *e.g.* Carillo Salcedo, Annuaire IDI 68-I (1999), at 281

220 Legal Consequences of the Construction of a Wall in the Occupied Palestinian Territory, Advisory Opinion of 9 July 2004, not yet reported, para. 158.

Arguably, the duty to ensure respect for the 1949 Geneva Conventions obliges troop contributing states which are states parties to the conventions to take steps to ensure that the peace support operation respects the provisions of these conventions. This obligation would go beyond the mere avoidance of aiding and assisting the operation in the violation of international humanitarian law. It is not clear which efforts such a 'due diligence' obligation requires a state to make to avoid responsibility. State practice[221] and the ICJ judgment in the *Nicaragua* case, in which the Court only required that the United States did not actively encourage others to act in violation of common Article 3, suggest a limited reach of the duty to ensure respect.

Such a limited reach implies that a state would not be responsible in every case it places troops at the disposal of the UN and the UN breaches international humanitarian law, because that in itself does not lead the organization to act in violation of the Geneva Conventions. Another case would be placing untrained or undisciplined troops at the disposal of the organization. Arguably the troop contributing state in question is responsible for violations of the Geneva Conventions by such troops.

State practice does not provide an example of responsibility of a troop contributing state for placing troops at the disposal of the UN, but it appears the possibility is in full conformity with the principles of state responsibility and the current interpretation of common Article 1 of the Geneva Conventions.[222]

Case law of the European Commission and Court of Human Rights demonstrates that already *de lege lata* the transfer of powers by a state to an international organization does not necessarily exclude that state's responsibility. The *M. & Co.* v. *Federal Republic of Germany* and *Matthews* v. *United Kingdom* cases in particular are relevant in this respect. In *M. & Co,* the applicant complained that the German authorities had issued a writ for the execution of a judgment of the European Court of Justice according to which it had to pay a heavy fine for having violated Article 85 of the EC Treaty. The applicant submitted that in this case the Court of Justice had violated Article 6 of the European Convention. According to the applicant the German authorities, before issuing a writ of execution, should have examined whether or not the judgment of the European Court of Justice had been given in proceedings respect-

221 See for example the statement by the Minister of Foreign Affairs of Norway who stated in connection with common article 1:

> The question has therefore been asked whether those who supply small arms to the violators of the provisions of international humanitarian law should share some responsibility with these violators. It has been argued that since availability of small arms may increase the risk of unlawful acts, supplier-states should take measures to reduce this and thereby strengthen respect for international humanitarian law. Although it may be difficult to argue that states have a legal obligation to do this, those who argue that they have a moral responsibility may, in my view, have a good case.

Minister of Foreign Affairs Knut Vollebaek, The Fridtjof Nansen Memorial Lecture, the Hague, 12 October 1998, <http//odin.dep.no/odinarkiv/norsk/dep/ud/1998/taler/032005-090222/index-dok000-b-n-a-html> .

222 Commissie van Advies inzake Volkenrechtelijke Vraagstukken, *supra* note 124, at 22, para 4.3.

ing the guarantees set out in Article 6 of the Convention. As this was not the case, the granting of the writ of execution, so the applicant company argued, gave effect to the violations complained of and therefore violated the provisions invoked. The respondent state argued *inter alia* that its responsibility could not be derived from the fact that it transferred part of its powers to the European Communities. Otherwise all Community acts would indirectly be subject to control by the Convention organs. It also pointed out that in any event, observance of fundamental rights is secured by the European Court of Justice. The Commission viewed the question before it from the perspective of the powers transferred by Germany to the European Communities. It asked itself whether Germany, by giving effect to a judgment reached in proceedings which allegedly violated Article 6, incurred responsibility on account of the fact that these proceedings against a German company were possible only because Germany had transferred its powers in this sphere to the European Communities.[223] In respect of this transfer of powers it held that:

> It has next to be observed that the Convention does not prohibit a Member State from transferring powers to international organisations. Nonetheless, the Commission recalls that "if a State contracts treaty obligations and subsequently concludes another international agreement which disables it from performing its obligations under the first treaty it will be answerable for any resulting breach of its obligations under the earlier treaty". The Commission considers that a transfer of powers does not necessarily exclude a State's responsibility under the Convention with regard to the exercise of the transferred powers. Otherwise the guarantees of the Convention could wantonly be limited or excluded and thus be deprived of their peremptory character. The object and purpose of the Convention as an instrument for the protection of individual human beings requires that its provisions be interpreted and applied so as to make its safeguards practical and effective. Therefore the transfer of powers to an international organisation is not incompatible with the Convention provided that within that organisation fundamental rights will receive an equivalent protection. [224]

The application of the 'equivalent protection' test by the Commission to the facts of the case in question demonstrates that the test is an abstract one. The Commission concluded on the basis of a joint declaration of the Parliament, the Council and the Commission of the European Communities that they attach prime importance to the protection of fundamental rights, and on the basis of case law of the Court of Justice of the European Communities according to which it is called upon to control Community acts on the basis of fundamental rights, that "the legal system of the European Communities not only secures fundamental rights but also provides for control of their observance."[225] Such an application has received criticism on the

223 *M. & Co.* v. *Federal Republic of Germany*, Decision of 9 February 1990, D.R. 64, 33 Yearbook ECHR , at 46.

224 *Id.*, at 52 (references omitted).

225 *Id.*, para. 53.

ground that it makes it unnecessary to examine whether there has been equivalent protection in individual cases.

Matthews v. *United Kingdom* concerned elections for the European Parliament. The applicant complained that she was not entitled to vote in the 1994 elections to the European Parliament. She invoked Article 3 of Protocol No. 1 to the Convention. Under European Community law, elections to European Parliament were governed by the EC Act on Direct Elections of 1976 annexed to Council Decision 76/787/ECSC, EEC, Euratom. The Council Decision itself was signed by the President of the Council and by the ministers representing the member states as members of the Council. Annex II, which is stated in the Act to be an integral part thereof, declares "The United Kingdom will apply the provisions of the Act only in respect of the United Kingdom" thereby excluding Gibraltar.

The applicant argued *inter alia* that the EC Act on Direct Elections with Annex II was a treaty like any other treaty and that by freely choosing to conclude the treaty which disabled it from performing its obligations under the Convention, the United Kingdom was answerable for any resulting breach of its obligations under the Convention. As to Annex II to the Act, the applicant underlined that the Annex was included in the Act as a result of the unilateral wish of the United Kingdom, that the United Kingdom was under no obligation to add Annex II, that the real aim of Annex II was to exclude the Channel Isles and the Isle of Man from the scope of EC elections (because the Channel Isles do not form part of the EU, unlike Gibraltar) and moreover, that nothing required the United Kingdom to interpret, or continue to interpret, Annex II in such a way as to exclude Gibraltar from the application of the Act on Direct Elections. The applicant recalled that Gibraltar is the United Kingdom's responsibility in the European Community, and in signing the treaty on direct elections, the United Kingdom had the power, and the obligation, to provide for the enfranchisement of citizens of the Union who live in Gibraltar.

The Grand Chamber of the European Court of Human Rights issued its judgment on 18 February 1999.[226] It decided that it had to consider whether, notwithstanding the nature of the elections to the European Parliament as an organ of the EC, the United Kingdom could be held responsible under Article 1 of the Convention for the absence of elections to the European Parliament in Gibraltar, that is, whether the United Kingdom is required to 'secure' elections to the European Parliament notwithstanding the Community character of those elections. The Court stated that:

> The Convention does not exclude the transfer of competences to international organisations provided that Convention rights continue to be "secured". Member States' responsibility therefore continues even after such a transfer.

The Court held that in the present case, the alleged violation of the Convention flowed *inter alia* from the Maastricht Treaty, which was freely entered into by the United Kingdom. The United Kingdom, together with all the other parties to the

---

226 *Matthews* v. *United Kingdom*, Judgment of 18 February 1999 (Application No. 24833/94).

Maastricht Treaty, was responsible *ratione materiae* under Article 1 of the Convention for the consequences of that Treaty. The Court considered that:

> In determining to what extent the United Kingdom is responsible for 'securing' the rights in Article 3 of Protocol No. 1 in respect of elections to the European Parliament in Gibraltar, the Court recalls that the Convention is intended to guarantee rights that are not theoretical or illusory, but practical and effective. It is uncontested that legislation emanating from the legislative process of the European Community affects the population of Gibraltar in the same way as legislation which enters the domestic legal order exclusively via the House of Assembly. To this extent, there is no difference between European and domestic legislation, and no reason why the United Kingdom should not be required to 'secure' the rights in Article 3 of Protocol No. 1 in respect of European legislation, in the same way as those rights are required to be 'secured' in respect of purely domestic legislation. In particular, the suggestion that the United Kingdom may not have effective control over the state of affairs complained of cannot affect the position, as the United Kingdom's responsibility derives from its having entered into treaty commitments subsequent to the applicability of Article 3 of Protocol No. 1 to Gibraltar, namely the Maastricht Treaty taken together with its obligations under the Council Decision and the 1976 Act. Further, the Court notes that on acceding to the EC Treaty, the United Kingdom chose, by virtue of Article 227(4) of the Treaty, to have substantial areas of EC legislation applied to Gibraltar (see paragraphs 11 to 14 above).[227]

On this basis the Court held that the United Kingdom was responsible under Article 1 of the Convention for securing the rights guaranteed by Article 3 of Protocol No. 1 to the Convention in Gibraltar regardless of whether the elections were purely domestic or European.

Matthews concerned the transfer of powers to the European Communities, but the principle that member states' responsibility continues even after the transfer of competences to an international organization can also be applied to the transfer of powers to other international organizations.[228] The judgment refers to the transfer of competences to 'international organizations', not to the European Communities. An example of the application of the principle to another international organization is *Waite & Kennedy* v. *Germany*,[229] in which the Court applied the principle to the transfer of immunities to the European Space Agency by Germany. In *Banković* the applicants invoked the principle in connection with the transfer of competences to NATO.

In *M. & Co.* the writ of execution given by the German authorities in accordance with Community law was attributable to the state, even though it was in application of Community law. *Matthews* v. *United Kingdom* demonstrates that a state party to

227 *Id.*, para. 34 (references omitted).

228 See also G. Cohen-Jonathan & JF Flauss, *A Propos de l'Arrêt Matthews c/ Royaume-Uni (18 février 1999)*, 35 Revue Trimestrielle de Droit Européen 637 (1999), at 643.

229 *Waite & Kennedy* v. *Germany*, *supra* note 34.

the European Convention can be responsible not only for an act but also for failure to ensure that the powers it has transferred to an international organization are exercized in conformity with its own international obligations.

To sum up, case law of the ECHR demonstrates that states can be held responsible for the consequences of the transfer of powers to international organizations. The European Convention on Human Rights does not contain a provision obliging states to ensure respect for the rights guaranteed by the Convention. *A fortiori*, because common Article 1 of the 1949 Geneva Conventions and Additional Protocol I does contain such a provision, the High Contracting Parties should be responsible for the transfer of powers to an international organization.

2.11 State practice of attribution of conduct of North Atlantic Treaty Organization peace support operations

2.11.1 Claims settlement procedures

NATO has developed procedures for the settlement of claims in the territory of host states of peace support operations. There is no standard procedure which applies to all peace support operations. The organization has yet to create a permanent claims structure to handle deployment claims.[230] Such procedures are negotiated for each individual peace support operation.

Settlement of claims against SFOR is governed by Annex 1A of the Dayton Peace Agreement[231] and the Status of Forces Agreements between NATO and Bosnia Herzegovina and Croatia in appendices to Annex 1A.[232] Article VI.9 of Annex 1A states that "the IFOR and its personnel shall not be liable for any damages to civilian or government property caused by combat or combat related activities." The SOFAs state that claims for damage or injury to government personnel or property, or to private personnel or property of the receiving state shall be submitted through governmental authorities of the receiving state to the designated NATO representatives.

The actual process to be followed in settling claims in Bosnia Herzegovina was addressed by Mr. Sergio Balanzino, acting Secretary-General of NATO, in a letter to the minister of foreign affairs of Bosnia Herzegovina. In this letter Mr. Balanzino

230 J. Prescott, *Claims*, in D. Fleck (Ed.), The Handbook of the Law of Visiting Forces 159 (2001), at 165.

231 Agreement on Military Aspects of the Peace Settlement, Annex 1A of the General Framework Agreement for Peace in Bosnia and Herzegovina, reproduced in 35 ILM 75 (1996).

232 Agreement between the Republic of Bosnia and Herzegovina and the North Atlantic Treaty Organisation Concerning the Status of NATO and its Personnel, Appendix B to Annex 1A of the General Framework Agreement for Peace in Bosnia and Herzegovina, reproduced in Office of the High Representative, Essential Texts 31 (2000), Art. 15 and Agreement between the Republic of Croatia and the North Atlantic Treaty Organisation Concerning the Status of NATO and its Personnel, Appendix C to Annex 1A of the General Framework Agreement for Peace in Bosnia and Herzegovina, reproduced in Office of the High Representative, Essential Texts 32 (2000), Art. 15.

noted that if civil suits were brought against NATO personnel for actions performed in their official capacity, the NATO commander could issue a scope certificate to that effect and remove the case to the standing claims commission to be established for that purpose.

Subsequent agreements spelled out the claims commission process in greater detail. These agreements included the claims annexes to the Technical Arrangements entered into between representatives of the peace support operation and Bosnia Herzegovina and Croatia. The claims annexes stated that payment orders were to be paid with either NATO or national contingent funds.

In practice, claims are the responsibility of the troop contributing states: third party claims are submitted to the contingent that caused the damage and payment for these claims is made by the contingent in question. Claims caused by the acts or omissions of force headquarters personnel are investigated and adjudicated by the force claims office and payment for these claims is made by the force.

2.11.2 The Legality of the Use of Force *cases*

In April 1999, the Federal Republic of Yugoslavia (FRY) instituted proceedings before the International Court of Justice against ten NATO member states. On the same day the FRY filed a request for provisional measures.

The application claimed *inter alia* that by taking part in the bombing of the territory of the FRY by NATO in Operation Allied Force, the states concerned violated several of their international obligations, including obligations under international humanitarian law. The application did not specify the precise acts or omissions that were considered attributable to the member states.

Strictly speaking this case did not concern a peace support operation. The case is nevertheless instructive because command and control relationships over military forces in Operation Allied Force were very similar to those in peace support operations.[233] In Operation Allied Force national forces were placed under the operational control of NATO. The overall NATO commander of the operation was the Supreme Allied Commander Europe (SACEUR). He delegated operational control to the Commander in Chief Allied Forces South (CINCSOUTH). SACEUR reported to the North Atlantic Council. It may be noted that this chain of command closely resembles the chain of command in NATO peace support operations.[234] Special arrangements were made in respect of United States forces however, for which a parallel national chain of command was established.[235]

233 See US Department of Defense, Kosovo/Operation Allied Force After-Action Report 16-20 (2000); UK Ministry of Defence, Kosovo: Lessons from the Crisis, para. 7.23 (2000); UK Parliament Select Committee on Defence Minutes of Evidence, 22 March 2000, para. 108.

234 See paras. 1.8.6 and 1.8.8.

235 US Department of Defence, *supra* note 23, at 16-20.

The FRY developed the question of attribution orally in the hearings concerning the request for provisional measures:

> Mr. President and Members of the Court, the acts of force are imputable to the Respondents.
>
> 5.1. The Respondents have used their military forces for bombing. The military forces are organs of a State and their acts are imputable to a State.
>
> 5.2. I refer to Article 5 of the 1949 North Atlantic Treaty, which reads as follows:
>
> > "The parties agree that an armed attack against one or more of them in Europe or North America shall be considered an attack against them all, and consequently they agree that, if such an armed attack occurs, each of them, in exercise of the right of individual or collective self-defense recognised by Article 51 of the Charter of the United Nations, will assist the Party or Parties so attached by taking forthwith, individually and in concert with the other Parties, such action as it deems necessary, including the use of force, to restore and maintain the security of the North Atlantic area."
>
> According to quoted basic rule, the Respondents are acting individually and in concert.
>
> 5.3. I believe that information offered by the NATO Handbook published in 1998, dealing with the functioning of that Organization, could be relevant for the matter. Describing "the principal policy and decision-making forum of NATO, the North Atlantic Council", the Handbook says:
>
> > "When decisions have to be made, action is agreed upon on the basis of unanimity and common accord. There is no voting or decision by majority. Each nation represented at the Council table or any of its subordinate committees retains complete sovereignty and responsibility for its own decision" (NATO Handbook, Brussels, 1998. p. 37).
>
> 5.4. And about the role of integrated military forces, the Handbook informs:
>
> > "In accordance with the fundamental principles which govern the relationship between political and military institutions within democratic states, the integrated military structure remains under political control and guidance at the highest level at all times." (Ibid., p. 245.)
>
> 5.5. So, even as a part of the integrated military force of NATO, military forces of the Respondents are under their control and guidance.[236]

In this statement the FRY seems to base attribution on alleged status of the military forces taking part in the bombing as organs of the member states, in accordance with

236 CR 99/14 of 10 May 1999.

article 4 of the draft articles on state responsibility or Article 91 of Additional Protocol I to the 1949 Geneva Conventions for those respondent states that are parties to the Protocol.

At a later moment in the same proceedings the FRY developed another ground for attribution to the member states:

> Several of the respondent States have contended that the actions of the NATO command structure are not imputable to individual member States of NATO. Three references will be in the transcript by way of examples (CR 99/17, p. 13, para. 6 (France), CR 99/16, p. 15, para. 34 (Canada), CR 99/22, p. 10 (Spain)).
> The general implications of such contentions call for some consideration. The North Atlantic Council directs the war against Yugoslavia as a joint enterprise. It constantly says so. It would be a legal and political anomaly of the first order if the actions of the command structure were not attributable jointly and severally to the member States. This joint and several responsibility is justified both in legal principle and by the conduct of the member States. Thus, after the destruction of the Chinese Embassy in Belgrade, the British Prime Minister apologized to the Chinese Government, although there had been no suggestion that a British plane had fired the missiles. More recently the German Chancellor has also apologized.
> In the case concerning *Certain Phosphate Lands in Nauru (Nauru* v. *Australia)*, this Court held that the possibility of a joint and several liability of the three States responsible for the administration of a Trust Territory at the material time did not render inadmissible *in limine litis* a claim brought against only one of them (*I.C.J. Reports 1992*, pp. 258-259, para. 48; see also President Jennings, p. 301).
> In closing on this issue of joint responsibility, I would point out that it is quite remarkable that States who have publicly associated themselves with a multilateral NATO campaign of coercion should now seek to avoid the legal responsibility involved.[237]

This argument seems to refer to the possibility of 'piercing the veil' of the organization and theories of member state responsibility for the conduct of an international organization discussed above.[238]

The respondent states approached the question of attribution in various ways. Some of the respondents seemed to accept that military actions were attributable to them. For example, the United Kingdom stated that it had acted in accordance with international law in its resort to force and the methods and means that it had adopted.[239] The United States also seems to have accepted that military actions were attributable to it.[240] Other respondents stated that the Federal Republic of Yugoslavia

---

237 CR 99/25 of 12 May 1999.

238 See para. 2.7.2.

239 CR 99/23 of 11 May 1999, para. 7.

240 CR 99/24 of 11 May 1999 ("the fact is that the Applicant has made no credible allegation that United States or other NATO forces have committed acts of genocide or are at all likely to do so", para 3.9; "the actions of the Members of the NATO Alliance find their justification in a number of factors", para. 1.7).

had not specifically imputed acts to that particular respondent state. For example, Portugal stated that the request for provisional measures was based on a list of apparently violated conventions and alleged damages attributed indistinctly to the Portuguese Republic without definition of its share of responsibility in the actions and alleged damages.[241] Belgium[242] and Canada[243] also made this argument.

Only two of the respondent states discussed the theory of joint and several responsibility in their pleadings. Canada stated that:

> No specific conduct – we said it two days ago – is alleged against Canada itself, as an independent sovereign State, or for that matter against any of the other Respondents. As a very poor substitute for the imputation of specific acts to any of the Respondents, the Applicant asserts broadly that joint and several liability can be imputed to each one of the Respondents for acts it may not have committed because of the integrated command structure of NATO.
>
> Mr. President, it was for the Respondent to demonstrate a basis in international law for that proposition, and it has not done so. Joint and several liability for acts of an international organization, or for the acts of other States acting within such an organization, cannot be established unless the relevant treaty provides for such liability. Article 5 of the 1949 NATO Convention, cited in the first round, provides no such indication of an assumption of joint and several liability, and neither do the provisions of the Handbook respecting the integrated military structure of the organization. The separate liability of Australia in *Nauru* was of course based on the specific terms of the trust instruments in issue in that case, not on general principles on international organizations. The work of the International Law Commission on State Responsibility provides no more support for the joint and several concept. I note as well that these concepts were canvassed in the Tin Council litigation in the United Kingdom, and the outcome would not support the Applicant in the present case.[244]

The Netherlands also rejected the theory of joint and several responsibility of the member states:

> On the question of joint and several responsibility, brought up by the FRY in its observations this morning, the Netherlands would like to observe, that this aspect is new and deviates from the Application submitted to the 10 countries individually on 29 April of this year. The Netherlands strongly rejects such a responsibility on the side of the Netherlands and observes that in the relevant instruments, invoked by the FRY, there is no legal basis for such a form of responsibility.[245]

---

241 CR 99/21 of 11 May 1999, para. 3.1.2.

242 CR 99/15 of 10 May 1999 ("nowhere have we seen evidence establishing prima facie that such facts are imputable to the military forces of the Kingdom of Belgium")

243 CR 99/16 of 10 May 1999, para. 34 ("there are no facts specifically imputed to Canada").

244 CR 99/27 of 12 May 1999.

245 CR 99/31 of 12 May 1999, para. 3.

On 2 June 1999 the Court decided that in two of the ten cases (*Yugoslavia* v. *Spain* and *Yugoslavia* v. *United States of America*) it manifestly lacked jurisdiction and ordered that these cases be removed from its list. In the other eight cases the Court found that it lacked *prima facie* jurisdiction, which is a prerequisite for the issue of provisional measures, and that it therefore could not indicate such measures.

The Court remained seized of those cases and held oral hearings on preliminary objections by the respondent states between 19 and 23 April 2004. During these hearings Serbia and Montenegro, as the FRY had been renamed in the meantime, elaborated on the two above-mentioned grounds for attribution. It maintained that the decision to use force and the decisions on the targets to be hit were taken by member states. These decisions were attributable to those states, in the view of Serbia and Montenegro.[246] It stated that:

> Each NATO Member State individually decided that the military operations should be initiated and continued, and made a sovereign decision on the use of armed force against Yugoslavia. That this was done within the framework of a military alliance does not alter the fact that decisions on the use of force were ultimately taken by the national governments.[247]

Concerning other possible grounds for attribution, Serbia and Montenegro contested the proposition that states members of an international organization, as a matter of principle, cannot be liable for acts of the organization. However, it stated that:

> the present cases do not concern the issue of liability of Member States for obligations of an international organization, that is, NATO. Rather, the issue in the present cases concerns liability of individual respondent States themselves for their own acts.[248]

It is uncertain whether the ICJ will have the opportunity to render judgment in the cases concerned. Reportedly, NATO has made dropping the case a condition for considering Serbia and Montenegro's candidacy for the so-called 'Partnership for Peace' program.[249]

2.11.3 The Banković *case*

On 20 October 1999 six citizens of the FRY lodged an application with the European Court of Human Rights against Belgium, the Czech Republic, Denmark, France, Germany, Greece, Hungary, Iceland, Italy, Luxembourg, the Netherlands, Norway, Poland, Portugal, Spain, Turkey and the United Kingdom in connection with

246 CR 2004/23 of 23 April 2004, paras. 6 -13.

247 CR 2004/14 of 21 April 2004, para. 25

248 *Id.*, para. 20.

249 See J. Chalmers, *Belgrade Offers to Aid NATO in Hunt for War Crime Suspect*, The Boston Globe, 23 July 2003.

Operation Allied Force. The applicants alleged that the strike on a radio and television station in Belgrade on 23 April 1999 by a missile from a NATO forces' aircraft that killed sixteen persons and seriously injured another sixteen was a violation by the respondents of Article 2 (the right to life), Article 10 (freedom of expression) and Article 13 (the right to an effective remedy) of the European Convention on Human Rights.

The plaintiffs claimed that the actions by NATO forces in Operation Allied Force were imputable, jointly and severally, to the governments of the respondent states. The application stated:

> The acts complained of in the present Application were not taken on the initiative of a single pilot or missile battery commander. They were approved and directed by the highest political authority of NATO, the North Atlantic Council, and the nationality of those who actually carried out a specific attack is irrelevant, in the context of the larger NATO command and control structure.
>
> Approval of the 'target list,' pursuant to which the attack on the RTS station was conducted, is the direct responsibility of the NAC and its member States. Within the NATO command structure, the Supreme Allied Commander Europe (SACEUR) delegated authority for the implementation of Operation Allied Force to the Commander in Chief of Allied Forces Southern Europe (CINCSOUTH), whose headquarters is in Naples, Italy. CINCSOUTH delegated control of the operation to the Commander, Allied Air Forces Southern Europe (COMAIRSOUTH), also based in Naples. Operational conduct of day to day missions during "Operation Allied Force" was delegated to the Commander 5th Allied Tactical Air Force, at Vicenza, Italy. To the best of the applicants' knowledge, target lists were initially prepared within this structure and, on a daily basis, forwarded through the NATO chain of command through the Supreme Allied Commander Europe (SACEUR) to the Military Committee and to the NAC. Every one of the 19 member States of NATO received the target lists on a daily basis, and each State had the legal authority to approve or object to any target on that list. To the best of the applicants' knowledge, either all of the Respondent States approved the target list on which the RTS station appeared or none of the Respondent States objected to listing the RTS station on the target list.
>
> The applicants refer to the Statement of Facts above. The RTS station could not and would not have been bombed without the prior approval of the NAC and, by extension, each of the Respondent States. Under the NATO Treaty, this is the case whether or not there was initial disagreement or dispute over the targeting of RTS.
>
> All of the information available to the Applicants confirms that the decision to bomb RTS was reached by unanimous consensus among NATO member States.[250]

The application also referred to the *M & Co* case discussed above. It may be recalled that in that case the European Commission of Human Rights considered that a trans-

---

250 Application, copy on file with the author.

fer of powers does not necessarily exclude a state's responsibility under the Convention with regard to the exercise of the transferred powers.[251] The transfer of powers to an international organization is not incompatible with the Convention, provided that within that organization fundamental rights will receive an equivalent protection, the Commission stated. The plaintiffs in the *Banković* case considered that the NATO structure offers neither substantive nor procedural protection for the fundamental rights guaranteed under the Convention. Thus, the respondent states could not argue that delegation of decision-making authority to NATO over as fundamental a right as the right to life in any way diminished their individual obligation to protect that right under the Convention.

The application seems to distinguish two bases of attribution. One is the decision by the representatives in the North Atlantic Council which is attributed to the member states. This argument raises the question whether national representatives to the North Atlantic Council act as agents of the member states or as members of the relevant decision-making organ of the organization. In the first case the vote of a national representative is attributable to the state on the basis of article 4 of the ILC draft articles on state responsibility. The latter case is referred to as *dédoublement fonctionnel*. It refers to the theory developed by Scelle according to which state officials act as state organs whenever they operate within the national legal system, and as international agents whenever they operate in the international legal system.[252] The position of national representatives in decision-making organs of international organizations was addressed during the work of the Institut de Droit International on the legal consequences for member states of the non-fulfillment by international organizations of their obligations toward third parties.[253] Rapporteur Higgins maintained that member state representatives should be considered as members of the relevant decision-making organ. As a consequence, the continuing role of states members qua organs should be regarded as neutral as regards the issue of members' responsibility for the acts of the international organization.[254] Several members of the Institut supported the position of the Rapporteur.[255] A number of other members considered that a state can be responsible for its vote in an international organization.[256] Salmon referred in this context to article 27 of the ILC draft articles on state responsibility. This article, which in 2001 ILC draft articles is draft article 16, provides that a state is responsible for aid or assistance in the commission of an internationally wrongful act by another state. There

251 See para. 2.10.3.

252 See G. Scelle, *Théorie et Pratique de la Fonction Exécutive en Droit International*, 55 Recueil des Cours (1936), at 91-106; G. Scelle, *Le Phénomène Juridique du Dédoublement Fonctionnel*, in W. Schätzel & H.J. Slochauer (Eds.), Rechtsfragen der Internationalen Organisation: Festschrift für Hans Wehberg zu seinem 70. Geburtstag 324 (1956); A. Cassese, *Remarks on Scelle's Theory of "Role Splitting" (Dédoublement Fonctionnel) in International Law*, 1 European Journal of International Law 210 (1990).

253 See para. 2.7.5.

254 Provisional report, Annuaire IDI 66-I (1995) 388.

255 Annuaire IDI 66-I (1995) 305 (Vignes); *Id.* 323 (Waelbroeck); *Id.* 331 (Seyersted).

256 Annuaire IDI 66-I (1995) 291 (Shihata); *Id.* 327 (Zemanek).

are two prerequisites for responsibility, namely that the state aiding or assisting does so with knowledge of the circumstances of the internationally wrongful act, and that the act would be internationally wrongful if committed by that state.

Writers point out that the theory of *dédoublement fonctionnel* is difficult to apply consistently.[257] If the conduct of member states of an international organization in the decision-making organs of that organization is not considered as state practice, for example, it cannot be maintained that UN General Assembly resolutions are a form of state practice, as Higgins does.[258]

There seems to be no other particular characteristic of international organizations which stands in the way of applying the principle in article 16 of the ILC draft articles to this case. In particular, it is possible to distinguish between the will of the member state as expressed through its vote, and the will of the decision-making organ of the organization as expressed in the result of the organ's voting procedure.

It seems that the application of the principle in article 16 of the ILC draft articles would only rarely lead to member state responsibility, however. Not only would the aiding or assisting state have to be aware of the circumstances making the conduct of the assisted organization internationally wrongful, the aid or assistance must also be given with a view to facilitating the commission of the wrongful act, and must actually do so. The latter requirement, that the state organ intended to facilitate the occurrence of wrongful conduct, will be difficult to establish.[259] It may also be pointed out that there is no state practice to support this theory. The courts in the *International Tin Council* and *Westland* cases did not find member states responsible for their votes. The Landgericht Bonn, in a 1992 judgment, also rejected an argument that Germany was responsible for its vote in favor of an EEC economic embargo that caused damage to a German company.[260] On the other hand, national law played an important role in all these judgments so that they are inconclusive as regards a rule of international law.

The other basis for attribution is the transfer of powers by the member states to the international organization that is attributed to those states. The application does not specify the precise transfer of powers in question. In the *M & Co* case the Commission had in mind the transfer of powers by the member states in the constituent instrument of the European Community. The application in the *Banković* case suggests that the applicants had in mind the delegation of certain decision-making powers to military organs of NATO specifically in connection with Operation Allied Force, rather than the transfer of powers effected in the constituent instrument of the organization.

The respondent governments disputed the admissibility of the case. They mainly contended that the court did not have personal jurisdiction because the applicants did not fall within the jurisdiction of the respondent states within the meaning of article 1 of the Convention. They also maintained that the court could not decide the merits of the case as it would be determining the rights and obligations of the United

---

257 Lawson, *supra* note 96, at 466-467.

258 R. Higgins, Problems & Process: International Law and How We Use It 23 (1994).

259 But see Klein, *supra* note 82, at 470.

260 Landgericht Bonn, Judgment of 26 February 1992 (1 O 446/90).

States, of Canada and of NATO itself, none of whom were contracting parties to the Convention. The French government further argued that the bombing concerned was not imputable to the respondent states but to NATO, an organization with an international legal personality separate from the respondent states.

On 12 December 2001 the Court declared the application inadmissible because it considered that it did not have jurisdiction *ratione personae*.[261] The Court considered that it was not necessary to examine the remaining submissions of the parties on the admissibility of the application, including the alleged several liability of the respondent states for an act carried out by an international organization of which they are members.

It may be concluded that the Court's decision in the *Banković* case does not provide any guidance on the question of state responsibility arising out of conduct of an international organization. The Court simply avoided this issue by declaring the application inadmissible *ratione personae*. In this regard, the decision is actually a 'non-decision'.[262] It has been suggested that the Court's restrictive stance on the question of jurisdiction in the sense of Article 1 of the European Convention was inspired by the desire to avoid the need to address states' responsibility for actions carried out within the framework of NATO.[263] If the Court would have considered this issue, it would arguably have been justified to hold member states responsible on the basis of the two theories of attribution put forward by the applicants discussed above, provided that the facts as stated by the applicants had been established. In particular, it would have been difficult for the Court not to find that member states were responsible on the basis of the delegation of powers over parts of their armed forces to certain organs of the Organization. This would be in accordance with the former Commission's and the Court's previous case law,[264] and in particular with the Court's holding in *Matthews* v. *United Kingdom* that the European Convention does not exclude the transfer of competences to international organizations provided that Convention rights continue to be secured.[265] As the applicants pointed out, unlike the European Community, NATO does not have any system for the protection of human rights that can provide protection equivalent to that of the European Convention.

2.12 Analysis of state practice in connection with North Atlantic Treaty Organization peace support operations

State practice so far in connection with NATO peace support operations is rare. Simply put, the international responsibility of the organization or states does not seem to have been invoked in connection with conduct by peace support operations.

---

261 *Supra* note 72.

262 G. Cohen-Jonathan, *Observations: La Territorialisation de la Jurisdiction de la Cour Européenne des Droits de l' Homme*, 12 Revue Trimestrielle des Droits de l'Homme 1069 (2002), at 1073.

263 A. Rüth & M. Trilsch, *Case Report: Banković v. Belgium*, 97 American Journal of International Law 168 (2003), at 172.

264 See para. 2.10.3.

265 *Matthews* v. *United Kingdom*, *supra* note 226, para. 32.

Claims settlement procedures in connection with NATO peace support operations were established by international agreement and do not necessarily reflect principles of state responsibility. In the case of the UN, the Secretary-General has expressly stated that claims settlement procedures were established in recognition of international responsibility of the organization for the activities of its forces. Troop contributing states to NATO peace support operations have not made such statements in connection with claims settlement procedures. Claims settlement procedures for SFOR expressly exclude combat-related damage. Troop contributing states which are parties to the Geneva Conventions could not rely on these agreements to absolve themselves from liability incurred in respect of grave breaches of the conventions.

Proceedings instituted by the FRY before the International Court of Justice and by *Banković* and others before the European Court of Human Rights do not concern a peace support operation. Arguments by the applicants in these cases concerning attribution of conduct are nevertheless instructive because control over forces in Operation Allied Force was governed by an arrangement quite similar to that in peace support operations, except for United States and Russian forces.

In its initial oral arguments in proceedings before the International Court of Justice the FRY appeared to deny separate international legal personality to NATO, so that military forces remained organs of a state. During the oral hearings on preliminary objections however it accepted NATO's international legal personality. It maintained that the decisions taken by representatives of member states in NATO decision-making organs were attributable to the member states concerned. Interestingly, the FRY has not claimed that responsibility of member states flows from the transfer of competences to the organization, even though it claims *inter alia* violations of the 1949 Geneva Conventions by the respondents. It could have argued that member states had violated their obligation in common Article 1 to ensure respect for the conventions. This obligation is as much applicable to troop contributing states in NATO operations as it is to troop contributing states in UN operations.[266]

2.13 Conclusion

Some writers make bold statements concerning responsibility of international organizations and their member states under international law. This study is primarily concerned with only part of the larger question of responsibility, responsibility for violations of international humanitarian law by peace support operations.

This part of the larger question is sometimes presented as providing a clear picture, at least concerning UN peace support operations.[267] As this chapter demonstrated, state practice in connection with UN peace support operations is relatively lacking, *inter alia* because the domestic case law which some writers treat as evidence of state practice does not meet the standard necessary to be seen as valid evidence.

266 But see A. Pellet, *supra* note 68, at 200.

267 5 EPIL (1983) 162-163.

268 Gaja, *supra* note 40, para. 57.

Consequently, caution is required when drawing conclusions with regard to responsibility for peace support operations, and *a fortiori* with regard to responsibility of international organizations and their member states in general, as demonstrated by the divergent conclusions by writers based on the same state practice.

At the same time, the need is felt to develop principles of responsibility of international organizations in general, and of responsibility for peace support operations in particular, as recognized by the ILC placing the topic of responsibility of international organizations on its program of work. Such a feeling is connected to an increase in operational activities of international organizations. Peace support operations are no longer deployed only by the UN. NATO is also deploying peace support operations, as well as the EU.

It became clear in paragraph 2.2 that international responsibility is premised on the capacity to possess rights and obligations under international law, in other words on international legal personality. Since the *Reparations for Injuries* case there is no doubt that the UN has international legal personality. Paragraph 2.3 demonstrated that NATO does as well.

State practice in connection with UN peace support operations demonstrates that the conduct of national contingents in these operations is attributed to the UN because the contingents have been placed at the disposal of the organization. The principle in article 6 of the draft articles on state responsibility is applied *mutatis mutandis*. Indeed, the ILC developed draft article 6 as corresponding to state practice in connection with UN peace support operations. Article 5 of the draft articles on the responsibility of international organizations, adopted on first reading by the ILC in 2004, takes the same approach. The commentary to that article makes extensive reference to state practice relating to UN peace support operations.

Transfer of command and control by a troop contributing state to the UN establishes a presumption that the contingent in question is placed at the disposal of and that its conduct is attributable to the organization. The presumption that a contingent is placed at the disposal of the organization is rebutted if it is established that the troops in question were acting in fact on behalf of a troop contributing state. It is not necessary that the sending state gave express instructions in this regard, because it is sufficient that the troops in question acted under the direction and control of the state. It is difficult to semantically further explicate direction and control, as demonstrated by the discussions in the IDI, and it may be necessary to take diverse elements into account.

State practice in connection with UN peace support operations also demonstrates that the principle in article 7 of the ILC draft articles on state responsibility is applied. Off-duty conduct of members of peace support operations, that is, conduct in an individual capacity and not attributable to the performance of official duties, is not attributed to the UN. The organization can be responsible for conduct of troops even if the conduct was in excess of authority or contravention of instructions. In that case attribution is justified by the apparent authority of the troops, in other words by the link between the individual or individuals in question and the organization that has conferred authority or power that they have abused. Article 6 of the ILC draft articles on the responsibility of international organizations conforms to the draft article on state responsibility. In the view of Special Rapporteur Gaja "there is no need to elaborate for international organizations, under this respect, a different rule from that applying to a State."[268]

The application of these principles to the UN demonstrates that in state practice the ILC draft articles on state responsibility are applied *mutatis mutandis* to the organization. Such an application is accepted by writers. More importantly, it is in conformity with the common basis for responsibility of states and international organizations: the capacity to possess rights and obligations under international law. In the specific case of peace support operations, application of draft article 6 is appropriate because it reflects the plurality of legal persons involved. In contrast to officials of the UN Secretariat, for example, contingents in peace support operations continue to have a functional connection with their state of nationality.

Lex specialis in Article 3 of Hague Convention (IV) and Article 91 of Additional Protocol I is not applied to peace support operations, which demonstrates that the law of state responsibility is applied *mutatis mutandis* to international organizations. The premises on which Articles 3 and 91 rest are not present in the case of peace support operations.

Responsibility of the international organization does not preclude the possibility of 'piercing the veil' of the organization in certain circumstances so that member states are responsible for conduct of the organization. State practice in connection with peace support operations does not contribute to establishing a clear rule of customary international law or general principle of law on this question, which cannot be deduced from practice outside the specific context of peace support operations either. In connection with UN operations a concurrent responsibility of member states has never been claimed, while the presence of claims settlement procedures may have prevented claims of secondary responsibility being raised.

In the absence of a clear rule of *lex lata* on member state responsibility, it is important to consider the *lex ferenda* on the topic. Arguments *de lege ferenda* will probably be important for the ILC when it progressively develops the law of responsibility of international organizations. Writers and courts have formulated such arguments primarily in connection with international corporations instead of international organizations that exercise public functions. The argument that those who engage in transactions of an economic nature are deemed liable for the obligations which flow therefrom, for example, does not apply to peace support operations unless such operations are seen as undertaken for economic profit.

On the other hand, the argument that member states will interfere unduly in the affairs of the organization if they are potentially responsible, applies to peace support operations. On one level member state responsibility could collapse the system of peace support operations, because member states could refuse to provide contingents. On another level, member state responsibility could lead national authorities to interfere in command and control in the field. Experience has demonstrated that when command in the field is divided, and military units receive guidance from national

269 Experience with the United Nations operation in Somalia does not support the argument

as well as UN headquarters, the difficulties inherent in an international operation are maximized and the risk of casualties rises. One example is UNOSOM II. The Lessons Learned Unit in the UN Department of Peacekeeping Operations concludes in its report concerning this operation that:

> Unity of command and purpose is a critical element if coalition operations such as UNOSOM are to succeed. With regard to the military component, there were at least two types of difficulties related to unity of command. First off, not all the national contingents operating in the area were placed under UNOSOM command, and this led to tragic consequences. Secondly, some contingents that were ostensibly part of UNOSOM were in fact following orders from their respective capitals; this made them unreliable in the mission area and reduced the mission's effectiveness.[269]

A policy argument used to support member state responsibility is the value of the protection of innocent third parties, and this argument also seems applicable to UN and NATO peace support operations. The third parties in question are states and not individuals. International law does not yet give individuals the right to invoke responsibility for a breach of international humanitarian law.

Whether or not member states are responsible for the conduct of an international organization, they remain responsible for their own conduct in connection with an international organization.

If a national contingent has nominally been placed at the disposal of an international organization but acts in fact on behalf of the troop contributing state, its conduct is attributable to the state. In that case the contingent remains an organ of the troop contributing state and its conduct is attributable to the state. In this case Article 3 of Hague Convention (IV) and Article 91 of Additional Protocol I apply for those states that are parties to the treaties in question. The conduct is attributed to states that are not parties to these treaties on the basis of article 4 of the draft articles on state responsibility.

State responsibility can also derive from the transfer of command and control over a national contingent to the UN or NATO. Such a transfer could be a violation of the duty to ensure respect for the provisions of the 1949 Geneva Conventions in common Article 1 of the conventions. The limited reach of the duty to ensure respect suggests that a state is not automatically responsible if a contingent that has been placed at the disposal of an organization breaches a provision of the conventions, but only if the state has not taken certain steps such as adequately training the contingent in question.

In the *Banković* case, applicants based their claim of state responsibility *inter alia* on the voting by states in the North Atlantic Council. Such a claim of responsibility is based on the attribution of conduct of the state's representatives in a decision-making organ of an organization and not on the attribution of conduct of the organization itself

that more control by officers of national contingents leads to more compliance with the law, because the most serious reports of unlawful conduct relate to this operation.

to the state.[270] It is an application of article 16 of the ILC draft articles, which states that a state which aids or assists another state in the commission of an internationally wrongful act by the latter, is internationally responsible.[271] In this case the state is responsible on the basis of the assistance given by its vote permitting an international organization to commit an internationally wrongful act.[272] In contrast to the theory discussed in paragraph 2.11.3, conduct by a state's representatives within an international organization instead of conduct by state officials outside the organization is attributed to the state. Other differences are that based on application of draft article 16 the conduct of the organization that receives the aid or assistance must be an internationally wrongful act itself, in other words the obligation breached must be in force for the state and for the organization, that the state votes with knowledge of the circumstances of the internationally wrongful act and that the aid or assistance is given with a view to facilitating the commission of the wrongful act, and must actually do so. Such a basis for responsibility was invoked by Milošević in interlocutory injunction proceedings against the Netherlands before the president of the District Court of the Hague.[273] Milošević claimed *inter alia* that the Netherlands acted unlawfully towards him by cooperating in the Security Council's decision to establish the ICTY. Because, according to Milošević, the Tribunal cannot be regarded as an independent and impartial tribunal, the Netherlands may therefore be regarded, in a sense, as a co-perpetrator of human rights violations. The President of the District Court held that he did not have jurisdiction, since the subject matter of the complaint fell within the exclusive competence of the ICTY which was entitled to immunity from jurisdiction in the Netherlands.

It is clear that the attribution of conduct in connection with a UN or NATO peace support operation is not an *a priori* exercise, but depends very much on the specific circumstances of the case. Depending on the circumstances, possible breaches of international humanitarian law by a peace support operation can be a basis of responsibility for troop contributing states, the international organization in question and/or member states.

---

270 See also T. Stein, *Kosovo and the International Community. The Attribution of Possible International Wrongful Acts: Responsibility of NATO or of its Member States?*, in C. Tomuschat (Ed.), Kosovo and the International Community 181 (2002), at 191.

271 Article 16

Aid or assistance in the commission of an internationally wrongful act

A state which aids or assists another State in the commission of an internationally wrongful act by the latter is internationally responsible for doing so if:

(a) That State does so with the knowledge of the circumstances of the internationally wrongful act; and

(b) The act would be internationally wrongful if committed by that State.

272 See Klein, *supra* note 82, at 469.

273 Judgment in the interlocutory injunction proceedings *Slobodan Milošević* v. *the Netherlands*, reproduced in 48 Netherlands International Law Review 357 (2001). In fact Milošević's claim went even further by claiming that the Netherlands was responsible for cooperating in decision making rather than voting. The Netherlands could not have voted for the establishment of the International Criminal tribunal for the former Yugoslavia because it was not a member of the Security Council in 1993.

3

Scope of application of international humanitarian law to peace support operations

3.1 Introduction

One element of international responsibility is that the conduct in question constitutes a breach of an international obligation of the entity to which the conduct is attributed. In other words, a state or an international organization can only be internationally responsible for a breach of international humanitarian law norms which bind it.

The obligations of states under international humanitarian law are relatively easy to determine. On the basis of the principle *pacta sunt servanda*, states are bound by the treaties to which they have expressed their consent to be bound.

States are also bound by customary international humanitarian law, unless they have persistently objected to be bound.[1] There is no question that at least certain parts of international humanitarian law constitute customary international law, although there is some controversy concerning which rules precisely.

The international obligations of international organizations are more difficult to determine than those of states, in particular because these organizations are generally not parties to multilateral rulemaking treaties. Another problem is that, while there is general agreement that in principle international organizations with an international legal personality are bound by customary international law, the precise consequences of this general assertion are controversial. In the case of the UN, finally, there is the question whether the Security Council is bound by customary international law. The question in respect of the Security Council is whether its special position in the UN collective security system, and the fact that its decisions are binding on member states, are compatible with the Council being bound by customary international law.

This chapter focuses in particular on the international humanitarian law obligations of the UN and NATO. The main reason is that, as stated, the obligations of states are relatively clear, although there is some controversy concerning the rules that are international customary law. The publication of a study by the International Committee of the Red Cross on the customary status of the provisions of Additional Protocols I and II is an important contribution in this regard. The obligation on states parties under common Article 1 of the 1949 Geneva Conventions to "respect and ensure respect" for the Conventions, which is of particular significance in the case of peace support operations, was discussed above.

1 J. Charney, *The Persistent Objector Rule and the Development of International Law*, 56 British Yearbook of International Law 1 (1985).

3.2 International humanitarian law norms[2]

International humanitarian law is the branch of international law which is also referred to as the law of armed conflict (LOAC), *ius in bello* or the law of war. The latter expression is not widely used anymore, mainly because recent treaties refer to 'armed conflict' instead of 'war' and because the term sits uncomfortably with the international prohibition of the use of force. International humanitarian law is defined by the ICRC as "a set of rules which seek, for humanitarian reasons, to limit the effects of armed conflict." [3]

Ius in bello must be distinguished from the *ius ad bellum*. The latter regulates the legitimate use of force, *i.e.* when force may be used. The former lays down rules which apply during the use of force, irrespective of the reasons for the conflict and whether or not the cause upheld by either party is just.

International humanitarian law is only applicable during an armed conflict. This is the principal difference between international humanitarian law and human rights law. The latter also strives to protect human beings, but is applicable in peacetime only, or at all times in the case of a number of 'non-derogable' rights.

The origin of customary rules of international humanitarian law reaches far back in time. Already in ancient times limits were placed on what was legitimate in war and these limits evolved into customary rules.[4] Customary rules still play a role in present international humanitarian law.

The codification of international humanitarian law began in the nineteenth century. The first treaty in this field was the 1864 Geneva Convention for the Amelioration of the Condition of the Wounded in Armies in the Field, followed by the 1868 St. Petersburg Declaration. In 1899 and in 1907 major codification efforts were undertaken at peace conferences in the Hague, leading *inter alia* to the adoption of the 1907 Convention (IV) on the Laws and Customs of War on Land and the Regulations annexed thereto. The above-mentioned treaties are considered the core of the so-called 'law of the Hague'. This is the part of international humanitarian law which relates to the conduct of war and permissible means and methods of war. Another part of the law is concerned with the protection of those who are not, or no longer, taking part in fighting, including civilians. This part of the law is referred to as the 'law of Geneva'. The principal elements of this part are the four Geneva Conventions of 1949. Each of these four Conventions deals with the protection of a different vulnerable group: the wounded and sick in armed forces on land; the wounded, sick and shipwrecked members of armed forces at sea; prisoners of war; and civilians. The Geneva Conventions have been almost universally ratified. In 1977 two Additional Protocols to the Geneva

---

2 See generally F. Kalshoven & L. Zegveld, Constraints on the Waging of War: An Introduction to International Humanitarian Law (2001); J. Pictet, Le Droit Humanitaire et la Protection des Victimes de la Guerre (1973).

3 ICRC Advisory Service on International Humanitarian Law, What is International Humanitarian Law? 1 (2002).

4 See G. Best, Humanity in Warfare: The Modern History of the International Law of Armed Conflicts (1980).

Conventions were adopted. The Protocols are a confluence of the Hague and Geneva law. They contain rules on methods and means of war as well as rules on the protection of civilians and other groups. The Protocols have not been as widely ratified as the 1949 Geneva Conventions, because they contain a number of controversial elements. Of particular importance is that the United States is not a party to the Protocols.[5]

Originally, international humanitarian law only applied to international conflicts, *i.e.* conflicts between two or more states. The law was only applicable between a state's armed forces and an armed opposition group if the latter's members were recognized as 'belligerents' by the state. The relationship between a state and its population, including armed opposition groups, was considered an internal affair and interference by other states was deemed to be a breach of that state's sovereignty. The adoption of Article 3 common to the 1949 Geneva Conventions was a departure from this situation. This article is applicable "in case of armed conflict not of an international character occurring in the territory of one of the High Contracting Parties." Although the article only contains a very limited number of rules which apply to non-international armed conflicts, the fact that it was the first regulation of these conflicts gave it major significance. Additional Protocol II of 1977 developed common Article 3, although its scope of application is formulated more restrictively.[6] The protection afforded by the Protocol is still much more limited than that provided by the regime which applies to international armed conflicts. At present there is a tendency to de-emphasize the distinction between the regimes for international armed conflicts on the one hand, and for non-international armed conflicts on the other hand. However, there is no reason to assume that the two will merge anytime soon.

In addition to the above-mentioned treaties, international humanitarian law comprises a number of other agreements which prohibit the use of certain weapons and military tactics or which protect certain categories of people and goods. These include the 1954 Convention for the Protection of Cultural Property in the Event of Armed Conflict and the two Protocols Additional to the Convention, the 1980 Convention on Prohibitions or Restrictions on the Use of Certain Conventional Weapons Which May be Deemed to be Excessively Injurious or to Have Indiscriminate Effects

---

5 See G. Aldrich, *Prospects for United States Ratification of Additional Protocol I to the 1949 Geneva Conventions*, 85 American Journal of International Law 1 (1991).

6 Article 1 of the Protocol provides:

> 1. This Protocol, which develops and supplements Article 3 common to the Geneva Conventions of 12 August 1949 without modifying its existing conditions or application, shall apply to all armed conflicts which are not covered by Article 1 of the Protocol Additional to the Geneva Conventions of 12 August 1949, and relating to the Protection of Victims of International Armed Conflicts (Protocol I) and which take place in the territory of a High Contracting Party between its armed forces and dissident armed forces or other organized armed groups which, under responsible command, exercise such control over a part of its territory as to enable them to carry out sustained and concerted military operations and to implement this Protocol.
> 2. his Protocol shall not apply to situations of internal disturbances and tensions, such as riots, isolated and sporadic acts of violence and other acts of a similar nature, as not being armed conflicts.

and its five Protocols, as well as the 1997 Convention on the Prohibition of the Use, Stockpiling, Production and Transfer of Anti-Personnel Mines and on their Destruction.

3.3 Sources of obligations for the United Nations and the North Atlantic Treaty Organization

The debate whether the UN in general, and the Security Council in particular, is or should be bound by international law is not new. The debate started during the drafting of the UN Charter. In the subsequent decades the debate continued mainly outside the organization itself. In particular, this debate focused on the application of international humanitarian law to operations authorized or established by the organization for the maintenance of international peace and security. In the 1990s, two developments in particular renewed the debate and shifted its focus slightly. The first was the application by Libya to the International Court of Justice (ICJ) in two parallel cases against the United States and the United Kingdom relating to the demands for surrender by that state of two of its nationals. The United States and the United Kingdom suspected the two of being responsible for the bombing of Pan Am flight 103 over Lockerbie, Scotland, and demanded that Libya surrender them for trial. When Libya refused, the UN Security Council adopted Resolution 731, urging Libya to immediately provide a full and effective response to the United States' and United Kingdom's requests. Libya then filed an application requesting the International Court of Justice to find that it had complied with all of its obligations under the Montreal Convention for the Suppression of Unlawful Acts against the Safety of Civil Aviation,[7] that the United Kingdom and the United States were in violation of their obligations under that convention, and that they were obliged to desist from the use of any force or threats against Libya. Libya also requested the indication of certain provisional measures. Shortly after the filing of the applications, the Security Council adopted Resolution 748 under Chapter VII of the UN Charter. The Council decided that Libya must comply with the request for surrender and that states should adopt certain sanctions against Libya if it had not complied by 15 April 1992. The central problem of the *Lockerbie* cases was whether the Court could review the legality of a Security Council resolution and which standards of review it should apply. The Court itself, in its orders of 14 April 1992[8] dismissing the request for provisional measures, and judgments of 27 February 1998[9] rejecting preliminary objections and finding jurisdiction, circumvented these questions to a large extent, leaving them

7 Convention for the Suppression of Unlawful Acts against the Safety of Civil Aviation, Montreal, 23 September 1971, reproduced in 1971 ILM 1151.

8 Questions of Interpretation and Application of the 1971 Montreal Convention arising from the Aerial Incident at Lockerbie (*Libya* v. *United Kingdom*; *Libya* v. *United States of America*), Provisional Measures, Order, 1992 ICJ Reports 4.

9 Questions of Interpretation and Application of the 1971 Montreal Convention arising from the Aerial Incident at Lockerbie (*Libya* v. *United Kingdom*; *Libya* v. *United States of America*), Preliminary Objections, Judgment, reproduced in 37 ILM 586 (1998).

for the merits stage.[10] On 10 September 2003, however, the cases were removed from the Court's List at the joint request of the Parties, so that there will be no judgment on the merits.[11] Nevertheless, the *Lockerbie* cases have given rise to an extensive literature on the legal limitations on the Security Council.[12]

The second development is related to the use of economic sanctions. The Security Council made extensive use of this instrument in the 1990s. The sanctions instrument was however criticized both inside and outside the UN for leading to humanitarian disasters, in particular in the case of Iraq.[13] This has led to a debate on the limits international law places on the use of economic sanctions[14] and a call for targeted or smart sanctions.[15]

The debate on legal limits to action by NATO is of much more recent origin. Generally, there was very little discussion of the application of international law to NATO action before 1999. This situation changed radically with Operation Allied Force, the air campaign conducted by the organization against the Federal Republic of Yugoslavia (FRY) in 1999. As a result, the FRY filed applications against ten members of the organization asking the ICJ *inter alia* to declare that rules of international humanitarian law had been violated. Operation Allied Force also gave rise to a report to the prosecutor of the ICTY[16] and to a body of literature which has started to address the legal contours of NATO.[17]

10 B. Martenczuk, *The Security Council, the International Court and Judicial Review: What Lessons from Lockerbie?*, 10 European Journal of International Law 517 (1999), at 525.

11 See ICJ press release 2003/29 of 10 September 2003.

12 See *e.g.* V. Gowlland-Debbas, *The Relationship between the International Court of Justice and the Security Council in the Light of the Lockerbie Case*, 88 American Journal of International Law 643 (1994); D. Akande, *The International Court of Justice and the Security Council: Is there Room for Judicial Control of Decisions of the Political Organs of the United Nations?*, 46 International & Comparative Law Quarterly 309 (1997); T. Gill, *Legal and Some Political Limitations on the Power of the UN Security Council to Exercise its Enforcement Powers under Chapter VII of the Charter*, 26 Netherlands Yearbook of International Law 33 (1995); D. Schweigman, The Authority of the Security Council under Chapter VII of the UN Charter: Legal Limits and the Role of the International Court of Justice (2001).

13 *Former UN Official Decries Sanctions on Iraq*, The Guardian, 27 January 1999; B. Crossette, *UN Council to Review its Policy on Sanctions*, New York Times, 18 April 2000.

14 See *e.g.* A. Reinisch, *Developing Human Rights and Humanitarian Law Accountability of the Security Council for the Imposition of Economic Sanctions*, 95 American Journal of International Law 851 (2001); E. de Wet, *Human Rights Limitations to Economic Enforcement Measures under Article 41 of the United Nations Charter and the Iraqi Sanctions Regime*, 14 Leiden Journal of International Law 277 (2001).

15 E. MacAskill, *UN Agrees Long-Awaited Smart Sanctions for Iraq*, The Guardian, 15 May 2002.

16 Final Report to the Prosecutor by the Committee Established to Review the NATO Bombing Campaign Against the Federal Republic of Yugoslavia, reproduced in 39 ILM 1257 (2000).

17 See *e.g.* P. Kovács, *Intervention Armée des Forces de l'OTAN au Kosovo: Fondement de l'Obligation de Respecter le Droit International Humanitaire*, 82 International Review of the Red Cross 103 (2000).

An aspect of commonality between these debates is that they look to the same sources for limitations under international law on action by the UN or NATO. These sources are mainly international humanitarian law treaties, the constituent instruments of the organizations and customary international law.

3.4 International humanitarian law treaties

The UN and NATO have both concluded treaties under international law. Such treaties are binding on them on the basis of the principle *pacta sunt servanda* as codified in Article 26 of the 1986 Convention on the Law of Treaties between States and International Organizations or between International Organizations.[18] Neither organization however is party to any treaty on international humanitarian law.

The question is whether the treaties themselves even provide for the possibility of accession by an international organization. Accession clauses of earlier international humanitarian law treaties provide only for accession by 'states'[19] or 'countries',[20] clearly excluding international organizations.[21] The 1907 Hague Conventions and the 1949 Geneva Conventions, and the 1977 Additional Protocols by reference to the Geneva Conventions, provide for accession by 'Powers'. Yet more recent treaties revert solely to the possibility of accession by 'states'.

Unlike the term 'state', the term 'Power' does not *a priori* exclude an international organization, and it has been suggested that the term should not be read restrictively and that consequently international organizations can accede to the 1907 Hague Conventions and the 1949 Geneva Conventions.[22] This possibility would then also extend to the 1977 Additional Protocols, because these refer to the 1949 Geneva Conventions. The question of accession by international organizations was simply not raised during the drafting of the 1907 Hague Conventions and the 1949 Geneva Conventions so that the *travaux préparatoires* are not conclusive. In practice, however,

---

18 Vienna Convention on the Law of Treaties between States and International Organizations or between International Organizations, 21 March 1986, reproduced in 25 ILM 543 (1986).

19 See Protocol for the Prohibition of the Use of Asphyxiating, Poisonous or Other Gases, and of Bacteriological Methods of Warfare, entered into force 8 February 1928, 94 LNTS 65 which states: "The High Contracting Parties will exert every effort to induce other States to accede to the present Protocol."

20 See Convention Relative to the Treatment of Prisoners of War, entered into force 19 June 1931, 118 LNTS 343, Article 93: "As from the date of its entry into force, the present Convention shall be open to accession notified in respect of any country on whose behalf this Convention has not been signed."

21 Cf. Reparation for Injuries Suffered in the Service of the United Nations, Advisory Opinion of 11 April 1949, 1949 ICJ Reports 174, at 179:

> The Court has come to the conclusion that the Organization is an international person. That is not the same as saying that it is a State, which it certainly is not, or that its legal personality and rights and duties are the same as those of a State.

22 F. Seyersted, United Nations Forces in the Law of Peace and War 350 (1966).

the UN has interpreted the term 'Power' as excluding international organizations, and this interpretation also finds extensive support in literature.[23]

The *travaux préparatoires* of Additional Protocol I reaffirm this interpretation. The ratification and accession clauses of the Protocol state that it is open to ratification or accession by any Party to the 1949 Geneva Conventions and thus by reference includes the concept of 'Power'. During the 1971 Conference of Government Experts, the ICRC mentioned the matter of the application of the Geneva Conventions to UN peacekeeping forces. Several statements were made on the subject and it was suggested that it be included in the agenda of the IVth Commission of the Conference.[24] At the second session of the Conference in 1972, the ICRC brought up the subject again. The representative of the UN Secretary-General then argued against the possibility of accession to the Conventions and Protocol by the UN. He stated that:

> Such accession would obviously pose problems as to the competence in general of the Organization to become a Party to a multilateral treaty, as well as with respect to the ratification procedure. But the main obstacle was the impossibility for the Organization to fulfill many of the obligations laid down in the Conventions of Geneva. ... The accession which had been suggested would therefore only raise false hopes, and in consequence, give rise to unjustified criticism of the United Nations.[25]

At the conference a proposal was introduced by Egypt to adopt the following provision:

> The United Nations Organization, the international specialized agencies and regional intergovernmental organizations may accede to the Conventions and the present Protocol.[26]

---

23 See *e.g.* 88 ASIL Proc. 349 (1994); B. Tittemore, *Belligerents in Blue Helmets: Applying International Humanitarian Law to United Nations Peace Operations*, 33 Stanford Journal of International Law 61 (1997), at 95; R. Simmonds, Legal Problems Arising from the United Nations Military Operations in the Congo 182-183 (1968); C. Greenwood, *International Humanitarian Law and United Nations Military Operations*, 1 Yearbook of International Humanitarian Law 3 (1998), at 16. But see D. Schindler, *United Nations Forces and International Humanitarian Law*, in C. Swinarski (Ed.), Etudes et Essais sur le Droit International Humanitaire et sur les Principes de la Croix-Rouge en l'Honneur de Jean Pictet 521 (1984), at 529.

24 International Committee of the Red Cross, Report on the Work of the Conference of Government Experts on the Reaffirmation and Development of International Humanitarian Law Applicable in Armed Conflicts, Geneva (1971), at 52, paras. 309-310 (Government Experts Conference Report, first session).

25 International Committee of the Red Cross, Report on the Work of the Conference of Government Experts on the Reaffirmation and Development of International Humanitarian Law Applicable in Armed Conflicts, Second Session, Geneva (1972), at 193-194, paras. 4.165-4.166 (Government Experts Conference Report, second session).

26 *Id.*, Vol. II (Annexes), at 108.

Most experts declared themselves against such a proposal. They stressed that the UN was not a party to any multilateral treaty and the capacity to become a party to such treaties raised difficult legal problems. It would be impossible for the UN to fulfill a great many of the obligations spelt out in the Conventions and the organization was not in a position to assume responsibility for the behavior of the contingents placed at its disposal.[27] The Egyptian proposal was not adopted. In other words, the delegates consciously excluded the possibility of accession by international organizations and gave a restrictive interpretation of the term 'Power'.[28]

Previously, the question of the accession of the UN had also arisen during negotiations on the 1954 Cultural Property Convention. At the diplomatic Conference, the legal advisor of UNESCO stated that the Convention would apply in the event of UN collective action, but only if the Security Council and the General Assembly adopted a resolution deciding to apply the Convention. The secretariat of the Conference envisaged the drafting of a text by which the UN itself would accept some of the provisions of the Convention.[29] The proposal was ruled out of order because it had not been introduced in writing. The French delegation proposed instead to adopt a resolution at the Conference recommending that the UN ensure application of the principles of the Conventions by the armed forces taking part in a military action in implementation of the Charter.[30] This resolution was adopted and reads:

> The Conference expresses the hope that the competent organs of the United Nations should decide, in the event of military action being taken in implementation of the Charter, to ensure application of the provisions of the Convention by the armed forces taking part in such action.[31]

Although the drafters expressed their concern that the UN ensure respect for the provisions of the convention, it is clear that they excluded the possibility of ratification or accession.

27 *Id.*, at 194, para. 4.168.

28 See also UNJY 1972, at 153: "Finally, the Commission IV of the Conference decided not to include in the draft Protocol any clause providing for accession of intergovernmental organizations. The position taken by the Secretariat on this matter has been nearly unanimously supported by all the delegations."

29 Where an international authority – by the terms of the Article (Final Provisions) -- would state its acceptance of all or some of the provisions of the present Convention, which it would be capable of applying, the High Contracting Parties shall be bound, in relation to the said international authority, by the provisions of the Convention accepted in the terms of the aforementioned statement, English translation, Actes de la Conférence Convoquée par l'Organisation des Nations Unies pour l'Education, la Science et la Culture tenue à la Haye du 21 Avril au 14 Mai 1954, at 187 (1954).

30 *Id.*, at 274-275.

31 United Nations Economic Social and Cultural Organization, Final Act of the Intergovernmental Conference on the Protection of Cultural Property in the Event of Armed Conflict 80 (1954).

3.5 Constituent instruments and derogation by the UN Security Council

In general, the constituent instrument of an international organization is a treaty and as such the organization and its organs must respect the division of competences and limitations on power in the treaty.[32] In this sense the constituent instrument of the organization performs a role similar to a constitution in domestic law. Although extreme care is required when comparing international organizations to states, the constitutional character of the UN Charter has recently been asserted in literature and in practice.[33] The Appeals Chamber of the ICTY affirmed that:

> The Security Council is an organ of an international organization, established by a treaty which serves as a constitutional framework for that organization. The Security Council is thus subjected to certain constitutional limitations, however broad its powers may be, those powers cannot, in any case, go beyond the limits of the jurisdiction of the Organization at large, not to mention other specific limitations or those which may derive from the internal division of power within the Organization. In any case, neither the text nor the spirit of the Charter conceives of the Security Council as *legibus solutus* (unbound by law).[34]

The assumption that an international organization is limited by its constituent instrument is in itself generally accepted. Problems arise, however, in defining the content of those limitations. This is primarily a matter of treaty interpretation, because the constituent instrument is generally a treaty.

The UN Charter contains a number of provisions which some writers have interpreted as imposing an obligation on the organization, and the Security Council in particular, to respect international humanitarian law. Legal limitations on the Security Council are of principal concern because in practice UN peace support operations are subsidiary organs of the Council.[35] Article 24 of the UN Charter provides that:

> In order to ensure prompt and effective action by the United Nations, its Members confer on the Security Council primary responsibility for the maintenance of international peace and security, and agree that in carrying out its duties under this responsibility the Security Council acts on their behalf.
> In discharging these duties the Security Council shall act in accordance with the Purposes and Principles of the United Nations.

---

32 I. Brownlie, Principles of Public International Law 697 (1998).

33 See *e.g.* B. Fassbender, *The United Nations Charter as Constitution of the International Community*, 36 Columbia Journal of Transnational Law 529 (1998); P.M. Dupuy, *The Constitutional Dimension of the Charter of the United Nations Revisited*, 1 Max Planck Yearbook of United Nations Law 33 (1997).

34 *Prosecutor* v. *Duško Tadić*, Decision on the Defence Motion for Interlocutory Appeal on Jurisdiction, Case No. IT-94-1-AR72, A. Ch., 2 October 1995, para. 28.

35 See para. 1.8.2.

The purposes and principles of the UN are set out in Article 1 and 2 of the Charter. Article 1 (1) provides that one of the purposes of the organization is:

> To maintain international peace and security, and to that end: to take effective collective measures for the prevention of threats to the peace, and for the suppression of acts of aggression or other breaches of the peace, and to bring about by peaceful means, and in conformity with the principles of justice and international law, adjustment or settlement of international disputes which might lead to a breach of the peace;

The ordinary meaning given to the terms of this article makes clear that the Security Council is only bound by the obligation to act in conformity with the principles of justice and international law in the adjustment or settlement of international disputes, and not when it takes collective measures for the prevention and removal of threats to the peace, and for the suppression of acts of aggression or other breaches of the peace.[36] The latter is clearly a reference to action under Chapter VII of the Charter.

The *travaux préparatoires* confirm this interpretation. The Dumbarton Oaks Proposals which laid the groundwork for the UN Charter did not include a reference to international law in its provisions on Purposes and Principles. A proposal was made at the United Nations Conference on International Organization by China, supported by the United Kingdom, the United States and the Soviet Union, to add that peaceful settlement of disputes must be brought about "with due regard for principles of justice and international law".[37] Other delegations thought that this phrase was inadequate, and that "a more explicit requirement for strict observance of the principles of justice, international law, and morality should be written into the Declaration of Purposes in the Charter."[38] In the subcommittee which was drafting the Purposes, it was proposed that the words "in conformity with the principles of justice and international law" be placed in the first line after the words "peace and security." This amendment received 19 votes in favor and 15 against, not enough for the two-thirds majority required.[39] The same amendment was later again introduced by the Egyptian delegation in Commission I. The Egyptian delegate said in support of the amendment that the "last argument with which we were today confronted was that if we asked the Security Council to respect justice and international law it might make the burden of the Organization heavier."[40] The delegate of the United Kingdom who opposed the amendment used:

36 See R. Wolfrum, *Article 1*, in B. Simma (Ed.), The Charter of the United Nations: A Commentary 49 (1995), at 52, M. Bedjaoui, *Article 1*, in J.P. Cot & A. Pellet (Eds.), La Charte des Nations Unies 23 (1985), at 25.

37 UNCIO III, at 622, Doc. 2 G/29.

38 Summary Report of Third Meeting of Committee I/1, doc. 197, 10 May 1945, UNCIO Documents VI, at 281, at 282.

39 Summary Report of the Ninth Meeting of Committee I/1, Doc. 742, I/1/23/ 1 June 1945, UNCIO VI, at 317, at 318.

40 Verbatim Minutes of First Meeting of Commission I, 14 June 1945, Doc. 1006, UNCIO.

> the illustration of the policeman or the gendarme who is concerned with dealing with a wrong that he sees arising. He does not stop at the outset of what he does to inquire where exactly lies the precise balance of justice in their quarrel. He stops it, and then, in order to make adjustment and settlement, justice comes into town.[41]

The United States delegation shared this opinion.[42] This opposition was an important element leading to the defeat of the Egyptian amendment by a vote of 21 for and 21 against.[43]

That Article 1 (1) may be interpreted to mean that the Security Council may derogate from the principles of international law when it acts under Chapter VII of the UN Charter was also understood by the Dutch government. It reported to parliament on the drafting of the article that:

> In the meanwhile the Delegations of Egypt, Panama and Uruguay had ... introduced two amendments, to the effect of naming the principles of justice and international law in the first part of paragraph 1, so that they could be considered to regard all the functions of the Organization, which, it seemed, could be doubted in the case of the proposed text. For the Dutch Delegation, which had been content with the amendment to paragraph 1 proposed by the Sponsoring Governments, there was initially no reason to support these amendments. When, however, the British Delegate challenged these amendments with the argument that in maintaining international peace and security one could not always respect these principles because the maintenance of international peace and security had a political dimension, the Dutch Delegation considered this so dangerous that it lent its support to the amendments. These were however unable to carry the required two-thirds majority in Committee 1.[44]

---

41 *Id.*

42 *Id*:

> It is our view that this Security Council ... will have two very important functions ... Those might be characterized somewhat as being the functions of a policeman and the functions of a jury. ... When you begin to function as a jury you must do so in conformity with justice and international law.

43 *Id.*

44 "Intussen waren door de Delegaties van Egypte, Panama en Uruguay ... twee amendementen ingediend, welke de strekking hadden om de grondslagen van rechtvaardigheid en van internationaal recht in lid 1 direct in de aanvang te noemen, zodat zij geacht konden worden op alle functies van de Organisatie betrekking te hebben, hetgeen, naar het scheen, van de voorgestelde bepalingen kon worden betwijfeld. Voor de Nederlandse Delegatie, die zich bevredigd had geacht door het door de Delegaties der Uitvoerende Mogendheden vastgestelde amendement op lid 1, bestond aanvankelijk geen aanleiding om deze amendementen te steunen. Toen echter bij het debat de Britse vertegenwoordiger die amendementen bestreed met het argument, dat men bij het handhaven van de internationale vrede niet altijd van deze grondslagen zou kunnen uitgaan, omdat het handhaven van de internationale vrede en veiligheid een politieke kant had, achtte de Nederlandse Delegatie dit betoog zo gevaarlijk, dat zij haar steun aan de amendementen gaf. Deze vermochten evenwel niet de vereiste tweederde meerderheid der stemmen in Comité 1 te behalen." Ministerie van Buitenlandse Zaken, Het Ontstaan der Verenigde Naties: San Francisco, 25 April – 25 Juni 1945, at 20-21 (1950) (English translation by the author).

In short, the Security Council, when acting under Chapter VII of the UN Charter can derogate from certain principles of international law.[45] As Judge Schwebel stated in his dissenting opinion to the 1998 judgment in the *Lockerbie* case, the omission of principles and justice of international law "was deliberately so provided to ensure that the vital duty of preventing and removing threats to and breaches of the peace would not be limited by existing law."[46]

The principle that the UN Security Council can derogate from international law which would otherwise be applicable, is supported by Article 103 of the Charter. This article provides that in case of conflicting obligations of member states under the UN Charter and under another international agreement, the obligations under the Charter prevail.[47] Obligations 'under the Charter' are understood to be not only obligations arising directly from provisions of the Charter, but also obligations arising from binding decisions of the UN Security Council.[48] This was confirmed by the ICJ in its order on provisional measures in the *Lockerbie* case.[49] The question arises whether in the latter case the Security Council must actually use the verb 'to decide' in the relevant paragraph of a resolution under Chapter VII of the UN Charter. This does not seem to be the case. Here it is important to recall that Article 25 concerns binding decisions of the Security Council. Speaking to that article, the ICJ stated in its advisory opinion in the *Namibia* case:

> The language of a resolution of the Security Council should be carefully analysed before a conclusion can be made as to its binding effect. In view of the nature of the powers under Article 25, the question whether they have been in fact exercised is to be determined in each case, having regard to the terms of the resolution to be interpreted, the discussions leading to it, the Charter provisions invoked and, in general, all circumstances that might assist in determining the legal consequences of the resolution of the Security Council.[50]

Consequently, although the Security Council need not use the verb 'to decide', there needs to be a clear indication that it intended to bind member states. Reisman has advocated that not only decisions, but also recommendations by the Security Council

---

45 G. Oosthuizen, *Playing the Devil's Advocate: the United Nations Security Council is Unbound by Law*, 12 Leiden Journal of International Law 549 (1999), at 552-553; H. Kelsen, The Law of the United Nations 294-295 (1951); Martenczuk, *supra* note 10, at 545.

46 *Supra* note 9, at 627.

47 Article 103 reads:

> In the event of a conflict between the obligations of the Members of the United Nations under the present Charter and their obligations under any other international agreement, their obligations under the present Charter shall prevail.

48 R. Bernhardt, *Article 103*, in Simma (Ed.), *supra* note 36, at 1120.

49 *Supra* note 8, at 16, para. 39.

50 Legal Consequences for States of the Continued Presence of South Africa in Namibia (South West Africa) notwithstanding Security Council Resolution 276 (1970), Advisory Opinion of 21 June 1971, 1971 ICJ Reports 16, at 53, para. 114.

should prevail over treaty obligations.[51] This seems a dangerous road to take. First, it overlooks the natural and close relationship between Article 103 and Article 25. Second, it gives much leeway to states to argue that their actions have the Council's blessing under Chapter VII of the Charter, at a time when there have been questionable invocations of Council resolutions to justify the use of force. Finally, it is not in conformity with the principle that exceptions should be interpreted narrowly.

It is striking that the wording of Article 103 only refers to treaty obligations and not to customary international law. At the San Francisco conference, a proposal to formulate the article in a such a way that all other commitments, including those arising under customary law, were to be superseded by the Charter, was ultimately not included.[52] Judge Bedjaoui concluded in his dissenting opinion in the ICJ's Order on provisional measures in the *Lockerbie* case, that Article 103 "does not cover such rights as may have other than conventional sources and be derived from general international law."[53] Combacau on the other hand offers another, and more probable, interpretation of the article, according to which its specific purpose is to set aside the rule that a later treaty prevails over an earlier treaty (*lex posterior derogat legi priori*).[54] If this is the specific purpose of the article, there is no need for it to refer to customary international law.[55]

In any event, Article 103 must be seen in the broader system of the Charter. Article 1 (1), Article 25 and Article 103 together make clear that the UN Security Council can derogate from customary international law. As Reisman states, "[t]he synergy of Articles 25 and 103 ... trumps all contrary non-Charter legal obligations."[56] This was confirmed by Judge Oda in his declaration in the *Lockerbie* case, in which he stated that "under the positive law of the United Nations Charter a resolution of the Security Council may have binding force, irrespective of the question whether it is consonant with international law derived from other sources."[57]

Certain writers argue that the Security Council is bound by peremptory norms of international law, also referred to as *ius cogens*. The concept of peremptory norms was first codified in the Vienna Convention on the Law of Treaties. Article 53 of that convention provides:

> A treaty is void if, at the time of its conclusion, it conflicts with a peremptory norm of general international law. For the purposes of the present Convention, a peremptory

51 M. Reisman, The Constitutional Crisis in the United Nations, 87 *American Journal of International Law* 83 (1993), at 89.

52 Bernhardt, *supra* note 48.

53 *Supra* note 8, Dissenting Opinion of Judge Bedjaoui, para. 29.

54 J. Combacau, Le Pouvoir de Sanction de l'O.N.U.: Étude Théorique de la Coercition non Militaire 282 (1974).

55 That Article 103 also covers customary international law is reaffirmed for example by the statement by the Russian Federation to the Security Council on 24 March 1999 concerning Kosovo: "Article 103, precisely establishing an absolute priority of the Charter obligations before any other international obligations of members of the Organization."

56 Reisman, *supra* note 51, at 93.

57 *Supra* note 8, Declaration of Acting President Oda, under I.

> norm of general international law is a norm accepted and recognized by the international community of States as a whole as a norm from which no derogation is permitted and which can be modified only by a subsequent norm of general international law having the same character.

It is argued that the non-derogatory character of peremptory norms means that all subjects of international law, including the Security Council, have to abide by them.[58]

Judge Lauterpacht declared in his separate opinion in the *Genocide* case that:

> The concept of *jus cogens* operates as a concept superior to both customary international law and treaty. The relief which Article 103 of the Charter may give the Security Council in case of conflict between one of its decisions and an operative treaty obligation cannot – as a matter of simple hierarchy of norms – extend to a conflict between a Security Council resolution and *jus cogens*.[59]

It has been argued that the concept of *ius cogens* partly explains the lack of reference to customary international law in Article 103 of the UN Charter.[60] However, at the time of drafting of the Charter this concept was not widely recognized, and it is therefore unlikely that the drafters took it into account. If they did, it is difficult to explain why Article 1 (1) does not mention peremptory norms. If the concept of peremptory norms gained currency only after the adoption of the UN Charter, it is not necessarily the case that the Security Council cannot derogate from such norms. At a minimum, there has been no attempt to amend the UN Charter to state that the Security Council is bound by peremptory norms when its acts under Chapter VII.

In addition, there is the question of the legal consequences of establishing that a particular norm is a peremptory norm. As noted, the concept of *ius cogens* was first anchored in conventional law in the Vienna Convention on the Law of Treaties, which sets out certain consequences in the field of treaty law. There is no consensus on other legal consequences of the determination that a particular norm is a peremptory norm. These consequences extend beyond the field of treaty law, as illustrated by Chapter III of Part Two of ILC draft articles on state responsibility. However, this does not mean that these consequences are unlimited. For example, the ICJ in the *Arrest Warrant* case declined to hold that immunity of a Minister of Foreign Affairs is set aside in case of a prosecution for genocide, even though the prohibition of genocide is widely regarded as one of the clearest examples of a peremptory norm.[61] In

58 See *e.g.* Schweigman, *supra* note 12, at 197.

59 Application of the Convention on the Prevention and Punishment of the Crime of *Genocide (Bosnia and Herzegovina* v. *Yugoslavia (Serbia and Montenegro))*, Separate Opinion of Judge Lauterpacht, 1993 ICJ Reports 4, at 440.

60 M. Shaw, *The Security Council and the International Court of Justice: Judicial Drift and Judicial Function*, in A. Muller, D. Raič & J. Thuránsky (Eds.), The International Court of Justice: Its Future after Fifty Years 219 (1997), at 229.

61 Arrest Warrant of April 11th 2000 (*Democratic Republic of the Congo* v. *Belgium*), Judgment, Merits, reproduced in 41 ILM 536 (2002).

other words, the mere determination that a norm is a peremptory norm does not automatically set aside all other international law.

Finally, it is uncertain which norms of international humanitarian law are peremptory norms. The ILC commentary to article 40 of the draft articles on state responsibility states that it would seem justified to treat as peremptory those basic rules of international humanitarian law referred to as 'intransgressible' in character by the International Court of Justice.[62] It may be recalled, however, that the Court refused to pronounce itself on the *ius cogens* nature of rules of international humanitarian law in the *Nuclear Weapons* case.[63] In its Advisory Opinion on the *Legal Consequences of the Construction of a Wall in the Occupied Palestinian Territory*, however, it did suggest that at least certain norms of international humanitarian law may have a peremptory character. The ICJ held that all states are under an obligation not to recognize the illegal situation resulting from the construction of the Wall, and that it is also for all states to see to it that any impediment created by the construction of the Wall is brought to an end.[64] This constituted an application of articles 40-41 of the ILC draft articles on state responsibility, which by their own terms apply "to the international responsibility which is entailed by a serious breach by a state of an obligation arising under a peremptory norm of general international law." Coupled with the ICJ´s conclusion that the law applicable to the Occupied Territories includes the law of occupation, this suggests that that branch of law may include peremptory norms.

In short, the proposition that the Security Council cannot derogate from peremptory norms is open to criticism. It may also be noted that in the context of the application of international humanitarian law to UN peace support operations, a conflict between basic, rather than more technical, norms of international humanitarian law and a Security Council decision is unlikely to arise.

Article 25 nor Article 103 of the UN Charter provides that if the Security Council derogates from particular rules of international law it should make clear which alternative regime applies. It is difficult to accept, however, that the drafters of the UN Charter intended to create a legal vacuum when the Council does derogate from international law. It could be argued that in case the Security Council authorizes states or an international organization to derogate from international law, it should indicate an alternative standard on the basis that, since the Council acts by delegation from the UN membership as a whole, it cannot delegate powers without continuing close scrutiny by the Council.[65] It has been argued that the Security Council must at all times retain overall authority and control over the exercise of delegated

62 Report of the International Law Commission on the work of its fifty-third session, 23 April – 1 June and 2 July – 10 August 2001 (A/56/10), at 284, para. 5.

63 Legality of the Threat or Use of Nuclear Weapons, Advisory Opinion of 8 July 1996, 1996 ICJ Reports 226, para. 83.

64 Legal Consequences of the Construction of a Wall in the Occupied Palestinian Territory, Advisory Opinion of 9 July 2004, not yet reported, para. 159.

65 See *e.g.* D. Bowett, *The Impact of Security Council Decisions on Dispute Settlement Procedures*, 5 European Journal of International Law 1 (1994), at 8.

powers under Chapter VII.[66] The Council should, according to this argument, provide a standard on the basis of which it can exercise scrutiny over the way in which the delegated powers are being exercised. It could also be argued that the Security Council has an obligation to act in good faith. Article 2 (2) of the UN Charter obliges member states to fulfill their obligations under the Charter in good faith. At first glance this obligation appears to address member states only, but read together with the first sentence of Article 2 it appears that it could apply to the UN as well.[67] In any event the principle applies to the member states participating in the decision-making process of the organization. The principle of good faith is difficult to define but at the very least, it seems to require the Council to act responsibly when it carries out its Charter-based functions.[68] It could be argued that an open-ended derogation from international humanitarian law would be irresponsible behaviour on the part of the Council.

Arguably, the Security Council has derogated from international humanitarian law in Resolution 1483.[69] This resolution was adopted after the United States and the United Kingdom invaded Iraq in early 2003. The resolution, which was adopted under Chapter VII of the UN Charter, included a number of paragraphs which were important to a legal characterization of post-conflict Iraq. In its preamble, it noted the letter of 8 May 2003 from the Permanent Representatives of the United States and the United Kingdom to the President of the Security Council and recognized "the specific authorities, responsibilities, and obligations under applicable international law of these states as occupying powers under unified command (the 'Authority')." The Council hereby observed that the US and the UK were occupying powers under international humanitarian law, and that consequently the provisions of the Hague Regulations 1907 and Geneva Convention (IV) of 1949 were applicable to them. Under international humanitarian law, an occupation is conceived of as a temporary administration of territory. For this reason the law, to a large extent, restricts the occupying power from interfering in state structures of the occupied territory. For example, Article 43 of the 1907 Hague Regulations provides that the occupying power shall respect, unless absolutely prevented, the laws in force in the country. Article 53 of the same regulations provides that an army of occupation can only take possession of cash, funds, and realizable securities which are strictly the property of the state, depots of arms, means of transport, stores and supplies, and, generally, all movable property belonging to the state which may be used for military operations. In other words, the law of occupation does not envisage changing the state structures of the occupied territory. Resolution 1483, however, called upon the Authority to:

---

66 D. Sarooshi, The United Nations and the Development of Collective Security: The Delegation by the Security Council of its Chapter VII Powers 34 (1999).

67 See *e.g.* E. de Wet, The Chapter VII Powers of the United Nations Security Council 195 (2004).

68 F. Kirgis, *Security Council Governance of Postconflict Societies: A Plea for Good Faith and Informed Decision Making*, 95 American Journal of International Law 579 (2001), at 581.

69 Security Council Resolution 1483 of 22 May 2003, UN Doc. S/RES/1483 (2003).

> promote the welfare of the Iraqi people through the effective administration of the territory, including in particular working towards the restoration of conditions of security and stability and the creation of conditions in which the Iraqi people can freely determine their own political future.[70]

In pursuance of this objective, the Authority made important changes to Iraqi structures, such as by establishing a 'Governing Council' and reforming the laws of the country. On the basis of these facts it has been maintained that Resolution 1483:

> has created a 'carve out' from the Hague Regulations and Fourth Geneva Convention, leaving other provisions of the treaties in force, but suspending with respect to the Authority those provisions that otherwise would curb its license to change the laws, institutions, and personnel of the occupied state.[71]

When the Security Council is not acting under Chapter VII of the Charter, as well as when it is acting under Chapter VII and has not derogated from the principles of international law, it is bound by those principles. What are the 'principles of international law'? At first sight the term 'principles' seems to refer to general principles of law recognized by civilized nations, which is only one subset of general international law. It seems that this is not what the drafters meant, however. The *travaux préparatoires* of the Charter make clear that the function of the principles in question is mainly to preserve the rights of states in the settlement of disputes.[72] This is illustrated *inter alia* by the debate in Commission III of the San Francisco Conference. The Norwegian delegate in this Commission stated that:

> The Security Council was vested with enormous powers and little restraint was placed upon their exercise by the Dumbarton Oaks Proposals. ... He felt that a basic rule of conduct must be formulated as a restraint on the Security Council and as a guarantee that it would not resort to a 'politique de compensation'. Whatever sacrifices the Security Council might require of a nation should not be of such a nature as to impair the confidence of that nation in its future.[73]

For this reason the Norwegian delegation proposed an amendment to Article 1 of the United Nations Charter which would have required that no solution should be imposed upon a state of a nature to impair its confidence in its future security or welfare.[74]

---

70 *Id.*, para. 4.

71 T. Grant, *Asil Insight: Iraq: How to Reconcile Conflicting Obligations of Occupation and Reform*, June 2003.

72 L. Goodrich, E. Hambro & A.P. Simons (Eds.), The United Nations Charter: A Commentary 28 (1969).

73 UNCIO Documents, 1945, Vol. XI, at 378.

74 UNCIO Documents 1945, Vol. XI, at 378.

The representative of the United Kingdom opposed the amendment and stated that:

> its purpose was already served by the amended principles in Chapter I, where it was stipulated that the Organization was to 'bring about by peaceful means, and with due regard for principles of justice and international law, adjustment or settlement…' etc.[75]

Clearly, the rights of states which must be preserved are not only found in general principles of law, but also in other sources of international law, in particular customary international law. In other words, the term 'principles of international law' in Article 1 (1) refers to all sources of international law.[76] This interpretation was reaffirmed by Judge Weeramantry in his dissenting opinion in the *Lockerbie* case. He stated that whatever Security Council Resolution 731, adopted under Chapter VI of the United Nations Charter, purported to do "was required by Article 24 (2) of the Charter to be in accordance with international law."[77] The obligations of international humanitarian law binding the UN and its organs under general international law, that is under customary international law and general principles of law, are discussed below.

The obligation for the Security Council to act in accordance with the principles and purposes of the Charter also extends to Article 1 (3) of the Charter. Unlike Article 1 (1), this paragraph does not exempt the Security Council when it is acting under Chapter VII of the Charter. Article 1 (3) states that one purpose of the organization is:

> To achieve international co-operation in solving international problems of an economic, social, cultural, or humanitarian character, and in promoting and encouraging respect for human rights and for fundamental freedoms for all without distinction as to race, sex, language, or religion;

Closely connected to this paragraph is Article 55 of the Charter which states that the UN shall promote *inter alia* universal respect for, and observance of, human rights and fundamental freedoms for all without distinction as to race, sex, language, or religion. Writers frequently base an obligation for the UN and the Security Council to respect human rights on these articles.[78] It is also argued that the term 'human rights' should be read extensively to include international humanitarian law. It is argued that the purposes and principles of the UN are evolutionary and should be read in the light of

75 *Id.*

76 Wolfrum, *supra* note 36, at 52. Wolfrum states that the words 'justice and international law' not only refer to treaties, customary law, and general principles of law, but also establish a connection to natural law.

77 *Supra* note 8.

78 See *e.g.* Gill, *supra* note 12, at 77; UN Doc. E/CN.4/Sub.2/2000/33, para. 26;

changes in international law since 1945, including the development of UN concern for international humanitarian law.[79] Gardam suggests that:

> the reference to human rights in the purposes of the Charter not only must be broad enough to include within its compass principles that have the potential to provide very real protection to individuals in that most destructive of activities – armed conflict – but should have a meaning outside the narrow context of how a State treats its own subjects.[80]

The question remains, however, whether the articles in question can be the basis for any obligation at all. A textual interpretation of the articles on the one hand seems to lead to the conclusion that the UN must promote human rights, not that it must respect them.[81] The *travaux préparatoires* on the other hand suggest that Article 1 (3) does impose an obligation on the organization. At the San Francisco Conference, Uruguay proposed an amendment to the purposes and principles of the organization that would oblige it "to promote the recognition of and guarantee respect for the essential human liberties and rights without distinction as to race, sex, belief, or social status."[82] The report of the debate concerning this amendment in the official records of the conference states:

> There was considerable discussion by other delegates of this point, with emphasis on the idea that respect for human rights should also be mentioned in Chapter II as a principle to be observed by all members. It was felt that if this statement were included only in Chapter I, it would bind only the Organization and would relieve member governments from the obligation to respect the fundamental freedoms of individuals within their own countries.[83]

The committee in question did not adopt the amendment. The report suggests that as a result only the organization is bound to respect human rights. In view of the debates and text of article 1 (1), however, presumably this does not include the Security Council when it is acting under Chapter VII of the Charter. If the Security Council is not bound by international law in that capacity, it is also not bound by human rights as a subset of that law.[84] This is also demonstrated by the *travaux préparatoires* of Article

79 V. Gowlland-Debbas, *Security Council Enforcement Action and Issues of State Responsibility*, 43 International & Comparative Law Quarterly 55 (1994), at 91.

80 J. Gardam, *Legal Restraints on Security Council Military Enforcement Action*, 17 Michigan Journal of International Law 285 (1996), at 301-302.

81 L. Goodrich, The United Nations 246 (1960).

82 UNCIO Documents Vol. VI, at 552.

83 Commission I, Committee 1, Doc. 308, I/1/14, May 15, 1945, UNCIO Documents Vol. VI, at 291.

84 A. Vradenburgh, *The Chapter VII Powers of the United Nations Charter: Do They "Trump" Human Rights Law?*, 14 Loyola of Los Angeles International and Comparative Law Journal 175 (1991), at 184.

1 (3). In respect of that article, Panama proposed an amendment at the San Francisco conference which would have obliged the Security Council:

> To maintain international peace and security in conformity with the fundamental principles of international law and to maintain and observe the standards set forth in the 'Declaration of the Rights and Duties of Nations', and the 'Declaration of Essential Human Rights' which are appended to the present Charter, and which are made an integral part thereof.

The amendment, which would have imposed an obligation on the Security Council to respect human rights even in the exercise of Chapter VII powers, was rejected.

In short, Article 1 (3) of the Charter only imposes an obligation on the Security Council to respect human rights, and possibly international humanitarian law, when it is not acting under Chapter VII of the Charter.[85] This conclusion however can also be reached, and arguably more strongly, on the basis of the applicability of general international law to the UN discussed below.

The constitutional documents of NATO are the 1949 Washington Treaty in which the member states establish the North Atlantic Council, and the 1951 Ottawa Treaty on the status of the organization, national representatives and international staff. There is no indication in either of these treaties that the member states intended that the organization would not be bound by international law. On the contrary, in the preamble to the Washington Treaty, the parties reaffirm their faith in the purposes and principles of the UN. The drafters of the treaty took much care to ensure that the treaty would be in conformity with the UN Charter, as is made clear in Article 5 by express reference to Article 51 of the UN Charter and the obligation to terminate action in self-defense when the Security Council has taken the measures necessary to restore and maintain international peace and security. The NATO Handbook, an official publication of the Organization, emphatically stresses the relationship between the UN Charter and the North Atlantic Treaty of 1949 (the Washington Treaty). The handbook states that the relevance of the UN Charter to the North Atlantic Alliance is twofold: "First, it provides the juridical basis for the creation of the Alliance, and second, it establishes the overall responsibility of the UN Security Council for international peace and security."[86] It also states that the UN Charter is the framework within which the Alliance operates.[87] In particular, Article 7 of the Washington Treaty

---

85 But see Judge *ad hoc* Lauterpacht in the Genocide case, *supra* note 59, at 440, para 101:

> Nor should one overlook the significance of the provision in Article 24 (2) of the Charter that, in discharging its duties to maintain international peace and security, the Security Council shall act in accordance with the Purposes and Principles of the United Nations. Amongst the Purposes set out in Article 1 (3) of the Charter is that of achieving international co-operation "in promoting and encouraging respect for human rights and for fundamental freedoms for all without distinction as to race, sex, language or religion."

86 NATO, NATO Handbook, Chapter 15, at www.nato.int/docu/handbook/2001/hb1501.htm.

87 *Id.*

reminds member states of their rights and obligations under the UN Charter and reaffirms the primary responsibility of the UN Security Council for the maintenance of international peace and security. Even if it is the case, as a number of authors assert, that the reference to the UN Charter was not a real commitment to the UN but only a formality,[88] this is not an indication that the Organization does not consider itself bound by international law including the UN Charter.

In particular, the organization has not claimed that its members should not respect international humanitarian law during NATO operations. This is illustrated by events during and after Operation Allied Force, the NATO air campaign in the FRY in 1999. During this operation NATO was accused of having violated a number of international humanitarian law norms. These accusations led to the establishment by the Prosecutor of the ICTY of a committee to assess the allegations and material accompanying them, and advise the Prosecutor and Deputy Prosecutor whether or not there was a sufficient basis to proceed with an investigation into some or all the allegations or into other incidents related to the NATO bombing.[89] In response to the allegations, the organization never claimed that international humanitarian law did not apply. Rather, it argued that the operation was conducted in accordance with the law.[90]

3.6 General international law

In principle, an organization with international legal personality is bound by general international law, that is customary international law and general principles of law.[91] The reason is that international organizations as subjects of international law are subject to general international law precisely because they partake of personality under this legal system. In the case of the UN, the ICJ determined in the *Reparations* case that states, "by entrusting certain functions to it, with the attendant duties and responsibilities, have clothed it with the competence to enable those functions to be effectively discharged."[92] The functions of the UN are those which are "specified or implied in its constituent documents and developed in practice."[93] In this sense the deployment of peace support operations is a function of the UN although it is not

---

88 See *e.g.* J. Granatstein, *The United Nations and the North Atlantic Treaty Organization*, in G. Schmidt (Ed.), A History of NATO – The First Fifty Years, Vol. I, 29 (2001), at 32.

89 *Supra* note 16. See for commentary P. Benvenuti, *The ICTY's Prosecutor and the Review of the NATO Bombing Campaign against the Federal Republic of Yugoslavia*, 12 European Journal of International Law 503 (2001).

90 See *e.g.* NATO press releases of 2 May 1999, 8 May 1999 and 15 May 1999.

91 See *e.g.* I. Brownlie, *supra* note 32, at 690; E. Butkiewicz, *The Premisses of International Responsibility of Inter-Governmental Organizations*, 11 Polish Yearbook of International Law 117 (1981-82), at 118-122; A. Bleckmann, *Zur Verbindlichkeit des Algemeinen Völkerrechts für Internationale Organisationen*, 37 Zeitschrift für ausländisches öffentliches Recht und Völkerrecht 107 (1977).

92 Reparations for Injuries Suffered in the Service of the United Nations, Advisory Opinion of 11 April 1949, 1949 ICJ Reports 174, at 180.

93 *Id.*, at 179.

expressly provided for in the UN Charter. In the same sense the deployment of peace support operations is a function of NATO although the organization was established for other purposes. In the case of the function of deploying peace support operations the 'attendant duties' to, or in other words law regulating, the conduct of hostilities, applies.[94] The law in question is international humanitarian law. Shraga states that the:

> principle of functionality which circumscribes the international personality of the organization and its legal capacity, also determines the scope of the applicable law to activities carried out by the United Nations in the performance of its functions. Indeed, the legal capacity of the United Nations to conclude international agreements, to bring international claims on behalf of its agents, to enjoy privileges and immunities and to incur international responsibility is thus governed, respectively, by the laws of treaties, diplomatic protection, privileges and immunities and state responsibility, as they were transposed and made applicable to it by analogy and mutatis-mutandis. In a similar vein, the ever-growing involvement of UN forces in situations of armed conflict, warrants that International Humanitarian Law be made applicable to them by analogy and as appropriate, when they, like states, are engaged in military operations as combatants.[95]

It can be said that international humanitarian law is a custom of the trade of being engaged in hostilities. Since the factual character of hostilities carried out on both sides during a peace support operation that is engaged in hostilities is hardly distinguishable from armed conflict between states, the situation calls for the application of the law of armed conflict.[96] In this sense the application of general international law rules of international humanitarian law to the UN is also consistent with, and could be said to depend on, the purposes of the organization.[97] The main purpose of the organization is the maintenance of international peace and security or, as expressed in the preamble of the Charter, saving succeeding generations from the scourge of war. In speaking of the need to prevent war the drafters of the Charter naturally had in mind the suffering inflicted during World War II which was aggravated to a large extent by many breaches of international humanitarian law. According to the rapporteur of the Committee which drafted the purposes "when we speak of the prevention of war we have, of course, in mind only what sufferings war is causing to humanity."[98] Respect

---

94 See *e.g.* J. Stone, Legal Controls of International Conflict: A Treatise on the Dynamics of Disputes and War Law 315 (1954).

95 D. Shraga, *The United Nations as an Actor Bound by International Humanitarian Law*, 5 International Peacekeeping 64 (1998), at 65.

96 D. Bowett, United Nations Forces: A Legal Study of United Nations Practice 498 (1964); F. Seyersted, *supra* note 22, at 209 (1966).

97 But see G. Draper, *The Legal Limitations upon the Employment of Weapons by the United Nations Force in the Congo*, 12 International & Comparative Law Quarterly 387 (1963), at 409.

98 Verbatim Minutes of First Meeting of Commission I, June 14, UNCIO, Doc. 1006, June 15.

for international humanitarian law would also be consistent with the organization's purpose of promoting respect for human rights and achieving international cooperation in resolving international problems of a humanitarian character, in particular if these purposes are considered as evolutionary.[99]

These arguments apply to NATO as well as to the UN. The preamble to the 1949 Washington Treaty makes clear that the organization was intended to be consistent with the purposes and principles of the UN Charter and founded to preserve, *inter alia*, the rule of law. Violating international humanitarian law would hardly be consistent with these principles.

The ICJ has reaffirmed the application of general international law to the UN on different occasions. In the *Interpretation of the Agreement of 25 March 1951 between the WHO and Egypt* case,[100] the Court was concerned with an envisaged transfer of a WHO regional office from Egypt. The Court rephrased the question before it as what "are the legal principles and rules applicable to the questions under what conditions and in accordance with what modalities a transfer of the Regional Office from Egypt may be effected?"[101] It considered that:

> International organizations are subjects of international law and, as such, are bound by any obligations incumbent upon them under general rules of international law, under their constitutions or under international agreements to which they are parties.[102]

The Court in this specific case held that mutual agreements between the WHO and Egypt constituted a contractual regime between the parties. Moreover, the legal relationship between the parties was that of a host state and an international organization, the very essence of which is a body of mutual obligations of co-operation and good faith. The Court then specified what these mutual obligations were. For this purpose it looked for guidance first to different host agreements, which it found to provide certain general indications of what the mutual obligations of organizations and host states to co-operate in good faith involve. Another source of guidance for the Court was the second paragraph of Article 56 of the Vienna Convention on the Law of Treaties and the corresponding provision in the ILC's draft articles on treaties between states and international organizations or between international organizations. The Court found that "these provisions are based on an obligation to act in good faith and have reasonable regard to the interests of the other party to the treaty."[103]

---

99 B. Tittemore, *supra* note 23, at 102-103.

100 Interpretation of the Agreement of 25 March 1951 between the WHO and Egypt, Advisory Opinion of 20 December 1980, 1980 ICJ Reports 4.

101 *Id.*, at 19.

102 *Id.*, at 20-21.

103 *Id.*, at 26.

The Court followed the written arguments presented to it by the United States in as far as it considered that obligations on the parties arose from general international law. The United States submitted that:

> The principle of pacta sunt servanda naturally governs the conduct of the parties as long as the Agreement remains in force. This principle is reflected in Article 26 of the Vienna Convention, which reads: 'Every treaty in force is binding upon the parties to it and must be performed by them in good faith.' The principle has also been repeatedly reaffirmed by the decisions of this Court and its predecessor.... The responsibilities discussed ... arise of general international law and came into being at the beginning of the relationship between the parties.[104]

In its Advisory Opinion of 21 June 1971 in the *Namibia (South West Africa)* case,[105] the ICJ applied general international law to the UN. In this case the Court dealt with, among other things, the legal consequences of General Assembly Resolution 2145,[106] which was concerned with the administration of the Mandated Territory of Namibia by South Africa. The resolution declared that South Africa had failed to fulfill its obligations under the mandate and that the mandate was therefore terminated. The Court held that the mandate over Namibia which had been conferred by the League of Nations on South Africa was an international agreement having the character of a treaty or convention. In examining this treaty relationship the Court stated that "it is appropriate to have regard to the general principles of international law regulating termination of a treaty relationship on account of breach."[107] In particular, the Court applied:

> the general principle of law that a right of termination on account of breach must be presumed to exist in respect of all treaties, except as regards provisions relating to the protection of the human person contained in treaties of a humanitarian character (as indicated in Art. 60, para. 5 of the Vienna Convention). The silence of a treaty as to the existence of such a right cannot be interpreted as implying the exclusion of a right which has its source outside of the treaty, in general international law, and is dependent on the occurrence of circumstances which are not normally envisaged when a treaty is concluded.[108]

---

104 Interpretation of the Agreement of 25 March 1951 between the WHO and Egypt (Pleadings, Oral Arguments, Documents), Written Statement of the United States of America, 182 (1951), at 205.

105 Legal Consequences for States of the Continued Presence of South Africa in Namibia (South West Africa) notwithstanding Security Council Resolution 276 (1970), Advisory Opinion of 21 June 1971, ICJ Reports 1971, at 16.

106 General Assembly Resolution 2145 of 27 October 1966, UN Doc. A/RES/2145 (1966).

107 *Supra* note 105, at 46.

108 *Id.*, at 47 (emphasis added).

The mandate was originally an agreement between the League of Nations and South Africa. The Court considered, however, that the relationship between the League and South Africa had been replaced on the basis of the UN Charter by a relationship between the UN and South Africa. Because the mandate was now an agreement to which the UN was party,[109] the general principle of law that a right of termination on account of breach must be presumed to exist in respect of all treaties applied to the UN.

There are several examples of general international law being applied *mutatis mutandis* to international organizations.[110] The law of treaties is one of these examples. From 1950 to 1960 the ILC prepared draft articles on the law of treaties. The question was frequently raised in the Commission whether the draft articles should apply not only to treaties between states but also to treaties concluded by international organizations. The Commission decided to exclude treaties concluded by international organizations from the draft articles. This course was also followed by the drafters of the 1969 Vienna Convention on the Law of Treaties.

In 1970 the ILC separately took up the question of treaties concluded between states and international organizations or between two or more international organizations. Paul Reuter was appointed Special Rapporteur for this topic and submitted eleven reports between 1971 and 1982. The approach taken by the Special Rapporteur was to take the 1969 Vienna Convention as a starting point. The general rules which applied to treaties concluded between states should in principle also apply to treaties to which international organizations were parties. He stated that "if international organizations were to be able to conclude treaties, general rules must be applied to them which, *a priori*, should be the same as those applicable to States."[111] For this reason the Commission followed as far as possible the articles of the 1969 Vienna Convention referring to treaties between states, for treaties between states and international organizations and between international organizations.[112] The Commission recognized that there are differences between international organizations and states which require modification of the rules for states to international organizations. It stated in its 1978 report that it should consider "what departures have to be made from the text of the Vienna Convention to take account of the inherent characteristics of international

109 *Id.*, at 37, 46.

110 See also Paul de Visscher, 54 (I) Annuaire IDI 43 (1971):

> L'extension analogique du droit interétatique aux activités des organisations internationales est un phénomène bien connu dont il existe de nombreux examples en matière de traités, de protection diplomatique et de responsabilité. Que cette extension doive se faire *mutatis mutandis*, en tenant compte de la condition spéciale des organisations internationales et de la compabilité de la norme en cause avec les finalités de ces organisations, est chose évidente.

111 YBILC 1979, Vol. I, at 66.

112 In his first report the Special Rapporteur stated as the first part of the work to be undertaken by the Commission: "all the provisions of the 1969 Convention must be examined article by article, in order to determine which of them would require drafting changes to adapt them to the agreements of international organizations."; YBILC 1972, Vol. II (Part One), at 78.

organizations, whose entire operation is based on functions and capacities less extensive than those of States."[113] The Commission adopted the draft articles on treaties between states and international organizations or between international organizations in 1982. These formed the basis for discussion in the Conference which negotiated the 1986 Convention on the Law of Treaties between States and International Organizations or between International Organizations.[114] The Conference took the same approach as the ILC in agreeing that the new instrument should make the general law of treaties applicable to international organizations, except in so far as there was a demonstrated need to adapt that law to the particularities of international organizations.[115] The Conference was even more limited in departing from the rules applicable between states than the ILC had been in its draft articles. This led one commentator to conclude that while:

> there had always been a certain assumption that agreements concluded by international organizations could and should be governed by the general international law of treaties, the Convention both confirms the assumption and circumscribed the questions with respect to which variations of the general rules are unavoidable.[116]

The application of rules of general international law to NATO can be based on the same considerations as apply to the WHO and the UN. The organization is an international legal person and in principle the relations of the organization with other persons of international law will be governed by international law.[117]

In this regard writers affirm that if the organization is an international legal person then it is subject to general international law rules of international humanitarian law.[118] These writers generally question whether NATO is an international legal person. As was discussed above, their arguments are not convincing.

The application of general international law to the UN is subject to the reservation that the Security Council may derogate from international law when it is acting under Chapter VII of the UN Charter when necessary to uphold or restore international peace and security. This was the specific intention of the drafters of the UN Charter as noted above.

---

113 YBILC 1978, Vol. II (Part Two), at 130.

114 Convention on the Law of Treaties between States and International Organizations or between International Organizations of 21 March 1986, reproduced in 25 ILM 543 (1986).

115 G. Gaja, *A 'New' Vienna Convention on Treaties between States and International Organizations or between International Organizations: A Critical Commentary*, 63 British Yearbook of International Law 253 (1987), at 258.

116 F. Morgenstern, *The Convention on the Law of Treaties between States and International Organizations or between International Organizations*, in Y. Dinstein (Ed.), International Law at a Time of Perplexity: Essays in Honour of Shabtai Rosenne 435 (1988), at 446.

117 See also L-A. Sicilianos, *L'Autorisation par le Conseil de Securité de Recourir à la Force: Une Tentative d'Evaluation*, 106 Revue Générale de Droit International Public 5 (2002), at 36.

118 See *e.g.* G. Moritz, *The Common Application of the Laws of War within the NATO-Forces*, 13 Military Law Review 1 (1961), at 5.

It may be noted that the application of international humanitarian law to international organizations is less revolutionary than the application of many other international rules, because international humanitarian law already provides for its direct application to non-state actors in the form of armed opposition groups.[119] Traditionally, the application of international humanitarian law to armed opposition groups remained very much within a state-centered system. It was dependent on formal recognition by states of the non-state group as belligerents.[120] Recognizing the status of belligerency placed the group on the same playing field as states. This state-centered system was abandoned with the adoption of common Article 3 to the 1949 Geneva Conventions, which states that certain rules apply in an armed conflict not of an international character. Common Article 3 notoriously does not define the term armed conflict, but it is clear that its field of application is determined by objective standards. It is generally recognized that the level of organization of the armed group or groups in question is an important aspect of the objective standard.[121] This aspect has been confirmed in the case law of the ICTY and ICTR. Trial Chamber I of the ICTR for example stated in its judgment in the *Akayesu* case in relation to common Article 3 that "an armed conflict is distinguished from internal disturbances by the level of intensity of the conflict and the degree of organization of the parties to the conflict."[122] Additional Protocol II to the 1949 Geneva Conventions, which develops and supplements common Article 3, sets out more clearly certain objective criteria for determining the field of application of the Protocol. The drafters of the Protocol considered it necessary to set out clear criteria because of the perceived ambiguity of the field of application of common Article 3, without modifying the existing conditions of application of that article. Most of the criteria listed in Article 1 of the Protocol, which defines its scope of application, refer directly or indirectly to the level of organization of the armed group involved in the conflict. This is obvious from the placement of the word 'organized' before the expression 'armed groups'. The existence of a responsible command and the exercise of control over part of a territory are also characteristics pointing to a certain level of organization. The article also makes clear that the requirement of a certain level of organization is not included for its own sake but because it makes it possible for the group in question to implement the substantive rules of the Protocol. The ICRC commentary to Article 1 states that the ability to implement the Protocol is "the fundamental criterion which justifies the other elements of the definition."[123] In other words, rules of international humanitarian law can be declared bind-

---

119 See generally L. Zegveld, Accountability of Armed Opposition Groups in International Law (2002).

120 H. Lauterpacht, Oppenheim's International Law: A Treatise, Vol. 2 (1952), at 249.

121 See para. 3.11.

122 *Prosecutor* v. *Jean-Paul Akayesu*, Judgment, Case No. ICTR-96-4-T, Tr. Ch. I, 2 September 1998, para. 625.

123 C. Pilloud *et al*, Commentary on the Additional Protocols of 8 June 1977 to the Geneva Conventions of 12 August 1949, at 1353 (1987). See also A. Castillo-Suárez, *Hors de Logique: Contemporary Issues in International Humanitarian Law as Applied to Internal Armed Conflict*, 15 American University International Law Review 1 (1999), at 91-92, and Zegveld, *supra* note 119, at 18.

ing on non-state actors because they are in a position to implement these rules. The elements of a number of amendments which were proposed at the 1949 diplomatic conference in the course of drafting common Article 3, including for example that the armed forces act under the direction of an organized authority and are prepared to observe the ordinary laws of war, support the conclusion that the ability of an armed group to implement the substantive obligations was considered important also for the application of common Article 3.[124] The requirement of a certain level of organization, which is derived from common Article 3, serves to establish that the armed group involved in the conflict is able to implement the substantive obligations of that article. In this context it is submitted that of the criteria mentioned in Article 1 of Additional Protocol II, the existence of a responsible command is relatively more important than control over part of the territory. It can be argued that humanitarian law is more easily applied by those who have a territorial base but that this does not mean that it cannot be implemented by a force which does not control a clearly defined area of territory.[125] A system of responsible command on the other hand seems indispensable.

Being under a responsible command is precisely a characteristic of peace support operations. UN peace support operations are under the exclusive operational command and control of the organization. On this basis it has been argued that:

> Only an entity that exercises command and control over military forces can order or fail to order compliance with humanitarian law, for example, what weapons are to be used, how civilian targets are to be avoided, and how prisoners of war and the wounded are to be treated. The United Nations exercises exclusive command and control over all troops comprising its forces, which are recruited and organized as national contingents. As a consequence of its command and control, the United Nations is deemed a party to armed conflict and thereby subject to the obligations of IHL.[126]

The operational control exercised by a NATO commander over a NATO peace support operation similarly makes that commander the principal person able to implement international humanitarian law.

This is not to argue that the fact that the ability of an international organization to implement the law makes it subject to that law, but simply that it is a small step from accepting the application of international humanitarian law to organized armed groups to accepting its application to international organizations.

---

124 See Final Record of the Diplomatic Conference of Geneva of 1949 , Vol. II-B, at 121.

125 C. Greenwood, *International Humanitarian Law, Revised Report for the Centennial Commemoration of the First Hague Peace Conference 1899*, in F. Kalshoven (Ed.), The Centennial of the First International Peace Conference: Reports & Conclusions 161 (2000), at 229-230.

126 R. Glick, *Lip Service to the Laws of War: Humanitarian Law and United Nations Armed Forces*, 17 Michigan Journal of International Law 53 (1995), at 97-98.

3.7 Equal application of international humanitarian law

It may be pointed out that for a number of decades after the establishment of the UN writers argued that international humanitarian law did not apply to the UN on the basis of a superior moral and legal position of the organization. Some members of a committee established in 1952 by the American Society of International Law to study the application of the laws of war to the organization for example held that:

> acceptance of the Charter by Member States meant acceptance by them of the superior legal position of the United Nations as regards the use of force and that, consequently, the United Nations may apply such rules as it wishes.[127]

On this view, a UN peace support operation is the equivalent of an international police force, and different standards should be applied to the police than to the criminal.[128] The doctrine of equal application that demands that international humanitarian law be applied in a similar manner to all parties to a conflict should make an exception for UN peace support operations.

Another version of this argument had the prohibition of the use of force as its starting point. The UN Charter in Article 2 (4) outlawed the use of force by states. Any state which had resorted to the prohibited use of force had, by its original criminality, forfeited the right to be treated according to the dictates of the law of war and toward such a state the UN could choose not to apply that law. In other words, a state had forfeited the right to be treated according to the law of war (*ius in bello*) because of its breach of the law against war (*ius ad bellum*).[129]

As a general proposition, these views no longer find much support. One reason is that the general view is that the *ius ad bellum* should be strictly distinguished from the *ius in bello*. A number of decisions by international and municipal tribunals after World War II rejected the view that an illegal aggressor cannot benefit from the rules

---

127 Report of Committee on Study of Legal Problems of the United Nations, *Should the Laws of War Apply to United Nations Enforcement Action?*, 46 ASIL Proc. 216 (1952), at 217.

128 A modern writer who adheres to this theory is Sharp. He states that:

> Coercive peace-keeping and peace-enforcement action under the Charter should not be viewed as mutual combat between states in a pre-Charter era when waging war was lawful. To the contrary, coercive peace-keeping and peace-enforcement actions are a concerted attempt by the international community to address a humanitarian crisis or thwart a threat to international peace and security. It is only a visceral fright of undermining the pre-Charter, outdated distinction between jus in bello and jus ad bellum that most rely upon to discredit a protected status for all U.N. forces, noncombatants and combatants alike.

Sharp does indicate that this view is not the *lex lata*, however. W. Sharp Jr., *Protecting the Avatars of International Peace and Security*, 7 Duke Journal of Comparative & International Law 93 (1996), at 164-165.

129 For a description and critique of this argument see D. Bowett, *supra* note 96, at 493-496.

of international humanitarian law.[130] The realization that the doctrine of equal application is essential to ensure respect for international humanitarian law gained increasing ground as it became clear that the prohibition of the use of force in Article 2 (4) of the UN Charter did not prevent armed conflicts from erupting and that forces fighting on behalf of the UN in Korea could not hope to benefit from international humanitarian law unless they themselves respected that law.[131] The doctrine was expressly reaffirmed in the preamble to Additional Protocol I of 1977, which states that the high contracting parties reaffirm:

> that the provisions of the Geneva Conventions of 12 August 1949 and of this Protocol must be fully applied in all circumstances to all persons who are protected by those instruments, without any adverse distinction based on the nature or origin of the armed conflict or on the causes espoused by or attributed to the Parties to the conflict.

A committee established by the prosecutor of the ICTY to review Operation Allied Force concluded the same in 2000:

> The precise linkage between *jus ad bellum* and *jus in bello* is not completely resolved. There were suggestions by the prosecution before the International Military Tribunal at Nuremberg and in some other post World War II war crimes cases that all of the killing and destruction caused by German forces were war crimes because the Germans were conducting an aggressive war. The courts were unreceptive to these arguments. Similarly, in the 1950's there was a debate concerning whether UN authorized forces were required to comply with the *jus in bello* as they represented the good side in a battle between good an evil. This debate died out as the participants realized that a certain crude reciprocity was essential if the law was to have any positive impact. An argument that the 'bad' side had to comply with the law while the 'good' side could violate it at will would be most unlikely to reduce human suffering in conflict.[132]

The gradual recognition that international humanitarian law must be applied equally between all parties is illustrated by studies by the Institut de Droit International from 1957 until 1975. These studies led to the adoption of resolutions supporting the equal application of international humanitarian law between a UN force and its opponent.[133]

---

130 See G. Schwarzenberger, *Legal Effects of Illegal War*, in K. Zemanek (Ed.), Völkerrecht und Rechtliches Weltbilt, Festschrift für Alfred Verdross 243 (1960), at 249.

131 J.L. Kunz, *The Laws of War*, 50 American Journal of International Law 313 (1956), at 319-320

132 *Supra* note 16, para. 32.

133 Resolution, Conditions of Application of Humanitarian Rules of Armed Conflict to Hostilities in which United Nations Forces may be Engaged, Annuaire IDI 54 (II) (1971) 465; Resolution, Conditions of Application of Rules, other than Humanitarian Rules, of Armed Conflict to Hostilities in which United Nations Forces may be Engaged, Annuaire IDI 56 (1975), at 541.

3.8 State practice and practice of the United Nations

3.8.1 A developing practice

Strictly speaking, the theory under which the organization is bound by international humanitarian law as an international person acting in a particular field does not require the international organization in question to contribute to the rules of customary international law concerned.[134] The organization is directly bound.[135] In practice, the policy of the organization is of course very important. However, until recently UN practice continued to give rise to questions concerning the legal basis and the extent of the applicability of international humanitarian law to UN peace support operations. Present practice by the UN and states is consistent with the view that the UN, its organs and peace support operations should be bound by rules of international humanitarian law. The development in practice started with the first United Nations Emergency Force and has for the moment culminated in the Statute of the Special Court for Sierra Leone of 2000.

3.8.2 Correspondence with the ICRC

After UNEF had been established in 1956, the President of the ICRC wrote a letter to the UN. He proposed that the force receive instructions ensuring that it comply with the 1949 Geneva Conventions if the circumstances should so require.[136] The UN replied that the force had been instructed to observe the principles and the spirit of the general international conventions concerning the behavior of military personnel. These instructions were included in the regulations issued for the force by the Secretary-General. The organization however did not specify the meaning of the term principles and spirit nor refer to specific conventions.

The President of the ICRC repeated his request after the establishment of ONUC. The ICRC also addressed a memorandum to the governments of states parties to the Geneva Conventions which were also members of the UN. This memorandum first referred to the undertaking by the UN to respect the principles and spirit of international humanitarian conventions. It noted that in reply to ICRC communications that:

> The International Committee of the Red Cross received assurances that the United Nations Organization would respect the principles of the international humanitarian Conventions and that instructions to that effect had been given to the troops placed under its command. It was pleased to place these assurances on record.[137]

---

134 N. Schermers & H. Blokker, International Institutional Law: Unity within Diversity 996 (2003).

135 Stone, *supra* note 94, at 315; C. Emanuelli, Les Actions Militaires de l'ONU et le Droit International Humanitaire 51 (1995).

136 Seyersted, *supra* note 22, at 190.

137 International Committee of the Red Cross memorandum, Application and dissemination of the Conventions, cited in Seyersted, *supra* note 22, at 191.

The memorandum not only asserted that the UN was bound by humanitarian law, but also that the troop contributing states remained bound with respect to the troops they contributed. It stated that:

> In fact, the United Nations Organization is not, as such, party to the Geneva Conventions. Consequently, each State is personally responsible for the application of these Conventions. It would therefore be highly desirable that such contingents receive, before leaving their own countries, instructions to conform to the provisions of the Geneva Conventions in the event of their finding themselves having to use force.[138]

The force's regulations contained a regulation on the observance of conventions. This regulation stated that the force would "observe the principles and spirit of the general humanitarian conventions."[139]

3.8.3 Practice in respect of ONUC

A clear recognition that the UN is bound by international humanitarian law are the lump sums which the organization paid to several states as a result of damages from the force's operations.[140] The lump sum agreements themselves did not refer to international humanitarian law, but in correspondence with the Soviet Union the Secretary-General stated that the policy of claims settlement in regard to the UN activities in the Congo was "reinforced by the principles set forth in the international conventions concerning the protection of the life and property of the civilian population during hostilities."[141] Apparently, the United Kingdom also considered a claim against the UN on the ground that actions of the UN force were contrary to the 1907 Hague Regulations.[142]

Seyersted describes that operations in the Congo gave rise to accusations from both sides of violations of international humanitarian law.[143] In his report on the developments in Elisabethville from 8 to 14 December 1961 for example, the Officer-in-Charge of the United Nations Operation stated that the "Katangese forces regularly abused the Red Cross symbol, contrary to the law of war."[144] Belgium urged the Secretary-General to issue immediate instructions that United Nations troops should scrupulously respect the obligations of the Geneva Convention and made a number of specific charges of breaches of international humanitarian law. In response, the UN refuted the factual accuracy of the charges but not the applicability of international

138 *Id.*

139 ONUC Regulations of 15 July 1963, UN Doc. ST/SGB/ONUC/1, Regulation 43.

140 See para. 2.9.1.

141 UN Doc. S/6589.

142 Simmonds, *supra* note 23, at 238.

143 Seyersted, *supra* note 22, at 192-197.

144 United Nations Review, IX, No. 1 (January 1962), at 52.

humanitarian law.[145] The ICRC maintained representatives in the Congo who intervened on a number of occasions in order to secure observance of international humanitarian law, *inter alia* by visiting persons detained by ONUC.[146]

3.8.4 UNFICYP Regulations

The regulations enacted for the United Nations Force in Cyprus, established in 1964, included a similar but slightly differently worded provision as the regulations for previous forces on the application of international humanitarian law.[147] The organization now also specified, albeit in a non-exhaustive manner, the general international conventions in question in the participating states agreements. The agreements stated in relation to the force regulations that:

> The international Conventions referred to in this Regulation include inter alia, the Geneva (Red Cross) Conventions of 12 August 1949 to which your Government is a party and the UNESCO Convention on the Protection of Cultural Property in the Event of Armed Conflict.[148]

3.8.5 Travaux préparatoires *of Additional Protocol I*

The matter of the application of humanitarian law to United Nations peace support operations arose during the 1971 Conference of Government Experts, leading up to the adoption of Additional Protocol I. The ICRC drew attention to the matter as it had done in respect of specific operations. In response, the representative of the Secretary-General of the UN at the Conference stated that:

> The problem of applying the Geneva Conventions to the United Nations Peace-Keeping Forces was not a topical issue and should not therefore concern the Conference. In fact, each regulation issued by the Secretary-General for those forces, such as that currently applying to the peace-keeping forces in Cyprus, implied not only respect for the letter of international Conventions applying to the conduct of military staff but also the most scrupulous respect for the spirit of such treaties.[149]

At the second session of the Conference in 1972, the representative of the Secretary-General repeated the explanations given during the first session. He added that since

145 UN Doc. S/5025 of 15 December 1961.

146 Annual Report of the International Committee of the Red Cross 1961, at 10-11.

147 UNFICYP Regulations of 25 April 1964, 555 UNTS 132, regulation 40. Observance of Conventions. "The Force shall observe and respect the principles and spirit of the general international Conventions applicable to the conduct of military personnel."

148 See Exchange of letters (with annexes) constituting an agreement concerning the service with the United Nations Peace-Keeping Force in Cyprus of the national contingent provided by the Government of Canada, New York, 21 February 1966, 555 UNTS 120, at 126.

149 *Supra* note 24, at 52, para. 311.

the UN had neither territorial authority nor criminal or disciplinary jurisdiction, it was for the time being incapable of implementing the Geneva Conventions. The representative underscored that:

> Though the United Nations might for the present lack the necessary authority to ensure respect for the Conventions of Geneva, guarantees to that effect were inscribed in the bilateral agreements with the Governments furnishing troops for the United Nations forces. Those Governments (which were Parties to the Conventions of Geneva) had in particular undertaken to furnish instructed troops and to ensure that their contingents respect the international humanitarian norms.[150]

At first sight this statement seems to reject the idea that principles or rules of international humanitarian law apply to the UN as an organization, and to state that only troop contributing states are bound by those rules. Yet this does not seem to have been UN policy in 1972. A legal opinion of the Secretariat of that year rather emphasizes the practical obstacles for the organization in fulfilling certain obligations of international humanitarian law which are an obstacle to becoming party to humanitarian law treaties, but it does not exclude that the organization is bound by certain rules of international humanitarian law:

> The United Nations is not substantively in a position to become a party to the 1949 Conventions, which contain many obligations that can only be discharged by the exercise of juridical and administrative powers which the Organization does not possess, such as the authority to exercise criminal jurisdiction over members of the Forces, or administrative competence relating to territorial sovereignty. Thus the United Nations is unable to fulfill obligations which for their execution require the exercise of powers not granted to the Organization, and therefore cannot accede to the Conventions.
> However, the United Nations by exchanges of letters, binds governments contributing contingents to its Forces to ensure respect for the Conventions by their respective contingents, and it has itself requested the Forces, in Regulations issued by the Organization, to respect the humanitarian principles and spirit of the Conventions.[151]

When in 1978 the Security Council established the United Nations Interim Force in Lebanon,[152] the President of the ICRC continued his practice of writing letters to the UN Secretary-General to draw attention to respect for international humanitarian law. In a letter of 23 October 1978 the Secretary-General replied that the principles of humanitarian law "must, should the need arise, be applied within the framework of the operations carried out by United Nations forces."[153]

---

150 *Supra* note 25, at 194, para. 4.166.

151 Question of the Possible Accession of Intergovernmental Organizations to the Geneva Conventions for the Protection of War Victims of 15 June 1972, 1972 UNJY 153-154.

152 Security Council Resolution 425 of 19 March 1978, UN Doc. S/RES/425.

153 U. Palwankar, *Applicability of International Humanitarian Law to United Nations Peacekeeping Forces*, 75 International Review of the Red Cross 227 (1993), at 232.

Several months earlier the organization had issued an interoffice memorandum to all commanders of UN forces. This memorandum specified that, in cases where the forces have to use their weapons in accordance with their mandate, the principles and spirit of the rules of international humanitarian law should apply, as laid down in the Geneva Conventions of 1949, the Additional Protocols of 1977 and elsewhere.[154]

3.8.6 Model Participating State Agreement

In 1991 the Secretary-General presented a model participating state agreement based on established practice and previous agreements.[155] Article 28 of the model agreement provides that:

> [The United Nations peace-keeping operation] shall observe and respect the principles and spirit of the general international conventions applicable to the conduct of military personnel. The international conventions referred to above include the four Geneva Conventions of 12 August 1949 and their Additional Protocols of 8 June 1977 and the UNESCO Convention of 14 May 1954 on the Protection of Cultural Property in the event of armed conflict. [The Participating State] shall therefore ensure that the members of its national contingent serving with [the United Nations peace-keeping operation] be fully acquainted with the principles and spirit of these Conventions.

This provision follows the practice developed between the UN and participating states. The model follows established practice in as much as previous contributing states agreements, in themselves or by reference to force regulations, included a similar obligation. In practice, however, formal agreements along the lines of the model agreement are not always concluded with troop contributing states.[156]

3.8.7 Status of Forces Agreements

In contrast to troop contributing agreements, status of forces agreements for a long time did not include a provision on international humanitarian law. The 1990 model status of forces agreement does not include such a provision either. These agreements did not entail the direct treaty-based responsibility of the organization toward host states to ensure respect for international humanitarian law by members of its forces.[157] In 1992 such a provision on international humanitarian law was included for the first time in the SOFA with Rwanda. Article 7 of the agreement stated that:

> The United Nations shall ensure that UNAMIR carries out its operations in Rwanda in a manner fully consistent with the principles and spirit of the general conventions

154 *Id.*

155 See para. 1.8.2.

156 Information provided to the author by Professor Paul Szasz.

157 Shraga, *supra* note 95, at 68.

> applicable to the conduct of military personnel. The relevant instruments include the four Geneva Conventions of 12 August 1949 and the additional Protocols thereto of 8 June 1977, and the UNESCO Convention for the Protection of Cultural Property in the event of Armed Conflict of 14 May 1954;[158]

Other status of forces agreements concluded since 1992 contained a similar clause on respect for international humanitarian law.[159]

It may be noted that all the statements and instruments relating to the application of international humanitarian law to UN peace support operations until this point use the term 'principles and spirit of international humanitarian law'. The precise content of the term however was never defined. On the one hand it definitely implied that not all the rules of the relevant conventions applied. On the other hand it was not clear which rules did apply, nor even which conventions other than the ones expressly named were relevant.[160] After the adoption of the 1977 Additional Protocols a reference to these conventions was included in relevant agreements, but did the principles and spirit of the 1980 Conventional Weapons Convention or the 1997 Ottawa Convention on the prohibition of anti-personnel landmines, for example, also become applicable?

3.8.8 Convention on the Safety of United Nations and Associated Personnel

The question of the applicability of international humanitarian law was indirectly addressed during the drafting of the Convention on the Safety of United Nations and Associated Personnel. The rationale of the convention is the concern over an increase in attacks on United Nations personnel in general, and members of peace support operations in particular, in the early 1990s, *inter alia* as a result of new types of peace support operations being deployed. The UN Secretary-General stated in his 1992 'An Agenda for Peace' that "innovative measures will be required to deal with the dangers facing United Nations personnel."[161] In 1993 the Secretary-General submitted a report to the Security Council at the request of the Council proposing *inter alia* the negotiation of a new legal instrument for the protection of UN personnel. [162]

In December 1993 the General Assembly established an *ad hoc* committee to elaborate such a convention. The convention drafted by the committee was adopted by the General Assembly on 9 December 1994, and entered into force on 15 January

158 Agreement between the United Nations and the Government of the Republic of Rwanda on the Status of the United Nations Assistance Mission for Rwanda of 5 November 1993, UNTS 1748.

159 For example the Agreement between the United Nations and the Government of the Republic of Croatia on the Status of the United Nations Confidence Restoration Operation in Croatia of 15 May 1995, UNTS 1864.

160 C. Greenwood, *supra* note 23, at 23.

161 UN Doc. S/24111 of 17 June 1992, reproduced in 31 ILM 953 (1992), para. 66.

162 UN Doc. A/48/349, para 34. See also UN Doc. A/AC.242/1, paras. 11-16 (1994).

1999.[163] The convention is not directly concerned with the application of international humanitarian law to UN operations. Its principal function is to oblige states parties to criminalize attacks on UN and associated personnel and to prosecute or extradite alleged offenders. Precisely this function made it necessary to consider the application of international humanitarian law. The negotiators realized that it was necessary to have a clear separation between the new legal regime under the instrument being drafted and international humanitarian law. One negotiator stated that:

> One important reason for this was to avoid undermining the Geneva Conventions, which rely in part for their effectiveness on all forces being treated equally. It was widely held that the new Convention should not criminalize attacks on UN forces engaged as combatants in an international armed conflict, as this could (by making the very act of waging war against the United Nations a criminal offense, and thus favoring one side over the other) lessen the willingness of opposing forces to adhere to the laws of war.[164]

In other words, the negotiators held that the convention should cease to apply where international humanitarian law starts to apply to members of UN operations as combatants.

In principle, the negotiators accepted the idea that UN operations can become a party to an armed conflict and rejected notions of the UN as an international police force morally and legally superior to its opponents. It remained to define the point at which an operation goes from being protected by the convention to being a party to an armed conflict. A number of provisions of the convention are relevant to this determination.

The first relevant provision is Article 1 (1). This article, together with Article 2 (1), defines the scope of application of the convention. The convention is applicable to UN operations, which are defined in Article 1 (1) as operations:

> established by the competent organ of the United Nations in accordance with the Charter of the United Nations and conducted under United Nations authority and control

The wording of this provision was much debated in the *ad hoc* committee. A number of states wanted to restrict the scope of application of the convention to operations mandated by the Security Council and under the command or the control of the UN itself. Other states felt that operations established by the General Assembly should also be included. Yet again other states advocated a broad approach whereby the convention would also cover operations authorized under Chapter VII of the UN Charter conducted under the control and supervision of the UN, presumably including opera-

---

163 Convention on the Safety of United Nations and Associated Personnel, reproduced in 34 ILM 482 (1995).

164 E. Bloom, *Protecting Peacekeepers: The Convention on the Safety of United Nations and Associated Personnel*, 89 American Journal of International Law 621 (1995), at 625.

tions under the command and control of states or regional organizations.[165] The final wording of the provision is a heavily negotiated compromise. While some writers state that the definition excludes operations authorized by the UN but controlled by individual member states or groups of member states, or by regional organizations, such as *Opération Turquoise* carried out under French command and control,[166] other writers maintain that such operations are covered by the convention.[167] States parties also interpret the provision differently. The government of the Netherlands for example holds that KFOR is not covered by the convention because it is not under the control of the UN.[168] The United States on the other hand would presumably consider that KFOR is in fact covered, as it considered that the multinational force in Haiti and assistance provided by NATO to UNPROFOR in Bosnia were covered.[169]

The second relevant provision is Article 2 (2) of the convention. This provision was intended as a demarcation between the application of the convention regime and international humanitarian law:

> This Convention shall not apply to a United Nations operation authorized by the Security Council as an enforcement action under Chapter VII of the Charter of the United Nations in which any of the personnel are engaged as combatants against organized armed forces and to which the law of international armed conflict applies.

This provision is also a compromise between opposing positions. Its deliberate ambiguity creates confusion about the scope of the exclusion clause and the point at which international humanitarian law starts to apply.

First, it is unclear how the term 'authorized' should be interpreted, especially if it is seen in relation to the term 'under United Nations control and authority' in Article 1. The view that seems to have prevailed in the discussions of the draft convention in the Sixth Committee of the General Assembly favors a strict interpretation of the term authorized, but the above-mentioned United States view cannot be discounted.[170]

Secondly, the wording of the provision suggests that operations established under Chapter VI, or VI 1/2, of the United Nations Charter are *a priori* covered by the convention and thus excluded from the regime of international humanitarian law. As noted, the drafters of the convention considered that the two regimes are mutually exclusive.[171] An interpretation in which operations under Chapter VI or VI 1/2 are *a*

165 Report of the Ad Hoc Committee on the Work carried out during the Period from 28 March to 8 April 1994 of 13 April 1994, UN Doc. A/AC.242/2, para. 47, 168.

166 C. Greenwood, *Protection of Peacekeepers: The Legal Regime*, 7 Duke Journal of Comparative & International Law 185 (1996), at 195.

167 Bloom, *supra* note 164, at 623.

168 Handelingen II 2001-02, 27454 (R 1668), nr. 7.

169 See United States explanation of vote, UN Doc. A/49/PV 84, at 15.

170 See Shraga, *supra* note 95, at 76.

171 C. Emanuelli, *The Protection Afforded to Humanitarian Assistance Personnel under the Convention on the Safety of United Nations and Associated Personnel*, 6 Humanitäres Völkerrecht Informationsschriften 4 (1990), at 6.

priori covered by the convention is supported by the statement by one of the sponsors of the draft convention:

> After pointing out that the instrument under elaboration was not intended to deal with situations where the United Nations would be acting as a party to a conflict, he observed that States parties to a conflict were always under an obligation to distinguish between civilians and combatants and between civilian objects and military objectives, the consequence being that United Nations personnel and their property could never be made the object of attack while conducting traditional peace-keeping operations or enforcement operations ... He added that if the United Nations, presumably further to a decision of the Security Council, assumed the status of a party to a conflict, then the normal laws of war would apply, with the opposing forces being placed on an equal footing.[172]

The delegation in question assumed that the mandate of an operation under Chapter VI or VI 1/2 does not allow it to become involved in hostilities and therefore such an operation will never become a party to an armed conflict. Its premise is the principle of the non-use of force except in self-defense in traditional peace support operations. Such an argument is also maintained by a number of authors, but it does not reflect the reality that even operations which are not established under Chapter VII of the UN Charter can become involved in protracted hostilities to which the law of armed conflict would apply if the hostilities took place between states. It may be recalled that the concept of self-defense is interpreted broadly in respect of UN peace support operations as including the use of force for a variety of purposes. In addition, the fact that the mandate of an operation only allows the limited use of force does not automatically guarantee that in practice there will be minimal use of force. The principle of the non-use of force except in self-defense is not always respected and the Brahimi Report seems to advocate a broad definition of the term. A peace support operation which exercises its right to self-defense might well find itself engaged in protracted hostilities with organized armed forces, which would be subject to the law of armed conflict. An interpretation of Article 2 (2) to the effect that personnel of operations under Chapter VI or VI 1/2 are never bound by international humanitarian law as combatants, would also run counter to the most widely held opinions and the practice of the UN itself. As noted, the UN has included provisions on the application of international humanitarian law in regulations and SOFAs in respect of operations not established under Chapter VII of the UN Charter. The government of the Netherlands therefore prefers to interpret the provision as not automatically excluding operations under Chapter VI or VI 1/2 from the application of international humanitarian law. It has stated that:

> In principle international humanitarian law will not be applicable to operations under Chapter VI of the Charter, since that Chapter exclusively concerns the peaceful settlement of disputes. However, it cannot be excluded that in case it exercises its

172 *Supra* note 165, para. 76.

> right to self-defense – even if based on Chapter VI – a United Nations peace support operation becomes engaged in hostilities, and that international humanitarian law becomes applicable.[173]

Article 2 (2) could also be read as excluding situations in which an operation is engaged as a party to a non-international armed conflict, because the article refers to the law of international armed conflict only. The wording suggests that if an operation would be engaged in hostilities with a non-state entity such an operation would not be excluded from the Convention's scope because the conflict would be non-international.[174] The *travaux préparatoires* of the convention suggest that some delegations considered this an appropriate interpretation of Article 2 (2). The report of the *ad hoc* Committee states in regard to a proposal that was included in the article that several delegations:

> noted that, under the proposal, the convention would not apply in respect of an operation: (a) authorized by the Security Council as an enforcement action; (b) involving an international armed conflict to which common article 2 of the 1949 Geneva Conventions applied; and (c) involving United Nations personnel as a party to the conflict.[175]

On the other hand, the chairman of the *ad hoc* Committee writes that the wording in Article 2 (2) proved acceptable in the end because it was generally agreed that it was impossible for the UN itself to be involved in an internal armed conflict since once UN or associated personnel became engaged in conflict with a local force the conflict becomes by definition international in character.[176] This appears to be a more acceptable interpretation.

The third relevant provision is Article 20 (a). This provision is a so-called 'savings clause' in respect of the application of international humanitarian law. It was introduced by five Nordic countries which saw the need for a provision on obligations relating to the observance of international humanitarian law by the UN itself.[177] Article 20 (a) of the convention states that nothing in the convention shall affect:

---

173 In beginsel zal het internationale humanitaire recht niet van toepassing zijn op operaties onder hoofdstuk VI van het Handvest, welk hoofdstuk immers uitsluitend de vreedzame regeling van geschillen betreft. Niet is echter per definitie uitgesloten dat in situaties van zelfverdediging een VN-operatie – hoewel gebaseerd op hoofdstuk VI – betrokken raakt bij het gebruik van geweld, en dat internationaal humanitair recht van toepassing is.

Bijlagen Handelingen II 2001-02, 27454 (R 1668), nr. 7. English translation by the author.

174 See C. Bourloyannis-Vrailas, *The Convention on the Safety of United Nations and Associated Personnel*, 44 International & Comparative Law Quarterly 561 (1995), at 568.

175 *Supra* note 165, para. 169.

176 P. Kirsch, *The Convention on the Safety of United Nations and Associated Personnel*, 2 International Peacekeeping 102 (1995), at 105.

177 M.J. Thwaites, *Negotiating a Convention on the Safety of UN Personnel*, in H. Smith (Ed.), International Peacekeeping; Building on the Cambodian Experience 169 (1994), at 170.

> The applicability of International Humanitarian Law and universally recognized standards of human rights as contained in international instruments in relation to the protection of United Nations operations and United Nations and associated personnel or the responsibility of such personnel to respect such law and standards.

The consequences of this provision are not entirely clear. The provision can be interpreted in the sense that in situations in which the convention is not applicable on the basis of Article 2 (2), UN personnel have a responsibility to respect international humanitarian law, adding nothing to what is already stated in Article 2 (2). An alternative interpretation is that international humanitarian law and the convention can apply simultaneously.[178] In this case however there is a contradiction with the purported objective of the negotiators to clearly distinguish between situations in which the convention is applicable and situations in which international humanitarian law applies. In any event, however, Article 20 (a) makes clear that although in such a case a UN operation could be a party to an armed conflict while its opponents would not have the combatant's privilege, *i.e.* be criminally responsible for taking part in the armed conflict, this would not release the UN operation from the obligation to respect international humanitarian law.

In short, the convention seems to reaffirm that a UN peace support operation can be a party to an armed conflict and be bound to respect international humanitarian law. The compromise wording of its most important provisions however creates ambiguity concerning the point at which international humanitarian law becomes applicable. In this respect the UN Secretary-General stated in 2000 that:

> It will eventually be for the practice of States or any of the competent national or international jurisdictions, to clearly delineate the distinction between the mutually exclusive regimes of International Humanitarian Law and the protective regime of the Convention. In the final analysis, it is not the nature of the conflict which should determine the applicability of International Humanitarian Law or that of the Convention, but whether in any type of conflict, members of United Nations peacekeeping operations are actively engaged therein as combatants, or are otherwise entitled to the protection given to civilians under the international law of armed conflict.[179]

3.8.9 Secretary-General's Bulletin on the Observance by United Nations Forces of International Humanitarian Law

The applicability of international humanitarian law to UN peace support operations was unequivocally reaffirmed by the promulgation by the United Nations Secretary-

---

178 As suggested by Bourloyannis-Vrailas, *supra* note 174, at 583-584, and by A. Bouvier, *Convention on the Safety of United Nations and Associated Personnel: Presentation and Analysis*, 35 International Review of the Red Cross 638 (1995).

179 Report of the Secretary-General, Scope of Legal Protection under the Convention on the Safety of United Nations and Associated Personnel of 21 November 2000, UN Doc. A/55/637, footnote 3.

General in 1999 of the Secretary-General's Bulletin on Observance by United Nations Forces of International Humanitarian Law.[180]

The negotiations for the Convention on the Safety of United Nations and Associated Personnel, as well as incidents in peace support operations in Somalia and the former Yugoslavia allegedly constituting breaches of international humanitarian law, demonstrated the need for a clear policy on the application of international humanitarian law to UN peace support operations. In 1995 the United Nations Special Committee on Peacekeeping Operations requested the Secretary-General to "complete the elaboration of a code of conduct for United Nations peace-keeping personnel, consistent with applicable International Humanitarian Law."[181] The ICRC, as a strong protagonist of such a code, played an important role in its drafting. It organized two meetings of experts on the applicability of international humanitarian law to UN forces in 1995. A half-dozen experts from academic and military circles and various UN representatives as well as legal experts from the ICRC attended the meetings. The participants analyzed provisions of humanitarian law in order to determine their applicability to peacekeeping forces and drew up a draft code of conduct. The project was subsequently reviewed jointly by the ICRC and the UN Secretariat. On 10 May 1996 the 'Guidelines for UN forces regarding respect for International Humanitarian Law' were presented to the Secretary-General.[182] The term 'Guidelines' was later replaced with 'Directives'. The Directives were circulated for comments by member states at the end of June 1999, followed by a meeting of the Office of Legal Affairs and the Department of Peacekeeping Operations with member states for a final exchange of views on the text.[183] The directives were then finalized and issued by the Secretary-General on 6 August 1999.

The Bulletin is subdivided into ten sections together comprising 34 articles. Sections 1 and 2 address the Bulletin's field of application and its relation to certain other instruments and sources of law. Sections 3 and 4 deal with Status of Forces Agreements and jurisdiction over personnel of a UN force. Sections 5-9 are concerned with different groupings of international humanitarian law provisions. Finally, section 10 states that the Bulletin shall enter into force on 12 August 1999, exactly fifty years after the adoption of the Geneva Conventions of 1949.

The preamble to the Bulletin declares that it is promulgated "for the purpose of setting out fundamental principles and rules of International Humanitarian Law applicable to United Nations forces conducting operations under United Nations command and control." The difference between the terms 'principles and rules', and

180 U.N. Secretary-General's Bulletin on the Observance by United Nations Forces of International Humanitarian Law, 38 ILM 1656. See generally A. Ryniker, *Respect du Droit International Humanitaire par les Forces des Nations Unies*, 81 International Review of the Red Cross 795 (1999); M. Zwanenburg, *The Secretary-General's Bulletin on Observance by United Nations Forces of International Humanitarian Law*, 39 Military Law and Law of War Review 14 (2000).

181 Report of the Special Committee on Peacekeeping Operations, UN Doc. A/50/230, para. 73

182 ICRC Press Release, 15 May 1996.

183 Report of the Secretary-General on the Implementation of the Recommendations of the Special Committee on Peacekeeping Operations of 6 January 2000, UN Doc. A/54/670, para. 42.

'principles and spirit' traditionally used by the UN, is immediately apparent. It underlines the fact that this is the first time the UN has issued specific rules of humanitarian law for its forces in contrast to the very general undertaking to respect the principles and spirit of humanitarian law. In a 2001 report the UN Secretary-General reaffirmed that the Bulletin signals "formal recognition of the applicability of International Humanitarian Law to United Nations peace operations."[184]

The Bulletin itself however does not state the legal basis for such a formal recognition. In particular, it does not specify whether the provisions of the Bulletin are simply a codification of customary international law that was already considered applicable, or whether the rules have a constitutive character. During one of the meetings of experts organized by the ICRC an expert remarked that the exercise amounted to identifying what rules were customary law, since those automatically applied to the UN, but other experts held that going through the rules to identify which applied tended in itself to support the position that unless the UN declared itself bound it was not bound by treaty rules or customary rules of international humanitarian law.[185]

From the perspective of the content of the substantive rules of the Bulletin it seems that not all the customary rules of international law are included, but rather a summary of what were considered the most important rules in the context of peace support operations.

It appears that there is agreement between states that at least a number of rules which are not included in the Bulletin constitute customary international law, and the Nuremberg Tribunal held that the entire 1907 Hague Regulations constitute customary international law. The ICRC for example holds that the Bulletin only summarizes some of the core rules of humanitarian law.[186] In this respect the choice of particular rules to be included, such as for example Section 7.3, which states that women shall be especially protected against any attack, in particular against rape, enforced prostitution or any other form of indecent assault, may have been influenced by specific incidents in peace support operations.

On the other hand, the Bulletin also includes several rules which are probably not of a customary law character. Shraga states in this respect that:

> concretizing the 'principles and spirit' of the Geneva Conventions and their Additional Protocols, the Secretary-General did not consider himself necessarily constrained by the customary international law provisions of the Conventions and Protocols as the lowest common denominator by which all national contingents would otherwise be bound.[187]

---

184 Road Map towards the implementation of the United Nations Millenium Declaration of 6 September 2001, UN Doc. A/56/326, para. 19.

185 Meeting of Experts on the Applicability of International Humanitarian Law to United Nations Forces, Geneva, 6-8 March 1995, at 26. Copy on file with the author.

186 Statement to the Fourth Committee of the General Assembly, 20 October 1999.

187 D. Shraga, *UN Peacekeeping Operations: Applicability of International Humanitarian Law and Responsibility for Operations-Related Damage*, 94 American Journal of International Law 406 (2000), at 408.

In this respect it must be noted that the Bulletin is intended especially as a teaching tool, in other words to acquaint members of UN peace support operations with the principles and rules of international humanitarian law.[188] The direct legal basis for the obligation to instruct personnel of peace support operations is found in Status of Forces Agreements, in which the UN undertakes to ensure that the members of the military section of an operation are made duly aware of the principles and spirit of the general conventions applicable to the conduct of military personnel.[189] The purpose of instruction may require that the provisions of international humanitarian law are summarized, in the same way as national armed forces have codes of conduct which include general references to international humanitarian law. The ultimate legal basis for the applicability of the majority of the rules in the Bulletin, however, is that they constitute customary international law.[190] Shraga states in respect of the rules in the Bulletin which are customary international law that "their inclusion amounted above all to an undertaking to abide by the highest standard of conduct within the general consensus of states."[191]

In short, the Bulletin reaffirms the applicability of the customary international law of armed conflict to the UN. It is not a unilateral act of the UN. This is clear from its main function as a teaching tool, as well as from its promulgation as a Secretary-General's Bulletin. A Secretary-General's Bulletin is an internal United Nations document, more specifically an administrative issuance by the Secretary-General.[192] It is a subsidiary instrument elaborating the Staff Rules issued by the Secretary-General as the highest administrative authority of the organization.[193] Staff Rules in turn elaborate Staff Regulations, which embody the fundamental conditions of service and the basic rights, duties and obligations of the Secretariat.[194]

---

188 See Report of the Secretary-General to the Security Council on the Protection of Civilians in Armed Conflict of 8 September 1999, UN Doc. S/1999/957, para. 61:

> I have also recently promulgated a Secretary-General's bulletin on the observance of International Humanitarian Law by members of United Nations forces, instructing them on the basic principles and rules governing means and methods of warfare and the protection of civilians and other protected persons.

189 See *e.g.* Agreement between the United Nations and the Government of the Republic of Rwanda on the Status of the United Nations Assistance Mission for Rwanda of 5 November 1993, UNTS 1748, Article 7.

190 Interview by the author with a senior United Nations official, 17 September 2002.

191 Shraga, *supra* note 187, at 408.

192 See: Secretary-General's Bulletin, Procedures for the Promulgation of Administrative Issuances of 28 May 1997, ST/SGB/1997/1.

193 C.F. Amerasinghe, The Law of the International Civil Service: As Applied by International Administrative Tribunals, vol. I, at 146 (1988).

194 *Id.*, at 1 (Scope and purpose of Staff Regulations of the United Nations). See also R. Zacklin, *United Nations Management of Legal Issues*, in J. Howard & B. Oswald (Eds.), The Rule of Law on Peace Operations 155 (2002), at 124.

3.8.10 Statute of the International Criminal Court

The Statute of the International Criminal Court (ICC), adopted in 1998 in Rome, also indirectly reaffirms the applicability of international humanitarian law to peace support operations. In 1995 the United Nations legal counsel stated that:

> The idea that the United Nations should be directly bound by the rules of International Humanitarian Law is certainly not new, and I am convinced that this matter will be discussed with renewed intensity in the context of the establishment of an international criminal court.[195]

The discussion the legal counsel referred to did not take place as extensively as he suggested. Prior to the Rome Conference, there were some suggestions that peace support operations should be excluded from the jurisdiction of the Court. France proposed the inclusion of a provision in the Statute according to which "persons who have carried out acts ordered by the Security Council or in accordance with a mandate issued by it shall not be criminally responsible before the Court."[196] This proposal did not enjoy much support, however, and a footnote to the report of the intersessional meeting of the Preparatory Committee in Zutphen in 1998 states that "There were widespread doubts about the contents and the placement of this paragraph."[197] The draft statute in the final report of the Preparatory Committee for an International Criminal Court, which formed the basis for negotiations at the Rome Conference, did not include a provision exempting peace support operations.[198] On the contrary, the draft statute provided that the official position of a person was irrelevant, indicating the members of peace support operations are not above the law. Articles 25 and 27 of the Rome Statute make clear that no person is exempted from the application of the Statute, in particular not on the basis of immunities or special procedural rules which may attach to the official capacity of a person. Although members of peace support operations are not expressly mentioned they obviously fall within the scope of these articles.[199]

The concerns of the United States regarding investigations and prosecutions by the ICC of United States personnel involved in peace support operations established or authorized by the UN are well known,[200] but these concerns have focused on

195 H. Corell, *Nuremberg and the Development of an International Criminal Court*, 149 Military Law Review 87 (1995), at 99.

196 Decisions taken by the Preparatory Committee at its session held from 1 to 12 December 1997, UN Doc. A/AC.249/1997/L.9/Rev.1, at 23.

197 Report of the Intersessional Meeting from 19 to 30 January 1998 in Zutphen, the Netherlands, UN Doc. A/AC.249/1998/L.13, at 54.

198 Final report of the Preparatory Committee for the Establishment of an International Criminal Court of 14 April 1998, UN Doc. A/CONF.183/2/Add.1.

199 C. Stahn, *The Ambiguities of Security Council Resolution 1422*, 14 European Journal of International Law 85 (2003).

200 See *e.g.* W. Lietzau, *International Criminal Law after Rome: Concerns from a U.S. Military Perspective*, 64 Law and Contemporary Problems 119 (2001).

immunity from jurisdiction of United States personnel instead of the applicable law. The United States from an early stage was concerned that the Court should only have jurisdiction over members of its armed forces in general, and those members involved in operations established or authorized by the UN in particular, in exceptional cases. An important reason given for this concern was the fear of politicized proceedings against United States armed forces personnel before the ICC.[201] To prevent such proceedings, the United States submitted several proposals before, during and after the Rome Conference, all of which concerned limits to the exercise of the ICC's jurisdiction, but not to the law applicable to peace support operations.[202] In other words, the United States has been concerned with achieving immunity from jurisdiction for peace support operations, implying that in principle jurisdiction exists. The United States' efforts culminated in the adoption of Security Council Resolution 1422 on 12 July 2002.[203] The very fact that the United States has been concerned with the possibility of prosecution of peace support operations' personnel by the Court implies that it considers that the personnel in question is bound by international humanitarian law and consequently is capable of committing war crimes within the jurisdiction of the Court. This is reaffirmed by the text of Resolution 1422 in which the Security Council, acting under Chapter VII of the United Nations Charter:

> Requests, consistent with the provisions of Article 16 of the Rome Statute, that the ICC, if a case arises involving current or former officials or personnel from a contributing State not a Party to the Rome Statute over acts or omissions relating to a United Nations established or authorized operation, shall for a twelve-month period starting 1 July 2002 not commence or proceed with investigation or prosecution of any such case, unless the Security Council decides otherwise;

Clearly, such a request would be unnecessary in respect of an investigation or prosecution concerning alleged breaches of international humanitarian law if that law is not applicable. The Security Council renewed the immunity conferred for conduct in UN established or authorized operations for another twelve months on 12 June 2003, in Resolution 1487.[204] The adoption of this resolution followed after strong diplomatic pressure from the United States.[205]

On 1 August 2003 the Security Council, acting under Chapter VII of the United Nations Charter, authorized a multinational force to support the implementation of

---

201 See Ambassador Bill Richardson, United States Permanent Representative to the United Nations Statement at the U.N. Plenipotentiaries Conference on the Establishment of an International Criminal Court, Rome, Italy, June 17, 1998, United States Mission to the United Nations Press Release No. 108 (98), June 17, 1998; Secretary Rumsfeld Statement on the ICC Treaty, United States Department of Defense News Release No. 233-02, 6 May 2002.

202 For an overview of these proposals see D. Scheffer, *Staying the Course with the International Criminal Court*, 35 Cornell International Law Journal 47 (2002).

203 Security Council Resolution 1422 of 12 July 2002, UN Doc. S/RES/1422.

204 Security Council Resolution 1487 of 12 June 2003, UN Doc. S/RES/1487.

205 C. Lynch, *US Confronts EU on War Crimes Court*, The Washington Post, 10 June 2003.

a ceasefire agreement in Liberia for a limited period of time. The authorizing resolution includes a decision by the Security Council that current or former officials or personnel from a contributing state, which is not a party to the Rome Statute of the International Criminal Court, shall be subject to the exclusive jurisdiction of that contributing State for all alleged acts or omissions arising out of or related to the Multinational Force or United Nations stabilization force in Liberia, unless such exclusive jurisdiction has been expressly waived by that contributing State.[206] Whereas Resolution 1487 granted a deferral of prosecution for a year, Resolution 1497 permanently bars the jurisdiction of the ICC, unless there is a waiver.[207] The United States delegation insisted on inclusion of the paragraph concerned in Resolution 1497, while France, Germany and Mexico vigorously objected. The latter stated that they supported the deployment of troops but that they could not support the provision on immunity, which they considered superfluous and flouting basic provisions of international law.[208]

3.8.11 Statute of the Special Court for Sierra Leone

The 2002 Statute of the Special Court for Sierra Leone provides more expressly for the prosecution of members of peace support operations for serious violations of international humanitarian law. This court is a treaty-based court established by agreement between the UN and the government of Sierra Leone. The court is part of the peace process in Sierra Leone aimed at bringing an end to the civil war in that country.[209]

The conflict in Sierra Leone was characterized by large-scale atrocities committed by the parties to the conflict. There were also reports of violations of humanitarian law by the Economic Community Monitoring Group (ECOMOG), a peace support operation introduced in the country by the Economic Community of West African States (ECOWAS).[210]

The impetus for the creation of a court was a letter from the government of Sierra Leone to the UN Secretary-General requesting the establishment of an international court similar to the ICTY and ICTR.[211] This request was denied, but on 14 August 2000 the Security Council requested the Secretary-General to negotiate an agreement with the government of Sierra Leone to create an independent special court to prosecute persons who bear the greatest responsibility for the commission of crimes

---

206 Security Council Resolution 1497 of 1 August 2003, UN Doc. S/RES/1497, para. 7.

207 See S. Zappalà, *Are Some Peacekeepers Better than Others? UN Security Council Resolution 1497 (2003) and the ICC*, 1 Journal of International Criminal Justice 671 (2003).

208 F. Barringer, *Security Council Support a Liberia Force*, The New York Times, 2 August 2003.

209 See generally S. Beresford & A. Muller, *The Special Court for Sierra Leone: An Initial Comment*, 14 Leiden Journal of International Law 635 (2001).

210 See *e.g.* J. Miller, *U.N. Monitors Accuse Sierra Leone Peacekeepers of Killings*, 12 February 1999.

211 Letter from the President of Sierra Leone to the Secretary-General of 12 June 2000, UN Doc. S/2000/786.

against humanity, war crimes and other serious violations of international humanitarian law, as well as crimes under relevant Sierra Leonean law committed within the territory of Sierra Leone.[212]

The Secretary-General presented a report on the establishment of the court, including a draft statute, to the Security Council on 4 October 2000.[213] He proposed the creation of a treaty-based *sui generis* court of mixed international and national jurisdiction and composition. He also proposed that the court be responsible for the prosecution of 'persons most responsible' for crimes within the jurisdiction of the court because this term reflects both a leadership or authority position of the accused, and a sense of the gravity, seriousness or massive scale of the crime. The Security Council, in its response of 22 December 2000 to the report, stated its continued preference for the arguably narrower term 'persons who bear the greatest responsibility for the commission of the crimes' used in Resolution 1315.[214] More importantly, the Council understood the proposed jurisdiction *ratione personae* of the court to include members of UN and regional peace support operations. It proposed the inclusion of language in the agreement to be concluded between the UN and the government of Sierra Leone and in the Statute that would only give the court jurisdiction over peacekeepers if authorized by the Security Council on the proposal of any state, in the event the sending state is unwilling or unable genuinely to carry out an investigation or prosecution.[215] The Secretary-General in a letter of 12 January 2001 objected to this proposal on the grounds that the amended article fell short of inducing an unwilling state to surrender an accused person situated in its territory and could politicize the legal process, but the Council did not agree.[216] As a consequence, the text of Article 1 of the Statute, annexed to the Agreement between the UN and the government of Sierra Leone concluded on 16 January 2002, provides:

> 1. The Special Court shall, except as provided in subparagraph (2), have the power to prosecute persons who bear the greatest responsibility for serious violations of International Humanitarian Law and Sierra Leonean law committed in the territory of Sierra Leone since 30 November 1996, including those leaders who, in committing such crimes, have threatened the establishment of and implementation of the peace process in Sierra Leone.
> 2. Any transgressions by peacekeepers and related personnel present in Sierra Leone pursuant to the Status of Mission Agreement in force between the United Nations and the Government of Sierra Leone or agreements between

212 Security Council Resolution 1315 of 14 August 2000, UN Doc. S/RES/1315.

213 Report of the Secretary-General on the Establishment of a Special Court for Sierra Leone of 4 October 2000, UN Doc. S/2000/915.

214 Letter dated 22 December 2000 from the President of the Security Council addressed to the Secretary-General, UN Doc. S/2000/1234, para. 1.

215 *Id.*

216 Letter dated 12 January 2001 from the Secretary-General addressed to the President of the Security Council, UN Doc. S/2001/40, para. 4-5; Letter dated 31 January from the President of the Security Council addressed to the Secretary-General, UN Doc. S/2001/95, para. 2.

Sierra Leone and other Governments or regional organizations, or, in the absence of such agreement, provided that the peacekeeping operations were undertaken with the consent of the Government of Sierra Leone, shall be within the primary jurisdiction of the sending State.

3. In the event the sending State is unwilling or unable genuinely to carry out an investigation or prosecution, the Court may, if authorized by the Security Council on the proposal of any State, exercise jurisdiction over such persons.

The Special Court itself will of course be competent to interpret the Statute, but the language in Article 1 (1) strongly suggests that international humanitarian law may apply to members of peace support operations in Sierra Leone.

At the same time, the subject-matter jurisdiction of the Special Court includes a crime taken from the Convention on the Safety of United Nations and Associated Personnel in Article 4, paragraph b, of the Statute:

> Intentionally directing attacks against personnel, installations, material, units or vehicles involved in a humanitarian assistance or peacekeeping mission in accordance with the Charter of the United Nations, as long as they are entitled to the protection given to civilians or civilian objects under the international law of armed conflict;

This article could prove especially interesting if it provokes debate on whether the United Nations operation and ECOMOG were entitled to the protection of the Convention or were engaged as a party to the conflict.[217] The Special Court may also make clear whether it is possible that the convention and international humanitarian law apply simultaneously. In this respect it may be noted that the charges in the indictment brought by the Special Court's prosecutor against Charles Taylor include unlawful killings and abduction of UNAMSIL personnel, which are charged *inter alia* as violations of Article 3 common to the Geneva Conventions.[218]

3.9 State practice and North Atlantic Treaty Organization practice

In contrast to the UN, NATO does not seem to consider itself bound by international humanitarian law as an international legal person. The organization's legal officials state that it is the individual member states and not the organization that have legal obligations.[219] Member states seem to share this opinion as confirmed in a number of interviews with officials involved in NATO peace support operations.[220] Certain

217 A. McDonald, *Sierra Leone's Shoestring Special Court*, 84 International Review of the Red Cross 121 (2002), at 130.

218 *Prosecutor* v. *Charles Ghankay Taylor*, Case No. SCSL-03-I, 13 March 2003, para. 59.

219 B. de Vidts, cited in Amnesty International, NATO/Federal Republic of Yugoslavia: Collateral Damage or Unlawful Killings, Violations of the Laws of War by NATO during Operation Allied Force, at 15.

220 Interview with Lieutenant-Colonel Gallup, Legal Advisor, SFOR Headquarters, 9 February 2001; Interview with B. Herfst, Legal Advisor, SFOR Headquarters

writers make the same point. Hampson for example states that for the purposes of the application of international humanitarian law:

> a regional organization does not function as one unit but consists of the total number of constituent units, unless the members work within a single command hierarchy and system of discipline.[221]

The idea that the organization itself is not bound by international humanitarian law seems to be related to the idea that the organization is not a subject of international law and refers to the ambiguity concerning the legal status of the organization. Moritz states that the organization:

> is not an international person by itself, and the necessity for a common application of the laws of war cannot be based on the theory that NATO is a subject of international law.[222]

It appears however that the idea that NATO is not an international legal person must be dismissed.[223]

Another element in thinking about the application of international humanitarian law within the organization seems to be the idea that a NATO peace support operation is not a party to the conflict. This is the same argument used by the UN at one time to deny the application of international humanitarian law to operations under its control. The NATO doctrine on peace support operations states in a section on international humanitarian law that:

> The Law of Armed Conflict (LOAC) is the body of international law that governs the conduct of hostilities during an armed conflict. The PSF [Peace Support Force] will not generally be a party to the conflict, yet certain LOAC principles may be applied. Individual civilians along with the civilian population must never be purposefully targeted unless they have taken active part in the armed conflict. When military force is used, every effort should be taken to minimise the risk of civilian casualties.[224]

Practice in NATO peace support operations reflects the member states' conception. The cases of IFOR, SFOR and KFOR are particularly illustrative.

Security Council Resolution 1031 authorized member states to take all necessary measures to effect the implementation of and to ensure compliance with Annex 1A of

---

Multinational Division South West, 12 February 2001; Interview with H. Boddens-Hosang, Directorate of Legal Affairs, Dutch Ministry of Defence, 12 July 2001.

221 F. Hampson, *States' Military Operations Authorized by the United Nations and International Humanitarian Law*, in L. Condorelli, A.M. La Rosa & S. Scherrer (Eds), Les Nations Unies et le Droit International Humanitaire 371 (1995), at 388.

222 Moritz, *supra* note 118, at 9.

223 See para. 2.3.

224 Allied Joint Publication-3.4.1 Peace Support Operations, (July 2001), para. 4B6.

the Dayton Peace Agreement and stated that the parties to the Yugoslav conflict shall be equally subject to such enforcement action by IFOR as may be necessary to ensure implementation of that Annex and the protection of IFOR. Annex 1A to the Dayton Peace Agreement also provided that the parties to the agreement shall be subject to such enforcement action by IFOR as may be necessary to ensure the implementation of the annex and the protection of the operation. The need for such powers was considered as reflecting a real possibility of the use of force. Many believed in 1995 that there was a serious risk of renewed fighting in Bosnia.[225] In other words, there was a serious possibility that IFOR could become engaged in hostilities. In addition, it could be argued that the law of occupation was applicable to, or at least could provide guidance for, IFOR.[226]

Despite of all this, the basic documents relating to IFOR and SFOR do not contain any reference to international humanitarian law. The SOFAs between NATO and Bosnia Herzegovina, Croatia and the FRY provide that personnel shall refrain from activities not compatible with the nature of the Operation, but this is a very vague obligation. Although rules from the law of occupation could have provided guidance to IFOR and SFOR in certain situations, policy decisions were made to deliberately avoid any reference to the law of occupation.[227]

Security Council Resolution 1244 authorized member states and relevant international organizations to establish the international security presence in Kosovo with all necessary means to fulfill its responsibilities. The responsibilities in question, described in paragraph 9 of the resolution, are very broad. Eide states that:

> in the absence of a final settlement, Kosovo is de facto occupied by NATO's KFOR and formally administered by the UN through its UNMIK mission. In choosing such a model, the international community has taken a much wider responsibility than it normally does for the future of the province.[228]

Similar to the case of IFOR, it appears that at least initially the possibility that the force would become engaged in hostilities with Yugoslav forces if the FRY would not respect the terms of Resolution 1244 and the Military Technical Agreement was considered real. There is also a case to be made for the application of the law of occupation to KFOR.[229]

The basic documents relating to KFOR, however, do not refer to international humanitarian law. In practice international humanitarian law or the law of occupation

---

225 See *e.g.* J. Mearsheimer & S. Van Evera, *The Partition that Dare not Speak its Name: When Peace Means War*, The New Republic, 5 December 1995.

226 See para. 3.12.

227 Information from interviews by the author with SFOR officials in February 2001.

228 E. Barth Eide, The Internal Security Challenge in Kosovo, paper prepared for UNA-USA/IAI Conference on 'Kosovo's Final Status'.

229 See *e.g.* M. Hoffman, *Peace-enforcement Actions and Humanitarian Law: Emerging Rules for "Interventional Armed Conflict"*, 82 International Review of the Red Cross 193 (2000).

also does not seem to be a point of reference, as described by a former KFOR battalion commander:

> In the reality of KFOR-1 the legal basis was not really discussed. The Dutch KFOR soldiers certainly did not think in terms of ... the law of occupation.[230]

It seems that if the peace does not hold and conflict breaks out anew, the troop contributing states would consider themselves bound by their treaty obligations.[231] This is consistent with the obligation on troop contributing states to respect and ensure respect for the 1949 Geneva Conventions, and if they are states parties, the 1977 Additional Protocols. Even when states place troops at the disposal of an international organization Article 1 of the Conventions remains applicable, but this does not preclude the international organization itself from having obligations under general international law.

3.10 International or non-international conflict

It was argued that international humanitarian law is in principle applicable to international organizations as general international law, in particular customary international law. International humanitarian law consists of separate regimes for international and non-international conflict. In recent years, the clear distinction between these two regimes has become increasingly blurred and there is a tendency to disregard the differences in the legal coverage of international and non-international armed conflicts.[232] The ICTY and ICTR have played an important role in this development, by identifying rules from the regime of international armed conflicts which are also applicable as customary international rules in non-international armed conflicts. The Appeals Chamber of the Yugoslavia Tribunal in its 1995 Decision on jurisdiction in the *Tadić* case stated that "in the area of armed conflict the distinction between interstate wars and civil wars is losing its value as far as human beings are concerned."[233] In treaty law there is also a tendency to apply the same rules to international and non-international armed conflicts, as illustrated by the scope of application of the Ottawa Convention on Anti-personnel Landmines and Protocol II to the 1954 Convention on the Protection of Cultural Property in the Event of Armed Conflict. The distinction between international and non-international armed conflicts has however not

230 "In de realiteit van KFOR-1 was de discussie over welke juridische basis nu moest gelden ook niet echt aan de orde. Het is zeker niet zo dat de Nederlandse KFOR-militairen in termen van [...] het bezettingsrecht gedacht hebben.", A. van Loon, *Kosovo Force-1: Tussen Trauma en Toekomst (II)*, 169 Militaire Spectator 656 (2000), at 659 (translation by the author).

231 See J. Burger, *International Humanitarian Law and the Kosovo Crisis: Lessons Learned or to be Learned*, 82 International Review of the Red Cross 129 (2000).

232 See *e.g.* T. Meron, *The Humanization of Humanitarian Law*, 94 American Journal of International Law 239 (2000), at 260-263.

233 *Prosecutor* v. *Duško Tadić*, Decision on the Defence Motion for Interlocutory Appeal on Jurisdiction, *supra* note 34, para. 96.

yet been abandoned, as the Appeals Chamber in the *Tadić* case reaffirmed by stating that the "emergence of the aforementioned general rules on internal armed conflicts does not imply that internal strife is regulated by general international law in all its aspects."[234] The dichotomy between international and non-international conflicts was also retained in the 1998 ICC Statute.[235]

The distinction between international and non-international armed conflicts, to the extent that it is still relevant, is not as obvious as it may seem. The 1949 Geneva Conventions and the first 1977 Additional Protocol apply in case of declared war or any other armed conflict which may arise between two or more of the High Contracting Parties. Customary international law of international armed conflict obviously does not require the involvement of contracting parties, but in principle it only applies between states. In the conventional law of non-international armed conflicts there are two regimes which become applicable at different thresholds. Common Article 3 to the Geneva Conventions becomes applicable in the case of armed conflict not of an international character occurring in the territory of one of the High Contracting Parties. Alhough the Conventions do not specify what the requirements for such a conflict are, they are generally considered to be lower than those required for the application of the second 1977 Additional Protocol to the Geneva Conventions. The Protocol applies, according to Article 1, to all armed conflicts which are not covered by Protocol I and which take place in the territory of a High Contracting Party between its armed forces and dissident armed forces or other organized armed groups which, under responsible command, exercise such control over a part of its territory as to enable them to carry out sustained and concerted military operations and to implement this Protocol. Article 1 (2) adds that the Protocol shall not apply to situations of internal disturbances and tensions, such as riots, isolated and sporadic acts of violence and other acts of a similar nature, as not being armed conflicts. The customary law of non-international armed conflict has come to be applicable to a broader set of situations than its conventional counterpart, including in particular to armed violence between non-state organized armed groups. The Appeals Chamber of the ICTY in the *Tadić* Decision on jurisdiction defined 'armed conflict' as "whenever there is a resort to armed force between States or protracted armed violence between governmental authorities and organized armed groups or between such groups within a State."[236] The Trial Chamber in its judgment in the same case specified that the intensity of the conflict and the organization of the parties to the conflict are relevant aspects in determining whether or not there is protracted armed violence between governmental forces and organized armed groups or between such groups under customary law. It stated that:

> In an armed conflict of an internal or mixed character, these closely related criteria are used solely for the purpose, as a minimum, of distinguishing an armed conflict from

234 *Id.*, para. 126.

235 H. Spieker, *The International Criminal Court and Non-International Armed Conflicts*, 13 Leiden Journal of International Law 395 (2000), at 398.

236 *Supra* note 34, para. 70.

> banditry, unorganized and short-lived insurrections, or terrorist activities, which are not subject to International Humanitarian Law. Factors relevant to this determination are addressed in the Commentary to Geneva Convention for the Amelioration of the Condition of the Wounded and Sick in Armed Forces in the Field, Convention I.[237]

The same criteria were referred to by Trial Chamber I of the Rwanda Tribunal in the *Akayesu* case in the context of a determination of the threshold of application of common Article 3.[238] In the *Musema* case the Trial Chamber further specified these criteria:

> First, a non-international conflict is distinct from an international armed conflict because of the legal status of the entities opposing each other: the parties to the conflict are not sovereign States, but the government of a single State in conflict with one or more armed factions within its territory. The expression 'armed conflicts' introduces a material criterion: the existence of open hostilities between armed forces which are organized to a greater or lesser degree. Internal disturbances and tensions, characterized by isolated or sporadic acts of violence, do not therefore constitute armed conflicts in a legal sense, even if the government is forced to resort to police forces or even armed units for the purpose of restoring law and order. Within these limits, non-international armed conflicts are situations in which hostilities break out between armed forces or organized armed groups within the territory of a single State. Having defined the term in an abstract manner, to the Chamber it is apparent that whether a conflict meets the criteria of Common Article 3 is to be decided on a case by case basis.[239]

These definitions do not refer to international organizations such as the UN and NATO, and the question arises whether the dichotomy between international and non-international conflicts applies to them as well.

It is generally accepted that in case of an armed conflict between an organization and the armed forces of a state the law of international armed conflict applies. Although the UN and NATO are not states, they are subjects of international law and as such a conflict with another subject of that law is regulated by the international regime.[240] The same logic would suggest that the law of non-international armed conflict applies to an armed conflict between an international organization and a non-state organized armed group, because there is only one subject of international law involved, but the question can also be seen from other perspectives. One possibility

237 *Prosecutor* v. *Duško Tadić*, Opinion and Judgment, Case No. IT-94-1-T, Tr. Ch. II, 7 May 1997, para. 562.

238 *Prosecutor* v. *Jean-Paul Akayesu*, Judgment, Case No. ICTR-96-4-T, Tr. Ch. I, 2 September 1998, para. 619-621.

239 *Prosecutor* v. *Alfred Musema*, Judgment and Sentence, Case No. ICTR-96-13, Tr. Ch. I, 27 January 2000, para. 246-249.

240 Greenwood, *supra* note 23, at 25; Emanuelli, *supra* note 135, at 34.

is to consider the international organization as analogous to a state intervening in another state in support of the latter state's government. The relationship between the opposition and the forces of a state intervening on behalf of the established government however creates an ambiguous legal situation in which it is unclear whether the law of international or non-international armed conflict applies, and as a consequence the analogy is not particularly instructive. Schindler for example states that in such a case only the rules of non-international armed conflict are applicable, but other writers maintain that the law of international armed conflict applies.[241]

Another perspective has its starting point in the reason behind the international-non-international armed conflict dichotomy, that is, state sovereignty. A majority of states are unwilling to subject what they consider their internal affairs to international scrutiny and are therefore unwilling to accept detailed regulation of non-international conflicts. Schindler states that a Norwegian proposal at the Conference of Experts in 1971 and 1972 to adopt one uniform protocol for all armed conflicts did not find much approval because:

> International law has to take into account that the world is divided into sovereign States, and that these States keep to their sovereignty. They are not willing to put insurgents within their territory on equal terms with the armed forces of enemy States, or members thereof.[242]

The UN and NATO, in contrast to states, do not have territorial sovereignty, and as a consequence sovereignty is not a reason for them not to apply the regime which offers the highest level of protection.[243] Such an interpretation is consistent with a more general development away from a state-sovereignty-oriented approach to international humanitarian law observed by the Appeals Chamber of the Yugoslavia Tribunal in the *Tadić* case.[244]

There is support in state practice for the idea that the law of international armed conflict applies to an armed conflict between a peace support operation and a non-state organized armed group. The negotiators of the 1994 Convention on the Safety of United Nations and Associated Personnel are reported to have held the view that it is impossible for the UN itself to be involved in an internal armed conflict since once UN or associated personnel become engaged in conflict with a local force, the conflict becomes by definition international in character.[245] In a case against two Belgian

---

241 *Pro* application of the law of international armed conflict *e.g.* Application of Humanitarian Law in Non International Armed Conflicts, 85 ASIL Proc. 83 (1991); E. David, Principes de Droit des Conflits Armés 135-137 (1994). *Contra*: D. Schindler, *The Different Types of Armed Conflicts According to the Geneva Conventions and Protocols*, 163 Recueil des Cours 125 (1979-II), at 150; D. Weissbrodt, *The Role of International Organizations in the Implementation of Human Rights and Humanitarian Law in Situations of Armed Conflict*, 21 Vanderbilt Journal of Transnational Law 313 (1988), at 337-338.

242 Schindler, *supra* note 241, at 154.

243 Glick, *supra* note 126, at 91.

244 *Supra* note 34, para. 97.

245 Kirsch, *supra* note 176, 105.

members of the United Nations Operation in Somalia accused of having mistreated a Somali child, the Belgian Military Court of Appeal was requested to find a breach of the 1949 Geneva Conventions and the 1977 Additional Protocols. The Court held that the operation in question had not become involved in permanent, generalized and structured combat operations against one or more rival armed factions. Importantly, the Court stated that if the operation had become involved in such operations the conflict would have had an international character.[246]

The Secretary-General's Bulletin takes another approach. It avoids the question of whether the conflict in which a peace support operation is involved is international or non-international because it applies a uniform set of rules to all conflicts in which personnel of a UN peace support operation becomes involved as combatants. It may be recalled that meetings of experts convened by the ICRC were the first real steps toward the Bulletin. The experts at these meetings were not certain which regime of international humanitarian law applies to a conflict between a UN operation and an organized armed group. The Chairman at one of the meetings concluded that "the distinction between international and non-international armed conflicts as far as United Nations operations were concerned was not totally clear."[247] The draft directives provided for the application of one set of rules to all conflicts, but it still contained a reference to the international/ non-international dichotomy by stating that the directives are applicable to international and non-international armed conflicts as may be relevant. This reference was not included in the final version of the Secretary-General's Bulletin. The Bulletin not only follows the tendency of the ICTY and ICTR to apply certain rules from the law of international armed conflicts to non-international armed conflicts, but even fails to distinguish between the two regimes.

At a meeting of experts on the application of international humanitarian law and international human rights law to UN-mandated forces, organized by the ICRC in December 2003, the issue was also taken up. Opinions were equally divided between experts who held that a UN-mandated operation, by definition, 'internationalizes' the whole conflict, and those for whom the latter's qualification will depend on the status of the other parties to the conflict.[248]

3.11 Threshold of application

It was argued that a UN or NATO peace support operation can become a party to an armed conflict and its personnel combatants, and also that such an armed conflict is an international armed conflict. This raises the question of the criteria for determining whether there is an armed conflict, in other words the threshold of armed conflict. International humanitarian law instruments, in particular the 1949 Geneva Conventions and the 1977 Additional Protocols, do not define the term 'armed conflict'. As noted,

246 Belgian Military Court of Appeal (Militair Gerechtshof), *Prosecutor* v. *C.K. and B.C.*, judgment of 17 December 1997, reported in Journal des Tribunaux 1998, 286-289.

247 *Supra* note 185, at 39.

248 *Application of International Humanitarian Law and International Human Rights Law to UN-mandated Forces*, 86 International Review of the Red Cross 207 (2004).

the Appeals Chamber of the Yugoslavia Tribunal in its Decision on jurisdiction in the *Tadić* case defined an armed conflict as "resort to armed force between States or protracted armed violence between governmental authorities and organized armed groups or between such groups within a State."[249] The main criteria used by the ICTY to determine the existence of an armed conflict are the intensity of the conflict and the organization of the parties involved. In general there is agreement that these are the criteria to determine whether there is an armed conflict, but not on the necessary level of intensity and organization. State practice is ambiguous because states rarely explain why they consider that a particular situation is an armed conflict or not.

The ICRC tends to interpret the term armed conflict as broadly as possible, but it seems that only when fighting reaches a level of intensity which exceeds that of isolated clashes will it be treated as armed conflict.[250] Situations which fall below this level of intensity are not armed conflicts but instances of internal disturbance and tension.

The parties to the conflict need to have a certain degree of organization. Such a level of organization probably must be such that they are capable of carrying out the various obligations which arise under international humanitarian law. The requirement of organization is illustrated for example by Israel, which claims it is engaged in an armed conflict with the Palestinians. The claim is based *inter alia* on the assertion that "attacks are carried out by a well-armed and organised militia, under the command of the Palestinian political establishment, operating from areas outside Israeli control."[251]

General definitions require application to specific facts. As the Trial Chamber of the Rwanda Tribunal stated in the *Rutaganda* case, the definition of armed conflict offered by the Yugoslavia Tribunal is still termed in the abstract and whether or not a situation can be described as an armed conflict is to be decided on a case-by-case basis.[252]

In the specific case of peace support operations the UN has never made clear statements concerning the application of international humanitarian law in specific circumstances.

ONUC was involved in hostilities with another non-state organized armed group, the secessionist forces of Katanga. The UN seems to have considered itself as involved in an armed conflict because it considered international humanitarian law applicable, but the organization did not state the criteria on which it based the existence of a conflict. The authorities in Katanga stated that they considered themselves in a state of war with the UN.[253]

249 *Supra* note 34, para. 70.

250 C. Greenwood, *Scope of Application of Humanitarian Law*, in D. Fleck (Ed.), The Handbook of Humanitarian Law in Armed Conflicts 39 (1995), at 42; M. Bothe, *Friedenssicherung und Kriegsrecht*, in W. Graf Vitzhum (Ed.), Völkerrecht 645 (2001); F. Siordet, *Commentaire de l'Article 3 de la IIIe Convention de Genève*, 40 International Review of the Red Cross 644 (1958).

251 Sharm El-Sheikh Fact-Finding Committee, First Statement of the Government of Israel, 28 December 2000, para. 287.

252 *Prosecutor* v. *Rutaganda*, Judgment, Case No. ICTR-96-3, Tr. Ch , 6 December 1999, para. 91.

253 UN Doc. S/4750, para. 11

In 1993, UNOSOM II was involved in hostilities with an armed group called the United Somali Congress/Somali National Alliance (USC/SNA). The hostilities were certainly of a high intensity, involving the use of helicopter gunships and tanks. There were considerable casualties on both sides. For example, five Moroccan soldiers were killed on 17 June, two Pakistani on 28 June and three Italians on 2 July 1993. In one single incident on 5 June 1993, twenty-four Pakistani members of the operation were killed in an ambush after returning from an inspection of weapons storage facilities. The non-governmental group responsible for these attacks was well organized. A Commission of Inquiry established by the Security Council to investigate the armed attacks described the group as "a reasonably well-organised and trained group under a good command structure."[254] The Commission described the conflict between the peace support operation and the armed group as a war, although it did not expressly state that international humanitarian law was applicable. It also stated that:

> the feeling of being at war is reflected in UNOSOM II fragmental orders (fragos). Until 8 July they refer to UNOSOM IIs adversaries as 'hostile forces'. After that date, the fragos use the phrase 'enemy forces'.[255]

The ICRC acted as a neutral intermediary between the operation and the SNA in organizing the release of a wounded Nepalese soldier who had been captured and detained by uncontrolled elements, in the same way it would between parties to an armed conflict.[256]

It seems however that the UN did not consider itself to be involved in an armed conflict in Somalia. The Security Council in Resolution 837 stated that it was gravely alarmed at the premeditated armed attacks against personnel belonging to the peace support operation and expressed "its outrage at the loss of life as a result of these criminal attacks."[257]

The United Nations Operation in Sierra Leone (UNAMSIL) has also been involved in hostilities with a non-governmental armed group called the Revolutionary United Front (RUF). In May 2000, the RUF detained a large number of peace support operation personnel. Around this time there were a number of armed clashes between the operation and the armed group, with the RUF using small arms, rocket-propelled grenades and mortars. There were a number of casualties on both sides. At least seven members of the peace support operation were killed and twenty-five were reported wounded.[258] There followed a number of smaller attacks by the RUF on the peace support operation, including an ambush during which one peacekeeper was

254 Report of the Commission of Inquiry established pursuant to resolution 885 (1993) to investigate armed attacks on UNOSOM II personnel of 1 June 1994, UN Doc. S/1994/653, para. 242.

255 *Id.*, para. 152.

256 International Committee of the Red Cross Annual Report 1995.

257 Security Council Resolution 837 of 6 June 1993, UN Doc. S/RES/837.

258 UN Doc. S/2000/455 of 19 May 2000, para. 56-71; C. Roy, *UN Troops Killed by Sierra Leone Rebels*, The Guardian, 4 May 2000.

killed and four were wounded on 30 June 2000. A major armed clash occurred on 15 July when the peace support operation launched a robust military operation to free a unit of Indian peacekeepers who were surrounded by the armed group and the operation traded heavy fire with the rebel forces.[259] The UN does not seem to have considered itself involved in an armed conflict in Sierra Leone. The Security Council in Resolution 1315 stated its deep concern at the very serious crimes committed within the territory of Sierra Leone against UN and associated personnel.[260]

The Secretary-General's Bulletin on the Observance of International Humanitarian Law by United Forces applies, according to Section 1 (1), to UN forces "in situations of armed conflict where they are actively engaged therein as combatants, to the extent and for the duration of their engagement." Experts at the meeting organized by the ICRC in July 1995 agreed that violence in which the UN is involved must reach a certain level of intensity before international humanitarian law applies, but they did not clearly define that level of intensity. Representatives of the ICRC suggested that Article 1 (2) of Additional Protocol II provided a useful analogy. Several experts stated that the intention behind the use of force was important. One expert maintained that in:

> a situation like the former Yugoslavia, for instance, where the United Nations force has been allowed to enter the territory in the first place, if shots were fired, then both the facts and the intention, within an appropriate time-scale, should be taken into account in combination to establish whether a state of armed conflict existed.[261]

A draft of the Bulletin, based on a code of conduct developed by the experts and reviewed by the ICRC and the UN secretariat, provided that the rules in question are applicable to UN forces "when in situations of armed conflict they are actively engaged therein as combatants."[262] The final version of the Secretary-General's Bulletin, in section 1 (1), is identical but adds the words "to the extent and for the duration of their engagement." If the term 'armed conflict' as used in this section is interpreted in accordance with the ordinary meaning given to the term, the threshold for the application of international humanitarian law to UN forces is the same as the threshold under general international law. The words "when … they are actively engaged therein as combatants" seem superfluous, because the armed forces of a party to an armed conflict are combatants. The words may have been included to distinguish the situation in which the Bulletin applies from the situation in which a UN operation is present in an ongoing conflict without becoming a party thereto.[263] They may also indicate that

259 UN Doc. S/2000/751 of 31 July 2000, para. 18-28.

260 Security Council Resolution 1315 of 14 August 2000, UN Doc. S/RES/1315.

261 *Supra* note 185, at 30.

262 Directives for UN Forces Regarding Respect for International Humanitarian Law, copy on file with the author, section 1 (1).

263 This distinction seems obvious, but some writers do not make it. See *e.g.* A. Weyemberg, *La Notion de Conflit Armé, le Droit International Humanitaire et les Forces des Nations Unies en Somalie (A Propos de l'Arrêt de la Cour Militaire du 17 Décembre 1997)*, 79 Revue de Droit Pénal et de Criminologie 177 (1999).

the hostilities require a certain level of intensity. The words "to the extent and for the duration of their engagement" seem to imply that UN peace support operation personnel can be combatants one moment and non-combatants the next. It implies that armed conflict to which the UN is a party can be intermittent. This would be contrary to customary international humanitarian law as interpreted by the Appeals Chamber of the Yugoslavia Tribunal, which stated in the *Tadić* case that international humanitarian law applies from the initiation of an armed conflict and extends beyond the cessation of hostilities until a general conclusion of peace is reached; or, in the case of internal conflicts, a peaceful settlement is achieved.[264] The implication is unfortunate because it may create confusion over the applicability of international humanitarian law in a particular situation. It is also difficult to apply in practice. It implies for example that if a peace support operation has detained opponents in an engagement, the provision on the humane treatment of those persons in section 8 of the Secretary-General's Bulletin ceases to apply at the end of that specific engagement. It is also not likely that the opponent of a peace support operation will accept the intermittent application of international humanitarian law.

At the meeting of experts organized by the ICRC in December 2003, some experts insisted that the use of force in self-defense, especially in isolated events, does not turn peacekeepers into combatants. It was noted, however, that self-defense can progressively lead to a situation where a peace support operation does become party to a conflict.[265]

It seems that a UN peace support operation will be regarded as a party to an armed conflict only if the hostilities in which it is involved are of a high level of intensity. This high level of intensity probably has its origin in the political desire of the organization to consider an operation as impartial, and as a consequence not a party to the conflict, as long as possible. In principle it seems to be accepted that the applicability of international humanitarian law to UN peace support operations is to be determined by the threshold in customary international law.[266]

Some writers imply that the threshold of armed conflict will not be reached in any event in case of a peacekeeping operation as distinguished from a peace enforcement operation. Van Hegelsom states that during traditional peace-keeping operations the law of armed conflict cannot and should not apply to the conduct of operations. "Should peace-keeping fail, peace-enforcement might prove necessary. It is submitted that the law of armed conflict is applicable in such cases."[267] A degree of consent is commonly understood as the most important difference between peacekeeping and peace enforcement. In other words, these writers seem to raise the question whether consent plays a role in determining whether or not there is an armed conflict between an operation and the opposing force. The idea that a peace support operation has received the consent of either the host state or the parties to the conflict and simulta-

264 *Supra* note 34, para. 97.

265 *Supra* note 248, at 208.

266 Schraga, *supra* note 95, at 76.

267 G. van Hegelsom, *The Law of Armed Conflict and UN Peace-keeping and Peace-enforcing Operations*, 6 Hague Yearbook of International Law 45 (1993), at 57.

neously be a party to a conflict may at first sight seem strange. On the other hand, the reference to consent implies that the intention of the parties plays a role in the determination of the existence of an armed conflict. This is contrary to the notion that the application of international humanitarian law is determined by objective standards. This notion is widely endorsed by writers.[268] The ICTY and ICTR also use a factual test to establish the existence of an armed conflict.[269] Finally, the drafters of the ICC Statute also considered that objective standards are conclusive. This is made clear by the introduction to the Elements of Crimes concerning Article 8 of the Statute. The introduction states with respect to the element that the conduct of the perpetrator took place in the context of and was associated with an armed conflict, which applies to all the war crimes in the Statute, that:

> There is only a requirement for the awareness of the factual circumstances that established the existence of an armed conflict that is implicit in the terms 'took place in the context of and was associated with'.[270]

The objective standards referred to were described as the intensity of the conflict and the degree of organization of the parties involved. The value of objective standards is that they limit the possibility that persons are deprived of the protection of international humanitarian law on the basis of a simple statement by a party that it does not consider itself as a party to an armed conflict. The March 1995 meeting of experts on the applicability of international humanitarian law to United Nations forces convened by the ICRC discussed the question whether the intention of the parties plays a role in determining whether there is an armed conflict in which the UN is involved. There was no consensus among the experts. Certain experts stated that intention had to be taken into account.[271] The Chairman of the meeting, a Red Cross official, on the other hand, took the view that intention did not matter in the event of an outbreak of hostilities. He considered that whether there is an armed conflict can be determined by the facts.[272] The Chairman's view is consistent with the present interpretation of the concept of armed conflict by writers and international tribunals.

Another consideration is that it may be very difficult to determine whether there is consent. Gray states that the notion of consent in UN military operations is a complex one.[273] The parties to the conflict may give their consent to the deployment of

---

268 See *e.g.* 3 EPIL 26 (1995).; M. Bothe, *Völkerrechtliche Eingrenzung von Gewalt – das Recht bewaffneter Konflikte (ius in bello)*, in W. Graf Vitzthum (Ed.), Völkerrecht 642 (2001), at 645.

269 *Supra* note 233, para. 70.

270 Finalized draft text of the Elements of Crimes, addendum to the Report of the Preparatory Commission for the International Criminal Court, 6 July 2000, UN Doc. PCNICC/2000/INF/3/Add.2, at 18.

271 *Supra* note 185, at 30.

272 *Id.*, at 30, 34.

273 C. Gray, *Host-State Consent and United Nations Peacekeeping in Yugoslavia*, 7 Duke Journal of Comparative & International Law 241 (1996).

an operation. If at a later moment that operation is given additional tasks and powers under Chapter VII of the UN Charter which do not have the consent of one or more of the parties, it may be unclear whether the original consent must be considered to have been withdrawn. It is also possible that the political authorities of the party to the conflict have expressed their consent but that this is not clearly communicated to the forces on the ground. The Brahimi Report recognizes the complexity of consent in peace support operations. It states that:

> consent may be manipulated in many ways by the local parties. A party may give its consent to United Nations presence merely to gain time to retool its fighting forces and withdraw consent when the peacekeeping operation no longer serves its interests. A party may seek to limit an operation's freedom of movement, adopt a policy of persistent non-compliance with the provisions of an agreement or withdraw its consent altogether. Moreover, regardless of faction leaders' commitment to the peace, fighting forces may simply be under much looser control than the conventional armies with which traditional peacekeepers work, and such forces may split into factions whose existence and implications were not contemplated in the peace agreement under the color of which the United Nations mission operates.[274]

Present military doctrine also recognizes that consent is not a switch that is either on or off but that there is a large gray area between the two.[275] It is clear that consent is a complex concept. As a consequence, it is not a clear criterion which is helpful to determine the existence of an armed conflict.[276]

It is also dangerous to base a determination of whether international humanitarian law applies simply on whether a peace support operation has been established under Chapter VI or Chapter VII of the Charter.[277] Chapter VI or Chapter VII is relevant to the range of situations in which an operation is entitled to use force. It does not determine whether an operation will actually make use of that entitlement to such an extent that the objective standards for the existence of an armed conflict are met. Greenwood observes that:

---

274 Report of the Panel on United Nations Peace Operations of 21 August 2000, UN Doc. S/2000/809, para. 48.

275 D. Jablonsky & J. McCallum, *Peace Implementation and the Concept of Induced Consent in Peace Operations*, 29 Parameters 54 (1999).

276 See H.P. Gasser, *Die Anwendbarkeit des Humanitären Völkerrechts auf Militärische Operationen der Vereinten Nationen*, 4 Schweizerische Zeitschrift für Internationales und Europäisches Recht 443 (1994), at 460.

277 This is suggested by Cottier, M. Cottier, *Attacks on Humanitarian Assistance or Peacekeeping Missions*, in O. Triffterer (Ed.), Commentary on the Rome Statute of the International Criminal Court: Observer's Notes, Article by Article 187 (1999), at 195. See also G. Cartledge, *Legal Constraints on Military Personnel Deployed on Peacekeeping Operations*, in H. Durman & T. McCormack (Eds.), The Changing Face of Conflict and the Efficacy of International Humanitarian Law 121 (1999), at 128.

> IHL applies in the event of an armed conflict, a factual concept which exists when certain hostilities take place ... whether or not it is applicable to a particular operation will be dependent upon the existence of an armed conflict to which the relevant United Nations force is a party, not on how the United Nations operation is classified for other United Nations purposes. It is the *fact* of participation in hostilities, not the existence of *authority* to do so which is significant.[278]

If the applicability of international humanitarian law depended on whether an operation was established under Chapter VII of the Charter, SFOR and KFOR would be parties to a conflict, which they are clearly not.[279]

The Secretary-General's Bulletin confirms the view that the applicability of international humanitarian law cuts across different chapters of the UN Charter. Section 1 (1) of the Bulletin expresses that UN troops can be engaged as combatants in a situation of armed conflict "in enforcement actions, or in peacekeeping operations when the use of force is permitted in self-defence."

For various reasons of dubious legal validity NATO and its member states do not seem to consider the organization as having obligations under international humanitarian law. If it is nevertheless accepted that the organization does have such obligations, the threshold for their applicability should be the same as that under customary international law.

3.12 Occupation

International humanitarian law applies during an armed conflict, but also during an occupation. Article 42 of the 1907 Hague Regulations states that:

> Territory is considered occupied when it is actually placed under the authority of the hostile army. The occupation extends only to the territory where such authority has been established and can be exercised.

The provision appears to be based on an assumption that a military occupation occurs in the context of an armed conflict, in particular by referring to the occupying power as a hostile army. Occupation was considered to be the result of an invasion, as illustrated by the judgment of the United States Military Tribunal in the *Hostages* case.[280] At the same time an important element to determine whether there is an occupation is effective control of the territory, and this element was also emphasized in the *Hostages* case. The Tribunal stated that "an occupation indicates the exercise of governmental authority to the exclusion of the established government."[281]

---

278 Greenwood, *supra* note 23, at 11.

279 Although it can be argued that KFOR is an Occupying Power. See para. 3.12.

280 *United States* v. *Wilhelm List and others (the Hostages Trial)*, United States Military Tribunal, Nuremberg, VIII Law Reports of Trials of War Criminals 55 (1949).

281 *Id.* See also E. Colby, *Occupation under the Laws of War*, 25 Columbia Law Review 904 (1925), at 907.

The 'contextual' element of armed conflict in occupation was attenuated in the 1949 Geneva Conventions, and more emphasis was put on the factual element of control of the territory.[282] Common Article 2 of the conventions provides:

> In addition to the provisions which shall be implemented in peacetime, the present Convention shall apply to all cases of declared war or of any other armed conflict which may arise between two or more of the High Contracting Parties, even if the state of war is not recognized by one of them.
> The Convention shall also apply to all cases of partial or total occupation of the territory of a High Contracting Party, even if the said occupation meets with no armed resistance.

The first paragraph covers territory which has been occupied during hostilities, in the sense of the Hague Regulations. The second paragraph extends the scope of the law of occupation to cases where the occupation has taken place without a declaration of war and without hostilities. This intention was made clearer in a proposal adopted by the 1947 Conference of Government Experts meeting to prepare for the 1949 Conference which provided that the Conventions would be applicable to "cases of occupation of territories in the absence of any state of war."[283] The final text expresses the same intention, as illustrated by the statement by the Rapporteur of the Committee at the 1949 Conference responsible for drafting this article that it "was perfectly well understood that the word 'occupation' referred not only to occupation during war itself, but also to sudden occupation without war, as provided in the second paragraph of Article 2."[284]

The extension of the concept of occupation was considered necessary to cover situations like the occupation of Denmark and Czechoslovakia during World War II. The ICJ adopted this interpretation of common Article 2 in its Advisory Opinion of 9 July 2004 on the *Legal Consequences of the Construction of a Wall in the Occupied Palestinian Territory*.[285]

Trial Chamber I of the ICTY, in its judgment in *Prosecutor* v. *Naletilic and Martinovic* of 31 March 2003, gave a two-fold definition of 'occupation'. It held that for the purposes of Article 42 of the Hague Regulations of 1907, actual control of the territory is required.[286] The Chamber enumerated a number of guidelines providing assistance in determining whether actual control is established. The Chamber adopted a different test in respect of occupation in the sense of Geneva Convention (IV) of 1949. According to the Chamber, the application of the law of occupation as it affects 'individuals' as civilians under Geneva Convention (IV) does not require

282 E. Benvenisti, The International Law of Occupation 4 (1993).

283 Report on the Work of the Conference of Government Experts for the Study of the Conventions for the Protection of War Victims (Geneva, April 14 – 26, 1947), Geneva, 1947, at 8.

284 Final Record of the Diplomatic Conference of Geneva of 1949, Vol. II-A, at 815.

285 *Supra* note 64, paras. 92-101.

286 *Prosecutor* v. *Mladen Naletilic and Vinko Martinovic*, Judgment, Case No. IT-98-34-T, Tr. Ch. I, 31 March 2003, para. 218.

that the occupying power have actual authority. For the purposes of those individual's rights, a state of occupation exists upon their falling into "the hands of the occupying power."[287] The Chamber adopted this definition on the basis of the ICRC commentary on Article 6 of Geneva Convention (IV).[288] The ICRC commentary maintains that the law of occupation becomes applicable even to a patrol which penetrates into enemy territory without any intention of staying there.[289] This appears to set the threshold for the application of the law of occupation too low. The Eritrea Ethiopia Claims Commission's approach in its Partial Award of 28 April 2004 was somewhat more nuanced. The Commission held that:

> On the one hand, clearly an area where combat is ongoing and the attacking forces have not yet established control cannot normally be considered occupied within the meaning of the Geneva Conventions of 1949. On the other hand, where combat is not occurring in an area controlled even for just a few days by the armed forces of a hostile Power, the Commission believes that the legal rules applicable to occupied territory should apply.[290]

The definition of occupation, based mainly on the fact of control of territory, applies to a wide range of situations, including occupations in times of so-called peace.[291] Arguably, it includes a situation in which a peace support operation exercises or is capable of exercising control over a territory. Kelly states that the customary law of occupation applies to a peace support operation if:

> the force present is not just passing through, is not engaged in actual combat, and is, in effect, the sole authority capable of exercising control over the civilian population, or if any remaining authority requires the approval or sanction of the force to operate.[292]

He considers that these elements were present in UNOSOM II and IFOR. The argument is that the thrust of the law of occupation seeks to regulate the relationship between a non-sovereign force in a territory and the population in that territory. The need for such a regulation reflects a potential conflict of interests between occupant and occupied which is largely independent of the process through which the occupant

287 *Id.*, para. 221.

288 J. Pictet (Ed.), The Geneva Conventions of 12 August 1949: Commentary, (IV) Geneva Convention relative to the Protection of Civilian Persons in Time of War 60 (1958).

289 *Id.*

290 Eritrea Ethiopia Claims Commission, Partial Award Central Front Eritrea's Claims 2, 4, 6, 7, 8 & 22, 28 April 2004, para. 57.

291 For an overview of these situations see A. Roberts, *What is a Military Occupation*, 55 British Yearbook of International Law 250 (1984).

292 M. Kelly, *Legitimacy and the Public Security Function*, in R. Oakley, M. Dziedzic & E. Goldberg (Eds.), Policing the New World Disorder 399 (1998).

established its control.[293] The potential conflict of interests is created by the exercise of authority by the occupant. In this sense the examples mentioned by Kelly seem to be proper occupants. UNOSOM II for example asserted a number of governmental or quasi-governmental powers in the state, including the rebuilding and resuscitation of key Somali institutions such as courts, the police force as well as political and administrative institutions that largely functioned under the operation's control.[294] The assertion of authority was based on the assumption that there was no sovereign authority in Somalia.[295]

The difference between traditional occupations and the presence of a peace support operation is that the presence of the latter is regulated by an alternative legal regime. The operation has a mandate under the Security Council resolution which established or authorized the operation. In addition there is in many cases a SOFA or Military Technical Agreement detailing the status, powers and responsibilities of the force. These elements raise questions concerning the appropriateness of applying the law of occupation. One question is whether the consent of the host state does not preclude the application of the law of occupation. Although the law of occupation has been dislodged from the context of armed conflict, it could be argued that its application still requires occupation against the will of the sovereign. In the case a peace support operation clearly has the consent of the government, for example UNEF, it seems that there is no occupation as the term has been used traditionally in international law.[296] This argumentation, at least in respect of the meaning of 'occupation' under the 1954 Convention for the Protection of Cultural Property in the Event of Armed Conflict, is supported by a report of a meeting of experts convened by the government of the Netherlands in July 1993. The report of the meeting states:

> The question was raised of whether the word 'occupation' in the 1954 Convention permits the application of the relevant provisions of the Convention to activities undertaken within the framework of peace-keeping activities. As long as the United Nations peace-keeping forces operate with the consent of the host State, such operations were not regarded as an occupation under the Convention.[297]

In the case of UNOSOM II, however, there was no government to give consent and it is disingenuous to claim that the operation acted with the consent of all the factions.

293 Benvenisti, *supra* note 282, at 4.

294 See S. Scott, *Legality in a Collapsed State: The Somali Experience*, 45 International & Comparative Law Quarterly 910 (1996).

295 M.J. Kelly, Restoring and Maintaining Order in Complex Peace Operations: The Search for a Legal Framework 67-68 (1999).

296 Roberts, *supra* note 291, at 291.

297 Final Report of the Meeting of Experts on the application and effectiveness of the Convention for the Protection of Cultural Property in the Event of Armed Conflict (The Hague, 14 May 1954), Annex to Report by the Director-General on the Reinforcement of UNESCO's Action for the Protection of the World Cultural and Natural Heritage of 18 August 1993, Doc. 142 EX/15, Ann., para. 6.1.

In the 1995 supplement to An Agenda for Peace, the UN Secretary-General stated that the mandate of the operation led it to forfeit the consent of the parties.[298]

In the case of KFOR, the FRY has given its consent to the presence of the operation in the Military Technical Agreement. It can be argued, however, that the government's consent was obtained by duress. Article 52 of the Vienna Convention on the Law of Treaties provides that a treaty is void if its conclusion has been procured by the threat or use of force in violation of the principles of international law embodied in the Charter of the United Nations. Consent to the Military Technical Agreement was certainly procured by the use of force during Operation Allied Force, and it can be argued that this use of force was a violation of the most important principle in the UN Charter, the prohibition of the use of force.[299] Cerone states that while the presence of the operation has been rendered legal by Security Council Resolution 1244 and must be accepted by the FRY, this does not directly affect the application of the 1949 Geneva Conventions.[300]

It can be argued that even in the absence of a valid SOFA the rights and duties of a peace support operation are derived exclusively from its mandate in a Security Council resolution and exclude the law of occupation, in particular in the case of a resolution under Chapter VII of the UN Charter.[301] A resolution under Chapter VII can override existing obligations under international humanitarian law, including the law of occupation, as Article 103 of the UN Charter makes clear. However, Security Council resolutions generally do not expressly depart from the law of occupation, and consequently do not replace that law.[302] In addition, Security Council resolutions only provide very general guidelines for a peace support operation. Security Council mandates are notoriously vague, as recognized most recently in the Brahimi Report.[303] They do not establish clear guidance for matters such as the handling of detainees, the procedure and standards applicable for dealing with local officials employed or

298 UN Doc. S/1995/1 of 3 January 1995, para. 34.

299 See *e.g.* I. Brownlie, *Kosovo: House of Commons Foreign Affairs Committee 4th Report, June 2000: Memoranda*, 49 International & Comparative Law Quarterly 876 (2000), para. 88-98 relating to the Rambouillet agreement. The same argument can be applied to the Military Technical Agreement.

300 J. Cerone, *Minding the Gap: Outlining KFOR Accountability in Post-Conflict Kosovo*, 12 European Journal of International Law 469 (2001), at 484.

301 D. Schraga, intervention in L. Condorelli, A.-M. La Rosa & S. Scherrer, Les Nations Unies et le Droit International Humanitaire 433 (1996).

302 See T. Irmscher, *The Legal Framework for the Activities of the United Nations Interim Administration in Kosovo: The Charter, Human Rights, and the Law of Occupation*, 44 German Yearbook of International Law 353 (2001), at 375-387.

303 UN Doc. S/2000/809 of 21 August 2000, para 56: As a political body, the Security Council focuses on consensus-building, even though it can take decisions with less than unanimity. But the compromises required to build consensus can be made at the expense of specificity, and the resulting ambiguity can have serious consequences in the field if the mandate is then subject to varying interpretation by different elements of a peace operation.

approved by the operation and the relationship between the force and the population.[304] The law of occupation may be required to give more specific guidance.

At the December 2003 Experts Meeting organized by the ICRC, experts drew attention to the traditional separation between the *ius ad bellum* and the *ius in bello*. In principle, the legal basis for an occupation has no bearing on the question of the applicability of the law of occupation. They underlined the difficulty of reconciling certain provisions of the law of occupation with the particular nature of UN mandated operations which are in control of a given territory. In this connection, they discussed the possibility that changes may be justified on the basis of international human rights law and the mandate entrusted to the force by the Security Council. They also envisaged the possibility that a clear mandate from the UN Security Council based on Article 103 could supersede, or even end, the application of the law of occupation.[305] As discussed above, in such a case the Council should deviate explicitly from occupation law, and provide an alternative standard of conduct.

State practice in general does not support the application of the law of occupation to peace support operations.[306] One possible exception appears to be Australia. The government of Australia stated at the 1998 Meeting of Contracting Parties to the Geneva Convention (IV) that the:

> Fourth Geneva Convention is a good model to use in peace operations involving deployment without consent as it is geared to take account of the exigencies of attempting to administer or restore order in war-like conditions as opposed to a peace time human rights regime. Australian troops in Somalia found this to be the case when they were deployed into, and given responsibility for, the Bay province during Operation Restore Hope in 1993. Following a determination that the Fourth Convention applied to that intervention, the Australian force relied on the Convention to provide answers to, and a framework for, many initiatives.

A Belgian Military Court of Appeal on the other hand held in 1997 that UNOSOM II could not be assimilated to an occupying power, because the operation did not have any of the powers or responsibilities that international treaties confer on an occupying power.[307]

It seems that NATO and troop contributing states do not consider the law of occupation applicable to KFOR.[308] Burger states that one reason is that the authority of the operation is not based on the imposition of military control by a state upon another state, but on the authorization by the UN to keep the peace.[309] It appears that

---

304 Kelly, *supra* note 295, at 70.

305 *Supra* note 248, at 209-210.

306 S. Vité, *L'Applicabilité du Droit International de l'Occupation Militaire aux Activités des Organisations Internationales*, 86 International Review of the Red Cross 9 (2004), at 21.

307 *Supra* note 246.

308 A. van Loon, *supra* note 230, at 656.

309 Burger, *supra* note 231, at 129.

one reason for governments and international organizations to oppose the application of the law of occupation to peace support operations is due to the positive obligations imposed by that regime. Lorenz states that the United States and most other governments are very reluctant to invoke and apply Geneva Convention (IV) and the law of occupation because the political, economic and legal ramifications of taking over functions of sovereignty and administration of another state are enormous.[310] The most important obligation arising under the law of occupation is the obligation to take all the measures in the power of the occupant to restore and ensure, as far as possible, public order and civil life.[311] This is a task which those operations claimed to be subject to the law of occupation are expressly mandated to undertake or find themselves undertaking in practice. Security Council Resolution 814 requested UNOSOM II to assume responsibility for the consolidation, expansion and maintenance of a secure environment throughout Somalia,[312] and Security Council Resolution 1244 states that one of the responsibilities of KFOR is to ensure public safety and order until the international civil presence can take responsibility for this task.[313] Other obligations under the law of occupation concern the welfare of the population. Kelly notes in relation to these obligations that Geneva Convention (IV):

> only obliges the force to assume responsibilities for the population in terms of health, sustenance, and welfare to the extent that it has the spare capacity to do so, beyond what it needs to deal with operational demands, and only to the maximum extent feasible. The role of meeting the needs of the population is more than adequately met by simply allowing the array of NGOs to do their job in these environments as they will always be present.[314]

3.13 Content of rules of general international law

It was argued that rules of general international law are applicable to UN and NATO peace support operations. This makes it important to indicate which rules of international humanitarian law are rules of general international law or in other words customary international law or general principles of law. It is clearly beyond the scope of this study to examine state practice in relation to every rule of international humanitarian law because of the sheer magnitude of the task. In addition, as the Appeals Chamber of the Yugoslavia Tribunal in the *Tadić* case emphasized, an examination of state practice in relation to rules of international humanitarian law is rendered extremely difficult by the fact that not only is access to the theatre of military operations normally refused to independent observers, but information on the actual conduct of hostilities is withheld by the parties to the conflict. The course recommended

310 F. Lorenz, *The U.S. Perspective of Operation Restore Hope*, in R. Oakley, M. Dziedzic & E. Goldberg (Eds.), Policing the New World Disorder (1998).

311 1907 Hague Regulations, Article 43.

312 Security Council Resolution 814 of 26 March 1993, UN Doc. S/RES/814, para. 14.

313 Security Council Resolution 1244 of 10 June 1999, UN Doc. S/RES/1244, para. 9, sub b.

314 Kelly, *supra* note 292, at 399.

by the Chamber, to place reliance primarily on such elements as official pronouncements of states, military manuals and judicial decisions, will mainly be followed.[315] Special emphasis will be placed on pronouncements of the ICJ.[316]

It may be recalled that the rules in question have developed through application to states. The factual differences between states and international organizations require that the rules are applicable *mutatis mutandis* to the organizations. In other words, the factual differences between a state and an international organization may require the modification of rules.[317] For example, the members of the UN and NATO have not conferred criminal jurisdiction on the organizations, requiring a modification of rules concerning criminal prosecution.

The rules in the 1907 Hague Regulations appear to be accepted as customary international law. The International Military Tribunal at Nuremberg stated that the 1907 Hague Regulations by 1939 were "recognized by all civilized nations, and were regarded as being declaratory of the laws and customs of war."[318] This was reaffirmed by the ICJ in its Advisory Opinion on the *Legal Consequences of the Construction of a Wall in the Occupied Palestinian Territory*.[319] It has also been suggested that the entire mass of rules in the 1949 Geneva Conventions are customary international law. In particular, the UN Secretary-General stated in his report on the establishment of the Yugoslavia Tribunal that the:

> part of conventional International Humanitarian Law which has beyond doubt become part of international customary law is the law applicable in armed conflict as embodied in: the Geneva Conventions of 12 August 1949 for the Protection of War Victims; the Hague Convention (IV) Respecting the Laws and Customs of War on Land and the Regulations annexed thereto of 18 October 1907.[320]

It is however unlikely that all the provisions of the 1949 Geneva Conventions are customary international law, if only because some of the technical rules in the conventions have never been implemented in practice. The Commission of Experts for the former Yugoslavia (the Kalshoven Commission) did not go so far as the Secretary-General, but only stated that the:

---

315 *Supra* note 34, para. 99.

316 See generally J. Gardam, *The Contribution of the International Court of Justice to International Humanitarian Law*, 14 Leiden Journal of International Law 349 (2001); V. Chetail, *The Contribution of the International Court of Justice to International Humanitarian Law*, 85 International Review of the Red Cross 235 (2003).

317 See *e.g.* Seyersted, *supra* note 22, at 202-203.

318 Trial of the Major War Criminals before the International Military Tribunal, vol. I, at 267 (1947).

319 *Supra* note 64, para. 89.

320 Report of the Secretary-General pursuant to paragraph 2 of Security Council Resolution 808 (1993) of 3 May 1993, UN Doc. S/25704, para. 35.

> body of customary international law applicable to international armed conflicts includes the concept of war crimes, and a wide range of provisions also stated in Hague Convention IV of 1907, the Geneva Conventions of 1949 and, to some extent, the provisions of Additional Protocol I.[321]

There is also state practice supporting a more limited scope of customary rules.[322] Nevertheless, the great majority of the rules in the 1949 Geneva Conventions undoubtedly have a customary character. These include common Article 3 of the 1949 Geneva Conventions. The ICJ in the *Nicaragua* case held that these rules constitute a minimum yardstick which applies in all armed conflicts and that they reflect 'elementary considerations of humanity'.[323] This customary character of common Article 3 in international and non-international armed conflicts has been reaffirmed in the case law of the Yugoslavia Tribunal.[324] The Appeals Chamber emphasized that common Article 3 is the quintessence of the 1949 Geneva Conventions in the *Čelebići* case:

> It is indisputable that common Article 3, which sets forth a minimum core of mandatory rules, reflects the fundamental humanitarian principles which underlie International Humanitarian Law as a whole, and upon which the Geneva Conventions in their entirety are based. These principles, the object of which is the respect for the dignity of the human person, developed as a result of centuries of warfare and had already become customary law at the time of the adoption of the Geneva Conventions because they reflect the most universally recognised humanitarian principles.[325]

The ICJ in the *Nicaragua* case also held that the 1949 Geneva Conventions are "in some respects a development, and in other respects no more than an expression" of "fundamental general principles of humanitarian law."[326]

In its Advisory Opinion in the *Nuclear Weapons* case the ICJ also discussed the character of certain rules of international humanitarian law. It stated that:

> It is undoubtedly because a great many rules of humanitarian law applicable in armed conflict are so fundamental to the respect of the human person and "elemen-

321 Final report of the Commission of Experts established pursuant to Security Council Resolution 780 (1992) of 24 May 1994, UN Doc. S/1994/674.

322 See *e.g.* oral statement by Australia to the International Court of Justice in the Nuclear Weapons case, 30 October 1995, para. 8.

323 Military and Paramilitary Activities in and against Nicaragua (*Nicaragua* v. *United States of America*), Merits, 1986 ICJ Reports 14, at 114, para. 218.

324 See *e.g. Prosecutor* v. *Tadić, supra* note 237, para. 609; *Prosecutor* v. *Miroslav Kvočka, Milojica Kos, Mlađo Radić, Zoran Žigić and Dragoljub Prcać*, Judgment, Case No. IT-98-30, Tr. Ch. I, 2 November 2001, para. 124.

325 *Prosecutor* v. *Zejnil Delalić, Zdravko Mucić, Hazim Delić and Esad Landžo ("Čelebići Case")*, Case No. IT-96-21, Judgement, A. Ch., 20 February 2001, para. 143.

326 *Supra* note 323.

> tary considerations of humanity" as the Court put it in its Judgment of 9 April 1949 in the *Corfu Channel* case (*I.C.J. Reports 1949*, p. 22), that the Hague and Geneva Conventions have enjoyed a broad accession. Further these fundamental rules are to be observed by all States whether or not they have ratified the conventions that contain them, because they constitute intransgressible principles of international customary law.[327]

The Court specifically isolated the principle of distinction between combatants and non-combatants, and the prohibition of the use of weapons causing unnecessary suffering, as the "cardinal principles contained in the texts constituting the fabric of humanitarian law."[328] The term 'intransgressible principles' as used by the Court, is confusing because it is unfamiliar to international lawyers, at least in conventional international law. Despite this ambiguity, it is clear that the Court recognized that the corpus of international humanitarian law contained in the major conventions essentially comprises general and customary international law.[329]

It is generally recognized that many but not all of the rules in Additional Protocol I are customary international law, but there is controversy over precisely which rules do not have a customary character.[330] ICTY case law has contributed significantly to the identification of these rules. Trial Chamber III for example stated in the *Kordić and Čerkez* case that there is no possible doubt that Article 15 (1-2) of the Protocol forms part of customary international law.[331] Trial Chamber I held in the *Strugar* case that it had no doubt that Articles 51 and 52 of the Protocol constitute a reaffirmation of existing norms of customary international law.[332] The methodology used by the Tribunal has however been criticized, because it relies almost exclusively on statements rather than operational practice.[333] The Tribunal seems to only formally adhere to the traditional theory of custom, requiring practice and *opinio iuris*.

For this reason states and international organizations may attach more importance to the results of a study undertaken by the ICRC published in 2005.[334] The

327 Legality of the Threat or Use of Nuclear Weapons, *supra* note 63, para. 79.

328 *Id.*, para. 78.

329 See L. Condorelli, *Nuclear Weapons: A Weighty Matter for the International Court of Justice*, 79 International Review of the Red Cross 9 (1997).

330 "Although the United States is not a party to the Additional Protocols, many of those provisions form part of international customary law." Reply by the Minister of Foreign Affairs, Question No. 224, South African National Assembly, 16 October 2002; Aldrich, *supra* note 5, at 19.

331 *Prosecutor* v. *Dario Kordić & Mario Čerkez*, Decision on Joint Defence Motion to Dismiss the Amended Indictment for Lack of Jurisdiction based on Limited Jurisdictional Reach of Articles 2 and 3, Case No. IT-95-14/2-PT, Tr. Ch. III, 2 March 1999.

332 *Prosecutor* v. *Pavle Strugar et al*, Decision on Defence Preliminary Motion Challenging Jurisdiction, Case No. IT-01-42-PT, Tr. Ch. I, 7 June 2002.

333 See *e.g.* T. Meron, *The Continuing Role of Custom in the Formation of International Humanitarian Law*, 90 American Journal of International Law 238 (1996).

334 J-M. Henckaerts, *Study on Customary Rules of International Humanitarian Law: Purpose, Coverage and Methodology*, 81 International Review of the Red Cross 660 (1999).

study was undertaken pursuant to an invitation by the 1995 International Conference of the Red Cross and Red Crescent, which endorsed a recommendation of the Intergovernmental Group of Experts for the Protection for War Victims. The recommendation proposed that:

> The ICRC be invited to prepare, with the assistance of experts in IHL representing various geographical regions and different legal systems, and in consultation with experts from governments and international organisations, a report on customary rules of IHL applicable in international and non-international armed conflicts, and to circulate the report to States and competent international bodies.

The study specifically concerns the customary character of the rules in the 1977 Additional Protocols. The conclusions in the report are based on research using both national and international sources. The sources in question include not only verbal statements but also operational practice.

3.14 Conclusion

The focus in this chapter has been on the obligations of the UN and NATO under international humanitarian law. Only if the organizations actually do have such responsibilities can they be responsible for conduct which is attributable to them and which breaches international humanitarian law.

The question whether international organizations as international legal persons are bound by international humanitarian law has mainly focused on the UN, and less on NATO. The legal contours of the latter organization are beginning to be the subject of public and academic, if not diplomatic, discussion, after Operation Allied Force and applications to the International Court of Justice, the European Court of Human Rights and national courts related to that campaign.

In the last decade, the discussion concerning international law obligations of the UN in general, and the Security Council in particular, has to a large extent taken place in the context of economic sanctions imposed by the Security Council. Economic sanctions in general, and in particular the economic sanctions imposed on Iraq after the invasion of Kuwait, were recognized as leading in certain cases to humanitarian disasters and encroachments upon basic principles of humanity.[335] In this context certain writers even identified a human rights paradox, in the sense that after the end of the Cold War the UN increasingly reacted to violations of human rights by imposing sanctions, while the sanctions themselves seemed to breach human rights. Emphasizing international law obligations of the Security Council is considered as one possible avenue to achieve mitigation of the sanctions and their effects.

Writers taking this avenue often simply assert international law limitations on the Security Council, and do not analyze the origin, scope and existence of the obliga-

335 See N. Schrijver, *The Use of Economic Sanctions by the United Nations Security Council: An International Law Perspective*, in H. Post (Ed.), International Economic Law and Armed Conflict 123 (1994).

tion in any detail. This is not problematic if the criticism of sanctions is from a moral or ethical perspective,[336] but it is not sufficient as a matter of legal argument.

Obligations do not arise from international humanitarian law treaties. These treaties only bind the contracting parties, and the organizations in question are not states parties. The accession clauses of the main modern international humanitarian law treaties, the 1949 Geneva Conventions and the 1977 Additional Protocols, also exclude the possibility of accession of international organizations. This is implied in the ordinary meaning of the term 'Powers' used in the clauses in question, and reaffirmed by the *travaux préparatoires* of the Additional Protocols. In this context it is also relevant that the evolution in UN practice towards a recognition of the applicability of international humanitarian law to peace support operations has not resulted in serious consideration of the possibility of accession but in a separate instrument for these operations.

Another possible source of humanitarian obligations is the constituent documents of the UN and NATO. In the case of the UN there is a distinction between action taken by the Security Council under Chapter VII of the UN Charter and other action. In the case of the former, Articles 24 and 1 (1) provide that the Security Council can derogate from international law. The *travaux préparatoires* of Article 1 (1) reaffirm that this was the intention of the drafters. The committee concerned with the drafting of Article 1 (1), at the San Francisco Conference took a decision to move the phrase 'in conformity with the principles of justice and international law' from the first part of paragraph 1 to the latter part, so that it would apply only to the 'adjustment or settlement of international disputes or situations'. This change was made to ensure that existing law would not limit the vital duty of preventing and removing threats to and breaches of the peace. In this context the importance attached to the maintenance or restoration of international peace and security by the negotiators can hardly be overestimated. Goodrich explains that one of the sponsoring governments of the Dumbarton Oaks proposals, the Soviet Union, at first considered that the organization should be exclusively limited in its functions to the maintenance of international peace and security and that while the great powers eventually agreed to give the organization additional functions, those who wrote the Charter were "convinced that the first job of the new organization, both in time and in importance, was to keep the peace."[337]

The possibility for the Security Council to derogate from international law when it is acting under Chapter VII may be excluded in the case of peremptory norms. This, however, hardly constitutes a broad limitation on the powers of the Council, *inter alia* because it appears that only a limited number of international humanitarian law rules are *ius cogens*.

In the exercise of powers other than under Chapter VII of the Charter, the UN and the Security Council are expected to act in conformity with principles of justice

336 See J. Gordon, *A Peaceful, Silent, Deadly Remedy: The Ethics of Economic Sanctions*, 13 Ethics & International Affairs (1999); D. Cortright & G. Lopez, *Are Sanctions Just? The Problematic Case of Iraq*, 52 Journal of International Affairs 33 (1999).

337 L. Goodrich, The United Nations 23, 159 (1960).

and international law. This includes action for the peaceful settlement of disputes under Chapter VI of the UN Charter.[338]

Article 1 (3) of the UN Charter provides an obligation for the UN to respect human rights. The *travaux préparatoires* suggest that an obligation for the member states was rejected but that it was retained for the organization itself. Arguably, the scope of this obligation extends to international humanitarian law. In this context it is relevant that the recent development of international humanitarian law has been influenced by human rights to such an extent that some writers speak of a convergence between the two fields of law. Article 1 (3), does not affect the conclusion that the Security Council is not bound by international law in the exercise of powers under Chapter VII of the United Nations Charter. The Charter must be read as a whole, and the phrasing of Article 1 (1) received close attention of the drafters of the Charter, such that if they had intended paragraph 3 as an exception to that rule they would have stated this expressly.

NATO, and the UN, except in the exercise of powers under Chapter VII of the Charter, are both bound by customary rules and general principles of international humanitarian law. As international legal persons they are subject to the general rules which apply in the system in which they operate. Their member states have entrusted certain functions to them but also the attendant duties and responsibilities, as the ICJ states in the *Reparations for Injuries* case. The duty to respect international humanitarian law is attendant to the use of force once it crosses a certain level of intensity. In this regard it is not relevant that the organization in question has not participated in the development of the rules concerned.

The precise contours of the body of customary rules and general principles of international humanitarian law is subject to debate, but there are also many rules that clearly belong in this category. ICJ case law has identified the core of these rules. The case law of the ICTY and ICTR is useful to identify a broader category of customary rules, and the publication of the study on customary international humanitarian law by the ICRC brings additional guidance.

State practice in relation to UN peace support operations supports the idea that such operations are bound by rules of international humanitarian law. Such recognition has been incremental, in the sense that it was first ambiguous and became increasingly clear. First the organization undertook to respect the principles and spirit of international humanitarian law conventions in agreements between the organization and states contributing troops. Although the precise content of these principles and spirit remained unclear, practice in relation to ONUC makes clear that it was not an empty undertaking. In particular, the organization admitted legal responsibility for crimes committed by members of the operation with reference to the principles of international humanitarian law. Although the drafters of Additional Protocol I rejected the possibility of accession of international organizations to the protocols, neither the UN nor member states rejected the idea that the organization has obliga-

338 R. Higgins, *The Place of International Law in the Settlement of Disputes by the Security Council*, 64 American Journal of International Law 1 (1970). See also the dissenting opinion of Judge Weeramantry in the *Lockerbie* cases (Provisional Measures), *supra* note 8.

tions under international humanitarian law which are separate from those of states. The obligation of states under common Article 1 of the 1949 Geneva Conventions does not cease to operate after the transfer of powers to an international organization, in accordance with the position of the ICRC, but this obligation co-exists with those of the UN under general international law.

The adoption of the Convention on the Safety of United Nations and Associated Personnel in 1994 constituted the first recognition that international humanitarian law, and not only its principles and spirit, is applicable to peace support operations established by the UN. The exclusion clause in Article 2 (2) implicitly recognizes the applicability of international humanitarian law. The savings clause in Article 20 (a) of the convention recognizes the applicability of international humanitarian law to peace support operations, although it does not clearly determine when personnel cross the dividing line between protected persons and combatants.

The 1999 Secretary-General's Bulletin on the Observance of International Humanitarian Law by United Nations Forces is an explicit recognition of the applicability of international humanitarian law to UN peace support operations. The preamble to the Bulletin presents a departure from the traditional reference to 'principles and spirit' where it states that the document sets out the 'fundamental principles and rules' of international humanitarian law to UN forces. The majority of the provisions of the Bulletin reflect customary international law, but many other rules of customary international law are not included in the document. It seems that this is related to the fact that the Bulletin is mainly intended as a tool for instruction, rather than an exhaustive list of all the applicable rules.

The Statute of the ICC implicitly also recognizes the applicability of international humanitarian law to UN peace support operations. Under Article 8 of the Statute, attacking personnel involved in a peacekeeping mission is a war crime within the jurisdiction of the Court, but only if such personnel was entitled to protection given to civilians under the international law of armed conflict. This implies that there are situations in which the personnel in question is not entitled to this protection, in other words that they are combatants who are bound by the rules of international humanitarian law. It is also relevant that the United States chose to veto the extension of the mandate of the United Nations Mission in Bosnia Herzegovina as one of the steps in its efforts to exempt United States military personnel from the jurisdiction of the Court.[339] The choice of an operation under UN command and control implies that the personnel in such operations are capable of committing crimes within the jurisdiction of the Court, including serious violations of international humanitarian law. This is reaffirmed by a letter from UN Secretary-General Kofi Annan to United States Secretary of State Colin Powell in which the Secretary-General expressed his concern at the United States veto. The letter recognizes that in principle personnel of a United Nations peace support operation could commit crimes within the jurisdiction of the Court, though in practice this is "highly improbable."[340]

---

339 See C. Lynch, *U.S. Fails to Get Support on Immunity for Its Peacekeepers*, Washington Post, 4 July 2002.

340 Letter from the Secretary-General to Secretary of State Powell, 3 July 2002.

The Statute of the Special Court for Sierra Leone also expressly recognizes that transgressions by personnel of peace support operations may come within the jurisdiction of the Special Court, which includes serious violations of international humanitarian law.

Almost no state practice in relation to NATO peace support operations supports the idea that the organization has obligations under international humanitarian law separate from its member states.[341] Documents relating to the status of IFOR, SFOR,and KFOR lack reference to international humanitarian law. More fundamentally, it seems that officials of the organization and member states consider that in the context of international humanitarian law the organization cannot have obligations because it does not have international legal personality. In other contexts however it seems that they do recognize that the organization is an international legal person. Moreover, there is a strong argument that the organization has international legal personality. If the organization does have an international legal personality and its functions include the deployment of military operations, it seems that the inevitable conclusion must be that the organization itself must respect customary rules and general principles of international humanitarian law.

State practice supports the idea that the international/non-international dichotomy in international humanitarian law is not relevant to UN peace support operations. This practice is consistent with the idea that the ground for making the distinction, deference to state sovereignty, is not an attribute of international organizations. This is quite apart from, but consistent with, the increasing tendency to de-emphasize a clear dichotomy between international and non-international armed conflicts in legal instruments and in the case law of international tribunals.

In principle, it seems to be accepted that the threshold of application of international humanitarian law to the UN is to be determined by the threshold in customary international law. Under customary international law, it is required that hostilities reach a certain level of intensity and that the opponent is a state, or a non-governmental armed group with a certain degree of organization, making it capable of carrying out the various obligations that arise under international humanitarian law. The case law of the ICTY and ICTR provides indicators for the existence of an armed conflict, though a final determination remains to be made on a case-by-case basis.

State practice in relation to UN peace support operations makes clear that hostilities need to reach a relatively high level of intensity before personnel of a peace support operation are considered combatants. The UN does not seem to have considered personnel of UNOSOM II as combatants for example, though hostilities between the operation and United Somali Congress/Somali National Alliance involved heavy armor and resulted in a number of casualties. Greenwood states on the basis of this and other examples that it seems:

> that there is a tendency to treat the threshold for determining whether a force has become party to an armed conflict as being somewhat higher in the case of United

---

341 But see para. 2.3.

> Nations and associated forces engaged in a mission which has a primarily peace-keeping or humanitarian character than in the normal case of conflicts between states.[342]

It is difficult to determine whether there is a consistent tendency because the organization does not make clear statements on whether the personnel of a peace support operation are combatants in specific situations. If such a tendency exists, it is presumably the result of the desire of the organization and member states to insist as long as possible on the impartiality of peace support operations, a desire which at least politically does not sit well with the status of party to an armed conflict.

The majority of state practice does not support the application of the law of occupation to peace support operations. Only Australia has suggested that it may consider the law of occupation to be applicable to peace support operations. *De lege ferenda* the development of a broad concept of occupation according to which the law of occupation would apply to peace support operations which are present in territory without the consent of the government and that exercise similar functions as a military government seems to offer many advantages. The law of occupation provides a legal framework which addresses many issues that the UN and NATO have encountered in peace support operations.[343] For example, it offers a sound basis to detain or intern persons posing a security threat. Such a sound basis has been lacking in relation to peace support operations.

It is useful at this point to recall the importance of the determination of the applicable standards to international organizations. It is often stated that there is no right without a remedy, although as discussed in chapter 5 this is presently not the case for rights of persons that have been violated by peace support operations. At the same time there is also generally no remedy without a right, at least in the context of state responsibility. The principles of state responsibility distinguish between primary and secondary rules, but draft article 3 makes clear that there is no responsibility without an international obligation of the state, and this also applies to international organizations. Accountability also requires standards of accountability. For this reason it is important to determine the rules of international humanitarian law that bind the UN and NATO.

---

342 Greenwood, *supra* note 23, at 24.

343 See *e.g.* B. Levrat, *Le Droit International Humanitaire au Timor Oriental: Entre Théorie et Pratique*, 83 International Review of the Red Cross 77 (2001).

4

Legal consequences of accountability for breaches of international humanitarian law by peace support operations

4.1 Introduction

It was concluded in the previous chapters that the UN and NATO as well as states can be responsible for violations of international humanitarian law by members of peace support operations in certain circumstances. In case they are responsible, the question arises what the consequences are under international law.

4.2 The ILC's draft articles on state responsibility and legal consequences

4.2.1 Regulation of legal consequences

The legal consequences of an internationally wrongful act of a state are governed by Part Two of the ILC draft articles on state responsibility. The core legal consequences of an internationally wrongful act set out in this Part are the obligations of the responsible state to cease the wrongful conduct, and to make full reparation for the injury caused by the internationally wrongful act, as provided in draft articles 30-31.[1]

---

1 Draft articles 30 and 31 state:

Article 30
Cessation and non-repetition

The State responsible for the internationally wrongful act is under an obligation:
(a) To cease that act, if it is continuing;
(b) To offer appropriate assurances and guarantees of non-repetition, if circumstances so require.

Article 31
Reparation

1. The responsible State is under an obligation to make full reparation for the injury caused by the internationally wrongful act.
2. Injury includes any damage, whether material or moral, caused by the internationally wrongful act of a State.

Chapter II of Part Two deals with the forms of reparation for injury, spelling out in further detail the general principle stated in draft article 31.[2]

Chapter III of Part Two provides that there are additional legal consequences in case of a serious breach by a state of an obligation arising under a peremptory norm of general international law.[3]

The forms of reparation dealt with in Chapter II of Part Two represent ways of giving effect to the underlying obligation in draft article 31 and must be seen against this background. It is for this reason that the ILC points out that some flexibility is shown in practice in terms of the appropriateness of requiring one form of reparation rather than another, subject to the requirement of full reparation for the breach in accordance with draft article 31.[4] In other words, Chapter II provides a flexible system for implementing the obligation to make full reparation.

4.2.2 Cessation

Draft article 30 (a) of the draft articles presents the obligation to cease an internationally wrongful act as an aspect of the restoration and repair of the legal relationship affected by the breach of an international obligation.[5] Obviously, this obligation can only arise in case of an internationally wrongful act which is continuing. Examples of a continuing violation of international humanitarian law are the treatment of detainees in contravention of the applicable standards, maintaining in effect orders preventing

---

2 See draft article 34 which provides:

Article 34
Forms of reparation

Full reparation for the injury caused by the internationally wrongful act shall take the form of restitution, compensation and satisfaction, either singly or in combination, in accordance with the provisions of this chapter.

3 See draft article 41 which provides:

Article 41
Particular consequences of a serious breach of an obligation under this chapter

1. States shall cooperate to bring to an end through lawful means any serious breach within the meaning of article 40.
2. No State shall recognize as lawful a situation created by a serious breach within the meaning of article 40, nor render aid or assistance in maintaining that situation.
3. This article is without prejudice to the other legal consequences referred to in this Part and to such further consequences that a breach to which this chapter applies may entail under international law.

4 Report of the International Law Commission on the work of its fifty-third session, 23 April – 1 June and 2 July – 10 August 2001 (A/56/10), at 237.

5 See generally C. Deman, *La Cessation de l'Acte Illicite*, 23 Revue Belge de Droit International 476 (1990).

the free passage of medical and hospital stores and using the immediate surroundings of cultural property as a base.

Cessation is often confused with restitution. This has to do with the fact that a claim to restitution during a continuing violation of international law to a large extent coincides with the claim to stop the violation. Although the result of cessation may be indistinguishable from restitution, there is nevertheless a difference. Cessation is only concerned with the future while restitution is also concerned with the period before it is demanded.[6]

4.2.3 Assurances and guarantees of non-repetition

Similar to cessation, assurances and guarantees of non-repetition in draft article 30 (b) are an aspect of continuation and repair of the legal relationship affected by the breach. The focus is on the future, not on the past. This legal consequence of an internationally wrongful act has featured in the draft articles since it was proposed by Special Rapporteur Arangio-Ruiz in 1989.[7] Until 2000, assurances and guarantees were presented as an aspect of reparation rather than in the context of the continuation and repair of the legal relationship affected by the breach. Certain writers maintained that this legal consequence is not an autonomous legal consequence but a form of satisfaction.[8] If it is maintained, as Brownlie does, that satisfaction may be defined as any measure which an author of a breach of duty is bound to take apart from restitution or compensation, this is a logical conclusion.[9] The 1996 ILC draft articles on state responsibility separated assurances and guarantees of non-repetition from satisfaction, on the ground that they are future-oriented and have a preventive rather than a remedial function. Special Rapporteur Crawford took this observation to its logical conclusion and proposed to connect this legal consequence to cessation rather than place it in the chapter on reparation,[10] and the ILC followed the Special Rapporteur's conclusions.

The question whether the obligation to offer assurances or guarantees of non-repetition may be a legal consequence of an internationally wrongful act was debated in the *LaGrand* case.[11] The relief requested by Germany in this case included asking the Court to adjudge and declare that the United States should provide Germany with a

6 *Id.*, at 487-488.

7 See G. Arangio-Ruiz, Second Report on State Responsibility, YBILC 1989, Vol. II (Part 1), at 42, paras. 148-163 and at 56, para. 191.

8 See *e.g.* F. Przetacznik, *La Responsabilité Internationale de l'État à Raison des Préjudices de Caractère Moral et Politique Causés a un Autre État*, 78 Revue Générale de Droit International Public 919 (1974), at 966; P. Bissonnette, La Satisfaction Comme Mode de Réparation en Droit International 85 (1952).

9 I. Brownlie, System of the Law of Nations, State Responsibility, Part I, 208 (1983).

10 J. Crawford, Special Rapporteur, Third Report on State Responsibility of 15 March 2000, UN Doc. A/CN.4/507, at 26.

11 See G. Palmisano, *Les Garanties de Non-Répétition entre Codification et Réalisation Juridictionelle du Droit: A Propos de l'Affaire Lagrand*, 106 Revue Générale de Droit International Public 753 (2002).

guarantee of the non-repetition of the illegal acts, in this case the failure by the United States to notify an accused of his right to consular assistance. The United States disputed that such a remedy exists in the law of state responsibility.[12] In its judgment the Court seems to have accepted the existence of assurances and guarantees of non-repetition as a legal consequence of an internationally wrongful act:

> The Court considers that the commitment expressed by the United States to ensure implementation of the specific measures adopted in performance of its obligations under Article 36, paragraph 1 *(b)*, must be regarded as meeting Germany's request for a general assurance of non-repetition.[13]

Despite the judgment in *LaGrand* it is uncertain whether the obligation to provide assurances or guarantees of non-repetition is customary international law.[14] Although draft article 30 (b) has not attracted much comment by states, some question its existence under customary international law. Even Germany in its pleadings in the *LaGrand* case conceded that "some doubts might exist about its anchoring in customary law."[15] Some members of the drafting committee of the ILC held that the provision lacks substantial roots in existing state practice and that there is no clear evidence of an emerging principle of international law in this direction.[16] The drafting committee decided to retain article 30 (b) in the draft articles not because of its roots in state practice but because it thought the provision introduced a useful policy.[17] State practice with regard to assurances and guarantees of non-repetition is found in particular in connection with responsibility for breaches of human rights. In a number of cases the United Nations Human Rights Committee has required states to provide guarantees in its decisions on individual complaints. In *Paul* v. *Guyana*, for example, the Committee stated that the "State party is under an obligation to take appropriate measures to ensure that similar violations do not occur in the future."[18] The Inter-American Court of Human Rights in constant jurisprudence also requires states to provide assurances and guarantees. The Court finds the power to do so in the law of state responsibility. In the *Suárez Rosero* case it stated:

---

12 Verbatim Record, CR 2000/29, 14 November 2000, para. 5.23.

13 LaGrand case (*Germany* v. *United States of America*), reproduced in 40 ILM 1069 (2001), para. 124.

14 See also C. Dominicé, *La Satisfaction en Droit des Gens*, in Mélanges Georges Perrin 91 (1984), at 109.

15 Verbatim Record, CR 2000/30, 16 November 2000, para. 5.

16 Second statement made by Mr. Giorgio Gaja on behalf of the Chairman of the Drafting Committee, at the 2701st meeting, held on 3 August 2001.

17 *Id.*

18 *Paul* v. *Republic of Guyana*, 21 December 2001, UN Doc. CCPR/C/73/D/728/1996, Communication No. 728/1996. Other recent examples are *Des Fours Walderode* v. *Czech Republic*, 2 November 2001, UN Doc. CCPR/C/73/D/747/1997, Communication No. 747/1997, para. 9.2 and *Winata* v. *Australia*, 16 August 2001, UN Doc. CCPR/C/72/D/930/2000, Communication No. 930/2000, para. 9.

> In the matter of reparations, the applicable provision is Article 63(1) of the American Convention, which codifies one of the fundamental principles of general international law, and is repeatedly applied in case law. (Factory at Chorzów, Jurisdiction, Judgment No. 8, 1927, P.C.I.J., Series A, No 9, p.21 and Factory at Chorzów, Merits, Judgment No. 13, 1928,P.C.I.J., Series A, No. 17, p 29; Reparations for Injuries Suffered in the Service of the United Nations, Advisory Opinion, I.C.J. Reports 1949, p. 184). This is the sense in which this Court has applied that provision. [...] When a wrongful act occurs that is imputable to a State, the State incurs international responsibility for the violation of international law, and thus incurs a duty to make reparation.
> Reparations is a generic term that covers the different ways (restitutio in integrum, compensation, satisfaction, and assurances or guarantees that the violations will not be repeated, among others) in which a State can redress the international responsibility it has incurred.
> The obligation to make reparations established by international courts is governed, as has been universally accepted, by international law in all its aspects: scope, nature, forms, and the determination of beneficiaries, none of which the respondent State may alter by invoking its domestic law.[19]

The obligation to provide assurances and guarantees of non-repetition is not a legal consequence of every internationally wrongful act. The commentary to draft article 30 (b) states:

> Assurances and guarantees of non-repetition are not always appropriate, even if demanded. Much will depend on the circumstances of the case, including the nature of the obligation and of the breach. The rather exceptional character of the measures is indicated by the words 'if the circumstances so require' at the end of subparagraph (b).[20]

Some guidance on the conditions under which a duty to provide guarantees and assurances arises is given by the ILC commentary to the provision on assurances and guarantees in the draft articles adopted on first reading.[21] The commentary states that:

> Circumstances to be taken into consideration include the existence of a real risk of repetition and the seriousness of the injury suffered by the claimant State as a result of the wrongful act.[22]

---

19 Inter-American Court of Human Rights, *Suárez Rosero* v. *Ecuador*, Reparations, Judgment of 20 January 1999, Series C, No. 44, para. 40-42.

20 *Supra* note 4, para. 13.

21 See also *LaGrand* case, Verbatim Records, CR 2000/27, 13 November 2000, para. 25.

22 YBILC 1993, vol. II (Part Two), at 83, para. 5.

4.2.4 Reparation

As noted, article 31 of the ILC draft articles on state responsibility codifies the obligation of reparation. This article, as well as the articles describing specific forms of reparation, is formulated as an obligation of the responsible state. In contrast, the 1996 ILC draft articles formulated reparation as a right of the injured state.[23] The immediate reason for the change is the bifurcation in the 2001 draft articles between the injured state and the state which has a legal interest in invoking responsibility.[24] There is also a more fundamental policy choice behind it which reflects the function of state responsibility of upholding the international rule of law. Formulating reparation as a right of the injured state implies that that state can choose not to ask for reparation, and this is not in the interest of the international rule of law.[25] In contrast, the ILC commentary maintains that the obligation of reparation is the immediate corollary of a state's responsibility. This is in conformity with the PCIJ's pronouncement in the *Chorzów Factory* case that it:

> is a principle of international law that the breach of an engagement involves an obligation to make reparation in an adequate form. Reparation therefore is the indispensable complement of a failure to apply a convention and there is no necessity for this to be stated in the convention itself.[26]

The article on reparation is but one of a number of articles in which the ILC has had difficulty in maintaining the strict separation between primary and secondary obligations. The commentary acknowledges that the definition of injury in article 31 leaves it to the primary obligations to specify what is required in each case.[27]

As ILC draft article 34 makes clear, restitution, compensation and satisfaction are forms of reparation. They are *species* of the *genus* reparation.

4.2.5 Restitution

The ILC presents restitution as the principal form of reparation in article 35 of the ILC draft articles.[28] It reflects the primacy of restitution expressed in the *Chorzów Factory* case, in which the PCIJ stated that:

---

23 See also F. Mann, *The Consequences of an International Wrong in International and National Law*, 48 British Yearbook of International Law 1 (1976), at 10; R. Jennings & A. Watts, Oppenheim's International Law, Vol 1, at 528 (1992).

24 See para. 5.2.1.

25 Reitzer presents reparation from a third perspective. He states that a request for reparation is an obligation of the injured state that must be fulfilled before the injured state is entitled to take countermeasures. L. Reitzer, La Réparation comme Conséquence de l'Acte Illicite en Droit International 48 (1938).

26 Factory at Chorzów (*Germany* v. *Poland*), Jurisdiction, 1927, P.C.I.J. Series A, No. 9, at 21.

27 *Supra* note 4, at 226, para. 8.

28 Draft article 35 reads:

> reparation must, so far as possible, wipe-out all the consequences of the illegal act and re-establish the situation which would, in all probability, have existed if that act had not been committed. Restitution in kind, or, if this is not possible, payment of a sum corresponding to the value which a restitution in kind would bear; the award, if need be, of damages for loss sustained which would not be covered by restitution in kind or payment in place of it – such are the principles which should serve to determine the amount of compensation due for an act contrary to international law.[29]

Certain writers have raised the question whether restitution should be considered as the primary form of reparation, considering that in practice compensation is more frequently demanded and given than restitution.[30] The ILC has nonetheless opted for making restitution the first form of reparation because restitution most closely conforms to the general principle that the responsible state is bound to wipe out the legal and material consequences of its wrongful act by re-establishing the situation that would exist if that act had not been committed.[31]

The obligation to make restitution can be formulated as the obligation to establish the situation which would have existed if the wrongful act had not been committed, as the PCIJ did in the *Chorzów Factory* case. The ICJ continues to apply this formulation in relation to reparation, for example in the *Arrest Warrant (Yerodia)* case.[32] The obligation can also be considered as the obligation to establish the situation which existed prior to the occurrence of the wrongful act. The ILC has chosen not to adopt the former definition because, as the commentary to article 35 states, it absorbs into the concept of restitution elements of full reparation and tends to conflate restitution as a form of reparation and the underlying obligation of reparation itself.[33] This choice is not in conflict with the ICJ judgments if it is considered that restitution in itself may not lead to full reparation, and that the ILC draft articles recognize that loss of profits may be an appropriate head of compensation.

Even though restitution is the primary form of reparation, there are situations where it is not appropriate. These situations are set out in draft article 35 and essentially concern the situations where restitution is either impossible or impracticable. Apart from the situations set out in article 35, the ILC draft articles provide that

---

> A State responsible for an internationally wrongful act is under an obligation to make restitution, that is, to re-establish the situation which existed before the wrongful act was committed, provided and to the extent that restitution:
>
> (a) Is not materially impossible;
>
> (b) Does not involve a burden out of all proportion to the benefit deriving from restitution instead of compensation.

29 Factory at Chorzów (*Germany* v. *Poland*), Indemnity, 1928 PCIJ Series A, No 17, at 47.

30 C. Gray, *The Choice Between Restitution and Compensation*, 10 European Journal of International Law 413 (1999), at 418.

31 *Supra* note 4, at 238, para. 3.

32 Case concerning the Arrest Warrant of 11 April 2000 (*Democratic Republic of the Congo* v. *Belgium*), Judgment of 14 February 2002, reproduced in 41 ILM 536 (2002), para. 76.

33 *Supra* note 4, at 238, para. 2.

the state invoking international responsibility may choose the form the reparation it wants to receive in article 43 (2) (b). The 1996 draft articles did not provide for an express right of choice, although such a right was implied.[34]

4.2.6 Compensation

Where restitution is not provided or does not fully eliminate the consequences of the injury, the responsible state must make compensation, as provided in article 36 of the ILC draft articles.[35] In the *Gabčikovo-Nagymaros Project* case the ICJ held that:

> It is a well-established rule of international law that an injured State is entitled to obtain compensation from the State which has committed an internationally wrongful act for the damage caused by it.[36]

In state practice, compensation is the form of reparation which is most frequently asked and given: it is the usual standard of reparation.[37] It may be noted that the jurisprudence of the Iran – United States Claims Tribunal has made a particular contribution to the law on compensation.[38] The function of compensation is to address the actual losses incurred as a result of the internationally wrongful act. The ILC defines the actual losses as 'financially assessable damage'. Financially assessable damage is contrasted with what is sometimes referred to as 'moral damage' to the state, *i.e.* the affront or injury caused by a violation of rights not associated with actual damage to property or persons. This may lead to confusion because in national systems non-material damage such as loss of loved ones, pain and suffering are referred to as 'moral damage'. Under international law such damage is compensable and must be distinguished from moral damage to the state.

As noted above, draft article 43 provides that a state invoking responsibility can legitimately prefer compensation to restitution, but this freedom is not unlimited. The ILC commentary states that there are cases where a state may not, as it were, pocket compensation and walk away from an unresolved situation, for example one involving the life or liberty of individuals or the entitlement of a people to their territory or to self-determination.[39] The first situation seems to be characterized by the *LaGrand*

---

34 Gray, *supra* note 30, at 416.

35 Draft article 36 reads:

1. The State responsible for an internationally wrongful act is under an obligation to compensate for the damage caused thereby, insofar as such damage is not made good by restitution.
2. The compensation shall cover any financially assessable damage including loss of profits insofar as it is established.

36 Gabčikovo-Nagymaros Project (*Hungary* v. *Slovakia*), 1997 ICJ Reports 7, at 81, para. 152.

37 C. Eagleton, The Responsibility of States in International Law 189 (1929).

38 See R. Lillich & D. Magraw (Eds.), The Iran – United States Claims Tribunal: Its Contribution to the Law of State Responsibility (1998).

39 *Supra* note 4, at 304, para 6.

case, in which Germany renounced its right to material compensation. Although this was never expressly stated by Germany during the proceedings, its decision seems to have been related to its contention that the rights at issue constituted individual rights of foreign nationals and are to be regarded as human rights of aliens.[40] The ILC commentary does not provide guidance concerning other situations in which a state would not be entitled to prefer compensation, but it may be noted that the common element in the examples it gives is that the rights in question are owed to individuals or peoples. If the ILC intended this fact to have consequences for the choice between restitution and compensation, states are not free to prefer compensation in case of certain breaches of international humanitarian law, even if they do not involve the life or liberty of individuals.

4.2.7 Satisfaction

Article 37 of the ILC draft articles provides that the state responsible for an internationally wrongful act is under an obligation to give satisfaction for the injury caused by that act insofar as it cannot be made good by restitution or compensation.[41] Subject to the freedom of a state to choose a form of reparation under article 43, satisfaction is the last head of reparation in the hierarchy of forms of reparation. Paragraph 2 of article 37 lists acknowledgement of the breach, an expression of regret, and a formal apology as examples of satisfaction, but this list is not exhaustive. The ILC commentary gives a number of other examples, including due inquiry into the causes of an accident resulting in harm or injury and disciplinary or penal action against the individuals whose conduct caused the internationally wrongful act, but in theory the forms satisfaction may take are unlimited.[42] Satisfaction is the remedy generally given for moral, political or other non-material injury to the state.[43] The demand made by the Democratic People's Republic of Korea (North Korea) for an apology by Japan for its policy con-

---

40 Though it is implicit in the following statement by Simma on behalf of Germany made during the oral proceedings:

> Turning to compensation, Germany has decided not to raise a claim in this regard because the policy it pursues in lodging the present Application is to ensure that German nationals will be provided with adequate consular assistance in the future, and thus be protected against the fatal consequences following from breaches of Article 36 in circumstances like those leading to the death of the brothers LaGrand.

CR 2000/27, 13 November 2000, para. 14.

41 Draft article 37 reads:

> 1. The State responsible for an internationally wrongful act is under an obligation to give satisfaction for the injury caused by that act insofar as it cannot be made good by restitution or compensation.
> 2. Satisfaction may consist in an acknowledgement of the breach, an expression of regret, a formal apology or another appropriate modality.
> 3. Satisfaction shall not be out of proportion to the injury and may not take a form humiliating to the responsible State.

42 *Supra* note 4, at 265-266, para. 5.

43 Przetacznik, *supra* note 8, at 960.

cerning so-called 'comfort women' during World War II is an example of a claim for an apology based on a violation of international humanitarian law.[44] Another example is Eritrea's request to the Eritrea Ethiopia Claims Commission that Ethiopia be obligated to apologize for certain alleged violations of international humanitarian law.[45]

4.2.8 Lex specialis

Chapter II of the ILC draft articles on state responsibility is intended to provide for the legal consequences of all internationally wrongful acts of states. However, draft article 55 provides that they do not apply where the content of international responsibility is governed by special rules of international law. This provision recognizes the residual character of the draft articles. In principle states are free, when establishing or agreeing to be bound by a rule, to specify that its breach shall entail only particular consequences and thereby to exclude the ordinary rules of responsibility.[46] With regard to the legal consequences of an internationally wrongful act *lex specialis* can have two effects. One is to exclude one or more of the legal consequences provided in Chapter II. The other is to change the content of one or more particular consequences provided in Chapter II without affecting the other consequences. Whether there is *lex specialis* with regard to the legal consequences of violations of international humanitarian law will be discussed below.

4.2.9 Legal consequences of serious breaches of peremptory norms

Chapter III of Part Two (articles 40 and 41) of the draft articles on state responsibility set out certain legal consequences of serious breaches of an obligation arising under a peremptory norm of general international law. These consequences are additional to the consequences set out in chapters I and II (including restitution, compensation, satisfaction and guarantees of non-repetition). Articles 40 and 41 are closely related to article 48 which provides that any state can invoke responsibility if the obligation breached is owed to a group of states including that state, and is established for the protection of a collective interest of the group, or the obligation breached is owed to the international community as a whole. These articles are the result of a major debate in the ILC about whether a qualitative distinction should be recognized between different breaches of international law.[47] The debate was caused by the development of the doctrines of peremptory norms of international law and obligations *erga omnes*.

44 Letter from the Permanent Representative of the Democratic People's Republic of Korea to the United Nations Office at Geneva, addressed to the Chairman of the Commission on Human Rights of 9 April 1996, UN Doc. E/CN.4/1996/148.

45 Eritrea Ethiopia Claims Commission, Partial Award, Central Front, Eritrea's Claims 2, 4, 6, 7, 8 & 22, 28 April 2004, para. 114.

46 *Supra* note 4, at 62, para. 5.

47 For an overview see N.H.B. Jørgensen, The Responsibility of States for International Crimes (2001). See also various articles in the symposium on state responsibility, 10 European Journal of International Law 339 (1999).

The ILC recognized that these developments had implications for the secondary rules of state responsibility. Initially this recognition took the form of a distinction between 'international crimes of state' and 'international delicts'. This highly controversial distinction was abandoned by the Commission in 1998. What remains in the draft articles is the recognition that there are certain consequences flowing from the basic concepts of peremptory norms of general international law and obligations to the international community as a whole.[48]

Whether draft articles 40 and 41 merit discussion here depends first on whether rules of international humanitarian law are peremptory norms of general international law. Chapter III of Part Two only applies to the international responsibility which is entailed by a serious breach by a state of an obligation arising under a peremptory norm of general international law. According to the commentary to article 40:

> In light of the International Court's description of the basic rules of international humanitarian law applicable in armed conflict as 'intransgressible' in character, it would also seem justified to treat these as peremptory.[49]

The ICJ also suggested that certain obligations under international humanitarian law are of a peremptory nature in its Advisory Opinion on the *Legal Consequences of the Construction of a Wall in the Occupied Palestinian Territory*. In relation to the obligation to respect the right of self-determination and certain obligations under international humanitarian law, the Court stated that:

> Given the character and the importance of the rights and obligations involved, the Court is of the view that all States are under an obligation not to recognize the illegal situation resulting from the construction of the wall [and] not to render aid or assistance in maintaining the situation created by such construction.[50]

The Court thus appears to have attached certain of the legal consequences in article 41 to the breach of certain obligations under international humanitarian law. The implication is that the obligations concerned are peremptory norms.

Although this justifies the conclusion that the legal consequences set out in draft article 41 attach to at least certain violations of international humanitarian law, these are not discussed here. One reason is that there are serious doubts whether the legal consequences in article 41 are a codification of customary international law rather than a progressive development of the law.[51] At the very least the legal regime of serious breaches is in a state of development, as the ILC states in the commentary to article

48 See J. Crawford, P. Bodeau & J. Peel, *The ILC's Draft Articles on State Responsibility: Toward Completion of a Second Reading*, 94 American Journal of International Law 660(2000).

49 *Supra* note 4, at 284, para. 5.

50 *Legal Consequences of the Construction of a Wall in the Occupied Palestinian Territory*, Advisory Opinion of 9 July 2004, not yet reported, para. 159.

51 See *e.g.* D. Shelton, *Righting Wrongs: Reparations in the Articles on State Responsibility*, 96 American Journal of International Law 833 (2002), at 842.

41.[52] Comments by governments on the legal regime of serious breaches also suggest that the legal consequences set out in article 41 may not reflect present-day international law. The United Kingdom for example in its statement to the Sixth Committee of the General Assembly on the topic of state responsibility in 2001 stated that "the provisions relating to serious breaches of fundamental obligations go far beyond codification of customary international law."[53] A second reason for not discussing articles 40 and 41 in this book is that for the regime to apply there must be a breach of an obligation arising under a peremptory norm of general international law that is 'serious'.[54] A breach of an obligation is serious if it involves a gross or systematic failure by the responsible state to fulfill the obligation. The term 'systematic' refers to a breach carried out in an organized and deliberate way, whereas 'gross' denotes the intensity of the breach or its effects. Although it is not unlikely that a peace support operation may breach international humanitarian law, it seems unlikely that such a breach will be gross or systematic.

4.3 The law of international responsibility of international organizations and legal consequences

The law on the international responsibility of international organizations is still underdeveloped. This is the case with regard to the element of attribution of conduct, and maybe even more so with regard to the legal consequences of an internationally wrongful act. The underdevelopment is partly due to the lack of standing of international organizations before international courts and tribunals with the result that these judicial bodies are rarely called upon to consider the international responsibility of international organizations. It is also partly due to the immunities enjoyed by international organizations with the result that domestic courts rarely consider the responsibility of the organizations.[55] As discussed above, the ILC decided in 2001 to include the responsibility of international organizations in its long-term program of work.

---

52 *Supra* note 4, at 292, para. 14; See also S. Wittich, *The ILC's Articles on the Responsibility of States for Internationally Wrongful Acts Adopted on Second Reading*, 15 Leiden Journal of International Law 891 (2002).

53 Statement by the United Kingdom to the Sixth Committee of the General Assembly, 29 October 2001, <http//www.ukun.org/xq/asp/SarticleType.17/Article_ID.340/qx/articles_show.htm>. See also the comments by Japan and the United States, Comments and observations received from Governments, 19 March 2001,UN Doc. A/CN.4/515, at 48, 52. Statement by Israel to the sixth committee in 2000, <http://www.israel-un.org/committees/sixth/6_102400.htm>, and statement by the Netherlands to the sixth committee in 2001, stating that: "while recognizing that the introduction of the concept of 'serious breaches' is an acceptable compromise, what in my view is still insufficiently elaborated, are the specific legal consequences to be attached to the commission of a serious breach", <http://www.pvnewyork.org/archive/c_responsibility.htm>.

54 For a critique of the requirement of 'seriousness', see W. Czapliński, *UN Codification of Law of State Responsibility*, 41 Archiv des Völkerrechts 62 (2003), at 73.

55 See also M.H. Arsanjani, *Claims against International Organizations: Quis custodiet ipsos custodes*, 7 The Yale Journal of World Public Order 131 (1981), at 174: "A corollary of the principle of responsibility is the principle of remedy. The point, which would appear to be self-evident, often is overlooked, in part because of enforcement problems."

The application of the rules on legal consequences in the draft articles on state responsibility to international organizations is in principle possible, and corresponds to the general idea that there is merit in applying, as much as possible, the same secondary rules of responsibility to all subjects of international law.[56] The rules of state responsibility have been developed to a large extent as rules governing responsibility of subjects of international law. The international responsibility of a state is closely linked to its international legal personality. Only because a state has international legal personality does it have the capacity to have obligations under international law. Only because a state has obligations under international law can it be responsible for breach of those obligations. The development of rules of international responsibility has taken place with special regard to states at least in part because until relatively recently international lawyers considered that only states are subjects of international law. There is no reason why they cannot in principle also be applied to other subjects of international law. Traces of such an approach to the topic of international responsibility can be found in Special Rapporteur García Amador's first report on state responsibility for the ILC.[57] In his report he presented a summary of his research and some of the conclusions reached in the form of 'bases of discussion' including the conclusion that international organizations may be subjects of international responsibility in respect of acts or omissions of their organs so far as the duty to make reparation for the injury caused is concerned.[58] In another 'basis of discussion' concerning the character, function and measure of reparation, the Special Rapporteur did not distinguish between international organizations and states.[59] The ILC subsequently limited the scope of the topic to state responsibility. It has stated moreover that the draft articles on state responsibility are without prejudice to any question which may arise in regard to the responsibility under international law of an international organization as provided in draft article 57. Nevertheless, it is still possible to find traces of a more unitary approach to international responsibility that starts from the concept of international legal personality. The commentary on the draft articles for example includes the statement that "It may be that the notion of responsibility for wrongful conduct is a basic element in the possession of international legal personality."[60] In a report to the ILC on the need to include the topic of responsibility of international organizations in the commission's agenda, Pellet also recognizes that the "principles embodied in Chapter I of Part Two of the draft articles on State responsibility can probably be transposed."[61]

56 See para. 2. 2. See also E. Butkiewicz, *The Premisses of International Responsibility of Inter-Governmental Organizations*, 11 Polish Yearbook of International Law 117 (1981-82).P. Klein , La Responsabilité des Organisations Internationales dans les Ordres Juridiques Internes et en Droit des Gens 305 (1998).

57 International Responsibility, Report by Special Rapporteur F.V. García Amador, YBILC 1956, at 173.

58 *Id.*, at 220.

59 *Id.*

60 *Supra* note 4, at 67-68, para. 7.

61 *Id.*, at 303.

The ILC study on the responsibility of international organizations will have to make clear precisely to what extent the rules of state responsibility apply to international organizations. The present study is limited to a discussion of state practice and practice of the UN and NATO concerning the consequences of alleged breaches of international humanitarian law by peace support operations.

4.4 *Lex specialis* in international humanitarian law

There are several provisions in conventional international humanitarian law which concern legal consequences of a violation of a primary rule, which could operate as *lex specialis* in the sense of draft article 55. For the *lex specialis* principle to apply, it is not enough that the same subject matter is dealt with by two provisions. There must be some actual inconsistency between them, or else a discernible intention that one provision is to exclude the other. In other words, it will depend on the special rule to establish the extent to which the more general rules on state responsibility as set out in the articles are displaced by that rule.

One special rule on the legal consequences of a breach of international humanitarian law is Article 3 of 1907 Hague Convention (IV) Respecting the Laws and Customs of War on Land. This article provides that a belligerent party which violates the provisions of the Regulations annexed to the Convention shall, if the case demands, be liable to pay compensation. The article appears to be consistent with article 36 of the ILC draft articles, although the meaning of the phrase 'if the case demands' is not immediately clear.[62] The phrase was not included in the original German proposal for the article. A number of commentators interpret the phrase as excluding from compensation damage that is not financially assessable.[63] A Greek court also found that the provision in Article 3 according to which the belligerent party shall pay compensation if the case demands specifically underlines that financially assessable damage must have been caused as a result.[64] This interpretation is consistent with draft article 36 which covers any financially assessable damage including loss of profits in so far as this is established in the given case.[65]

Article 3 does not exclude other legal consequences than an obligation of compensation as arising from a violation of the Hague Regulations. The contrary is suggested by a statement of the president of the subcommittee of the Second Hague Peace Conference, suggesting that the German proposal was of great interest because

62 M. Sassòli, *State Responsibility for Violations of International Humanitarian Law*, 84 International Review of the Red Cross 401 (2002), at 418.

63 J. Kunz, Kriegsrecht und Neutralitätsrecht 35 (1935); M. Hüber, *Die Fortbildung des Völkerrechts auf dem Gebiete des Prozeß- und Landkriegsrechts*, 2 Das Öffentliche Recht der Gegenwart 471 (1908), at 575.

64 *Prefecture of Voiotia* v. *Federal Republic of Germany*, Case No. 137/1997, Court of First Instance of Leivadia, Greece, 30 October 1997.

65 Sassòli gives another interpretation. He states that the 'if the case demands' refers to the subsidiary character of compensation. Only if restitution in integrum is not possible is compensation in order. Sassòli, *supra* note 62, at 418.

it attached a sanction to rules, for which there was not yet a sanction in place.[66] Kalshoven submits:

> It may be the case, though, that at the time of the Second Hague Peace Conference the general rules were of little practical import in relation to the problem the delegates sought to solve, so that in tackling it they were more or less oblivious of such general rules. At any rate, the rule they purported to lay down in Article 3, with its special characteristics adapted to the perceived needs of the situation, even today is entirely capable of coexisting with, and supplementing, the general rules on State responsibility.[67]

Another special rule on the legal consequences of a breach of international humanitarian law is Article 51 of Geneva Convention I, which is reproduced in the other three Geneva Conventions in Articles 52, 131, and 148 respectively.[68] There is no inconsistency between this article and draft article 36 of the ILC draft articles. The article reaffirms draft article 36 by excluding any contractual exemption from claims for compensation by a vanquished state. With regard to the question whether the article excludes other legal consequences of an internationally wrongful act, the *travaux préparatoires* make clear that compensation was only considered as one of different legal consequences. The report of the Committee which drafted Article 51 states:

> The State remained responsible for breaches of the Convention and could not refuse to recognise its responsibility on the ground that individuals concerned have been punished. There remained, for instance, the liability to pay compensation.[69]

A third special rule with regard to legal consequences for violation of international humanitarian law is Article 91 of Additional Protocol I. The preparatory work of the article indicates that it was intended to have the same meaning as Article 3 of 1907 Hague Convention (IV). This was stated among others by the delegation of Viet Nam when it introduced the article.[70] There is no actual inconsistency between Article 91

---

66 Original French: "Cette proposition est très intéressante puisqu'elle tend à attacher une sanction à des prescriptions, qui en sont actuellement dépourvues", Deuxième Conférence internationale de la Paix, La Haye 15 juin – 18 octobre 1907, Actes et Documents (Actes), Vol. III, at 144.

67 F. Kalshoven, *State Responsibility for Warlike Acts of the Armed Forces: From Article 3 of the Hague Convention IV of 1907 to Article 91 of Additional Protocol I of 1977 and Beyond*, 40 International & Comparative Law Quarterly 827 (1991), at 838.

68 These Articles provide:

> No High Contracting Party shall be allowed to absolve itself or any other High Contracting Party of any liability incurred by itself or by another High Contracting Party in respect of breaches referred to in the preceding Article.

69 Fourth Report drawn up by the Special Committee, 12 July 1949, Final Report, Vol. IIB, at 118.

70 Official Records of the Diplomatic Conference on the Reaffirmation and Development of International Humanitarian Law Applicable in Armed Conflicts, Geneva (1974-1977) (Official Records), Vol. 9, at 355 (CDDH/I/SR.67, paras. 67, Mr. Van Luu).

and draft article 36 nor a discernible intention that the provision is to exclude other legal consequences.

A final *lex specialis* in international humanitarian law is Article 1 (3) of Protocol I to the Hague Convention on Protection of Cultural Property in the Event of Armed Conflict. This paragraph obliges state parties to return, at the close of hostilities, to the competent authorities of the territory previously occupied, cultural property which is in their territory, if such property has been exported by the occupying power.[71] The rule limits the freedom of the state invoking international responsibility to prefer compensation in lieu of restitution.

4.5 Practice in respect of conduct of peace support operations

4.5.1 Introduction

This section discusses practice in respect of the consequences of internationally wrongful acts by peace support operations. It will seek to determine whether the framework discussed above is reflected in practice.

In some of the situations to be discussed international humanitarian law was considered applicable by the parties to the dispute. These situations are of course of particular interest. In other situations the parties to the dispute did not refer to international humanitarian law, even if that body of law may have been applicable. A discussion of these cases is justified by the fact that the principles with regard to legal consequences of an internationally wrongful act are the same for all internationally wrongful acts unless *lex specialis* applies.

The discussion does not follow the classification of legal consequences in the ILC draft articles on state responsibility. It will rather examine striking features of state and organization practice in particular peace support operations.

4.5.2 ONUC

In 1966 the UN concluded agreements with Belgium, Greece, Italy, Luxembourg and Switzerland relating to the settlement of claims filed against the UN by nationals of these states.[72] The Status of Forces Agreement between the UN and the Congo pro-

---

71 See G. Carlucci, *L'Obligation de Restitution des Biens Culturels et des Objets d'Art en Cas de Conflit Armé: Droit Coutumier et Droit Conventionnel Avant et Après la Convention de la Haye de 1954*, 104 Revue Générale de Droit International Public 289 (2000).

72 Exchange of letters constituting an agreement relating to the settlement of claims filed against the United Nations in the Congo by Swiss nationals of 3 January 1966, 564 UNTS 193; Exchange of letters constituting an agreement relating to the settlement of claims filed against the United Nations in the Congo by Greek nationals of 20 January 1966, 565 UNTS 3; Exchange of letters constituting an agreement relating to the settlement of claims filed against the United Nations in the Congo by Luxembourg nationals of 28 December 1966, 585 UNTS 147; Exchange of letters constituting an agreement relating to the settlement of claims filed against the United Nations in the Congo by Italian nationals of 18 January 1967, 588 UNTS 197.

vided that if as a result of any act performed by a member of the force or an official in the course of his duties, it was alleged that loss or damages which might give rise to civil proceedings had been caused, the UN would settle the dispute by negotiation or any other method agreed between the parties, and if it was not found possible to arrive at an agreement in that manner, the matter should be submitted to arbitration at the request of either party.[73] The procedure was open to nationals and to residents of the host state. It seems that pursuant to this agreement the UN established local claims review boards to settle claims. These were not responsible for the settlement of claims by nationals of the above-mentioned states for injury as a result of the activities of ONUC, for unknown reasons.[74]

Instead, the governments of the states of nationality of these individuals exercised their right of diplomatic protection. In this capacity they entered into negotiations with the UN. These negotiations resulted in exchanges of letters between the states concerned and the UN in which the latter agreed to pay certain sums to the governments in outright and final settlement of claims lodged by the nationals of these governments. The agreements provided that the distribution of the sum paid to the government concerned would be effected by the government.

The agreements do not refer expressly to breaches of international humanitarian law as the basis of UN responsibility, but there are several indications that this was, in fact, the case.[75] First, the Belgian government had previously complained that the UN did not respect the obligations of the Geneva Convention to take all necessary measures to safeguard the lives and property of the civilian population. It complained in particular of the death of several Belgian civilians killed by UN forces.[76] It is very likely that some of the claims arose from the facts complained about by the Belgian government. Secondly, the agreements between the UN and the various governments provide that the UN agrees to settlement of claims arising from harmful acts committed by ONUC personnel and not arising from military necessity. The expression 'military necessity' is an expression which derives from international humanitarian law and which is not used in any other field of international law. It is widely recognized as one of the underlying principles of modern international humanitarian law.[77] A third indication is the reference by the UN Secretary-General to international humanitarian law in connection with the agreements. In a reply to a diplomatic note by the Soviet Union concerning the agreements, he stated that the policy of compensation

73 Agreement between the United Nations and the Republic of the Congo Relating to the Legal Status of the United Nations in the Congo, 27 November 1961, UN Doc. S/5004, Art. 10 (b).

74 J. Salmon, *Les Accords Spaak-U Thant du 20 Février 1965*, 11 Annuaire Français de Droit International 468 (1965), at 485.

75 *Id.*, at 480-482.

76 See F. Seyersted, United Nations Forces in the Law of Peace and War 194 (1966).

77 See *e.g.* H. McCoubrey, *The Nature of the Modern Doctrine of Military Necessity*, 30 Revue de Droit Militaire et de Droit de la Guerre 215 (1991).

was reinforced by the principles set forth in the international conventions concerning the protection of the life and property of civilian population during hostilities.[78]

4.5.3 UNPROFOR

In 1998, the United Nations General Assembly requested the Secretary-General to submit a report on Srebrenica. It contains a description of the events in Srebrenica as well as an assessment of these events. The assessment repeatedly uses the word 'responsibility'. In particular the report concludes that:

> The international community as a whole must accept its share of responsibility for allowing this tragic course of events by its prolonged refusal to use force in the early stages of the war. This responsibility is shared by the Security Council, the Contact Group and other Governments which contributed to the delay in the use of force, as well as by the United Nations Secretariat and the Mission in the field.

In 1996 the Netherlands government commissioned a report on the events prior to, during and after the fall of Srebrenica by the Netherlands Institute for War Documentation, an independent body. The Institute was requested to list and classify the relevant factual material in order to present a historical perspective of the causes and events which led to the fall of Srebrenica and the dramatic developments which ensued. For this reason the report submitted by the Institute does not speak in terms of responsibility.[79] The report submitted by the parliamentary commission of inquiry, established in 2002 to examine the events in Srebrenica, does speak of responsibility in its report submitted in January 2003.[80] This is a consequence of the objective of the report to give a definite judgment concerning the political responsibility for the events.[81] One of the main conclusions is that the Netherlands has accepted political responsibility through the resignation of the government.[82]

A report submitted by a French parliamentary commission of inquiry examines the role, and possible responsibility, of France in the Srebrenica drama.[83] The conclusion of the report discusses the findings in terms of responsibility, of persons, structures and states.[84] In particular, the report finds that France has a share of political responsibility for the events in Srebrenica.[85]

---

78 UN Doc. S/6589.

79 Srebrenica, A 'Safe' Area: Reconstruction, Background, Consequences and Analyses of the Fall of a Safe Area (2002).

80 Rapport Enquete Srebrenica, Bijlagen Handelingen II 2002-03, 28506, nr. 3.

81 *Id.*, at 413.

82 *Id.*, at 452.

83 Rapport d'Information par la Mission d'Information Commune sur les Evénements de Srebrenica (2001).

84 *Id.*, at 184.

85 *Id.*, at 189.

More generally, at a memorial ceremony in Sarajevo on 11 October 1999 the UN Secretary-General expressed his regrets on behalf of the organization for the failure of the international community to take decisive action to halt the suffering and end a war that had produced so many victims.[86]

Although the majority of the above-mentioned reports and the Secretary-General's statement refer to responsibility, it seems that this expression is not used in the sense of international legal responsibility. The reports and the statement do not refer to the attribution of conduct to states or the organization, nor do they refer to any international norms allegedly breached by the UN or governments. In particular, no connection is made with allegations that the conduct of the peacekeeping contingent in Srebrenica was in breach of an obligation under international humanitarian law. There is only one brief paragraph in the Dutch parliamentary report stating that there have been accusations that Dutch military personnel committed crimes, but that no evidence has been found to substantiate these accusations and the crimes concerned were likely to have been committed by Bosnian Serb personnel dressed in UN attire.[87]

This conclusion is not fully consistent with a memorandum by the public prosecutor's office in Arnhem concerning alleged crimes committed by members of the Netherlands contingent deployed in Srebrenica (Dutchbat).[88] The memorandum gives an overview of investigations by the public prosecutor into the alleged crimes.[89] These investigations were based on the information contained in a factual account of declarations by members of Dutchbat released by the Ministry of Defense to the public prosecutor's office in September 1998. The memorandum states that information in the factual account called for criminal investigations. In particular, the office investigated five categories of incidents: allegations of civilians being run over by Dutchbat vehicles; an allegation by a member of Dutchbat that civilians had been pushed off a Dutchbat vehicle and run over; allegations of withholding medical aid to civilians; allegations of aid to the Bosnian Serb Army and allegations of threats or mistreatment of civilians. In respect of all these allegations the public prosecutor's office found that there was no ground for prosecution. In some cases there was lack of evidence, in some *mens rea* was lacking, in some cases a statute of limitation applied and, finally, in some cases a prosecution was not appropriate because it would not be within a reasonable time-period. It may be recalled that the public prosecutor's office considered that the applicable law was the Dutch Penal Code. In particular, it held that international humanitarian law was not applicable because the force did not become a party to the conflict and the personnel did not become combatants. It considered in this respect that the combat activities in which the Netherlands personnel

86 UN Press Release SG/SM/7168, 11 October 1999.

87 *Supra* note 80, at 442.

88 Bijlagen Handelingen II 1999-00, 26122, nr. 17.

89 See also A. Simons & B. Vandenberghe, *Der Fall der UN "Safe Area" Srebrenica und die Rolle des niederländischen Bataillons Dutchbat – Eine Zusammenfassung der niederländischen Untersuchungen*, 61 Zeitschrift für ausländisches öffentliches Recht und Völkerrecht 681 (2001).

were involved did not exceed their mandate under Security Council Resolution 836, which implied that they could not have committed war crimes. It has also been noted that this observation is not directly relevant to the determination of the applicability of international humanitarian law.

Responsibility in relation to the events in Srebrenica was raised during the consideration of the third periodic report submitted by the Netherlands to the United Nations Human Rights Committee. In its concluding observations the Committee stated that:

> The Committee remains concerned that, six years after the alleged involvement of members of the State party's peacekeeping forces in the events surrounding the fall of Srebrenica, Bosnia and Herzegovina, in July 1995, the responsibility of the persons concerned has yet to be publicly and finally determined. The Committee considers that in respect of an event of such gravity it is of particular importance that issues relating to the State party's obligation to ensure the right to life be resolved in an expeditious and comprehensive manner (articles 2 and 6 of the Covenant).
> The State party should complete its investigations as to the involvement of its armed forces in Srebrenica as soon as possible, publicize these findings widely and examine the conclusions to determine any appropriate criminal or disciplinary action.[90]

4.5.4 UNOSOM

Practice in respect of accusations against members of UNOSOM relates in particular to Belgian and Italian personnel. In respect of accusations against Belgian personnel, the Belgian Minister of Defense in September 1993 established an administrative commission of inquiry following press reports of incidents involving Belgian soldiers in UNOSOM. Civil servants and military officers were appointed to serve on the commission. Their mandate was to investigate the conduct of the Belgian UNOSOM contingent as well as circumstances and factors directly or indirectly leading to that conduct. The main objective was to "examine whether collective or individual reprehensible acts had been committed against the Somali population, and also to attempt to reconstruct and analyze the specific context of the operations". The report of the commission of 24 November 1993 was discussed in parliament. One of the conclusions was that there had been isolated cases of unacceptable conduct which had been addressed by the command and/or the military magistrate, and that "during the whole operation there was never any serious problem in respect of the application of the law of armed conflict."[91]

Belgium did not pay compensation to victims of the incidents involving Belgian soldiers in UNOSOM. Claims by third parties were processed and paid by the United

90 Concluding Observations of the Human Rights Committee: Netherlands, 27 August 2001, UN Doc. CCPR/CO/72/NET, para. 8.

91 Translation by the author. Original Dutch text: "Alhoewel er tijdens het ganse verloop van de aktiviteiten nooit een ernstig probleem werd vastgesteld inzake de toepassing van het oorlogsrecht." Report Commission of Inquiry Somalia, Chapter 3 (Synthesis and conclusions), para. 3.6, copy on file with the author.

Nations.[92] After consultations with the Belgian Ministry of Defense a sum of US $ 2,800,000 was paid.[93]

In 1998 a Belgian Military Tribunal convicted Dirk N. of acts of racism, of intentionally causing personal injury to a child and of threatening the child with an attack on the child's person or property.[94] The sergeant was accused of forcing a Muslim child to eat pork and of ordering his subordinates to tie another child behind a truck and driving the truck a short distance while he was a member of UNOSOM II. He was sentenced to a year in prison of which six months suspended and suspension of civil rights for five years. In the operative part of its judgment the Tribunal found that the accused had interfered with the right to freedom of religion which the child enjoyed under the Universal Declaration of Human Rights and the African Charter on Human and Peoples Rights.

In 1997 the same Tribunal reaffirmed the acquittal by Court Martial of C.K. and B.C. They were accused of having held a Somali child above a fire while they were members of UNOSOM II, thereby intentionally causing personal injury and threatening the child with an attack on its person or property. The proceedings were joined by the Center for Equal Opportunity and Combat against Racism (Centrum voor Gelijke Kansen en Racismebestrijding) as a civil party (*partie civile*). The Center requested a requalification of the alleged facts as violations of the Belgian law implementing the 1949 Geneva Conventions and the 1977 Additional Protocols, as well as the Belgian law against racial discrimination. The Tribunal held that it had no evidence to conclude that UN forces in Somalia were involved *de facto* in sustained, general and structured combat operations against one or more armed groups, so that international humanitarian law was not applicable. It also held that UNOSOM II could not be assimilated to an occupying power.

In 1995 a Court Martial convicted two persons on a count of having intentionally caused personal injury (Articles 66 and 392 of the Belgian criminal code).[95] They were accused of having ill-treated a detained Somali whom they were guarding at their base in Kismayo. The indictment stated that they had kicked and punched the handcuffed detainee and subjected him to electric shocks. One of the accused was sentenced to three month's suspended imprisonment and the other to two month's suspended imprisonment.

In 1995 a Belgian Military Tribunal acquitted a soldier of involuntary manslaughter on appeal from a Court Martial.[96] The soldier had killed an unarmed Somali man with the board gun of a helicopter while firing a warning shot. These criminal cases were considered by the United Nations Human Rights Committee in 1999 during the

92 Letter to the author from J. Vergauwen, Belgian Ministry of Defense, Legal Division, Directorate of International Affairs, 19 December 2001.

93 Letter to the author from J.Y. Mine, Auditor-General at the Military Court at Brussels, 21 January 2002.

94 Brussels Military Tribunal (Krijgshof), Military Prosecutor CGKR v. Dirk N., 7 May 1998, copy on file with the author.

95 Reported in Rechtskundig Weekblad 1995-1996, nr. 26, 9 March 1996, at 949.

96 *Id.*

examination of Belgium's report under Article 40 of the International Covenant on Civil and Political Rights (ICCPR). A representative of the Belgian government submitted to the Committee that:

> Many members had asked how Belgium's commitments under the Covenant and other international instruments could be implemented when Belgian nationals committed certain acts outside the country – for instance in Somalia. Irrespective of where an act was committed, Belgian jurisdiction applied, as could be seen by the proceedings instituted in Belgium against a number of Belgian nationals in which some had been convicted and others acquitted.[97]

In its concluding observations the Committee "acknowledges that the State party has recognized the applicability of the Covenant in this respect and opened 270 files for purposes of investigation."[98]

The Italian government established a governmental fact-finding Commission by a Decree of the Ministry of Defense on 16 June 1997 to investigate reports of ill treatment by Italian personnel in UNOSOM and Operation Restore Hope. The Commission had five members and was chaired by a former President of the Constitutional Court. The Commission collected evidence in Italy, Ethiopia and Kenya but not in Somalia. Its report was presented on 8 August 1997 and found that several allegations of ill treatment were credible but that superior officials were not aware of the ill-treatment and therefore not responsible.[99]

Days after the publication of the report, there were new reports of ill treatment by Italian troops in Somalia. The Minister of Defense asked the Commission to reopen its inquiry. The Commission presented its final report on 26 May 1998.[100] The report concludes that incidents of ill treatment by Italian personnel were sporadic and localized.[101] Neither the 1997 report nor the final report addressed issues of state responsibility or the applicability of international humanitarian law.

Criminal proceedings were also initiated in Italy in response to accusations of mistreatment of Somalis by Italian personnel in UNOSOM and UNITAF.[102]

The criminal law division of the Livorno Tribunal on 13 April 2000 convicted Valerio Ercole on a count of abuse of authority over arrested or detained persons.[103]

---

97 Summary Record of the 1707th Meeting of the Human Rights Committee, 27 October 1998, UN Doc. CCPR/C/SR.1707, para. 22.

98 Concluding Observations of the Human Rights Committee, 19 November 1998, UN Doc. CCPR/C/79/Add.99, para. 14.

99 See N. Lupi, *Report by the Enquiry Commission on the Behaviour of Italian Peace-keeping Troops in Somalia*, 1 Yearbook of International Humanitarian Law 375 (1998).

100 Commissione Governativa d'Inchiesta per i fatti di Somalia, Relazione Conclusiva, 26 May 1998, copy on file with the author.

101 *Id.*, at 109.

102 See F. Lattanzi, *Le Accuse al Contingente Italiano in Somalia alla Luce del Diritto Internazionale*, Diritto Penale e Processo 1131 (1997).

103 Tribunal of Livorno, Criminal Division, Sentence No. 439, 13 April 2000, copy on file with the author.

As a member of the Italian contingent of Operation Restore Hope Ercole had participated in the illtreatment of Aden Abukar Ali by administering electrical shocks to the victim's testicles. He was sentenced to eighteen months suspended imprisonment.

On 9 February 1997, an investigating judge of the Livorno Tribunal discontinued criminal proceedings against Italian members of UNOSOM. The soldiers were accused of having killed three Somalis in a car on 3 June 1993.[104] Criminal proceedings in connection with a gang rape by Italian members of the UN operation at a checkpoint in Mogadishu in June 1993 were also closed because it was not possible to identify the perpetrators or the victim.

Criminal proceedings in connection with the peace support operation were reported by the government to the Committee against Torture in Italy's third periodic report in 1998. The report did not distinguish between acts committed by members of Operation Restore Hope and acts committed by members of the United Nations Operation. It reported that:

> Thorough and complex investigations are currently being carried out by various Italian judicial authorities in connection with the acts of violence committed by Italian soldiers in Somalia. Four such investigations are currently in progress at the Public Prosecutor's Office attached to the Court of Livorno.
> As regards the proceedings for alleged torture suffered by a Somali man arrested at Jhoar and the alleged rape of a Somali woman by soldiers at a roadblock in Mogadishu, a probatory hearing was arranged so as to have the testimonies of the victims and a witness collected directly by the judge. Expert examinations are being carried out to ascertain the after-effects of the violence on the victims and also to see whether they corresponded to the photographs published by a weekly journal. The expert work is now in progress. Investigations are also being continued in the other two proceedings.
> The Public Prosecutor's Office attached to the Court of Milan, for its part, is diligently continuing its investigations regarding an alleged case of carnal violence committed by an Italian soldier in Mogadishu.
> By means of a decree dated 9 February 1997, the Preliminary Examination Judge of the Court of Leghorn ordered that the case based on the facts denounced by Abdi Hasn Addò be filed. Addò had accused Italian soldiers of having shot and killed three Somalis in a car on 3 June 1993. But the investigations showed that on the day in question the soldiers had been engaged in a military operation known as 'Illach 26' that was taking place in another part of Somalia from that indicated by Addò.[105]

The Committee against Torture, in its Concluding Observations on Italy's report, expressed its concern over the lack in training in the field of human rights, in particular, the prohibition against torture to the troops participating in peacekeeping opera-

104 Third periodic report of Italy to the Committee against Torture, 15 December 1998, UN Doc. CAT/C/44/Add.2, para. 79.

105 *Id.*, paras. 76-79.

tions and the inadequate number of military police accompanying them, which was responsible in part for the unfortunate incidents that occurred in Somalia.[106]

On 16 November 1993 the United Nations Security Council established a Commission of Inquiry to investigate armed attacks on UNOSOM II.[107] Unlike the commissions of inquiry established by Belgium and Italy, the mandate of the Commission seems to have been focused on abuses committed against, rather than by, UNOSOM personnel. Resolution 885, which established the Commission, used neutral language to describe its mandate, which was "to investigate armed attacks on personnel of the United Nations Operation in Somalia II which led to casualties among them."[108] In a previous resolution adopted under Chapter VII of the United Nations Charter, however, the Security Council had already strongly condemned the attacks to be investigated by the Commission, and described them as 'criminal attacks' and as "unprovoked armed attacks ... which appear to have been part of a calculated and premeditated series of cease-fire violations to prevent by intimidation UNOSOM II from carrying out its mandate."[109]

In response to reports of 'allegations of criminality in peacekeeping missions', an apparent reference to accusations against UNOSOM personnel, the United Nations Under-Secretary-General for Peacekeeping Operations, Bernard Miyet, stated in 1997 that when troops are in the field "the United Nations had the responsibility to investigate to cover all the aspects and determine what was going on."[110] He also stated that even in case of the slightest doubt over allegations of crimes committed by personnel of a peace support operation the UN would ask the troop contributing country to repatriate its troops, make investigations, take disciplinary measures or begin a judiciary process, as appropriate. It is not clear to what extent UN practice in response to accusations of crimes committed by peace support operations is in conformity with official policy as stated by the Under-Secretary-General. There is no evidence that the organization investigated accusations against members of UNOSOM.

4.5.5 SFOR

In 1997 SFOR personnel from the United Kingdom stole a Bosnian flag. SFOR itself started an investigation into the incident and apologized.[111] Similarly, the SFOR commander is reported to have sent a letter of apology to the Croatian Minister of

---

106 Concluding Observations of the Committee against Torture: Italy, 7 May 1999, UN Doc. A/54/44, paras. 163-169, at para. 168.

107 Security Council Resolution 885 of 16 November 1993, UN Doc. S/RES/885.

108 *Id.*, para. 1.

109 Security Council Resolution 837 of 6 June 1993, UN Doc. S/RES/837, preambular para. 5 and para. 1.

110 *Allegations of Criminality in Peacekeeping Missions: 'UN Cannot be Indifferent'*, 34 United Nations Chronicle no. 3 (1997), at 39.

111 "Our investigation into the allegations is now complete, and SFOR would like to apologize for any offense caused by the actions of members of the Stabilization Force", SFOR Press Conference Transcript, 3 December 1997.

Foreign Affairs in December 2002. The letter expressed deepest regrets after SFOR personnel damaged a monument to Croatians who were killed or disappeared in the 1991-1995 war. Croatia then lodged a protest with SFOR, urging a thorough investigation.[112]

4.5.6 KFOR

Investigations have been conducted and disciplinary and criminal action have been taken by authorities of troop contributing states concerning alleged crimes committed by KFOR personnel. Some of the conduct concerned would seem to constitute human rights violations.

In 1999 a team from the United Kingdom ministry of defense special investigation branch investigated three British soldiers serving in KFOR for the murder of two men and malicious injury of three others.[113]

Belgian military police conducted an inquiry into the alleged killing of a man by Belgian KFOR personnel in December 2000.

In 2000 United States authorities conducted an investigation into allegations of abuses committed by United States KFOR personnel.[114] The report presenting the findings of the investigation stated *inter alia* that personnel intimidated and beat the members of the local population.

In 2000 a member of United States troops in KFOR was prosecuted and convicted by national authorities for the rape and murder of a local girl.[115]

4.6 Conclusion

It is difficult to draw conclusions from the practice examined above, because it is unclear in respect of the majority of measures described whether they were taken in recognition of international responsibility, and can consequently be considered as legal consequences of international responsibility. The payment of compensation by the UN for harm resulting from actions of ONUC is the only measure which was accompanied by a clear recognition of international responsibility. As a matter of principle the legal consequences of an internationally wrongful act arise automatically from the wrongful act itself. In other words, their coming into existence does not depend on a claim being pressed. The new legal relationship created by the internationally wrongful act comes into existence before any injured subject would press a claim for reparation.[116] The coming into existence of the obligation to make full reparation for

---

112 *NATO Commander Apologises to Croatia for Vandalism by Soldiers*, Agence France Presse, 12 December 2002.

113 *Kosovo's Love Affair with NATO Keeps Tempers Down*, The Guardian, 4 December 2000.

114 *Army Report Says Soldiers Abused Civilians in Kosovo*, Washington Post, 17 September 2000, at section A, at 8.

115 G. Boehmer, *Ohio GI Gets Life Sentence for Killing Ethnic Albanian Girl in Kosovo*, Washington Post, 2 August 2000, Section A, at 25.

116 See Mann, *supra* note 23, at 14.

the injury caused by the internationally wrongful act can *a fortiori* not depend on the admission of responsibility by the responsible entity. The automatic coming into existence of legal consequences is underlined by the wording of article 28 of the ILC draft articles on state responsibility.[117] In practice, however, it is difficult to conclude that a specific measure is a legal consequence of an internationally wrongful act unless the responsible entity states that it is, or the measure is imposed by an international tribunal.

It may be noted that in as far as the measures described above can be regarded as legal consequences of internationally wrongful acts, in all cases except the compensation of injury caused by ONUC, responsibility seems to have been considered to arise from the breach of international norms other than international humanitarian law. In the case of criminal investigations into conduct by Dutchbat personnel for example, which could possibly be a form of satisfaction, the public prosecutor held explicitly that international humanitarian law was inapplicable. This does not lead to the conclusion that the practice is not relevant to this study. It has already been established that the provisions in international humanitarian law on the legal consequences of a breach of its rules are consistent with the general principles concerning legal consequences of an internationally wrongful act. It seems that the legal consequences of a breach of international humanitarian law would not necessarily have been different from the legal consequences of the breach of another international obligation. In the present case it seems that in as far as the measures described are reactions by the author state or organization to an internationally wrongful act, the obligations involved were in most cases obligations under human rights law. The ILC does state in its commentary to article 34 of the draft articles that the "primary obligation breached may also play an important role with respect to the form and extent of reparation",[118] but in the present case it is not obvious that this would have led to a different result if the primary obligation were an obligation under international humanitarian law.

The above-mentioned practice is especially interesting to the extent that it can shed light on two questions. The first is whether the practice is in conformity with the conclusions in Chapter 2 concerning attribution of conduct of peace support operations. If a state or international organization takes measures to meet the secondary obligations arising from responsibility, this implies that conduct is attributed to that entity. Without attribution there would be no responsibility and consequently no legal consequences. The second is whether the practice confirms the application of the principles in Part Two, Chapters I and II of the draft articles on state responsibility, to responsibility of states and international organizations for breaches of international law committed by a peace support operation.

---

117 The draft article reads:

> The international responsibility of a State which is entailed by an internationally wrongful act in accordance with the provisions of Part One involves legal consequences as set out in this Part.

118 *Supra* note 4, at 236. See also I. Brownlie, System of the Law of Nations: State Responsibility, Part I, at 236 (1983).

With regard to UN peace support operations, the legal consequence of compensation for internationally wrongful acts seems to be borne by the UN. A clear example is the compensation for violations of international humanitarian law committed by ONUC personnel to the state of nationality of the victims. This payment of lump sums by the UN was accompanied by recognition of its international responsibility. It seems to confirm the application of the general principles concerning legal consequences of state responsibility to the UN. Salmon observes that the analogy between the agreements, and agreements concluded between states at the conclusion of the World War II concerning compensation, is striking.[119]

The refusal by Belgium to provide compensation in connection with alleged wrongful acts committed by Belgian personnel in UNOSOM suggests that troop contributing states consider that the UN should bear the legal consequence of an obligation to compensate for wrongful acts committed by UN peace support operations.[120]

The official policy of the UN to investigate alleged crimes committed by peace support operation personnel could be considered as a form of satisfaction if the crime was a breach of an international obligation of the UN. In this regard it may be noted that a UN official confirmed the need for the Secretary-General to take action in response to internationally wrongful acts by UN peace support operations. She added that the kind of action taken by the Secretary-General depended *inter alia* on the nature of the act committed. If this act was very serious then an apology by the Secretary-General might be appropriate, but no conduct of peace support operation personnel had hitherto been of such a serious character.[121]

It may be added that while the UN official policy in principle may confirm the conclusion that the organization bears the legal consequences of internationally wrongful acts by peace support operations, in practice official policy frequently does not seem to be followed. Amnesty International for example concluded that in respect of accusations against UNOSOM personnel investigations by the UN into killings or abuses were in most cases non-existent or minimal.[122]

The national authorities of troop contributing states undertook criminal investigations and prosecutions of alleged crimes committed by personnel in UNPROFOR and UNOSOM. This raises questions from the perspective of international responsibility. The ILC recognizes disciplinary or penal action against the individuals whose conduct caused an internationally wrongful act as a form of satisfaction. As a consequence it seems that in this case it is implied that troop-contributing states are responsible. This would however not be a correct conclusion. That the UN does not prosecute

119 Salmon, *supra* note 74, at 487.

120 Another example is the case brought by families of persons killed in Srebrenica against the Netherlands, discussed in para. 5.5.3, in which the government of the Netherlands claims that in principle the United Nations is responsible for the conduct of a peace support operation under UN command and control.

121 Interview with an official in the United Nations Office of Legal Affairs, 18 September 2002.

122 Amnesty International, Peace-keeping and Human Rights 14 (1994).

the perpetrators of breaches of human rights or international humanitarian law is not a result of disowning responsibility. It is rather a result of participating state agreements between the UN and troop contributing states and the absence of a full-fledged criminal justice system in the UN. The UN has consistently held that from a practical perspective it cannot take disciplinary or penal action against peace support operation personnel. This position has been articulated in respect of international humanitarian law conventions which impose an obligation to prosecute or extradite persons responsible for grave breaches of those conventions as a primary obligation, but it also applies to disciplinary or penal action as a secondary obligation, that is as a legal consequence of international responsibility. The UN position is set out *inter alia* in a memorandum by the Office of Legal Affairs drafted in connection with the possible accession of the organization to the 1949 Geneva Conventions. This memorandum states that:

> the United Nations is not substantively in a position to become a party to the 1949 Conventions, which contain many obligations that can only be discharged by the exercise of juridical and administrative powers which the Organization does not possess, such as the authority to exercise criminal jurisdiction over members of the Forces.[123]

It seems that the UN not only considers that there is no mechanism available to the organization to exercise disciplinary or criminal jurisdiction, but that the organization does not have the power to establish such a mechanism. A UN official states that:

> It is not a question of a lack of certain mechanisms, but it is a question which goes to the roots of the competence, powers and legal nature of the Organization. This is why it cannot penalize in the way that you understand it in all criminal systems.[124]

This suggestion that somehow the establishment of criminal jurisdiction and a mechanism to exercise that jurisdiction is incompatible with the competence, powers and legal nature of the UN must be rejected. There is no *legal* obstacle preventing the organization from establishing such a mechanism.[125] In general, the power to create such a mechanism could be based on an implied power of the organization. In the *Reparations* case the ICJ described 'implied powers' as "those powers which, though not expressly provided in the Charter, are conferred upon it by necessary implication as being essential to the performance of its duties."[126] In other words, a functional

123 Question of the Possible Accession of Intergovernmental Organizations to the Geneva Conventions for the Protection of War Victims, UNJY 1972, at 153.

124 D. Schraga, in L. Condorelli, A.M. La Rosa & S. Scherrer (Eds), Les Nations Unies et le Droit International Humanitaire: Actes du Colloque International à l'Occasion du Cinquantième Anniversaire de l'ONU 436 (1996).

125 M. Bothe, *Peacekeeping and International Humanitarian Law: Friends or Foes?*, 3 International Peacekeeping 91 (1996), at 94.

126 Reparations for Injuries Suffered in the Service of the United Nations, Advisory Opinion of 11 April 1949, 1949 ICJ Reports 174, at 182.

criterion is commonly used to determine whether a particular power qualifies as an 'implied power'.[127] It can be argued that such a functional criterion necessitates a UN mechanism. A parallel can be drawn with the ICJ's Advisory Opinion in the *Effect of Awards* case. In that case the ICJ held that the General Assembly had the implied power to create an independent administrative tribunal for UN staff. According to the ICJ:

> It would, in the opinion of the Court, hardly be consistent with the expressed aim of the Charter to promote freedom and justice for individuals and with the constant preoccupation of the United Nations Organization to promote this aim that it should afford no judicial or arbitral remedy to its own staff for the settlement of any dispute which may arise between it and them.[128]

It is not clear why the constant preoccupation of the UN with the promotion of freedom and justice of individuals should apply only to UN staff and not to victims of the conduct of a UN peace support operation.

The argument that the UN does not have the competence to establish judicial mechanisms also flies in the face of the establishment by the Security Council of the ICTY and ICTR. Both these Tribunals, in exercising their '*compétence de la compétence*', have examined the legality of their establishment and concluded that the Security Council can establish subsidiary organs with judicial powers. Moreover, the scope of jurisdiction of these tribunals would comprise any serious violation of international humanitarian law committed by peace support operation personnel in the former Yugoslavia or Rwanda in a specified period. The ICTY actively investigated certain accusations against UNPROFOR personnel from the Netherlands, although this did not lead to an indictment.[129]

It may be concluded that if the Security Council wanted to establish a UN mechanism to exercise disciplinary and criminal jurisdiction over peace support operation personnel, there would be no legal impediment. That such a mechanism has not been established is a reflection of political rather than legal impediments. The UN depends on states to contribute troops for peace support operations, and those states make exclusive national jurisdiction a condition for such contributions.

To the extent that an obligation to take disciplinary or penal action against peace support operation personnel arises, either as a primary norm or as a legal consequence of international responsibility, the UN delegates the execution of this obligation to troop contributing states.[130] To this end it makes arrangements with troop contributing states that those states will exercise their jurisdiction. In exchanges of letters

---

127 H.G. Schermers & N.M. Blokker, International Institutional Law: Unity Within Diversity 177 (2003).

128 Effect of Awards of Compensation by the UN Administrative Tribunal, Advisory Opinion of 13 July 1954, 1954 ICJ Reports 55, at 57.

129 Bijlagen Handelingen II 1999-00, 26122, nr. 17, at 35.

130 See *e.g.* C. Emanuelli, Les Actions Militaires de l'ONU et le Droit International Humanitaire 66 (1997).

between the UN and troop contributing states concerning the status of troops, the Secretary-General requests assurances that the government of a troop contributing state will be prepared to exercise firm and effective jurisdiction with respect to any crime that might be committed by a member of the contingent and to report to the UN in each case on the action taken.[131] Statements by UN officials suggest that the organization would remind a troop contributing state of its obligation in case of specific allegations.

The delegation of the obligation to take disciplinary or penal action by the UN implies a duty to supervise the execution of that obligation. The UN should ensure that an appropriate authority carries out prosecutions when warranted, even if an individual's national government is unable or unwilling to do so.[132] To this end the organization has recently started to monitor the follow-up in troop contributing states to reports of crimes committed by members of peace support operations.

In summary, the exercise of disciplinary and penal jurisdiction over peace support operation personnel by troop contributing states does not constitute recognition of responsibility by those states. It is an example of the application *mutatis mutandis* of a principle of state responsibility to an international organization necessitated by the absence of a UN court martial structure.

The practice of human rights treaty monitoring bodies, referred to in paragraphs 4.5.3 and 4.5.4, calls for careful scrutiny, because it suggests that these bodies have focused on legal consequences for troop contributing states arising from conduct by UN peace support operations. Unless the conduct in question was carried out under the effective control of a troop contributing state, this would be inconsistent with the proposition that the legal consequences of the international responsibility of the UN fall on the organization itself.

The first instance of practice is the concluding observations of the Committee against Torture concerning Italian personnel in UNOSOM. In these observations the Committee expressed its concern over the lack of training of troops participating in peacekeeping operations and the inadequate number of military police accompanying them, and it recommended that Italy inform the Committee of the progress and result of the judicial proceedings resulting from the incidents in Somalia. It is interesting to note that the concerns expressed by the Committee relate to conduct by Italian authorities prior to the actual deployment of the troops under United Nations command, and not to conduct taking place while the troops were under the organization's control. The Committee's recommendation relates to Italy's obligation under Article 7 of the Convention to prosecute any person alleged to have committed torture present in its territory. This obligation extends to all cases of torture and not only cases of tor-

131 See *e.g.* Exchange of letters constituting an agreement between the United Nations and Canada concerning the service with the United Nations Peace-keeping Force in Cyprus of the national contingent provided by the Government of Canada, 21 February 1966, 555 UNTS 120.

132 B. Tittemore, *Belligerents in Blue Helmets: Applying International Humanitarian Law to United Nations Peace Operations*, 33 Stanford Journal of International Law 61 (1997), at 111; Emanuelli, *supra* note 130, at 66.

ture for which the state is internationally responsible. In summary, the Committee's observations can be reconciled with the proposition that only the United Nations is responsible for the conduct of the Italian personnel in UNOSOM.

The second instance of practice is the Concluding Observations of the Human Rights Committee on the third periodic report submitted by the Netherlands. The Committee expresses its concern about the "alleged involvement of members of the State Party's peacekeeping forces in the events surrounding the fall of Srebrenica", and the Committee states that these events relate to the state party's obligation to ensure the right to life under Articles 2 and 6 of the Covenant. In this case the Committee does seem to base obligations, including an obligation to complete its investigations as to the involvement of its armed forces in Srebrenica as soon as possible, on conduct under the command and control of the UN. It may be recalled however that initially there have been allegations that the Dutch government directly gave orders to the Dutch troops in Srebrenica, which would make the Netherlands responsible for conduct resulting from those orders, allegations that the Dutch government denied.[133] These allegations may have played a role in the Concluding Observations of the Committee. The government, in its reply to the Human Rights Committee's Concluding Observations, did not make any statement on whether or not the conduct concerned could be attributed to the Netherlands. Rather, it argued that the citizens of Srebrenica did not fall within the jurisdiction of the Netherlands in the sense of Article 2 of the International Covenant on Civil and Political Rights.[134]

The final instance of practice is the Concluding Observations of the Human Rights Committee on the third periodic report of Belgium. The Committee in its observations expressed its concern about the behavior of Belgian soldiers in Somalia under the aegis of UNOSOM and acknowledges that Belgium has recognized the applicability of the Covenant in this respect and opened a number of investigations. The Committee suggested that Belgium has an obligation to investigate the conduct of personnel under the effective control of the United Nations on the basis of the Covenant. There is no evidence that the Committee applied the theory that a state is responsible for breaches of the Covenant if that state has transferred powers to an international organization without adequate guarantees that the organization will respect the Covenant, in which case the transfer of powers is attributed to the state. Rather, the Committee seems to have based legal consequences for Belgium on conduct attributable to the United Nations.

The inquiries and the expression of regret by the UN Secretary-General relating to the fall of Srebrenica seem to be consequences of accountability and of political responsibility rather than of international responsibility in the legal sense. Reports submitted by the UN, French and Dutch commissions of inquiry use the expression 'responsibility' but do not refer to any international norm that the UN or states would have breached. The monitoring of conduct of international organizations and states

133 R. Siekmann, *The Fall of Srebrenica and the Attitude of Dutchbat from an International Legal Perspective*, 1 Yearbook of International Humanitarian Law 301 (1998), at 303-305.

134 Replies of the Government of the Netherlands to the Concerns Expressed by the Human Rights Committee of 29 April 2003, UN Doc. CCPR/CO/72/Net/Add.1.

through the submission of reports, the collection and dissemination of information and inspections carried out is an essential component of accountability.[135]

Practice in respect of NATO peace support operations is so limited that extreme caution must be taken in drawing any conclusions from it. Nevertheless, the apology offered by SFOR for an incident involving the theft of a Bosnian flag merits special attention. It seems that the apologies were offered by SFOR to the state of Bosnia Herzegovina.[136] The conduct concerned seems to be a clear example of an insult to the symbol of a state giving rise to international responsibility. In other cases in which international responsibility arose from the insult to the flag of a state an apology was generally considered as appropriate reparation or at least part of the measures constituting reparation.[137] This similarity is an indication that the apology could be considered as a legal consequence of international responsibility. In view of the arguments by NATO that it cannot be internationally responsible, it is remarkable that the apology was made by SFOR and not by the United Kingdom.

Criminal investigations and prosecutions can in certain cases constitute a form of satisfaction for an internationally wrongful act. In the case of SFOR and KFOR disciplinary and penal action is exclusively exercised by the authorities of the troop contributing states. This is not necessarily an indication that troop-contributing states bear the legal consequences of an internationally wrongful act attributable to NATO. Like the UN, NATO presently does not have a criminal justice system. Investigation or prosecution by the organization is presently not an alternative. As in the case of the UN, however, impediments to the establishment of a NATO criminal justice system are political rather than legal.

---

135 International Law Association Committee on Accountability of International Organizations, First Report 18 (1998).

136 See also the transcript of SFOR joint press conference of 27 November 1997, in which a reporter asks "Will SFOR make an official apolgize [sic] to Bosnian state because two SFOR soldiers played game with the Bosnian flag on the national holiday?"

137 Compare the case that arose from the insult to the French flag in Berlin discussed in C. Eagleton, The Responsibility of States in International Law 186-187 (1928).

5

Existing mechanisms for invoking accountability for violations of international humanitarian law by peace support operations

5.1 Introduction

This chapter discusses the implementation of international responsibility and of accountability for violations of international humanitarian law by peace support operations. Responsibility is a component of accountability for which there is a relatively formal framework in international law.[1] Within this framework, implementation of responsibility relates to the ways and means of giving effect to the obligations which arise for a responsible state or international organization by virtue of its commission of an internationally wrongful act.

A discussion of implementation of responsibility and accountability must address troop contributing states, as well as the UN and NATO. Chapters 2 and 3 demonstrated that violations of international humanitarian law by a peace support operation can be attributable to one or the other or both, depending in particular on which entity exercises effective control.

Another distinction which needs to be made concerns the actor wishing to implement responsibility or accountability. Traditionally, the invocation of international responsibility is a prerogative of states. The regime of the ILC draft articles on state responsibility only extends to implementation of responsibility of states by states, although in draft article 33 it expressly leaves the possibility open that a right to invoke responsibility may accrue to any person or entity other than a state. The corpus of law concerning the implementation of responsibility of international organizations is small, because few claims have been made against international organizations.[2] Because the concept of accountability has only recently been discussed in the context of international law, the situation with respect to implementation of accountability, whether of states or international organizations, is much the same.

Between the responsibility and accountability of states and international organizations, there is potentially a large number of implementing mechanisms. Particularly the flexibility of the concept of accountability imposes few limits on potential means of implementation. This chapter does not presume to discuss all potential mecha-

1 See para. 2.3.

2 P. Klein, La Responsabilité des Organisations Internationales dans Les Ordres Juridiques Internes et en Droit des Gens 567 (1998). See generally K. Wellens, Remedies Against International Organisations (2002).

nisms. Rather, it focuses on those mechanisms which have in practice played a role in implementation of responsibility and accountability for unlawful conduct by peace support operations on the one hand, and on mechanisms which have the potential to effectively implement responsibility or accountability on the other hand.

This chapter takes a broad view of implementation of responsibility for violations of international law, in the sense that it also discusses implementation of responsibility under private law which is based on an underlying violation of international law. Strictly speaking it is contestable whether such a procedure is a means of implementing international responsibility. On the other hand, it can at a minimum be qualified as a mechanism of implementing accountability.

5.2 The general principles of invocation of international responsibility by a state

5.2.1 Invocation of international responsibility of a state by another state: Part Three of the draft articles on state responsibility

The implementation of the international responsibility of a state is regulated in Part Three of the ILC draft articles on state responsibility. Chapter I of Part Three deals with the invocation of state responsibility by states and with certain associated questions. Chapter II deals with countermeasures taken in order to induce the responsible state to cease the conduct in question and to provide reparation.

The traditional paradigm of international law as law between states still has its consequences for the law of international responsibility. As Brownlie states in respect of individuals as potential claimants in international law:

> Although there is no rule that individuals cannot have procedural capacity before international jurisdictions, the assumption of classical law that only states have procedural capacity is still dominant and affects the content of most treaties providing for the settlement of disputes which raise questions of state responsibility.[3]

This traditional paradigm is reflected in the ILC draft articles. These deal exclusively with the invocation of international responsibility by a state. It may be noted that the first Rapporteur of the ILC on the topic of state responsibility, García Amador, did not exclude the possibility that the draft articles would deal with the invocation of state responsibility by individuals or international organizations.[4] He submitted that the traditional view, that only the state itself can be considered as the passive subject of international responsibility, was incompatible with certain contemporary legal realities and theories, as well as patently inconsistent with itself. He referred in particular to the recognition of fundamental human rights and freedoms, which he held amounts to recognition of the individual as a legal person independent of the state.

3 I. Brownlie, Principles of Public International Law 585 (1998).

4 Report of the International Law Commission on the work of its eighth session, 23 April to 4 July 1956, Vol II, UN Doc. A/3159, at 194.

This did not necessarily mean that the individual has the capacity to bring an international claim in all cases. Certain prerequisites could be considered.

It is well known that the Commission chose to deal exclusively with states as active and passive subject of international responsibility and that it has been criticized for this choice as not taking into account developments in international law.[5] Even without taking into account the added complexities of non-state actors, however, the drafting of articles on invoking responsibility proved an arduous task. The principal reason was that the ILC wished to recognize the multilateral dimension of state responsibility. As stated, the classical conception of state responsibility, of which Anzilotti is considered the main intellectual author, was as a relationship between states. More specifically, it was a conception of state responsibility as a bilateral relationship between the author state and the state whose subjective right has been violated. In the course of the ILC's work on state responsibility it came to be recognized that state responsibility also has a multilateral dimension: other states than the state whose subjective right had been violated could also be concerned by an internationally wrongful act. This recognition was closely connected to the introduction of the notion of *erga omnes* obligations. The ICJ stated in the *Barcelona Traction* case:

> An essential distinction should be drawn between the obligations of a State towards the international community as a whole, and those arising vis-à-vis another State … By their very nature the former are the concern of all States. In view of the importance of the rights involved, all States can be held to have a legal interest in their protection; they are obligations *erga omnes*.[6]

In the specific context of state responsibility Rapporteur Ago introduced the notion of 'crime of state' to express the community dimension. As is well known, the ILC in 2000 dropped the notion of crime of state, but not the idea that state responsibility is more than a bilateral relationship. The ILC came to recognize that the multilateral dimension should have consequences for the rules on the invocation of responsibility, but there was much controversy concerning which consequences.[7]

One important question in this respect was whether states other than those whose subjective right had been breached could be considered to be 'injured states'. The draft articles adopted by the ILC in 1996 as well as the draft articles on invocation of 2000 answered the question in the positive. At the same time it was clear that not all the states concerned were in a similar position. A state which has a legal interest in invoking responsibility merely because a crime of state has been committed, is in another position than the state whose subjective interest has been directly affected by

5 E. Brown Weiss, *Invoking State Responsibility in the Twenty-First Century*, 96 American Journal of International Law 798 (2002), at 816.

6 Barcelona Traction, Light and Power Company, Limited (*Belgium* v. *Spain*), Judgment, 1970 ICJ Reports 3, para 32.

7 See *e.g.* D. Bederman, *Article 40 (2) (E) & (F) of the ILC Draft Articles on State Responsibility: Standing of Injured States under Customary International Law and Multilateral Treaties*, 92 ASIL Proc. 291 (1998).

that crime. In other words, they are not equally injured. More concretely, a state victim of aggression is clearly not in the same position as a state which merely has a legal interest in upholding the prohibition of aggression. This difference in position found its expression in the different legal consequences to be attached to the commission of an international crime toward the different states. Certain commentators maintain that the difference can be expressed by stating that a state whose subjective interest is not injured can nevertheless be 'legally' injured.[8] The 'legal injury' would consist of the fact that an obligation to which it subscribes has been breached and its status could therefore be threatened unless action is taken to enforce the obligation. This however begs the question, because this reasoning can be applied to all international obligations, and not only a limited category. The same criticism applies to the distinction between 'directly' and 'indirectly' injured states.[9] For this reason it is fortunate that the ILC on the suggestion of Special Rapporteur Crawford,[10] chose to distinguish between injured states and states with a legal interest in the 2001 draft articles.

In the 2001 draft articles on state responsibility the basic principle is that an 'injured state' in the strict sense is entitled to invoke international responsibility. This is the state whose individual right has been denied or impaired by the internationally wrongful act or which has otherwise been particularly affected by that act. Article 42 of the draft articles identifies three cases of an injured state.[11] In the first case, in order to invoke the responsibility of another state as an injured state, a state must have an individual right to the performance of an obligation, in the way that a state party to a bilateral treaty has toward the other state party. Secondly, a state may be specially affected by the breach of an obligation to which it is a party, even though it cannot be said that the obligation is owed to it individually. The ILC commentary mentions as an example a case of pollution of the high seas in breach of Article 194 of the United Nations Convention on the Law of the Sea which may particularly impact on one or several states whose

8 B. Stern, *Et Si l'On Utilisait le Concept de Préjudice Juridique? Retour sur une Notion Délaissée à l'Occasion de la Fin des Travaux de la CDI sur la Responsabilité des Etats*, 47 Annuaire Français de Droit International 3 (2002).

9 See on this distinction M. Spinedi, *From One Codification to Another: Bilateralism and Multilateralism in the Genesis of the Law of Treaties and the Law of State Responsibility*, 13 European Journal of International Law 1099 (2002), at 1112-1113. In addition, this distinction creates the risk of confusion with the distinction between moral and material injury.

10 See J. Crawford, *Responsibility to the International Community as a Whole*, 8 Indiana Journal of Global Legal Studies 303 (2001), at 319-320.

11 Draft article 42 reads:

> A State is entitled as an injured State to invoke the responsibility of another State if the obligation breached is owed to:
>
> (a) That State individually; or
>
> (b) A group of States including that State, or the international community as a whole, and the breach of the obligation:
>
> (i) Specially affects that State; or
>
> (ii) Is of such a character as radically to change the position of all the other States to which the obligation is owed with respect to the further performance of the obligation.

beaches may be polluted by toxic residues or whose coastal fisheries may be closed.[12] Thirdly, it may be the case that performance of the obligation by the responsible state (or organization) is a necessary condition of its performance by all the other states. Such obligations are so-called 'integral' or 'inderdependent' obligations.[13] Examples are disarmament conventions or agreements demilitarizing certain regions. This category is based on Article 60 (2) (c) of the 1969 Vienna Convention on the Law of Treaties, which recognizes a category of treaties of such a character that a material breach of its provisions by one party radically changes the position of every party with respect to the further performance of its obligations. Pierre-Marie Dupuy includes conventions prohibiting certain weapons or methods of warfare in this category, presumably referring to conventions such as the 1980 Certain Conventional Weapons Convention.[14] A breach of this convention however does not seem to radically change the position of the other parties to the Convention. Rather, another state would be injured if a prohibited weapon was used against it, which would constitute a situation falling under draft article 42 (b) (i) rather than subparagraph (ii). It seems that only the adverse party in an international armed conflict, the state on the territory of which a violation has occurred or the national state of the victims can be considered as injured.[15]

Article 48 of the draft articles provides for the invocation of responsibility by states which are not injured but which do have a legal interest.[16] Invocation by these

---

12 Report of the International Law Commission on the work of its fifty-third session, 23 April – 1 June and 2 July – 10 August 2001 (A/56/10), at 299, para. 12.

13 L.A. Sicilianos, *Classification des Obligations et Dimension Multilatérale de la Responsabilité Internationale*, in P.M. Dupuy, (Ed.) Obligations Multilatérales, Droit Impératif et Responsabilité Internationale des Etats 57 (2003), at 65.

14 P.M. Dupuy, *A General Stocktaking of the Connections between the Multilateral Dimension of Obligations and Codification of the Law of Responsibility*, 13 European Journal of International Law 1053 (2002), at 1071.

15 M. Sassòli, *State Responsibility for Violations of International Humanitarian Law*, 84 International Review of the Red Cross 401 (2002), at 423.

16 Draft article 48 reads:

1. Any State other than an injured State is entitled to invoke the responsibility of another State in accordance with paragraph 2 if:
   (a) The obligation breached is owed to a group of States including that State, and is established for the protection of a collective interest of the group; or
   (b) The obligation breached is owed to the international community as a whole.
2. Any State entitled to invoke responsibility under paragraph 1 may claim from the responsible State:
   (a) Cessation of the internationally wrongful act, and assurances and guarantees of non-repetition in accordance with article 30; and
   (b) Performance of the obligation of reparation in accordance with the preceding articles, in the interest of the injured State or of the beneficiaries of the obligation breached.
3. The requirements for the invocation of responsibility by an injured State under articles 43, 44 and 45 apply to an invocation of responsibility by a State entitled to do so under paragraph 1.

states is possible in the first place if the obligation is owed to a group of states including that state, and is established for the protection of a collective interest of the group. According to the ILC commentary, the obligations coming within the scope of this provision are not limited to arrangements established only in the interests of the member states, but would extend to agreements established by a group of states in some wider common interest. The commentary adds that the principal purpose of obligations falling within subparagraph (1) (a) will be to foster a common interest, over and above any interests of the states concerned individually. Customary international humanitarian law rules binding on the author state, as well as the 1949 Geneva Conventions and the 1977 Additional Protocols seem to be included in this category. The principal purpose of these obligations is protecting the victims of armed conflict. It may be noted that the right to invoke responsibility for violations of international humanitarian law in the 2001 draft articles is broader than in draft article 40 of the 2000 draft. The latter provided that if the right infringed by the act of state arises from a multilateral treaty, any other state party to the multilateral treaty could invoke responsibility, if it was established that the right had been expressly stipulated in that treaty for the protection of the collective interests of the states parties thereto. It thereby excluded obligations under customary international law.[17]

Secondly, under draft article 48 any state other than an injured state is entitled to invoke the responsibility of another state if the obligation breached is owed to the international community as a whole. According to the ILC commentary, this subparagraph intends to give effect to the *Barcelona Traction* case, in which the ICJ held that all states have a legal interest in obligations owed to the international community as a whole. Whereas subparagraph (a) concerns so-called obligations *erga omnes partes*, subparagraph (b) concerns obligations *erga omnes*.

The ILC does not state which obligations have an *erga omnes* character, stating that it is not the function of the draft articles to provide a list of those obligations. This raises the question whether obligations under international humanitarian law are owed to the international community as a whole, and the related question whether the category of *erga omnes* obligations is identical to the category of peremptory norms referred to in article 40 of the ILC draft articles on state responsibility. To start with the last question, the ILC commentary does not answer it. It merely states that:

> whether or not peremptory norms of general international law and obligations to the international community as a whole are aspects of a single basic idea, there is at the very least substantial overlap between them.[18]

There is certain logic to the idea that two concepts which express a hierarchy between international obligations should have the same content. A practical advantage of identical categories would be that it would facilitate the identification of obligations

---

17 Bederman, *supra* note 7, at 292.

18 *Supra* note 12, at 281, para. 7.

erga omnes.[19] In the *Barcelona Traction* case, the ICJ did not state how obligations *erga omnes* are to be identified, other than on the basis of their content. Article 53 of the Vienna Convention on the Law of Treaties on the other hand does provide for a primitive procedure for the identification of a peremptory norm, in stating that it is a norm accepted and recognized by the international community of states as a whole as a norm from which no derogation is permitted and which can be modified only by a subsequent norm of general international law having the same character. If the categories of obligations to which the concepts of *erga omnes* and *ius cogens* refer are identical, then there is only a difference in the concepts to the extent that they attach different consequences to those obligations: one concerning the legal consequences of their breach, and the other concerning the states entitled to invoke responsibility of a breach of the obligation.

However, there is no reason why as a matter of principle the two consequences have to attach to precisely the same obligations. The international community is not precluded from considering that all states should be able to invoke the responsibility of the author state for a breach of a particular obligation but that additional legal consequences are not attached to that breach. Consistent with this view a number of writers maintain that the circle of *erga omnes* obligations is broader than the circle of peremptory norms.[20]

With respect to the second question, it is not clear to what extent obligations under international humanitarian law are obligations *erga omnes*. There is evidence in state practice that states consider at least certain obligations under international humanitarian law to have an *erga omnes* character.[21] The Statute of the ICC supports this. The preambular paragraph to the Statute, which states that "the most serious crimes of concern to the international community as a whole must not go unpunished", is clearly a reference to obligations *erga omnes* and implies that the states parties to the Statute consider that the war crimes in Article 8 of the Statute constitute breaches of obligations *erga omnes*.[22] The ICJ in its Advisory Opinion on the *Legal*

19 See A. De Hoogh, Obligations Erga Omnes and International Crimes: A Theoretical Inquiry into the Implementation and Enforcement of the International Responsibility of States 45-48 (1995).

20 G. Gaja, *Obligations Erga Omnes, International Crimes and Jus Cogens: A Tentative Analysis of Three Related Concepts*, in J. Weiler, A. Cassese & M. Spinedi (Eds.), International Crimes of States: A Critical Analysis of the ILC's Draft Article 19 on State Responsibility 151 (1989); L.A. Sicilianos, *The Classification of Obligations and the Multilateral Dimension of the Relations of International Responsibility*, 13 European Journal of International Law 1127 (2002), at 1136-1137.

21 At the Expert Meeting on the Fourth Geneva Convention held in Geneva on 27-29 October 1998 for example, the German representative stated that the "respect for International Humanitarian Law, and the respect for human rights, is an obligation erga omnes, an obligation owed to the international community and to each of its members." See also the statement by Canada during the oral proceedings in the *Legality of the Use of Force* case, CR 99/16 of 10 May 1999, para. 42.

22 But note Article 10 of the Statute, which provides that "Nothing in this Part shall be interpreted as limiting or prejudicing in any way existing or developing rules of international law for purposes other than this Statute."

Consequences of the Construction of a Wall in the Occupied Palestinian Territory held that certain obligations under international humanitarian law are obligations *erga omnes*:

> The Court recalls that in its Advisory Opinion on the Legality of the Threat or Use of Nuclear Weapons, it stated that "a great many rules of humanitarian law applicable in armed conflict are so fundamental to the respect of the human person and 'elementary considerations of humanity'...", that they are "to be observed by all States whether or not they have ratified the conventions that contain them, because they constitute intransgressible principles of international customary law" (*I.C.J. Reports 1996 (I)*, p. 257, para. 79). In the Court's view, these rules incorporate obligations which are essentially of an *erga omnes* character.[23]

5.2.2 *The concept of injured state in international humanitarian law*

Some writers state that common Article 1 to the 1949 Geneva Conventions makes all contracting parties to the conventions injured states in case of a breach of the conventions.[24] In other words, common Article 1 is *lex specialis* in respect of article 42 of the draft articles on state responsibility. In this case all contracting parties to Additional Protocol I would also be injured states in case of a breach of the Protocol, because Article 1 (1) of the Protocol repeats common Article 1 of the 1949 Conventions.

Claims that common Article 1 makes all contracting parties injured states must be seen against the background of the earlier broad definition of injured state used by the ILC. Draft article 40 adopted by the Commission in 1996 included in its definition of 'injured state' any state party to a multilateral treaty or bound by the relevant rule of customary international law, if it was established that the right infringed had been created or established for the protection of human rights and fundamental freedoms. In case of an international crime all other states were also injured states. Draft article 40 was binary in the sense that a state was either an injured state with all the connected rights concerning invocation of responsibility, or a state was not injured and consequently did not have any right concerning invocation of responsibility. Article 40 was also closely connected to the very controversial concept of crime of state.

In the draft articles adopted in 2001, the ILC abandoned this system together with the concept of international crimes of states.[25] Draft article 42 gives a much narrower definition of 'injured state'. By way of compensation, the Commission introduced a special rule on the invocation of responsibility by a state other than an injured

---

23 *Legal Consequences of the Construction of a Wall in the Occupied Palestinian Territory*, Advisory Opinion of 9 July 2004, not yet reported, para. 157.

24 K. Sachariew, *States' Entitlement to Take Action to Enforce International Humanitarian Law*, 29 International Review of the Red Cross 177 (1989), at 184 and N. Levrat, *Les Conséquences de l'Engagement Pris par les Hautes Parties Contractantes de "Faire Respecter" les Conventions Humanitaires*, in F. Kalshoven & Y. Sandoz (Eds.), Implementation of International Humanitarian Law 263 (1989), at 274.

25 See Report of the International Law Commission Report on the work of its fifty-second session, 1 May-9 June and 10 July-18 August 2000 (A/55/10), Chapter IV (State Responsibility), 37-48.

state with a legal interest in draft article 48, abandoning the system of former draft article 40.

In the system of the draft articles adopted in 2001 it seems much more appropriate to consider common Article 1 as a forerunner of draft article 48 (1).[26] Contracting parties have a legal interest in the invocation of responsibility, but they are not injured states in the strict sense. They do not have a subjective right that has been breached.

Article 89 of Additional Protocol I also seems relevant as potential *lex specialis*.[27] The article deals directly with questions of consequences of international responsibility, including the right to take countermeasures, rather than with the invocation of international responsibility. However, this implies that responsibility has been invoked in a prior phase and that the states entitled to take action are *a fortiori* entitled to invoke responsibility. In relation to draft article 48 (1) (a) of the ILC draft articles, Article 89 is both broader and narrower. It is broader because it is in the form of an undertaking rather than a right. It is narrower because it only attaches to serious violations. As far as invocation of responsibility is concerned, Article 89 adds nothing to common Article 1 of the Geneva Conventions and Additional Protocol 1.

As far as legal consequences of responsibility are concerned, Article 89 corresponds to article 41 (1) of the ILC draft articles, which provides that states shall cooperate to bring to an end through lawful means any serious breach of an obligation arising under a peremptory norm of general international law.[28] Whether or not Article 89 is *lex specialis* in this respect depends on whether all serious violations of the Geneva Conventions and the Protocol are also serious breaches of peremptory norms. The similarities between draft article 41 and Article 89 are striking. Both mainly seem to call for an institutionalized reaction through the UN, but seem not to exclude action outside that forum.[29] The ILC commentary to draft article 41 states that "Cooperation should be organized in the framework of a competent international organization, in particular the United Nations. However, paragraph 1 also envisages the possibility of non-institutionalized cooperation."[30] The text of Article 89 refers to action "in co-operation with the United Nations". The *travaux préparatoires* do not remove the ambiguity of this expression. According to one of the sponsors of the article, there was no need to spell out the nature of the action proposed. The action concerned:

---

26 Sassòli, *supra* note 15, at 424.

27 Article 89 reads:

> In situations of serious violations of the Conventions or of this Protocol, the High Contracting Parties undertake to act, jointly or individually, in co-operation with the United Nations and in conformity with the United Nations Charter.

28 Sassòli, *supra* note 15, at 430.

29 See on draft article 41 P. Klein, *Responsabilité pour Violation Grave d'Obligations Découlant de Normes Impératives de Droit International et Droit des Nations Unies*, in P.M. Dupuy, (Ed.) Obligations Multilatérales, Droit Impératif et Responsabilité Internationale des Etats 189 (2003).

30 *Supra* note 12, at 287, para. 2.

> was, in fact, the action prescribed by the United Nations Charter and could not be undertaken without the consent of the General Assembly or the Security Council. General international law would apply during a legal vacancy, in other words when neither the General Assembly nor the Security Council was in session. [31]

On the other hand, many delegations stated that the wording of the article was unclear and a number of them abstained during the vote on the article for that reason.[32]

5.2.3 *Diplomatic protection*

A state can be injured directly, for example because of legal injury to its agent in breach of international law. Legal injury to a national of the state who is *not* an agent of that state in contravention of international law, is an indirect injury to the state and gives rise to the right of diplomatic protection. The ILC is presently addressing the topic of diplomatic protection under the guidance of Special Rapporteur Dugard. In 2002 the Commission adopted the text of draft articles 1 to 7. In 2003, the ILC adopted three more draft articles on first reading. Draft article 1 (1) describes diplomatic protection as follows:

> Diplomatic protection consists of resort to diplomatic action or other means of peaceful settlement by a State adopting in its own right the cause of its national in respect of an injury to that national arising from an internationally wrongful act of another State.[33]

The right of diplomatic protection is occasioned by the legal injury to an individual but it is not a procedural right of the individual. The doctrine of diplomatic protection, at least as it is traditionally conceived, rests on the assumption that the national of a state constitutes a legal interest of the state; it is a corollary of the personal jurisdiction of the state over its population. An individual may benefit from the exercise of diplomatic protection but it is his state of nationality which is exercising a procedural right. The classical formulation of this position was stated by the Permanent Court of International Justice in the *Mavrommatis Palestine Concessions* case:

> It is an elementary principle of international law that a State is entitled to protect its subjects, when injured by acts contrary to international law committed by another State, from whom they have been unable to obtain satisfaction through the ordinary channels. By taking up the case of one of its subjects and by resorting to diplomatic

31 Official Records of the Diplomatic Conference on the Reaffirmation and Development of International Humanitarian Law Applicable in Armed Conflicts (1974-1977), Vol. VI, CDDH/SR.46, at 347, para. 46.

32 *Id.*, at 374 (India), at 376 (Italy).

33 Report of the International law Commission on the Work of its Fifty-fourth Session, 2002, (A/57/10), at 169.

> protection or international judicial proceedings on his behalf, a State is in reality asserting its own right – its right to ensure, in the person of its subjects, respect for the rules of international law.[34]

The consequence of the classical position on diplomatic protection is that an individual does not have any guarantee that his state of nationality will protect him. His state is entitled to exercise diplomatic protection but it is not obliged to do so.[35] In this respect the concept of diplomatic protection is an expression of the fact that, while it is increasingly recognized that individuals have substantive rights under international law, their remedies are limited.[36]

This classical position was questioned by Special Rapporteur Dugard in his first report to the ILC. He formulated a draft article providing for a number of situations in which the exercise of diplomatic protection would be mandatory, in particular if the injury to the national resulted from a grave breach of a *ius cogens* norm attributable to another state.[37] Although he underlined that the proposal was *de lege ferenda* in the field of progressive development of the law, a majority of the Commission was not willing to accept it. It was reiterated that diplomatic protection is a sovereign prerogative of the state, exercised at the state's discretion.[38]

5.3 Invocation of international responsibility of an international organization by a state

5.3.1 General principles

There is little practice in respect of the implementation of international responsibility of an international organization. Claims are not frequently made against international organizations. In this context, one UN official stated that one of the reasons for persistent ambiguity concerning the binding nature of international humanitarian law for UN peace support operations has been that few claims have been lodged against the organization.[39]

The ILC established a working group on responsibility of international organizations following the decision to include the topic in the Commission's program of

---

34 Mavrommatis Palestine Concessions Case (Jurisdiction) (*Greece* v. *United Kingdom*), 1924 P.C.I.J., series A, No. 2, at 12.

35 *Supra* note 6, at 44.

> The State must be viewed as the sole judge to decide whether its protection will be granted, and to what extent it is granted, and when it will cease. It retains in this respect a discretionary power the exercise of which may be determined by considerations of a political or other nature, unrelated to the particular case.

36 See First Report on Diplomatic Protection by Mr. John R. Dugard, Special Rapporteur, of 7 March 2000, UN Doc. A/CN.4/506, at 8, para. 24.

37 *Id.*, at 27-34.

38 *Supra* note 33, at 156-158.

39 Interview by the author with an official in the Office of Legal Affairs, 17 September 2002.

work. In its report, which was considered and adopted by the Commission,[40] the working group set out a general orientation of the topic intended as guidance to the Special Rapporteur.[41] The report noted the complexities of implementation of responsibility and suggested to leave open the question of whether the Commission's study should include matters relating to implementation of responsibility of international organizations and, in the affirmative, whether it should consider only claims by states or also claims by international organizations.[42] The complexities signaled by the working group appear to relate in particular to claims that international organizations may submit against other organizations. With respect to the issue of states' entitlement to invoke responsibility, articles 42 and 48 of the draft articles on state responsibility do not appear to present insurmountable problems if applied in the context of the responsibility of international organizations. Such application is consistent with the basic assumption that the principles of state responsibility should be applied in the context of responsibility of international organizations unless other special rules are required.[43]

Writers on the responsibility of international organizations do not hesitate to apply the principles derived from state responsibility.[44] Applied to breach of international humanitarian law, the consequences are that potentially injured states include the adverse party in an international armed conflict, the state on the territory of which a violation has occurred or the national state of the victims. In case of a breach of an obligation *erga omnes*, any other state is also entitled to invoke the responsibility of the organization.

5.3.2 *Diplomatic protection*

In case an international organization has committed an internationally wrongful act causing harm to a state's national, that state is entitled to exercise diplomatic protection. In practice there have been few instances in which states have exercised this right. One of these instances was the espousal by Belgium and a number of other states of claims of their nationals for damage caused by ONUC. These cases of diplomatic protection resulted in the conclusion of agreements between the UN and the states concerned in which the organization agreed to pay lump-sum compensation. The work of the ILC on diplomatic protection is limited to action taken by a state against another state.

---

40 *Supra* note 33, at 228, para. 464.

41 Report of the Working Group on Responsibility of International Organizations of 6 June 2002, UN Doc. A/CN.4/L.622.

42 *Id.*, at 8, para. 24.

43 Special rules may be required for the implementation of responsibility of an organization by a state that has not recognized the organization as a separate international legal person. See also M. Perez-Gonzalez, *Les Organisations Internationales et le Droit de la Responsabilité*, 92 Revue Générale de Droit International Public 63 (1988), at 76-77. Non-recognition seems unlikely in the case of the United Nations or the North Atlantic Treaty Organization.

44 Klein, *supra* note 2, at 529-531.

In spite of the relative lack of practice, there seems to be no doubt concerning the possibility of diplomatic protection in respect of an international organization. The UN recognized the possibility in an *amicus curiae* brief in the case of *Broadbent* v. *Organization of American States*.[45] Writers also reaffirm the possibility.[46]

The modalities of diplomatic protection are the same whether a state or an international organization is the respondent. This means that the right to exercise diplomatic protection is at the discretion of the state. An individual does not have a right to diplomatic protection, unless his state has created such a right under domestic law. This was illustrated in the *Manderlier* case, which arose from the agreement concluded between Belgium and the UN referred to above. Manderlier was one of the Belgian nationals whose claims had been espoused by his government. He was not satisfied with the part of the lump sum the government allocated to him and sought an order from the Brussels Court of First Instance, and subsequently the Court of Appeals, against the UN for the payment of compensation for damage to his property in the Congo and a declaration against Belgium that it had failed to fulfill its obligation of diplomatic protection. It can be implied from the fact that the Court of First Instance examined whether there was a specific source of an obligation in this case that it considered that there was no general obligation on Belgium. The Court found neither a specific obligation in domestic legislation nor did it find that statements by government officials, that they would exert their best efforts to protect Belgian nationals and their property in the Congo, resulted in such an obligation.[47] The Court of Appeals also considered that Manderlier was unable to establish the existence of the alleged undertaking which he invoked.[48]

The applicability of the local remedies rule to diplomatic protection in respect of an international organization raises special problems and is a modality which cannot simply be transposed.[49] The principle that an international organization should have the opportunity to give redress is acknowledged by writers. In the case of states this is usually achieved through the domestic courts of the state which are able to exercise jurisdiction over the individual when an injury has been inflicted on that individual. International organizations usually lack this possibility. This difference in institutional structure leads to an interpretation of the local remedies rule which is not centered on domestic courts, but is more flexible.[50] An individual needs to exhaust any judicial

45 Brief for the United Nations as Amicus Curiae, UNJY 1980, at 227.

46 See *e.g.* J.P. Ritter, *La Protection Diplomatique à l'Egard d'une Organisation Internationale*, 8 Annuaire Français de Droit International 427 (1962).

47 *Manderlier* v. *United Nations and Belgium*, Court of first instance of Brussels, 11 May 1966, 81 Journal des Tribunaux No. 4553 (1966), 723. See also J. Salmon, *De Quelques Problèmes Posés aux Tribunaux Belges par les Actions des Citoyens Belges contre l'O.N.U. en Raison des Faits Survenus sur le Territoire de la République Démocratique du Congo*, 81 Journal des Tribunaux 713 (1966), at 718-719.

48 *Manderlier* v. *United Nations and Belgium*, Court of Appeals of Brussels, 15 September 1969, reproduced in 69 ILR 139 (1985).

49 C. Eagleton, International Organization and the Law of Responsibility, 76 Recueil des Cours (1950-I), 352.

50 Klein, *supra* note 2, at 536.

mechanisms of redress which are available within the organization, as long as they are effective. In the case of the European Community for example an individual has recourse to the European Court of Justice.[51] In the UN and NATO, there are no judicial bodies to which individuals, other than employees of the organization, have access in case they have been injured by a breach of international humanitarian law for which the organization is responsible. An individual will also have to exhaust special mechanisms put in place by the organization to resolve disputes with individuals, including arbitral and administrative procedures.[52] These include claims settlement procedures established in peace support operations. In respect of the UN, Amrallah states that procedures such as the local claims review boards "should be considered as local remedies which must be exhausted before the individual's state could be allowed to interpose a claim on his behalf."[53] It must be noted, however, that although UN claims settlement procedures do not explicitly exclude non-nationals of the host state, NATO claims settlement procedures are exclusively open to nationals of the host state.[54]

5.4 Interim conclusion

The paragraphs above discussed the possibilities for a state to invoke the responsibility of another state or an international organization for a breach of international humanitarian law by a peace support operation. It is however unlikely that injured states, and even less states with a more indirect interest, will use the available possibilities. One reason is that an injured state may not have a government to invoke responsibility, such as Somalia in 1993. Another reason is that if a state submits a claim against an international organization of which it is a member, the state may end up paying part of the compensation itself. A third reason is that the exercise of diplomatic protection is a discretion of the state and not a right of the individual. There are many policy reasons why a state may not be inclined to exercise diplomatic protection. Claimants are therefore likely to prefer remedies which they are entitled to pursue in their own name, whether under an individual complaints mechanism or at the international level or through civil litigation.[55]

---

51 See P. Pescatore, *Les Relations Extérieures des Communautés Européennes*, 103 Recueil des Cours (1961-II), at 232; M. Jones, *The Non-Contractual Liability of the EEC and the Availability of an Alternative Remedy in the National Courts*, 1 Legal Issues of European Integration 1 (1981).

52 Ritter, *supra* note 46, at 454.

53 B. Amrallah, *The International Responsibility of the United Nations for Activities Carried out by U.N. Peace-Keeping Forces*, 32 Revue Egyptienne de Droit International 57 (1976), at 76.

54 See Claims Annex to the Technical Agreement between the Republic of Bosnia and Herzegovina Ministry of Justice and the Implementation Force, Art. 2; Agreement between the Government of the Republic of Albania and NATO Concerning the Status of NATO and its Personnel Present on the Territory of the Republic of Albania of 25 June 1999, Art. 17 (copy on file with the author).

55 C. Wickremasinghe & G. Verdirame, *Responsibility and Liability for Violations of Human Rights in the Course of UN Field Operations*, in C. Scott (Ed.), Torture as Tort: Comparative Perspectives on the Development of Transnational Human Rights Litigation 465 (2001).

5.5 Invocation of international responsibility by an individual

5.5.1 A rights-based perspective of international humanitarian law

International humanitarian law was traditionally considered as governing relations between states. It set out rights and obligations of the belligerent states. Individual persons were the objects and beneficiaries of the law rather than subjects. They did not have rights or obligations under international law.

Such a traditional view was connected with the consideration that states were the only subjects of international law. Until the beginning of the nineteenth century, it was firmly established that an individual was not a subject of international law in the sense of having rights under international law. Today it is generally accepted that the individual is capable of having rights under international law, although there is a discussion whether this makes him a subject of international law *per se*. International humanitarian law is considered as a branch of international law conferring rights on individuals.[56] Meron explains that while:

> even the early Geneva Conventions conferred various protections on individuals, as well as on States, whether those protections appertained to the contracting states or to the individuals themselves remained unclear at best. The treatment to be accorded to persons under the Conventions was not necessarily seen as creating a body of rights to which those persons were entitled. The 1929 POW Convention paved the way for recognition of individual rights by using the term "right" in several provisions. It was not until the adoption of the 1949 Conventions, however, that "the existence of rights conferred on protected persons was affirmed" through several key provisions.[57]

Of particular interest in this regard is Article 6 of Geneva Convention (I) of 1949, and the corresponding Articles 6, 6, and 7 of Geneva Conventions (II), (III), and (IV), respectively. This article provides that protected persons may in no circumstances renounce in part or in entirety the rights secured to them by the present conventions, and by the special agreements provided for in the conventions. It clarifies that the rights referred to are granted to individuals instead of to their governments, since only the holder of a right is entitled to renounce it. This conclusion can also be drawn from the fact that the article in Geneva Convention (III) speaks not only to the relationship between a prisoner of war and the detaining power, but also to the relationship between the prisoner and his state of origin. The prisoner is not bound by a special agreement to which his state of origin has consented, if that agreement encroaches on the rights of the former.

---

56 L. Zegveld, *Remedies for Victims of Violations of International Humanitarian Law*, 85 International Review of the Red Cross 497 (2003); G. Aldrich, *Individuals as Subjects of International Humanitarian Law*, in J. Makarczyk (Ed.), Theory of International Law at the Threshold of the 21st Century: Essays in Honour of Krzysztof Skubiszewski 851 (1996). See also R. Teitel, *Humanity's Law: Rule of Law for the New Global Politics*, 35 Cornell International Law Journal 355 (2002), at 362-363.

57 Th. Meron, *The Humanization of Humanitarian Law*, 94 American Journal of International Law 239 (2000), at 251.

The ICRC commentary on Article 7 of Geneva Convention (III) even suggests that a prisoner of war could have a legitimate claim against his state of origin if violations of his rights are the consequence of an agreement signed by his state of origin.[58]

Other articles in the conventions also use the term 'right', including Articles 5, 52, 72, 73, 75 and 101 of Geneva Convention (IV), as does Additional Protocol I. Other provisions of the 1949 Conventions and Additional Protocol I use analogous terms such as 'entitlement', 'privilege' and 'claim'.

Article 118 of Geneva Convention (III) provides that prisoners of war shall be released and repatriated without delay after the cessation of active hostilities. The article does not use the term 'right' or a similar term. Nevertheless, repatriation of prisoners of war has been interpreted as an individual right of those prisoners. The United Nations Command determined after the Korean conflict that many prisoners of war in its custody were opposed to being repatriated to North Korea or China. The latter insisted that the obligation to repatriate was owed to them and not to the prisoners of war themselves. The prisoners should therefore be repatriated without consideration of their wishes. The UN Command however determined that force would not be used against prisoners of war to prevent or effect their return to their homelands. This interpretation was reaffirmed in a UN General Assembly Resolution of 3 December 1952.[59] The United States interpreted Article 118 similarly after Operation Desert Storm. The official Department of Defense after action report notes that:

> Article 118, GPW [Geneva Convention of Prisoners of War], establishes a POW's right to be repatriated. In conflicts since the GPW's adoption, this principle has become conditional: Each POW must consent to repatriation rather than being forced to return.[60]

The Eritrea Ethiopia Claims Commission, established to decide among others claims between the governments for loss, damage or injury resulting from violations of international humanitarian law, including the 1949 Geneva Conventions, or other violations of international law, handed down a partial award on Eritrea's claim concerning prisoners of war on 1 July 2003. The award noted that on 29 November 2002 Ethiopia released all prisoners of war registered by the ICRC remaining in its custody.[61] It also stated that some chose to remain in Ethiopia for family or other reasons, apparently accepting that this was their choice and not that of their government.

ICTY case law also provides an example of the concept of individual rights in the interpretation of the 1949 Geneva Conventions. In the *Čelebići* case, for exam-

58 J. Pictet (Ed.), The Geneva Conventions of 12 August 1949; Commentary; III Geneva Convention Relative to the Treatment of Prisoners of War 92 (1960).

59 General Assembly Resolution 610, UN Doc. A/2361 (1952).

60 United States Department of Defense Report to Congress on the Conduct of the Persian Gulf War – Appendix on the Role of the Law of War, 10 April 1992, reproduced in 31 ILM 612 (1992), at 631.

61 Eritrea Ethiopia Claims Commission, Partial Award, Prisoners of War, Eritrea's Claim 17, 1 July 2003, at 33, para. 144.

ple, the accused Delić contended *inter alia* that because Bosnia Herzegovina acceded to the 1949 Geneva Conventions after the events alleged in the indictment, his acts committed before that date could not be prosecuted under the treaty regime of grave breaches. The Prosecution contended that Bosnia Herzegovina was bound by the conventions as a result of their instrument of succession deposited on 31 December 1992, which took effect on the date on which Bosnia Herzegovina became independent, 6 March 1992. The Appeals Chamber examined the question on the basis of the 1978 Vienna Convention on Succession of States in Respect of Treaties. It held that Bosnia Herzegovina formally succeeded to the 1949 Geneva Conventions on 6 March 1992 on the basis of Article 23 paragraph 1 of the Vienna Convention. It also stated that:

> irrespective of any findings of formal succession, Bosnia and Herzegovina would in any event have succeeded to the Geneva Conventions under customary law, as this type of convention entails automatic succession, i.e., without the need for any formal confirmation of adherence by the successor State. It may be now considered in international law that there is automatic State succession to multilateral treaties in the broad sense, i.e., treaties of universal character *which express fundamental human rights*.[62]

5.5.2 *Procedural capacity*

Being a bearer of a right under international law must be distinguished from being able to enforce that right on the international level. The ILC has recognized this distinction. Article 33 (2) of the draft articles provides that Part Two of the draft articles, concerning the content of state responsibility, is without prejudice to any right, arising from the international responsibility of a state, which may accrue directly to any person or entity other than a state. In the system of the draft articles, this provision merely makes clear that the draft articles do not deal with the possibility of the invocation of responsibility by persons or entities other than states, but it has much wider implications, as the ILC commentary makes clear:

> In cases where the primary obligation is owed to a non-State entity, it may be that some procedure is available whereby that entity can invoke the responsibility on its own account and without the intermediation of any State.[63]

The commentary gives human rights treaties which provide for a right of petition to a court or some other body as an example. But not every case of responsibility for breach of a primary obligation owed to a non-state entity can be invoked by that entity:

62 *Prosecutor* v. *Zejnil Delalić, Zdravko Mucić, Hazim Delić and Esad Landžo*, Judgment, Case No. IT-96-21, A. Ch, 20 February 2001, para. 111 (emphasis added).

63 *Supra* note 12, at 234, para. 4.

> It will be a matter for the particular primary rule to determine whether and to what extent persons or entities other than States are entitled to invoke responsibility of their own account.[64]

ILC Special Rapporteur on Diplomatic Protection Dugard considers that the lack of procedural rights for individuals under international law is an argument for retaining diplomatic protection. He states that "while the individual may have rights under international law, her remedies are limited".[65]

International humanitarian law at present does not provide for the possibility for an individual to invoke international responsibility on her own account.[66] Article 3 of Hague Convention (IV) of 1907 and Article 91 of the first Additional Protocol do not provide for a private right of action,[67] although some writers maintain the contrary. Kalshoven for example states that:

> the records of the conference that adopted the text, i.e. the Second Hague Peace Conference 1907, provide convincing evidence that the delegates sought not so much to lay down a rule relating to the international responsibility of one State vis-à-vis another, as one relating to a State's liability to compensate the losses of individual persons incurred as a consequence of their direct (and harmful) contact with its armed forces.[68]

Applicants in national court proceedings have also made such an argument. In an *amicus curiae* brief to the United States Supreme Court in *Lindo Maduro S.A. and others* v. *United States*, for example, the government of Panama stated that Article 3 sought to provide individual victims of violation of the regulations with a cause of action against the responsible party to the Convention.[69]

The *travaux préparatoires* of the Convention however do not support such an interpretation. A statement by Belgium at the Hague Peace Conference suggests that this delegation considered Article 3 as relating to inter-state responsibility by referring to the settlement of cases by the states concerned.[70] Other delegations did not

---

64 *Id.*

65 First Report on Diplomatic Protection by Mr. John R. Dugard, Special Rapporteur, of 7 March 2000, UN Doc. A/CN.4/506, at 8, para. 24.

66 See *e.g.* R. Dolzer, *The Settlement of War-Related Claims: Does International Law Recognize a Victim's Private Right of Action? Lessons after 1945*, 20 Berkeley Journal of International Law 296 (2002).

67 N. Ronzitti, *Compensation for Violations of the Law of War and Individual Claims*, 12 Italian Yearbook of International Law 39 (2002).

68 F. Kalshoven, *State Responsibility for Warlike Acts of the Armed Forces: From Article 3 of Hague Convention IV of 1907 to Article 91 of Additional Protocol I of 1977 and Beyond*, 40 International & Comparative Law Quarterly 830 (1991).

69 Brief of the Government of Panama as amicus curiae in support of petition for writ of certiorari, reproduced in M. Sassòli & A. Bouvier, How Does Law Protect in War 944 (1999).

70 "Le règlement des indemnités dues à des neutres pourra, le plus souvent, avoir lieu sans retard, par la simple raison que l'Etat belligérant responsable est en paix avec leur pays et

object to this statement, nor did they make it clear that they interpreted the article differently, which would have been a radical departure from contemporary theories of international responsibility.

In a great majority of cases in which individual claimants have based their claim on Article 3, national courts have rejected such an interpretation of the article. United States courts have held that Article 3 does not create a right to invoke international responsibility for individuals.[71] In *Princz* v. *Federal Republic of Germany*, for example, the plaintiff, a Holocaust survivor, brought suit against the defendant to recover damages for injuries suffered while he was a prisoner in a concentration camp.[72] The Court of Appeals considered whether the respondent could claim immunity under the relevant United States legislation, the Federal Sovereign Immunities Act. Princz argued that the compensation provisions of the Hague Convention provided for a right of action for individuals, which would bring the case within an exception to the Act's immunity provision. The Court held that nothing in the Convention even impliedly grants individuals the right to seek damages for violation of its provisions and that consequently there was no exception to the rule of immunity.[73]

In a series of complaints against the Japanese government for violations of the Hague Convention toward individuals, the Japanese courts have held that there is no private right of action for these violations and that compensation may be claimed only by another state.[74] Such an interpretation of Article 3 was also given by the Tokyo district court in *Shimoda and others* v. *Japan*:

> Indeed, international law permits a state to demand from the other country reparations for damage caused to its nationals, in the name of the state for the sake of its nationals. This is called diplomatic protection, as is generally known. Diplomatic

---

continue avec ce dernier des relations pacifiques qui permettront *aux deux Etats* de liquider aisément et sans délai tous les cas venant à se présenter. La même facilité ou possibilité n'existe pas entre les belligérants, par le fait même de la guerre, et, bien que le droit à une indemnité naisse en faveur de leurs ressortisants respectifs aussi bien qu'en faveur de neutres, le règlement des indemnités, *entre belligérants*, ne pourra guère être arrêté et effectué qu'à la conclusion de la Paix.", Deuxième Conférence internationale de la Paix, La Haye 15 juin – 18 octobre 1907, Actes et Documents (Actes), Vol. III, at 147 (emphasis added).

71 *Goldstar (Panama) S.A.* v. *United States*, 967 F.2d 965 (4th Cir. 1992).

72 *Princz* v. *Federal Republic of Germany*, 307 U.S. App. D.C. 102; 26 F.3d 1166.

73 See also *Handel* v. *Artukovic*, 601 F. Supp. 1421, 1425 (C.D. Cal. 1985) and *Tel-Oren* v. *Libyan Arab Republic*, 233 U.S. App. D.C. 384, 726 F.2d 774, 810 (D.C. Cir. 1984 (Bork, J., concurring).

74 See M. Igarashi, *Post-War Compensation Cases, Japanese Courts and International Law*, 43 Japanese Annual of International Law 1 (2000). See also the case of *Daniković et al.* v. *the Netherlands*, Supreme Court of the Netherlands, 29 November 2002 (copy on file with the author). In this interlocutory judgment the Supreme Court held that no action before the civil court in interlocutory proceedings lies for individuals against the state for breach of international humanitarian law. This raises the question whether this would be possible in regular (not interlocutory) proceedings. See also *Prime Minister's Office* v. *Marković et al.*, Court of Cassation of Italy, 5 June 2002, discussed in 12 Italian Yearbook of International Law 292 (2002).

> protection is, however, an act based on the state's own right of diplomatic protection and the individual's claim itself is not asserted by this act. The claim for damages is asserted as the state's own claim. Whether the state exercises the right of diplomatic protection is decided by the state in its own judgment, and the state exercises the rights in its name. It does not follow that the state acts on behalf of its nationals. Borchard and others call this phenomenon "immersion of the individual's claim into the state's claim." In this case, the state is not interfered with at all by the nationals in regard to how and what the state claims, and how it solves the question of the claim. With regard to the amount of compensation which the state claims, it does not always claim the compensation for the whole damage caused to the nationals. Further, the state can determine freely by its intention how the state distributes the compensation thus obtained. Therefore, in this case, we must say that there is no room for regarding the individual as the subject of right in international law.

The German Supreme Court (Bundesgerichtshof) held in a decision of 26 June 2003 that on the basis of Article 3 a 'Party to the conflict' has an obligation to compensate another 'Party to the conflict', and not individuals.[75] The case concerned a claim for damages by Greek nationals for a massacre committed by the German armed forces during World War II. They based their claim on, *inter alia*, Article 3 of the 1907 Hague Convention (IV). A German Court of Appeals rejected the claim on the grounds that Germany was immune from prosecution, and that individuals do not have legal standing to make claims regarding violations of international humanitarian law. The Supreme Court upheld both arguments. With respect to the latter argument, however, it limited its analysis to the state of law at the time of the events concerned. The Court stated that:

> In case of breaches of international law arising from acts in respect of aliens it is not the victims themselves, but their state of nationality that can make a claim. The state asserts its own right to respect for international law vis-à-vis its nationals. This principle, that only states have rights, also applied to the breach of human rights between 1943 and 1945. ... As a consequence, on the basis of Article 2 of the Hague Convention on the Laws and Customs of War on Land of 18 October 1907 (Hague Regulations [sic]) its provisions "do not apply except between Contracting Powers", and in accordance with Article 3 of the Hague Regulations [sic] a "Belligerent Party" is liable to pay compensation (to another Belligerent Party).[76]

75 Bundesgerichtshof, Judgment of 26 June 2003, III ZR 245/98.

76 *Id.*, at 19. Translation by the author. The original wording is:
Bei völkerrechtlichen Delikten durch Handlungen gegenüber fremden Staatsbürgern steht ein Anspruch nicht dem Betroffenen selbst, sondern nur seinem Heimatstaat zu. Der Staat macht im Wege des diplomatischen Schutzes sein eigenes Recht darauf geltend, daß das Völkerrecht in der Person eines Staatsangehörigen beachtet wird. Dieses Prinzip einer ausschließlichen Staatenberechtigung galt in den Jahren 1943 bis 1945 auch für die Verletzung von Menschenrechten ... Dementsprechend finden nach Art. 2 des Abkommens betreffend die Gesetze und Gebräuche des

The Court did not specify whether the situation had changed since 1945, although it did state that only recent developments in international law conferred rights on individuals and created treaty-based systems of protection, on the basis of which an individual could make a claim. This statement implies that such a right to make a claim does not (yet) exist outside the framework of treaty-based systems.[77] This implication was made explicit in the judgment of the Landesgericht Bonn of 10 December 2003 concerning the attack on a bridge during Operation Allied Force. The court held that states have created treaty-based individual claims procedures in the field of human rights. Where such a procedure has not been created, an individual cannot invoke the breach of an individual right under international law against a state. Article 3 of the 1907 Hague Convention (IV) and Article 91 of Additional Protocol I do not create a remedy for individuals.[78]

The discrepancy has led some writers to argue for a general individual complaints procedure for violations of international humanitarian law, arguing that individual humanitarian rights should be justiciable and subjected to the scrutiny of a supervisory organ on the basis of the principle that where there is a right there must be a remedy. [79] This notion of 'no right without a remedy' is already deeply rooted in human rights law. The right to an effective remedy is itself a human right, recognized in Article 8 of the Universal Declaration of Human Rights and Article 2 (3) of the International Covenant on Civil and Political Rights. Whether the right to an effective remedy also operates as a general principle outside the human rights sphere is contestable.

Wellens maintains that an important reason why international organizations should provide appropriate remedies for those entities whose interests have been or may have been affected by their conduct emanates from the 'right to a remedy'.[80] As stated, the right to a remedy is set out in a number of international human rights instruments, and it is claimed that in this particular context it is part of the corpus of customary international law.[81] The right to a remedy has been discussed in the Sub-Commission on the Promotion and Protection of Human Rights (previously the Sub-Commission on the Prevention of Discrimination and Protection of Minorities). In 1989 the Sub-Commission entrusted Theo van Boven with the task of undertaking a study concerning the right to restitution, compensation and rehabilitation of victims

---

Landkriegs vom 18. Oktober 1907 (Haager Landkriegsordnung – HKLO) deren Bestimmungen "nur zwischen den Vertragsmächten Anwendung", und gemäß Art. 3 HKLO ist gegebenenfalls "die Kriegspartei" (gegenüber der anderen Kriegspartei) zum Schadenersatz verpflichtet.

77 *Id.*, at 20.

78 Landgericht Bonn, Case no. 1 O 361/02 of 10 December 2003, reproduced in Neue Juristische Wochenzeitschrift 2004, at 525.

79 J. Kleffner & L. Zegveld, *Establishing an Individual Complaints Procedure for Violations of International Humanitarian Law*, 3 Yearbook of International Humanitarian Law 384 (2000); J. Kleffner, *Improving Compliance with International Humanitarian Law Through the Establishment of an Individual Complaints Procedure*, 15 Leiden Journal of International Law 237 (2002).

80 Wellens, *supra* note 2, at 16-19.

81 D. Shelton, Remedies in International Human Rights Law 358 (2001).

of gross violations of human rights and fundamental freedoms. In 1993 he presented a final report in which he proposed a set of 'basic principles and guidelines.'[82] The report encompassed breaches of international humanitarian law as 'gross violations of human rights'. In the body of the report, van Boven concluded that:

> The obligations resulting from State responsibility for breaches of international human rights law entail corresponding rights on the part of individual persons and groups of persons who are under the jurisdiction of the offending State and who are victims of those breaches.[83]

This finding is hardly convincing, since most of the evidence adduced by van Boven for such a principle is from the case law of human rights monitoring bodies, whose jurisdiction has expressly been accepted by states parties to human rights conventions. The lack of state practice is acknowledged by van Boven who states that "the perspective of the victim is often overlooked."[84] Nevertheless, general principle 2 of the proposed basic principles and guidelines states that every "State has a duty to make reparation" in case of the obligation to respect and to ensure respect for human rights and fundamental freedoms, and that the obligation to ensure respect includes "the duty to afford remedies to victims". Interestingly, a footnote to this principle notes that "where these principles refer to States, they also apply, as appropriate to other entities exercising effective power", thus apparently providing for their application to international organizations. In 1996 van Boven, at the request of the Sub-Commission, presented a revised set of basic principles. This set was unequivocal on the right to a remedy. Principle 4 provided that:

> Every State shall ensure that adequate legal or other appropriate remedies are available to any person claiming that his or her rights have been violated. The right to a remedy against violations of human rights and humanitarian norms includes the right of access to national and international procedures for their protection.[85]

The revised principles no longer included a reference to 'other entities exercising effective power'. In 1998 the Commission on Human Rights, the Sub-Commission's parent body, appointed Cherif Bassiouni to prepare a revised version of the basic principles with a view to their adoption by the General Assembly. Bassiouni presented his final report in 2000, including a proposed set of principles. Principle 11 of the 'Bassiouni principles' states that:

---

82 Final Report submitted by Mr. Theo van Boven, Special Rapporteur, Study concerning the right to restitution, compensation and rehabilitation for victims of gross violations of human rights and fundamental freedoms of 2 July 1993, UN Doc. E/CN.4/Sub.2/1993/8.

83 *Id.*, at 19, para. 45.

84 *Id.*, at 53, para. 133.

85 Revised set of basic principles and guidelines on the right to reparation for victims of gross violations of human rights and humanitarian law prepared by Mr. Theo van Boven pursuant to Sub-Commission decision 1995/117 of 24 May 1996, UN Doc. E/CN.4/Sub.2/1996/17.

> Remedies for violations of international human rights and humanitarian law include the victim's right to:
> (a) Access justice;
> (b) Reparation for harm suffered; and
> (c) …[86]

In Resolution 2000/41 the Commission called "upon the international community to give due attention to the right to restitution, compensation and rehabilitation for victims of grave violations of human rights", and requested the Secretary-General to circulate to all member states the text of the principles and to request that they send their comments thereon to the Office of the United Nations High Commissioner for Human Rights.[87] In the Commission's 2002 resolution on the topic, 2002/44, the Commission repeated the request to the Secretary-General to circulate the 'Bassiouni principles' and:

> Calls upon the international community to give due attention to the right to a remedy and, in particular, in appropriate cases, to receive restitution, compensation and rehabilitation, for victims of violations of international human rights law.[88]

In October 2002, the United Nations Office of the High Commissioner for Human Rights convened an international consultation meeting on the 'Bassiouni principles'. The final outcome of the meeting included a summary of the discussion during the meeting as well as the Chairperson's conclusions,[89] but not a final document codifying the principles. One of the Chairperson-Rapporteur's conclusions is that:

> It was recognized that, in international law, while the forms and modalities of reparation may differ, the right to reparation applies both to violations of human rights and violations of humanitarian law.[90]

The Commission on Human Rights in 2003 took note of the report of the Chairperson-Rapporteur, and requested him to prepare a revised version of the principles. The Commision also requested the United Nations High Commissioner for Human

86 Basic principles and guidelines on the right to a remedy and reparation for victims of violations of international human rights and humanitarian law, Annex to Report of the Special Rapporteur, Mr. M. Cherif Bassiouni, The right to restitution, compensation and rehabilitation for victims of gross violations of human rights and fundamental freedoms of 18 January 2000, UN Doc. E/CN.4/2000/62.

87 Commission on Human Rights Resolution 2000/41 of 20 April 2000, UN Doc. E/CN.4/RES/2000/41, para. 1.

88 Commission on Human Rights Resolution 2002/44 of 23 April 2002, UN Doc. E/CN.4/RES/2002/44.

89 Report of the Consultative Meeting on the Draft Basic Principles and Guidelines on the Right to a Remedy and Reparation for Victims of Violations of International Human Rights and Humanitarian Law of 27 December 2002, UN Doc. E/CN.4/2003/63.

90 *Id.*, at 11, para. 47.

Rights to hold a second consultative meeting, which, if appropriate, could consider options for the adoption of these principles and guidelines.[91] The Commission resolution also repeated the call on the international community to give due attention to the right to a remedy, and, in particular, in appropriate cases, to receive restitution, compensation, and rehabilitation, for victims of grave violations of international human rights law and international humanitarian law.[92] The second consultative meeting took place on 23 October 2003. The revised text of the principles submitted to this meeting included the principle that the victim of a 'serious violation of humanitarian law' has a right to 'reparation for harm suffered or other appropriate remedy' as well as 'access to justice'.[93] In its resolution on this topic of 2004, the Commission again called upon the international community to give due attention to the right to a remedy and, in particular, in appropriate cases, to receive restitution, compensation and rehabilitation.[94] The Commission also requested that a third consultative meeting be held.[95]

It may be noted that the Human Rights Commission has not stated that the 'Bassiouni principles' reflect the content of the right to a remedy. Moreover, its resolutions suggests that a right to receive restitution, compensation and rehabilitation, only exists in 'appropriate cases'. This is hardly an unequivocal adoption of the 'Bassiouni principles' and its formulation of the right to a remedy in particular. In other words, there is reason to doubt that states recognize an unbounded right of access to justice and to reparation for harm suffered even in the field of human rights, unless they have expressly accepted such a right in conventional law. On the other hand, there is unquestionably a development to pay more attention to remedies for individual victims, as illustrated for example by the establishment of a Committee on Compensation for the Victims of War by the International Law Association in 2003. This increased attention may, and should, eventually lead to increased remedial rights for victims.

5.5.3 Procedural capacity under national law implicating a violation of international law

In the absence of a private right of action under international law, national law can confer such a right. Generally speaking, such an opportunity can be created in the national law of torts. In such a case the action by an individual is grounded directly on a domestic tort but implicates an international law violation. Such a possibility is

91 United Nations Commission on Human Rights Resolution 2003/34 of 23 April 2003, UN Doc. E/CN.4/RES/2003/34.

92 *Id.*, para. 1.

93 Basic principles and guidelines on the right to a remedy and reparation for victims of gross violations of international human rights law and serious violations of international humanitarian law, Rev. 23 October 2003 (copy on file with the author), para. 12 (b).

94 United Nations Commission on Human Rights Resolution 2004/34 of 19 April 2004, UN Doc. E/CN.4/RES/2004/34, para. 1.

95 *Id.*, para 4.

only available in exceptional cases. In 1999 a Canadian judge decided on such a claim in connection with the illtreatment and killing by Canadian Forces personnel of a Somali national, Shidane Arone, during Operation Restore Hope (UNITAF). Justice Cunningham of the Ontario Superior Court of Justice struck out a claim on behalf of the family of Shidane Arone against the Canadian government.[96] Abubakar Arone Rage and Dahabo Omar Samow, the parents of Shidane Arone, claimed damages founded in negligence as well as assault, battery and fiduciary duty for the torture, wrongful death and/or murder of their son. Justice Cunningham determined that the action was improperly commenced because the claim was submitted on behalf of the parents by a litigation guardian appointed by them living in Ontario and the rules of the court made no provision for the commencement of legal proceedings by a litigation guardian for persons of full age and capacity. In other words, the parents should have gone to Canada to start proceedings themselves. Justice Cunningham also held that action was barred by statute because under section 7 of the Public Authorities Act and section 269 (1) of the National Defence Act it could not be instituted after six months after the cause of the action arose.

This case illustrates some of the procedural difficulties involved in tort proceedings against governments under national law. It does not seem reasonable for example to personally require the parents of a victim in Somalia to travel to the troop contributing state concerned. Such a requirement effectively discriminates against victims who cannot afford travel to the state in question.

Attorney-General v. *Nissan* is another example of the limitations of an action under the domestic law of torts.[97] In that case the House of Lords could only give redress to Nissan because he was a United Kingdom national. Lord Reid stated that the:

> other case which is, I think, clear is where the act complained of was done against an alien outside her majesty's dominions. Since Buron v. Denman it has been accepted that if the act was ordered or has been ratified by the British government the English courts cannot give redress to that alien. He may enlist the support of his own government who may make diplomatic representations, but he has no legal remedy in England.[98]

Another possible obstacle is immunity from jurisdiction of states and international organizations before national courts. *Manderlier* v. *United Nations and Belgium* is an example of immunity barring an action under national law.[99]

On 9 November 2003, lawyers representing families of persons killed in Srebrenica announced that they would file suit against the UN and the Netherlands before appropriate courts for breaching international laws and the European Convention

96 Abubakar Arone Rage and Dahabo Omar Samow by their Litigation Guardian Abdullahi Godah Barre v. The Attorney General of Canada (unreported, 6 July 1999, Ontario Superior Court of Justice, Cunningham J.) (copy on file with author).

97 See also para. 2.9.3.

98 *Attorney-General* v. *Nissan*, House of Lords, 11 February 1969, [1969] 1 All ER 629, at 634.

99 *Supra* note 48.

of Human Rights.[100] The families hold the UN and the Netherlands responsible for failing to protect the enclave. Pursuant to this announcement, lawyers for the families initiated a procedure before the Court of First Instance of the Hague on 29 August 2003, with a view to obtaining an injunction to hear a number of witnesses.[101] They contended that hearing the witnesses concerned was necessary to establish certain facts, necessary to determine whether the facts of the case justified a claim against the Netherlands. In this regard, the plaintiff noted that it had the intention of submitting a claim against the Netherlands under tort law on the grounds that:

the Netherlands in July 1995 had the opportunity to take upon itself the evacuation of the Muslim population, which would have prevented their deportation; the compound of the Dutch contingent had room for more persons that had been admitted and there were no other obstacles to admitting more; the Dutch soldiers did not offer sufficient protection to those not admitted to the compound, though they received signals of executions and abuse; and the Netherlands facilitated the deportation of the population from the safe area, *inter alia* by expelling them from the compound, even though there was an alternative to forced expulsion.

The plaintiff maintained that the Netherlands exercised insufficient supervision over respect for fundamental norms of international law, as well as that it interfered in the UN command structure.

The respondent submitted that the conduct concerned related to the relationship between states and the UN on the one hand, and the state where the conduct occurred on the other. This relationship, the state maintained, is governed by international law. According to the respondent, only the UN could be responsible for this conduct.

The Court, in its decision of 27 November 2003, noted that the plaintiff agreed with the respondent that in principle the UN is exclusively responsible for conduct by UN peace support operations. The plaintiff however pointed to a report by an advisory committee to the government of 14 February 2002, which formulated certain exceptions to this principle. One exception is the situation where a state has interfered in UN command and control. Another exception is that a troop contributing state is responsible in case of violations of international humanitarian law, if the state has transferred powers without guarantees that the Geneva Conventions will be respected. It may be noted that this is precisely the ground for responsibility discussed above.[102] The Court noted that the plaintiff assumed that the views of the commission state the current law. The Court however stated that, in the absence of any case law in this field, it first has to be decided whether, and if so in which cases, the state can be responsible for the conduct of a contingent under UN command and control. The Court concluded that the hearing of witnesses was premature and unnecessary as long as there is no legal certainty concerning these complex questions, and rejected the application.

100 *Srebrenica Survivors to Sue UN*, AFP, 9 November 2003.

101 Court of First Instance of the Hague, Decision of 27 November 2003, case no. 03.531 (copy on file with the author).

102 Para. 2.10.3.

Claims settlement procedures established by peace support operations are in a sense analogous to tort proceedings under national law. The practice in UN operations has been to base claims review board decisions on the types of injury and loss compensable under local law of the host state and the prevailing practice in the mission area, in particular, as well as on the past practice of the organization. Claims settlement procedures in NATO peace support operations also use the local law of the host state as reference.[103]

In contrast to a court, however, the bodies created by claims settlement procedures are not *per se* independent. Sorel states that the replacement in practice of claims commissions by local claims review boards is a transition from a quasi-judicial to a unilateral system.[104] Wellens also underlines that the fact that local claims review boards are composed exclusively of United Nations staff members raises concerns over the boards' independence and the objectivity of their rulings, which are two elements in assessing any kind of claims settlement procedure as an adequate alternative system for protection.[105] The lack of any obligation to make their decisions public also contributes to the assessment that they do not function as proper mechanisms of accountability. Under the SFOR claims settlement procedure as it has developed in practice, claims are adjudicated in first instance by officers of the operation, although a claims commission can hear appeals from the claimant when a claims dispute cannot be resolved between the claimant and the unit responsible for the loss or damage. A claims commission consists of four members: two SFOR representatives and two receiving state representatives.[106] An appeal is possible from a decision of the claims commission to an Arbitration Tribunal. Under the Technical Arrangements and the subsequent agreements, the decisions of the SFOR Claims Commissions and Arbitration Tribunals[107] are supposed to be final and binding, but in the first case before the Croatian Arbitration Tribunal, the United States informed the Tribunal that it did not accept the final and binding nature of any decision the Tribunal might reach.

5.6 Using human rights machinery to invoke international responsibility for violations of international humanitarian law by peace support operations

5.6.1 Availability of human rights monitoring bodies

Some writers argue that human rights machinery could be used indirectly to enforce international humanitarian law. Greenwood for example states that:

103 J. Prescott, *Claims*, in D. Fleck (Ed.), The Handbook of the Law of Visiting Forces 159 (2001).

104 J.M. Sorel, *La Responsabilité des Nations Unies dans les Opérations de Maintien de la Paix*, 3 International Law Forum 127 (2001), at 134.

105 Wellens, *supra* note 2, at 104.

106 Prescott, *supra* note 103, at 175.

107 See para. 2.11.1.

> Various mechanisms for the enforcement of international human rights law may be able to offer a measure of assistance in improving compliance with the laws of war. Although such bodies have no jurisdiction to apply the laws of war as such, it is possible that in cases involving allegations of human rights violations during an armed conflict (international or internal), a human rights tribunal will look to the laws of war for guidance in relation to such issues as whether the deprivation of life in a particular case was arbitrary.[108]

In the field of human rights a number of monitoring bodies exist which are independent and which bypass the need for governments to act. In other words, individuals can invoke state responsibility before these bodies. Some of these agencies are linked to a regional human rights instrument. The European Court of Human Rights (ECHR) may receive applications from any person, non-governmental organization or group of individuals claiming to be the victim of a violation by one of the High Contracting Parties of the rights set forth in the European Convention for the Protection of Human Rights and Fundamental Freedoms or the Protocols thereto. Under the American Convention on Human Rights any person or group of persons may lodge petitions with the Inter-American Commission on Human Rights containing denunciations or complaints of violation of the Convention by a state party. Only the states parties and the Commission have the right to submit a case to the Inter-American Court of Human Rights. Human rights monitoring agencies which are not limited to a geographic area include the UN Human Rights Committee established under the International Covenant on Civil and Political Rights. A state which is party to the Optional Protocol to the Covenant recognizes the competence of the Committee to receive and consider communications from individuals subject to its jurisdiction who claim to be victims of a violation by that state. The Committee against Torture established under the United Nations Convention against Torture and other Cruel, Inhuman or Degrading Treatment or Punishment may receive and consider individual complaints against those states which have expressly accepted its jurisdiction.

A number of human rights treaties also provide for a state's obligation to submit reports on measures adopted to give effect to the rights recognized by the treaty in question. Several cases were considered above in which violations of human rights by peace support operations were considered in state reporting procedures. State reporting procedures such as those in the International Covenant on Civil and Political Rights and the United Nations Convention against Torture consist of a mandatory submission of reports by contracting states, examination of the reports by the monitoring body in question and the adoption of concluding observations that are made

---

108 C. Greenwood, *International Humanitarian Law*, in F. Kalshoven (Ed.), The Centennial of the First International Peace Conference 161 (2000), at 251. See also F. Hampson, *Using International Human Rights Machinery to Enforce the International Law of Armed Conflicts*, 31 Military Law and Law of War Review 117 (1992), F. Martin, *Application du Droit International Humanitaire par la Cour Interaméricaine des Droits de l'Homme*, 83 International Review of the Red Cross 1037 (2001).

public.[109] Monitoring bodies cannot enforce these observations and recommendations but rely on political pressure on governments in a human rights dialogue.

So-called 'charter-based mechanisms' are another part of the UN human rights monitoring machinery. The United Nations Commission on Human Rights is the principal charter-based human rights body.

Reports by the Special Rapporteur on the situation of human rights in Somalia are an example of a Commission procedure. The Special Rapporteur is an example of the so-called 'special public procedures' of the Commission.[110] Special procedures are individuals or groups of individuals appointed by the Commission to study the situation of human rights in a specific country or a specific theme. The names given to these individuals or groups of individuals[111] vary considerably as well as the mandate conferred on them depending on the resolution creating it, but they have in common that their main function is fact-finding and reporting the facts to the Commission.[112] In practice a Special Rapporteur has considerable freedom concerning the methodology of his or her inquiry and the form of the report. The Commission has not adopted specific rules of procedure for Rapporteurs and in practice they have a role in interpreting their own mandate.

Special procedures are not judicial or quasi-judicial procedures. Their function is to report to the Commission. Action by the Commission on the basis of a report consists mainly of adoption of a resolution. The Commission is a political organ which does not make legally binding findings of state responsibility giving rise to a claim of reparation in the same way as for example the ECHR. The most important instruments at the disposal of the Commission are political and moral pressure.

The availability of procedures for invoking international responsibility or accountability in the field of human rights and the undisputed correspondence with international humanitarian law strengthened by a rights-based perspective of international humanitarian law raise the question whether human rights monitoring bodies can play a role in enforcing international humanitarian law in general, and in respect of peace support operations in particular.

---

109 See R. Bank, *International Efforts to Combat Torture and Inhuman Treatment: Have New Mechanisms Improved Protection?*, 8 European Journal of International Law 613 (1997) and I. Boerefijn, The Reporting Procedure under the Covenant on Civil and Political Rights: Practice and Procedures of the Human Rights Committee (1999).

110 See M. Bossuyt, *The Development of Special Procedures of the United Nations Commission on Human Rights*, 6 Human Rights Law Journal 179 (1985).

111 Names include Special Rapporteur, Independent Expert, Special Representative and Special Envoy for individuals and Special Committee and Working Group for groups. I will use the term Special Rapporteur to refer to all Special Procedures whatever their name because in the context of peace support operations the Special Rapporteur on the situation of human rights in Somalia has been most active. Note that the Commission has now renamed the Special Rapporteur on Somalia Independent Expert on Somalia.

112 J. Pastor Ridruejo, *Les Procédures Spécialisées de la Commission des Droits de l'Homme des Nations Unies*, 228 Recueil des Cours 183 (1991-III), at 238.

5.6.2 Subject-matter jurisdiction as an obstacle

One obstacle to such use of human rights machinery is that the subject-matter jurisdiction or mandate of the various agencies in question does not expressly include international humanitarian law. Human rights monitoring bodies nevertheless sometimes take into account international humanitarian law, but to a varying extent. So far, the Inter-American Commission on Human Rights has been the sole human rights monitoring body to directly apply international humanitarian law. In its report in the *Tablada* case, the Commission gave several arguments why it could apply international humanitarian law without an explicit legal basis in the American Convention on Human Rights.[113] In 2000 however, the Inter-American Court of Human Rights held that the Commission's approach could not stand up to scrutiny. In its decision on preliminary objections in the *Las Palmeras* case, the Court admitted the preliminary objections by the respondent state to the effect that the Commission and the Court are not competent to apply international humanitarian law.[114] The Commission argued before the Court that international humanitarian law could be applied as customary international law. It also argued that international humanitarian law could be applied as *lex specialis* in relation to the American Convention. It considered that, in an armed conflict, there are cases in which the enemy may be killed legitimately, while, in others, this was prohibited. The Commission stated that the American Convention did not contain any rule to distinguish one hypothesis from the other and, therefore, the Geneva Conventions should be applied. Colombia on the other hand emphasized the importance of the principle of consent. The Court accepted the Colombian argument in the sense that a state which is a party to the American Convention and which has accepted the contentious jurisdiction of the Court has not accepted the competence of the Court to determine whether the acts or the norms of the state are compatible with the 1949 Geneva Conventions.[115] The Court stated:

> When a State is a Party to the American Convention and has accepted the contentious jurisdiction of the Court, the Court may examine the conduct of the State to determine whether it conforms to the provisions of the Convention, even when the issue may have been definitively resolved by the domestic legal system. The Court is also competent to determine whether any norm of domestic or international law applied by a State, in times of peace or armed conflict, is compatible or not with the American Convention. In this activity, the Court has no normative limitation: any legal norm may be submitted to this examination of compatibility.

---

113 IACHR Report No. 55/97, Case No. 11.137, Argentina, OEA/Ser/L/V/II.97, Doc. 38, October 30, 1997. See for an analysis L. Zegveld, *The Inter-American Commission on Human Rights and International Humanitarian Law: A comment on the Tablada Case*, 38 International Review of the Red Cross 505 (1998).

114 *Las Palmeras* case (Preliminary Objections), 4 February 2000, Inter-American Court of Human Rights, Series C, No 67.

115 See for a discussion of the *Las Palmeras* case Martin, *supra* note 108.

> In order to carry out this examination, the Court interprets the norm in question and analyzes it in the light of the provisions of the Convention. The result of this operation will always be an opinion in which the Court will say whether or not that norm or that fact is compatible with the American Convention. The latter has only given the Court competence to determine whether the acts or the norms of the States are compatible with the Convention itself, and not with the 1949 Geneva Conventions.[116]

Short of applying international humanitarian law directly, human rights monitoring bodies may use it indirectly as authoritative guidance in interpretation of human rights norms. It appears that the Inter-American Court of Human Rights did not exclude this possibility in the *Las Palmeras* case.[117] In several cases the European Commission and Court of Human Rights have used concepts from that body of law to interpret states' obligations under the European Convention. But they have been careful not to refer to international humanitarian law directly. Applicants in the *Banković* case invited the ECHR to use international humanitarian law more explicitly in its interpretation of Article 2 and Article 15 of the Convention. Article 15 of the Convention provides that states parties can derogate from the Convention in time of emergency. The second paragraph states that no derogation can be made from the right to life (Article 2) except in respect of deaths resulting from lawful acts of war. Applicants stated that in the case in question Article 15 was not applicable. In the alternative, they stated that the attack in question was not a lawful act of war. According to the applicants, in determining what constitutes a lawful act of war, the Court should have regard to the conventional and customary law of war obligations of states as *lex specialis*.[118]

Special Rapporteurs appointed by the UN Commission on Human Rights do not apply international humanitarian law consistently.[119] One obvious reason is that the mandate of some of them includes that body of law, while the mandate of others is limited to human rights. Special Rapporteurs whose mandate does not include international humanitarian law nevertheless do apply it, but not consistently. Some use it as a means of interpretation of human rights. In his 1992 report, for example, the Special Rapporteur on Extrajudicial, Summary or Arbitrary Executions explained that he applied the Geneva Conventions and their Protocols, in particular common Article 3 to the Conventions, Article 51 of Additional Protocol I and Article 13 of Additional Protocol II, because these standards could be used to determine whether deaths occurring in the context of armed conflict were 'arbitrary' or not, and thus whether or not they violated the right to life.[120]

---

116 *Supra* note 114, paras. 32-33.

117 Kleffner & Zegveld, *supra* note 79, at 389.

118 Application, file on copy with the author.

119 See D. O'Donnell, *Trends in the Application of International Humanitarian Law by United Nations Human Rights Mechanisms*, 38 International Review of the Red Cross 481 (1998).

120 UN Doc. E/CN.4/1992/30, paras 19-28.

Other Special Rapporteurs apply international humanitarian law directly. The Special Rapporteur on the situation of human rights in Afghanistan, for example, in his 2002 report urged all parties in Afghanistan and members of the international coalition to respect the provisions of the Geneva Conventions notwithstanding the fact that his mandate does not refer to international humanitarian law.[121]

In the specific context of peace support operations, the Special Rapporteur on Somalia, in her 1998 report, also applied international humanitarian law. In the first section of her report she reviewed her mandate to report on the human rights situation in Somalia, but in the section on allegations against Belgian, Canadian and Italian troops she stated that she:

> believes that it is essential for the credibility of international action in the field of human rights in Somalia that these allegations are fully investigated, the complete truth about the behaviour of the international troops in Somalia is revealed, and all the perpetrators of unlawful acts are brought to justice. In addition to the legal obligations imposed on States to respect international law, it is essential that proper action is taken with regard to the alleged violations of international law by the international forces because the international community ought to send positive signals to and set correct examples for Somalis with regard to maintaining full respect of human rights and humanitarian law.[122]

In her report, the Special Rapporteur focused specifically on the obligation in the 1949 Geneva Conventions to investigate and prosecute grave breaches of the conventions. She concluded that the perpetrators of wrongful acts which amount to grave breaches of the Geneva Conventions, and other serious violations of international humanitarian law, must be brought to justice.

Her successor, in his 2002 report to the Commission on Human Rights, repeated concern for allegations of violations of international law by the United Nations Operations in Somalia.[123] In his report he referred expressly to human rights as well as to international humanitarian law, but in the context of allegations against the United Nations operation he did not make this distinction but rather referred to 'past atrocities'. He stated that given the widespread support for the idea of pursuing serious and independent investigation into past atrocities, he had urged the Security Council to consider a proposal for the establishment of a committee of experts to investigate alle-

---

121 Report on the Situation of Human Rights in Afghanistan by Mr. Kamal Hossain, Special Rapporteur, of 6 March 2002, UN Doc. E/CN.4/2002/43, para. 12. The Special Rapporteur's mandate is "to examine the human rights situation in Afghanistan, with a view to formulating proposals which could contribute to ensuring full protection of the human rights of all residents of the country, before, during and after the withdrawal of all foreign forces", see UN Doc. E/RES/1984/37, para. 1.

122 Situation of Human Rights in Somalia, Report of the Special Rapporteur, Ms. Mona Rishmawi, of 16 January 1998, UN Doc. E/CN.4/1998/96, para. VI (2).

123 Report by the Independent Expert on the situation of human rights in Somalia, Dr. Ghanim Alnajjar, of 14 January 2002, UN Doc. E/CN.4/2002/119.

gations of past atrocities in Somalia. He emphasized that the investigation should also include the conduct of the United Nations in Somalia.[124]

It seems that the strongest human rights monitoring bodies, courts which can make legally binding decisions concerning state responsibility and order reparation, are the bodies which are least likely to apply international humanitarian law. Special Rapporteurs on the other hand, who can only make their views public and recommend action by the Commission on Human Rights, a political organ, are more likely to do so.

5.6.3 Territorial application of human rights: another obstacle

A second potential obstacle to using human rights machinery to invoke state responsibility for violations of international humanitarian law is that states parties to human rights treaties are only obliged to secure human rights to persons within their jurisdiction. The ECHR's inadmissibility decision in the *Banković* case illustrates that a narrow interpretation of jurisdiction can limit the situations in which the treaty applies extraterritorially.[125] The Court held that Article 1 of the Convention, which states that the High Contracting Parties shall secure to everyone within their jurisdiction the rights and freedoms of the Convention, must be considered as reflective of an essentially territorial notion of jurisdiction, other bases of jurisdiction being exceptional and requiring special justification in the particular circumstances of the case. After reviewing its own case law, the Court concluded that it had recognized the exercise of extra-territorial jurisdiction by a contracting state only:

> when the respondent state, through the effective control of the relevant territory and its inhabitants abroad as a consequence of military occupation or through the consent, invitation or acquiescence of the Government of that territory, exercises all or some of the public powers normally to be exercised by that Government.[126]

In the case in question this test was not met. The ECHR did not elaborate on the meaning of 'public powers'. It appears that the respondent states accepted that arrest and detention are examples of 'public powers'.[127] An interpretation of the ordinary meaning of the words would appear to lead to a distinction between 'public' and 'private powers'. 'Public powers' would then be those powers which only state authorities are entitled to exercise. In any event, it seems that in certain cases peace support operations could meet the requirement concerned. For example, KFOR continues to

---

124 *Id.*, para. IX.

125 See para. 2.11.3.

126 *Vlastimir and Borka Banković, Živana Stojanović, Mirjana Stoimenovski, Dragana Joksimović and Dragan Suković* v. *Belgium, the Czech Republic, Denmark, France, Germany, Greece, Hungary, Iceland, Italy, Luxembourg, the Netherlands, Norway, Poland, Portugal, Spain, Turkey and the United Kingdom*, Decision of 12 December 2001 (Appl. No. 52207/99), para. 71.

127 *Id.*, para. 37.

exercise the powers of arrest and detention, On the other hand, there are indications in the decision that the Court will not easily find jurisdiction in the case of peace support operations. In particular, the Court stated that it finds:

> State practice in the application of the Convention since its ratification to be indicative of a lack of any apprehension on the part of the Contracting States of their extra-territorial responsibility in contexts similar to the present case. Although there have been a number of military missions involving Contracting States acting extra-territorially since their ratification of the Convention (inter alia, in the Gulf, in Bosnia and Herzegovina and in the FRY), no State has indicated a belief that its extra-territorial actions involved an exercise of jurisdiction within the meaning of Article 1 of the Convention by making a derogation pursuant to Article 15 of the Convention.[128]

The Court's decision concerning admissibility is open to criticism. The Court maintained that the applicant's submission, that the positive obligation under Article 1 of the Convention extends to securing the Convention rights in a manner proportionate to the level of control exercized in any given extra-territorial situation, is tantamount to arguing that anyone adversely affected by an act imputable to a Contracting State, wherever in the world that act may have been committed or its consequences felt, is thereby brought within the jurisdiction of that State for the purpose of Article 1.[129] It agreed with the respondents that the wording of Article 1 does not provide any support for the applicant's suggestion that the positive obligation in Article 1 can be divided and tailored in accordance with the particular circumstances of the extra-territorial act in question. Here, the Court correctly made a distinction between the scope of application of the Convention on the one hand, and the question whether an act which allegedly violates the Convention is attributable to a contracting state. In terms of state responsibility, Article 1 of the Convention sets out the obligations of the contracting parties and is not concerned with attribution. This distinction however in itself does not justify the Court's conception of jurisdiction, based principally on scholarly definitions of 'jurisdiction'. 'Jurisdiction' in these definitions is not necessarily identical with jurisdiction in Article 1. Under international law and as conceived in the publications the Court refers to, state jurisdiction concerns essentially the extent of a state's right to regulate, enforce or adjudicate. Article 1 of the Convention, however, is not concerned with the question of whether a state, when acting territorially, is lawfully entitled to do so with respect to another state, but with the question whether a state, when so acting, is bound to respect its obligations under the Convention.[130] A broader conception of jurisdiction, as proposed by the applicants, would be fully in line with a dynamic interpretation of the Convention. In constant case law, the Court has reiterated that the Convention is a living instrument to be interpreted in

---

128 *Id.*, para. 62.

129 *Id.*, para. 75.

130 A. Rüth & M. Trilsch, *Case Report: Banković v. Belgium*, 97 American Journal of International Law 168 (2003), at 172.

light of present-day conditions, as it recognizes in the *Banković* decision.[131] The Court however seemed to suggest that, for some unspecified reason, this approach is not applicable to Article 1. It is telling that the Court referred to the 'ordinary' notion of jurisdiction.[132] It is argued with some justification that this is a misunderstanding of the particular nature of the Convention.[133] It is arguable whether a broader conception of 'jurisdiction' would divide the obligation under Article 1, as the Court agrees with the respondents. Rather, it appears that the fact that a state would not in all cases be obliged to respect all the rights under the Convention, would be an application of the principle that no-one is held to perform the impossible ('*impossibilium nulla obligatio est*').

Under the approach advocated by the applicants, the extra-territorial actions of a contracting state would be subject to the Convention's standards under the same conditions which apply to attribution under the law of state responsibility. While the same standards would apply, however, this would not be a question of attribution proper. As explained above, Article 1 is concerned with the scope of a state's obligations, not with attribution. This doctrine may not have been in the minds of the drafters of Article 1, but it is certainly in accordance with a dynamic interpretation of the Convention. The Court's summary of its previous case law[134] is a recognition by the Court that it has departed from the purely territorial notion of jurisdiction which it attributes to the drafters of the Convention. The Court does not make clear why departures in other cases than the two it mentions would not be appropriate.

The Court arguably restricted the interpretation of jurisdiction under Article 1 even further. It distinguished its judgement in *Cyprus* v. *Turkey*, in which it held that persons in northern Cyprus fell within the jurisdiction of Turkey on the basis of the Turkish occupation, from the facts in *Banković*. According to the Court, the inhabitants of northern Cyprus would have found themselves excluded from the benefits of the Convention safeguards and system which they previously enjoyed, by Turkey's 'effective control' of the territory and by the accompanying inability of the Cypriot government, as a contracting state, to fulfil its obligations under the Convention.[135] The Court did not state whether this means that it regards persons affected by extra-territorial military operations to fall within the jurisdiction of contracting states only if they enjoyed the protection of the Convention prior to the operation. Certain authors interpret the Court's statement in this sense.[136] It is just as likely, however, that the Court merely distinguished the applicants in *Banković* from those in *Cyprus*

131 *Supra* note 126, para. 64.

132 *Id.*, para. 61.

133 G. Cohen-Jonathan, *Observations: La Territorialisation de la Jurisdiction de la Cour Européenne des Droits de l' Homme*, 12 Revue Trimestrielle des Droits de l'Homme 1069 (2002), at 1080.

134 *Supra* note 126.

135 *Id.*, para. 80

136 Rüth & Trilsch, *supra* note 130, at 171; H. Krieger, *Die Verantwortlichkeit Deutschlands nach der EMRK für seine Streitkräfte im Auslandeinsatz*, 62 Zeitschrift für ausländisches öffentliches Recht und Völkerrecht 669 (2002), at 683.

v. *Turkey* for the specific purpose of refuting the applicant's claim that any failure to accept that the applicants fell within the jurisdiction of the respondent states would defeat the *ordre public* mission of the Convention, without establishing an additional condition. The Court's judgement in the *Öcalan* case seems to confirm that the latter is the correct interpretation.[137] In that case, the Court accepted that the applicant fell within Turkey's jurisdiction when it abducted him from Kenya, a country which is not a contracting state to the Convention. The Court stated that:

> the circumstances of the present case are distinguishable from those in the aforementioned Banković and Others case, notably in that the applicant was physically forced to return to Turkey by Turkish officials and was subject to their authority and control following his arrest and return to Turkey.[138]

On 8 July 2004 the Grand Chamber of the ECHR delivered its judgment in *Ilaşcu, Leşco, Ivanţoc and Petrov-Popa* v. *Moldova and the Russian Federation.*[139] This case concerned an application by a number of Moldovan nationals detained in the breakaway 'Moldovan Republic of Transdniestra' (MRT) in Moldova, an entity of Transdniestran separatists which is allegedly supported by the Russian Federation. The applicants complained that the Russian Federation shared responsibility for violation of their rights under the European Convention caused by their unlawful detention, conviction and abuse while in detention, on the ground that the territory of Transdniestra was *de facto* under the Russian Federation's control. The Russian Federation argued before the Court that the Court had no jurisdiction to consider the merits of the case in so far as the application was directed against the Russian Federation, since the acts complained of did not come within the 'jurisdiction' of the Russian Federation within the meaning of Article 1 of the Convention. It maintained that the Russian military presence on the territory of Moldova, with the latter's consent, for the purpose of maintaining peace in the Republic, could not engage the Russian Federation's responsibility. The Russian forces in the area had been given peacemaking duties and had prevented the conflict from worsening and the number of victims among the civilian population from rising. It argued that the Russian Federation did not *de facto* control the territory of Transdniestra. The Court first recalled that although in the *Banković* case it emphasized the preponderance of the territorial principle in the application of the Convention, it had accepted that in exceptional circumstances the acts of contracting states performed outside their territory or which produce effects there may amount to the exercise by them of jurisdiction:

> According to the relevant principles of international law, a State's responsibility may be engaged where, as a consequence of military action – whether lawful or unlawful – it in practice exercises effective control of an area situated outside its national ter-

137 *Öcalan* v. *Turkey*, Judgement of 12 March 2003, (Appl. No. 46221/99).

138 *Id.*, para. 93.

139 *Ilaşcu, Leşco, Ivanţoc and Petrov-Popa* v. *Moldova and the Russian Federation*, Application No. 48787/99, Judgment of 8 July 2004, not yet reported.

> ritory. The obligation to secure, in such an area, the rights and freedoms set out in the Convention derives from the fact of such control, whether it be exercised directly, through its armed forces, or through a subordinate local administration.
> It is not necessary to determine whether a Contracting Party actually exercises detailed control over the policies and actions of the authorities in the area situated outside its national territory, since even overall control of the area may engage the responsibility of the Contracting Party concerned.
> Where a Contracting State exercises overall control over an area outside its national territory its responsibility is not confined to the acts of its soldiers or officials in that area but also extends to acts of the local administration which survives there by virtue of its military and other support.[140].

The Court held that the Russian Federation did exercise overall control over Transdniestra. Having examined the various forms of support given by the Russian Federation to the separatists, it concluded that:

> The "MRT", set up in 1991 – 1992 with the support of the Russian Federation, vested with organs of power and its own administration, remains under the effective authority, or at the very least under the decisive influence, of the Russian Federation, and in any event that it survives by virtue of the military, economic, financial and political support given to it by the Russian Federation.[141]

On this account the applicants fell within the jurisdiction of the Russian Federation, both regarding conduct of the separatists as well as regarding conduct of Russian soldiers *vis-à-vis* the applicants. The claim by the Russian Federation that its soldiers had acted in breach of disciplinary regulations made no difference "Regard being had to the principle of States' responsibility for abuses of authority."[142] It appears that the ECHR was referring to article 7 of the ILC draft articles on state responsibility, concerning attribution of *ultra vires* acts. It is unclear whether the ECHR would have considered the applicants to be within the jurisdiction of the Russian Federation if the latter would not have been in overall control of Transdniestra. Judge Loucaides in his partly dissenting opinion to the judgment appeared to suggest that it would not have done so. In any event, the judgment does not provide unequivocal support for the position that states may be held responsible under the Convention where their agents exercise *de facto* control over persons and property abroad in a more or less incidental, *ad hoc* fashion, irrespective of whether they exercise overall control over the territory.[143]

---

140 *Id.*, paras. 314-316 (references omitted).

141 *Id.*, para. 392.

142 *Id.*, para. 380.

143 As Lawson suggested it might, R.A. Lawson, *Life after Bankovic – On the Extraterritorial Reach of the ECHR*, in F. Coomans & M. Kamminga (Eds.), The Extraterritorial Scope of Human Rights Treaties 83 (2004).

The Court appears to espouse the above-mentioned approach to jurisdiction, whereby the extra-territorial actions of a contracting state would be subject to the Convention's standards under the same conditions which apply to attribution under the law of state responsibility. However, it does not apply that approach consistently when it does not clearly include conduct by individual state officials or agents in the absence of overall control of the territory. In sum, the judgment does not clearly attenuate the restrictive definition of 'jurisdiction' set out in *Banković*, except in one respect. It does not refer to the requirement in *Banković* for the state which has overall control of a territory to exercise "all or some of the public powers" normally to be exercised by the government of the territory concerned. This does not seem to be a requirement any longer.

It is possible but not certain that other human rights monitoring bodies could interpret the term 'jurisdiction' which also appears in the International Covenant on Civil and Political Rights (ICCPR) and the American Convention on Human Rights, broader than the ECHR has done in the *Banković* case, whereby the ECHR has arguably excluded most or all peace support operations. In 1995 the Human Rights Committee in commenting on the report submitted by the United States noted that it could not share the view of the United States government that the Covenant lacks extraterritorial reach under all circumstances.[144] In views resulting from communications concerning the alleged abduction by Uruguay of two persons from Argentina and Brazil, the Human Rights Committee held that it had jurisdiction over acts perpetrated on foreign soil.[145] The Committee held that the expression 'subject to its jurisdiction' refers not to the place where the violation occurred, but rather to the relationship between the individual and the state in relation to a violation of any of the rights set forth in the Covenant, wherever they occurred. It stated that:

> it would be the unconscionable to so interpret the responsibility under article 2 of the Covenant as to permit a State party to perpetrate violations of the Covenant on the territory of another State, which violations it could not perpetrate on its own territory.[146]

Israel has consistently maintained before the Human Rights Committee that the ICCPR does not apply to the Occupied Palestinian Territory.[147] In the face of this claim, the Committee held in its concluding observations on Israel's second periodic report that:

144 UN Doc. CCPR/C/79/Add.50 (1995), para. 19.

145 *Sergio Euben Lopez Burgos* v. *Uruguay*, Communication No. R.12/52 (6 June 1979), UN Doc. Supp. No. 40 (A/36/40) at 176 (1981); *Lilian Celiberti de Casariego* v. *Uruguay*, Communication No. 56/1979 (29 July 1981), UN Doc. CCPR/C/OP/1 at 92 (1984).

146 *Id.*, para. 10.3.

147 Second Periodic Report, Addendum, Israel, UN Doc. CCPR/C/ISR/2001/2 of 4 December 2001, para. 8.

> In the current circumstances, the provisions of the Covenant apply to the benefit of the population of the Occupied Territories, for all conduct by the State party's authorities or agents in those territories that affect the enjoyment of rights enshrined in the Covenant and fall within the ambit of State responsibility of Israel under the principles of public international law.[148]

The ICJ in its Advisory Opion on the *Legal Consequences of the Construction of a Wall in the Occupied Palestinian Territory* also accepted the application of the ICCPR to "acts done by a State in the exercise of its jurisdiction outside its own territory."[149] Acts by Israel in the Occupied Palestinian Territory constituted such exercise of jurisdiction.

On 29 March 2004 the Human Rights Committee adopted General Comment No. 31 on Article 2 of the Covenant, which defines the legal scope of the obligations undertaken by states parties to the Covenant. The General Comment makes clear that Article 2 (1) applies to anyone within the power or effective control of a state party, even if not situated within the territory of the state party. It explicitly states that this may include situations involving peace support operations:

> This principle also applies to those within the power or effective control of the forces of a State Party acting outside its territory, regardless of the circumstances in which such power or effective control was obtained, such as forces constituting a national contingent of a State Party assigned to an international peace-keeping or peace-enforcement operation.[150]

The Inter-American Commission on Human Rights in its report in *Coard et al* v. *United States* determined that its jurisdiction on the basis of the American Declaration of the Rights and Duties of Man is not limited to the territory of the states parties. In the case in question the Commission held that the United States was responsible for violations of human rights committed by its agents during the United States' intervention in Grenada. The reason given by the Commission to apply the Declaration to extraterritorial acts is also valid for the American Convention on Human Rights:

> The Commission finds it pertinent to note that, under certain circumstances, the exercise of its jurisdiction over acts with an extraterritorial locus will not only be consistent with but required by the norms which pertain. The fundamental rights of the individual are proclaimed in the Americas on the basis of the principles of equality and non-discrimination – 'without distinction as to race, nationality, creed or sex.' Given that individual human rights inhere simply by virtue of a person's humanity, each American State is obliged to uphold the protected rights of any person subject to its jurisdiction. While this most commonly refers to persons within a state's terri-

148 Concluding Observations of the Human Rights Committee, Israel, 21 August 2003, UN Doc. CCPR/C/79/ISR, para. 11.

149 *Supra* note 23, para. 111.

150 General Comment No. 31 on Article 2 of the Covenant, adopted on 29 March 2004, UN Doc. CCPR/C/74/CRP.4/Rev.6.

> tory, it may, under given circumstances, refer to conduct with an extraterritorial locus where the person concerned is present in the territory of one state, but subject to the control of another state – usually through the acts of the latter's agents abroad. In principle, the inquiry turns not on the presumed victim's nationality or presence within a particular geographic area, but on whether, under the specific circumstances, the State observed the rights of a person subject to its authority and control.[151]

5.6.4 Lack of jurisdiction over international organizations: a third obstacle

Human rights monitoring bodies are concerned mostly with states and not with international organizations. Even if human rights machinery can be used to invoke responsibility for violations of international humanitarian law, this possibility is limited in respect of the UN and NATO. Clear examples are treaty-based mechanisms such as the Human Rights Committee and the ECHR which have the task of monitoring respect for the rights in a particular treaty by the parties to that treaty. Only states can become parties to these treaties.[152] International organizations cannot appear as respondents before these bodies. The conduct of international organizations may be scrutinized indirectly in a case in which a troop contributing state is also responsible for its own act or omission in connection with an act of the organization, or possibly in a case in which a member state is held directly responsible for the conduct of an organization.

In such a case the theory of 'indispensable third parties' could be an obstacle to the exercise of jurisdiction by the court or body in question. According to this theory, a court cannot exercise jurisdiction in a case where the legal interest of a state not party to the proceedings would be affected.[153] The theory, developed in ICJ case law, has also been invoked by respondent states before other courts and tribunals. In the *Monetary Gold Removed from Rome in 1943* case, the ICJ refused to exercise jurisdiction because it would have to adjudicate upon the international responsibility of Albania. The Court stated that it can only exercise jurisdiction over a state with its consent. Noting that Albania had chosen not to intervene, the Court stated:

> In the present case, Albania's legal interests would not only be affected by a decision, but would form the very subject matter of the decision. In such a case, the Statute

---

151 *Coard et al* v. *United States*, Inter-American Commission on Human Rights, Case No. 10.951, Report No. 109/99, 29 September 1999, para. 37. The Commission stated the same interpretation of jurisdiction *ratione loci* in *Armando Alejandre Jr. et al* v. *Cuba*, Case No. 11.589, Report No. 86/99, 29 September 1999, para. 23. This case concerned the shooting down of two airplanes by the Cuban air force in international airspace.

152 See Article 48 paragraph 1 of the International Covenant on Civil and Political Rights, Article 59 of the European Convention and Article 74 of the American Convention.

153 S. Torres Bernárdez, *The New Theory of "Indispensable Parties" Under the Statute of the International Court of Justice*, in K. Wellens (Ed.), International Law: Theory and Practice: Essays in Honour of Eric Suy 737 (1998).

> cannot be regarded, by implication, as authorizing proceedings to be continued in the absence of Albania.[154]

This principle was also at issue before the ICJ in the *East Timor* case.[155] In that case, Australia objected that the application by Portugal would require the Court to determine the rights and obligations of a third state, Indonesia, in the absence of consent of that state. The Court emphasized that it is not necessarily prevented from adjudicating when the judgment it is asked to give might affect the legal interests of a state which is not a party to the case. However, in the present case it considered that Indonesia's rights and obligations would constitute the very subject-matter of such a judgment in the absence of that state's consent. For that reason, it concluded that it could not exercise jurisdiction.[156]

In the *Banković* case, the respondent states held that the application was inadmissible *inter alia* on the basis of this principle, because, they stated, the court cannot decide the merits of the case as it would be determining the rights or obligations of the United States, of Canada and of NATO itself, none of which are contracting parties to the Convention. In the case in question the ECHR did not consider it necessary to examine this question. Incidentally, the submission that a decision by the ECHR would determine the rights and obligations of NATO implies that the organization is capable of having international rights and obligations or, in other words, has international legal personality.

Special Rapporteurs of the UN Commission on Human Rights are not limited by strict procedural rules. Some Special Rapporteurs have addressed conduct by field operations of international organizations. One example is the Independent Expert on the Situation of Human Rights in Somalia's call for an investigation into the conduct of the UN in Somalia. Another example is found in the Special Representative on the situation of human rights in Bosnia and Herzegovina and the Federal Republic of Yugoslavia's 2002 report. In the section on Kosovo the Special Representative expresses a number of human rights concerns in relation to the United Nations Mission in Kosovo and KFOR.[157]

Human rights monitoring bodies can potentially play an important role in the implementation of responsibility and accountability where states are responsible for a breach of human rights by peace support operations. The more the idea that states have a due diligence obligation to ensure respect by an international organization for human rights and international humanitarian law is accepted, the more likely that

---

154 Monetary Gold Removed from Rome in 1943 (*Italy* v. *France, United Kingdom and the United States*), 1954 ICJ Reports 32.

155 Case concerning East Timor (*Portugal* v. *Australia*), Judgment, 1995 ICJ Reports 90.

156 See for an analysis N. Sybesma-Knol, *The Indispensable Parties Rule in the East Timor Case*, in E. Denters & N. Schrijver (Eds.), Reflections on International Law from the Low Countries: In Honour of Paul de Waart 442 (1998).

157 Report of the Special Representative of the Commission on Human Rights on the Situation of Human Rights in Bosnia and Herzegovina and the Federal Republic of Yugoslavia, José Cutileiro, 8 January 2002, UN Doc. E/CN.4/2002/41, paras. 90, 92.

there will be an important role for human rights monitoring bodies. Above, a number of cases were mentioned in which human rights monitoring bodies have addressed states concerning the conduct of troops placed at the disposal of the UN. One example was the concern expressed by the UN Human Rights Committee that several years after the alleged involvement of members of the Netherland's peacekeeping forces in the events surrounding the fall of Srebrenica, the responsibility of the persons concerned has not yet been publicly and finally determined. The Committee considered that in respect of an event of such gravity it is of particular importance that issues relating to the state party's obligation to ensure the right to life be resolved in an expeditious and comprehensive manner.[158] The factors discussed above may limit the role of human rights monitoring bodies in the implementation of the responsibility and accountability of troop contributing states.[159]

5.7 Conclusion

This chapter demonstrated that there are many potential obstacles to the invocation of international responsibility of a state or an international organization for a violation of international humanitarian law by a peace support operation.

Traditional international law is based on rights of redress by the state whose nationals are victims of a violation of the law and not for the victims themselves. Human rights law has changed this by granting individuals rights and, in some cases, the possibility to invoke a violation of those rights on the international level. International humanitarian law, influenced by human rights, now also recognizes individual rights, but so far without jettisoning the inter-state implementation scheme. On the international level, only states can invoke international responsibility for violations of international humanitarian law in accordance with the basic principle in article 42 of the draft articles on state responsibility. Central to the invocation of responsibility is the concept of the 'injured state', the state whose individual right has been denied or impaired by the internationally wrongful act or which has otherwise been particularly affected by that act. The recognition that other states, which are not injured states but do have a legal interest, may also invoke responsibility widens the circle of states entitled to invoke responsibility for breach of obligations under international humanitarian law, because these can be considered as obligations *erga omnes partes*. In addition, at least certain obligations under international humanitarian law seem to be obligations owed to the international community as a whole. Apart from these secondary rules, common Article 1 of the Geneva Conventions and Additional Protocol I as a primary rule gives all states parties the right to invoke responsibility for violations of the Conventions or the Protocol.

In case of a breach of international law by a peace support operation there are many policy reasons to prevent a state from invoking the responsibility of the responsible state or international organization, whether directly or in diplomatic protection

158 Concluding Observations of the Human Rights Committee, Netherlands, 27 August 2001, UN Doc. CCPR/CO/72/NET.

159 Ronzitti, *supra* note 67, at 50.

of a national of the state. In some cases, such as in Somalia, there may not even be a government to protect its interests or those of its nationals. In practice, diplomatic protection exercised by states in the United Nations operation in the Congo is the only example of such exercise.

Claims settlement procedures are a possibility for an individual – but often for those of the host state only – to pursue a claim based on a violation of the law by a peace support operation without the intermediation of his state of nationality. But such procedures are not established in every operation. In ONUC, for example, there was no claims settlement procedure, nor was there a clear policy until after some time in KFOR.

Claims settlement procedures principally use the national law of the host state as applicable law in their procedures. It is uncertain whether a claim could be based directly on a breach of international law, or whether this possibility is contingent on how international law is incorporated in the national law of the host state.[160] For this reason Wickremasinghe and Verdirame note that while:

> Such procedures would appear suitable to deal with straightforward private law claims, for example for personal injury, death, or damage to property resulting from road traffic accidents, it may be questioned whether the procedural regime is also appropriate to deal with cases in which allegations of serious violations of human rights are at issue, even though the conduct in question may be simultaneously characterised as falling within standard tort categories related to harm to persons.[161]

Other features of specific claims settlement procedures are also potential obstacles to a claim based on a breach of international humanitarian law, in particular the exclusion of claims relating to 'combat damage' from the scope of admissible claims. Claims settlement procedures also raise questions of independence because of the composition of claims settlement bodies. In the case of UN local claims review boards, which are composed exclusively of UN staff, the Secretary-General has admitted that the organization may, rightly or wrongly, be perceived as acting as a judge in its own case.[162] Lack of any clear formulation of the law to be applied by claims settlement bodies and the fact that their decisions are not made public also raises concerns over the objectivity of their rulings.

Domestic private law of the host state or the troop contributing state may give an individual a cause of action. In such a case the action is based directly on a domestic tort but implicates an international law violation. Causes of action under domestic law however are generally accompanied by onerous procedural and jurisdictional requirements.

---

160 A senior United Nations official interviewed by the author stated that local claims review boards have never dealt with violations of international humanitarian law. Interview on 17 September 2002.

161 Wickremasinghe & Verdirame, *supra* note 55, at 483.

162 UN Doc. A/51/903 of 21 May 1997, para. 10.

In many cases the international organization or troop contributing state in question will also have immunity from jurisdiction before a national court. In theory a national court could interpret jurisdictional immunity restrictively, but on the sole occasion on which the question has been raised in relation to the immunity of the United Nations, in *Manderlier* v. *United Nations and Belgium*, a restrictive interpretation was rejected.[163]

International human rights machinery can provide another forum in which to invoke international responsibility for violations of international humanitarian law by a peace support operation. Of special interest are independent judicial or quasi-judicial bodies before which individuals can invoke international responsibility such as the European Court of Human Rights, the Inter-American Court of Human Rights and the United Nations Human Rights Commission.

It may be questioned whether such procedures are effective in the case of an alleged violation of international humanitarian law by a peace support operation. Exercise of subject-matter jurisdiction by these bodies over breaches of international humanitarian law is contested by states on the ground that they have not consented to such subject-matter jurisdiction.

Another potential obstacle to the effectiveness of human rights bodies is that states parties to human rights treaties are only obliged to secure human rights to persons within their jurisdiction. A restrictive interpretation of which persons fall under the jurisdiction of a state such as the interpretation by the European Court of Human Rights in the *Banković* case may exclude victims of human rights violations by peace support operations from the protection of human rights treaties. Finally, the jurisdiction of judicial or quasi-judicial human rights monitoring bodies does not extend to international organizations.

In other words, there are not many effective possibilities for invoking the responsibility of a state or an international organization for a breach of international humanitarian law by a peace support operation. In particular, the invocation of responsibility of an international organization is constrained. This situation is patently at odds with the present discourse on the accountability of international organizations. It may be recalled that international responsibility is a component of accountability. Accountability, as well as responsibility as a component of the former, relate to both primary rules governing the conduct of organizations and secondary rules to enable those potentially affected in their interests to means of redress and remedies.[164] As Wellens states, the "efficacy of any accountability regime for international organisations depends to a large extent, if not entirely, on the nature of the remedies afforded."[165]

The system of remedies is particularly weak in respect of the rights of individuals. As stated above, accountability is increasingly considered from the perspective of individuals. In the case of international humanitarian law the position of individuals

163 See Wickremasinghe & Verdirame, *supra* note 55, at 475-478.

164 Second Report of the International Law Association Committee on Accountability of International Organisations 2 (2000).

165 Wellens, *supra* note 2, at 15.

is reinforced by the fact that they can be considered to enjoy rights in their own name under international law. These substantive rights are however not matched by procedural rights, despite claims that there is a 'right to a remedy' under human rights law and international humanitarian law. In respect of international humanitarian law, this is confirmed by a body of domestic case law holding that there is no right of individual action.[166]

Whether or not there is a legal obligation to provide an effective remedy to individuals for breaches of international humanitarian law by peace support operations, there is an undeniable practical need. The goodwill of the local population in the host state and of the population of the troop contributing states is crucial for the accomplishment of the mandate of a peace support operation. Implementation of accountability and responsibility can be an important contributing factor in preserving that goodwill. A UN report on lessons learned from peacekeeping operations states that:

> support of the local population is essential to the success of a peacekeeping operation. Lack of local support not only hinders the operation in the implementation of its mandate and the conduct of daily activities, but can also pose a physical danger to the mission's personnel.[167]

If the local population considers a peace support operation as not being accountable there is a grave risk that their support will be lost. The local population will not fail to see the contradiction between the mandate of peace support operations, which often contains an element of fostering a culture of accountability in the host state, and lack of accountability of the operations themselves. Wilde calls this a 'representational problem' which risks creating a perception that accountability is for 'us' the local people, not 'them' the international officials.[168] Or, as a United Nations report on the Operation in Somalia states, "The United Nations was perceived by many in Somalia to be 'above the law', which undercut its efforts to promote human rights".[169]

166 See para. 5.5.2.

167 United Nations Department of Peacekeeping Operations, Multidisciplinary Peacekeeping; Lessons from Recent Experience, para. O.

168 R. Wilde, *Accountability and International Actors in Bosnia and Herzegovina, Kosovo and East Timor*, 7 ILSA Journal of International & Comparative Law 455 (2001), at 459.

169 United Nations Department of Peacekeeping Operations, The Comprehensive Report on Lessons Learned from United Nations Operation in Somalia (UNOSOM), April 1992 – March 1995, para. 57.

6

Proposals for new mechanisms for invoking accountability

6.1 Introduction

There is a need to improve the mechanisms for implementing the accountability of both troop contributing states, and international organizations especially, for violations of international humanitarian law by peace support operations.

First, the prevailing accountability discourse requires that organizations are accountable to any group or individual who is affected by the activities of the organization. Deploying a peace support operation is an activity which has the potential to directly affect many individuals in the host state. International organizations cannot and should not isolate themselves from this discourse.

Secondly, accountability contributes to the credibility and accomplishment of peace support operation mandates by preserving the cooperation of the local population. Where accountability is not sufficiently guaranteed, the activities of international organizations will be affected as there is increased resistance to international organizations taking action without the possibility for those who experience the consequences to hold them accountable for such action. The credibility of peace support operations is compromised if they do not practice what they preach.

In respect of breaches of international humanitarian law, the responsibility component of accountability plays an important role. Individuals have certain rights under international humanitarian law, and states and international organizations have corresponding obligations. There may or may not be a legal obligation for states and international organizations to provide mechanisms of redress,[1] but in any case the practical need discussed previously also operates on this level. The Security Council cannot for example credibly discuss ways in which it can improve the legal protection of civilians in armed conflict while there are hardly any possibilities to hold the organization responsible when it breaches international humanitarian law.

Below, the establishment of effective mechanisms to ensure the accountability of states and international organizations for breaches of international humanitarian law by peace support operations is proposed. A distinction is made between UN and NATO operations. A distinction is also made between mechanisms to implement responsibility, and mechanisms to implement a broader notion of accountability. The latter distinction is, to some extent, arbitrary, because the components of accountability are interrelated and mutually supportive.[2] The distinction is nevertheless useful

1 See para. 5.5.7.

2 First Report of the International Law Association Committee on Accountability of International Organizations 17 (1998).

because it allows making use of existing mechanisms and expanding on them. This is likely to be more acceptable to states and international organizations than creating entirely new mechanisms.

6.2 A mechanism to implement the responsibility of the United Nations

In its 1971 resolution on the application of humanitarian rules of armed conflict to UN forces, the Institut de Droit International stressed the need for a complaints procedure for individuals injured by a breach of those rules. Article 8 of the resolution stated that it is:

> desirable that claims presented by persons thus injured be submitted to bodies composed of independent and impartial persons. Such bodies should be designated or set up either by the regulations issued by the United Nations or by the agreements concluded by the Organization with the states which put contingents at its disposal and, possibly, with any other interested State.[3]

The standing claims commission provided for in Article 51 of the UN Model Status of Forces Agreement does not meet these criteria, and in any case it has never been established in practice. However, it is an appropriate starting point for harnessing a mechanism which does. Article 51 provides for the establishment of a standing claims commission as a mechanism for the settlement of claims of a private law character to which the UN operation or any member thereof is a party and over which the local courts have no jurisdiction because of the immunity of the organization or its members. The commission is to be composed of three members: one member to be appointed by the UN Secretary-General, another by the government of the host state and a chairman jointly by the Secretary-General and the government. If no agreement is reached as to the chairman, the President of the ICJ may, at the request of either party, appoint the chairman. The article also provides for the competence of the commission to determine its own procedure and the legally binding nature of its awards.

Several modifications to the claims commission are required to make it an effective mechanism for implementing responsibility for violations of international humanitarian law by a peace support operation. The reference in Article 51 to a 'standing' claims commission does not appropriately describe the commission. The article envisages the establishment of a claims commission for each peace support operation and not a real standing commission. A real standing or central claims commission should be established which can receive claims against all peace support operations.[4] This would ensure that the establishment of a claims commission does not depend on the conclusion of a SOFA. Individual victims should not be deprived of the possibility

---

3 Conditions of Application of Humanitarian Rules of Armed Conflict to Hostilities in which United Nations Forces May be Engaged, 54 Annuaire IDI 465 (1971-II).

4 The 'Commissie van Advies inzake Volkenrechtelijke Vraagstukken' (CAVV) recommended the establishment of such a central claims commission. Advies Nr. 13, 14 februari 2002, at 19.

to submit claims because it is not possible to conclude an agreement or because there is no government to represent them. The permanent character of the institution would also make it possible to preserve gained expertise. If the claims commission becomes a permanent institution, the procedure for appointment of members in Article 51 can no longer be used. Another procedure will have to devised which guarantees the independence of the commission. The need for independence follows from the principle that justice should not only be done but also be seen to be done. Hence, it would be wise policy to involve independent persons and not to serve as judge in its own case. The UN Secretary-General has underlined the applicability of this principle to claims settlement in peace support operations.[5]

The claims commission in Article 51 only has jurisdiction over claims of a private law character. A claim based on a violation of international humanitarian law can only be made if the conduct in question can be simultaneously characterized as falling within standard tort categories. This is not an appropriate procedural regime for claims based on violations of international humanitarian law.[6] The mandate of the permanent claims commission should be enlarged to expressly include violations of international humanitarian law.

In practice, local claims review boards exclude compensation for claims which result from 'operational necessity'. 'Operational necessity' is defined as where damage results from necessary actions taken by a peacekeeping force in the course of carrying out its operations in pursuance of its mandate.[7] The Secretary-General has proposed to include this ground for exemption in Article 51 of the Model SOFA.[8] This proposal is undesirable for several reasons.[9] International humanitarian law does not recognize 'operational necessity' as a circumstance precluding wrongfulness. It does contain the concept of 'military necessity', which is however not a circumstance precluding wrongfulness: a given rule can only be set aside on grounds of military necessity when it expressly so permits.[10] It may be noted that the wording proposed by the Secretary-General to incorporate the principle of operational necessity in Article 51 does not distinguish between claims for the ordinary functioning of an operation and claims for combat-related activities.[11] Even if 'operational necessity' can only be invoked in case of claims for the ordinary operation of the force, as opposed to claims for combat-related damage, violations of the law of occupation could still fall in the

5 UN Doc. A/51/903 of 21 May 1997, para. 10.

6 Compare C. Wickremasinghe & G. Verdirame, *Responsibility and Liability for Violations of Human Rights in the Course of UN Field Operations*, in C. Scott (Ed.), Torture as Tort: Comparative Perspectives on the Development of Transnational Human Rights Litigation 465 (2001), at 483.

7 UN Doc. A/51/389 of 20 September 1996, para. 13.

8 *Id.*, para. 15.

9 See also J. Prescott, *Claims*, in D. Fleck (Ed.), The Handbook of the Law of Visiting Forces 159 (2001), at 173.

10 F. Kalshoven & L. Zegveld, Constraints on the Waging of War 37 (2001). On the principle of military necessity see H. McCoubrey, *The Nature of the Modern Doctrine of Military Necessity*, 30 Military Law and Law of War Review 215 (1991).

11 *Supra* note 7, para. 15.

first category. There also seems to be lack of clarity concerning the concept of 'operational necessity' which could lead to its being applied in situations in which international humanitarian law applies.

The permanent claims commission should have investigative capacities. The Secretary-General has proposed the establishment of *ad hoc* fact-finding commissions, as necessary, to examine reports on alleged breaches of international humanitarian law and human rights law committed by members of UN forces.[12] Giving the permanent claims commission an investigative branch would have a number of advantages over that proposal. It would make it possible to start an investigation immediately after an allegation has been made. It would also prevent political considerations from influencing the establishment, work or findings of an *ad hoc* committee.

The permanent claims commission should also have expansive remedial powers. The claims commission referred to in Article 51 can only award compensation, but sometimes reparation of the wrong may require other forms of reparation, for example guarantees of non-repetition or an apology, instead of, or in addition to, compensation.

The permanent claims commission should have jurisdiction over the UN as well as troop contributing states. The legal basis for jurisdiction over troop contributing states could be a provision in the participating state agreement between the UN and the troop contributing states. Submitting to the jurisdiction of the permanent claims commission would provide a mechanism for implementation of responsibility which would be available to victims, unlike in most cases the national courts of troop contributing states at present. It would also provide a mechanism which meets minimum standards of due process.

6.3 A mechanism to implement the responsibility of the North Atlantic Treaty Organization

In a similar vein, NATO should also establish a permanent claims commission. The member states of the organization and the international secretariat, in the *ad hoc* working group of legal experts, have formulated a general 'out-of-area' claims policy. The policy is intended as guidance for the establishment of claims settlement procedures in future operations. These discussions offered a unique opportunity for the creation of a permanent claims commission to implement the responsibility of the organization itself. It seems however that this is not the direction in which the discussions moved. The point of departure taken by the working group was the claims policies and procedures established in SFOR and KFOR. As discussed, these policies and procedures do not reflect the responsibility of the organization as the legal person which exercises effective control over the operations because they make settling claims primarily a function of troop contributing states, even though the conduct of personnel acting under the direction and control of NATO is attributable to the organization. It may be that one reason why the organization is not in favor of a system such as that of the UN is budgetary.[13]

12 UN Doc. S/1999/957 of 8 September 1999, para 61.

13 Interview with an official in the legal department of the Netherlands Ministry of Foreign Affairs, 31 January 2003.

The establishment of a permanent claims commission by NATO would avoid the need for complicated negotiations at the beginning of each peace support operation concerning a claims settlement mechanism. It would provide legal certainty for residents of the host state and it would ensure that a claims settlement mechanism exists from the start of the operation.

Existing claims mechanisms in NATO peace support operations only have jurisdiction over claims of a private law character. The jurisdiction of the permanent claims commission should expressly include violations of international humanitarian law. Existing claims procedures expressly disallow claims for damage arising from 'combat damage' or 'combat related activities'. Article VI (9) of Annex 1A to the Dayton Agreement for example states that "The IFOR and its personnel shall not be liable for any damages to civilian or government property caused by combat or combat related activities."[14]

In the context of claims settlement for IFOR this kind of damage has also been referred to as 'operational necessity'.[15] This demonstrates the confusion which can arise concerning the distinction between ordinary operations of a force and combat activities. It should be made clear that a permanent claims commission could receive claims based on alleged violations of international humanitarian law. Legally, absolution from responsibility incurred in respect of grave breaches of the 1949 Geneva Conventions and Additional Protocol I is not allowed.[16] As a matter of policy there should also be no absolution from responsibility for other violations.

The permanent claims commission should be an independent institution. A procedure will have to be devised to ensure this independence.

It should have jurisdiction over NATO as well as the troop contributing states. The legal basis for jurisdiction over troop contributing states could be a provision in the participating state agreement between the organization and the troop contributing states. Because the organization does not conclude participating state agreements with member states concerning their participation in peace support operations, a decision by the NAC would be an alternative way for member states to accept the jurisdiction of the claims commission.

Existing claims settlement procedures provide only for claims of nationals of the host state. There is no valid reason to continue such a discriminatory practice in relation to the permanent claims commission. The commission should be able to receive claims from all victims of violations of international humanitarian law by peace support operations even if they are not nationals of the host state.[17]

---

14 General Framework Agreement for Peace in Bosnia and Herzegovina with Annexes, reproduced in 35 ILM 75 (1996).

15 Private information of the author.

16 Article 51, 52, 131 and 148 respectively of the 1949 Geneva Conventions and Article 85 (1) of Additional Protocol I.

17 Compare B. Amrallah, *The International Responsibility of the United Nations for Activities Carried out by U.N. Peace-Keeping Forces*, 32 Revue Egyptienne de Droit International 57 (1976), at 80.

The permanent claims commission should have extensive remedial powers. It should be able to impose other forms of reparation than compensation where necessary.

If the organization and its member states do not adopt the above proposal or a similar proposal, they should consider dispensing with the principle that combat-related claims are inadmissible in claims settlement procedures.

6.4 A mechanism to ensure the accountability of peace support operations

6.4.1 Previous proposals

In addition to a mechanism for implementing responsibility there is also a need for a mechanism to implement accountability in a broader sense. In 1994, Childers and Urquhart proposed the establishment of an ombudsman-type mechanism for this purpose:

> The need for an ombudsman-type function is also increasingly obvious regarding UN peace and security operations. The greater the UN's involvement in peace-enforcement and other operations that may employ force, the more vital it becomes to have transparent and independent human rights supervision. This is needed as much to protect the organization from false or inflated charges of human rights abuse as to ensure that if these occur they are properly investigated and reported. A recent example of this need was the alleged actions and behavior involving civilians by UNOSOM II forces in Mogadishu, Somalia.[18]

More recently other writers have launched similar calls for the establishment of accountability mechanisms. One such proposal calls for the establishment of an international humanitarian ombudsperson, who would handle allegations of abuse by peacekeeping staff and peacekeeping missions at the global level, as well as for the creation of independent mission-based ombudsperson offices.[19]

The need to provide an accountability mechanism has recently started to receive recognition by the UN itself. A report by the Department of Peacekeeping Operations evaluating UNOSOM states that:

> In UNOSOM, no independent oversight existed which could serve as an ombudsman to consider grievances registered by the local population against the United Nations. Without such a mechanism, the United Nations was perceived by many in

18 E. Childers & B. Urquhart, Renewing the United Nations System 111 (1994).

19 F. Rawski, *To Waive or Not to Waive: Immunity and Accountability in U.N. Peacekeeping Operations*, 18 Connecticut Journal of International Law 103 (2002), at 129-130. See also C. Bongiorno, *A Culture of Impunity: Applying International Human Rights Law to the United Nations in East Timor*, 33 Columbia Human Rights Law Review 623 (2002), at 648-688; and B. Bedont, International Criminal Justice: Implications for Peacekeeping, Report for the Canadian Department of Foreign Affairs and International Trade (2001).

> Somalia to be "above the law", which undercut its efforts to promote human rights … It was suggested that consideration should be given to appointing an ombudsman to some peacekeeping operations.[20]

In 1999, the UN Secretary-General adopted this proposal. In his first report to the Security Council on the protection of civilians in armed conflict he made clear that although normally the activities of peace support operations contribute to the protection of civilians in armed conflict, abuses do occur.[21] He underlined that in order to protect civilians in armed conflict, as well as to protect the legitimacy and respect of peacekeeping operations and their personnel, the organization needs to address cases in which peacekeepers are involved in unacceptable behavior, including abuses of the civilian population. For this purpose the Secretary-General recommended that the Security Council:

> Support a public 'ombudsman' with all peacekeeping operations to deal with complaints from the general public about the behavior of United Nations peacekeepers and establish an ad hoc fact-finding commission, as necessary, to examine reports on alleged breaches of international humanitarian and human rights law committed by members of United Nations forces.[22]

The recommendation has not been received with much enthusiasm by members of the Security Council. The Council discussed the Secretary-General's report in open meetings in September 1999 and April 2000.[23] At these meetings no delegation spoke in favor of the recommendation and one delegation expressly stated that it was undesirable because of the financial implications it could have.[24] In January 2004 the Secretary-General repeated his recommendation, calling for the post of Personnel Conduct Officer, to act as the mission's ombudsman, to be created in each field mission.[25]

Nevertheless, an ombudsperson institution has been established in the United Nations Mission in Kosovo. This institution, with limited powers, is discussed below. At this point it is sufficient to note that the particular nature of the United Nations Operation in Kosovo, which acts as a surrogate government, seems to have been an important impetus for the establishment of the ombudsperson institution. These particular characteristics may not be reproduced in other, future, operations.

---

20 The Comprehensive Report on Lessons Learned from United Nations Operation in Somalia (UNOSOM), para. 57.

21 Report of the Secretary-General to the Security Council on the Protection of Civilians in Armed Conflict of 8 September 1999, UN Doc. S/1999/957, para. 61.

22 *Id.*

23 See Provisional Verbatim record of the 4046th Meeting of the Security Council, 16-17 September 1999, UN Doc. S/PV.4046; Provisional Verbatim Record of the 4130th Meeting of the Security Council, 19 April 2000, UN Doc. S/PV.4130.

24 *Id.*

25 Report of the Secretary-General, Implementation of the Recommendations of the Special Committee on Peacekeeping Operations of 26 January 2004, UN Doc. A/58/694, para. 72.

In contrast to the UN, NATO does not (yet) seem to be convinced of the need for accountability in its peace support operations. There have been no proposals for accountability mechanisms in the organization. In Kosovo the commander of KFOR has not made arrangements for the exercise of jurisdiction by the United Nations-established ombudsman over the Force.

6.4.2 The ombudsperson concept[26]

It may be noted that all the above-mentioned proposals refer to an ombudsperson or an ombudsperson-type institution. This is in conformity with the assertion which is frequently made that an ombudsperson is an appropriate mechanism to ensure accountability. This assertion implies that the characteristics of an ombudsperson correspond to the elements making monitoring and scrutiny of an international organization possible, such as transparency, including access to information, responsiveness and reporting. In order to determine whether this assertion is warranted, a closer analysis of the ombudsperson concept is required.

The ombudsman concept developed as a mechanism to ensure accountability of (parts of) national governments. The first ombudsman was established in Sweden in 1809. The institution was the result of a power struggle between parliament and the executive. In 1809 parliament gained the upper hand and an ombudsman was created in the new constitution to control the executive power and its administration on behalf of parliament. The word 'ombudsman' in Swedish means 'representative, agent, delegate'. The ombudsman was an agent of parliament to control the executive. The present commonly understood function of the ombudsman, to receive complaints from the public, was at that time not a major part of his work but developed over time.[27] The present legal basis for the Swedish ombudsman is found in Article 6 of Chapter 12 of the Instrument of Government or constitution. This article states that the parliament (Riksdag):

> Shall elect one or more Ombudsmen to supervise in accordance with the instructions laid down by the Riksdag the application in public service of laws and other statutes.

The instructions referred to are found in the Act with Instructions for the Parliamentary Ombudsmen of 13 November 1986.[28] The Swedish ombudsman has largely been the model on which other ombudsperson institutions have been based. In 1919 Finland also created an ombudsman, followed by Denmark in 1954. Since that time many other countries have established an ombudsman. This development is related to the proliferation of large government bureaucracies and the perceived

---

26 A number of institutions use the term 'ombudsman', while others use the term 'ombudsperson'. In the following, the terms will be used interchangeably.

27 T. Bull, *The Original Ombudsman: Blueprint in Need of Revision or a Concept with More to Offer?*, 6 European Public Law 334 (2000), at 335.

28 Lag [1986:765] med instruktion för Riksdagens ombudsmän of 13 November 1986.

need for an instrument of accountability. Most of the institutions established after 1954 follow the model of the Swedish and Danish institution. This model has become the archetypal or 'classical' ombudsman. Gottehrer and Hostina list as the irreducible characteristics of the classical ombudsman: independence, impartiality and fairness, credibility of the review process and confidentiality.[29] In practice, these requirements have the following consequences. The ombudsman is usually appointed by the legislative power to investigate the activities of the executive power. The institution is established in the constitution or a law to make it more difficult to challenge the legal basis of the office, because constitutions are often difficult to amend. The ombudsperson is not appointed by the organizations or arm of government he reviews. This is why he is almost always appointed by the legislative power and why he functions on behalf of that power. The ombudsman has a fixed, long term of office and may be reappointed. He can be removed only on specific grounds. This guarantees that he will not be removed for political reasons or because the results of his investigations have offended those in political power. The ombudsperson must to a certain extent also be financially independent.

To be impartial and fair and to be seen to avoid even the appearance of partiality the ombudsman must be highly qualified so that he will be respected among different groups. Complaints can be directed to the ombudsman without paying a fee so that there is no discrimination. The ombudsman has the right to criticize officials and make recommendations to resolve specific situations or prevent their reccurrence, and he is immune from liability and criminal prosecution for acts performed in his official capacity. The classical ombudsman does not have the power to make binding decisions. He relies on powers of persuasion, reason and criticism.

The ombudsman usually has the power to initiate an investigation on the basis of a complaint he has received, or on his own initiative. The authority to initiate an investigation allows him to act when information warranting an investigation comes to his attention in the absence of a willing complainant. The classical ombudsman has a number of powers to make an investigation effective. These usually include access to records and premises and the power to compel individuals to testify or produce evidence. The standards used by the ombudsman to conduct a review are usually stated broadly and in terms of maladministration. Fairness, in the sense of broader notions of justice than mere compliance with relevant statutory law, is also an important component of the standards under which complaints are investigated. The ombudsman should also be accountable, for example through an obligation to report annually.

The classical ombudsman may determine that certain information, in particular the identity of a complainant, should remain confidential. Officials who are the subject of a complaint may also warrant protection during the process of investigation. As stated, the standard of review of the ombudsman is traditionally whether there has been a case of maladministration. The precise wording of the standard varies. The mission of the Greek ombudsman for example is the protection of citizen's rights,

29 D. Gottehrer & M. Hostina, Essential Characteristics of a Classical Ombudsman, Annex 1 to Ombudsman and Human Rights Protection Institutions in OSCE Participating States, OSCE Human Dimension Implementation Meeting October 1998, Background paper.

opposition to maladministration and observance of legality,[30] the ombudsman in the Netherlands "shall determine whether or not the administrative authority acted properly in the matter under investigation,"[31] and the Norwegian ombudsman's task is to "endeavour to ensure that injustice is not committed against the individual citizen by the public administration."[32] Although the wording varies, the standard in all these cases is whether there has been a violation of law or administrative rules and principles.

The ombudsman traditionally does not have an express human rights or international humanitarian law mandate. In the past decades, however, he has increasingly been considered as an instrument for the protection of rights of the individual. This development has accompanied a general trend in international institutions which recognizes the importance of national human rights institutions.[33] One important step in this development was a 1991 UN international workshop on national institutions for the promotion and protection of human rights. The workshop resulted in the drafting of guiding principles referred to as the 'Paris principles' which were adopted by the General Assembly in 1993 and which reaffirm the importance of developing, in accordance with national legislation, effective national institutions for the promotion and protection of human rights.[34] Other international organizations have also stressed the role of the ombudsman as a tool for the promotion and protection of human rights. The Committee of Ministers of the Council of Europe adopted a recommendation to member states in 1985 to consider the possibility of appointing an ombudsman and to consider empowering the ombudsman, where this is not already the case, to give particular consideration to the human rights matters under his scrutiny.[35] In 1997 the Committee of Ministers recommended that the governments of member states consider the possibility of establishing effective national human rights institutions, in particular human rights commissions or ombudsmen.[36] The OSCE has also supported the importance of the ombudsman as a way to promote and protect human rights.

30 Law No. 2477 signed by the President on 17 April 1997 The Ombudsman and the Public Administration Inspectors-Controllers Body, Art. 1.

31 National Ombudsman Act, Act of 4 February 1981 (Bulletin of Acts and Decrees 1981, 35), most recently amended by Act of Parliament of 12 May 1999 (Bulletin of Acts and Decrees 1999, 214), Art. 26.

32 Act concerning the Storting's Ombudsman for Public Administration of 22 June 1962 No. 8, amended by Acts of 22 March 1968 No. 1, 8 February 1980 No. 1, 19 December 1980 No. 63, 6 September 1991 No. 72, 11 June 1993 No. 85 and 15 March 1996 No. 13, Art. 3.

33 See L. Reif, *Building Democratic Institutions: The Role of National Human Rights Institutions in Good Governance and Human Rights Protection*, 13 Harvard Human Rights Journal 1 (2000).

34 UN Doc. A/RES/48/134 of 20 December 1993, para. 2.

35 Recommendation No. R (85) 13 of the Committee of Ministers to member states on the institution of the ombudsman, 23 September 1985.

36 Recommendation No. R (97) 14 of the Committee of Ministers to member states on the establishment of independent national institutions for the promotion and protection of human rights of 30 September 1997, para. a; see generally Council of Europe Directorate of Human Rights, Non-judicial means for the protection of human rights at the national level, May 1998, H/INF (98) 3.

The member states of the CSCE, the forerunner of the OSCE, agreed at the Second Meeting on the Human Dimension of the CSCE to "facilitate the establishment and strengthening of independent national institutions in the area of human rights and the rule of law."[37] Since that time, support for national human rights institutions, expressly including the ombudsman, has been part of the human dimension.[38]

As a result of this development, human rights protection has become a major focus of national ombudsmen. Many pre-existing ombudsmen have started to put a stronger emphasis on human rights and interpret their mandate accordingly.[39] Many of the more recently established ombudsman institutions have been given an express human rights mandate. Especially in Latin America, where the creation of an ombudsman was considered an important mechanism to prevent the recurrence of human rights violations such as those pervasive on that continent in the 1970s and 1980s. For example, in 1991 Colombia established the 'Defensor del Pueblo', El Salvador a 'Procurador para la Defensa de los Derechos Humanos' in 1992 and Argentina a 'Defensor del Pueblo' in 1993. These ombudsperson institutions were based to a large extent on the model of the Spanish and Portuguese ombudsmen.[40] The Spanish ombudsman (Defensor del Pueblo) *inter alia* protects the human rights contained in the constitution for which purpose he may supervise the activity of the administration. These rights include civil and political rights, economic, social and cultural rights as well as certain collective rights.

Another region in which many ombudsmen have been established with a human rights mandate is Central and Eastern Europe. Ombudsman institutions have been established in Poland, Hungary, Croatia, Bosnia Herzegovina and Slovenia. These have specific human rights mandates, often combined with more traditional functions. The Human Rights Ombudsman of Slovenia for example was established to "protect human rights and fundamental freedoms against the state bodies, local self-government bodies, and bodies entrusted with public authorities",[41] but while intervening he may also invoke "the principles of equity and good administration."[42] The Polish Commissioner for Civil Rights Protection also has an express human rights mandate. Article 208 of the Polish Constitution states that he "shall safeguard the freedoms and rights of persons and citizens specified in the Constitution and other normative acts."[43]

---

37 Document of the Copenhagen Meeting of the Conference on the Human Dimension of the CSCE, 5 June – 29 July 1990, para. 27.

38 See *e.g.* Consolidated Summary, Human Dimension Implementation Meeting, Warsaw, 9-19 September 2002, IV.

39 See *e.g.* M. Oosting, *The National Ombudsman of the Netherlands and Human Rights*, 12 International Ombudsman Journal 1 (1994).

40 F. Alvarez de Miranda y Torres, *Human Rights and their Functioning in the Institutional Strengthening of the Ombudsman*, 2 International Ombudsman Yearbook 146 (1998).

41 Law on the Ombudsman, Official Journal of the Republic of Slovenia, No. 71/1993, Art. 1.

42 *Id.*, Art. 3.

43 See generally E. Letowska, *The Polish Ombudsman (The Commissioner for the Protection of Civil Rights)*, 39 International & Comparative Law Quarterly 206 (1990).

6.4.3 *The ombudsman concept and international humanitarian law*

The development of the ombudsman as a national human rights institution demonstrates that it is generally considered as an appropriate mechanism to ensure accountability for the violation of individual rights. Does this also include rights under international humanitarian law? The author is not aware of any ombudsman mandate which expressly includes the protection of international humanitarian law. On the other hand, at least two ombudsmen do apply that branch of law as a standard of review in their investigations.

One is the Peruvian ombudsman ('Defensor del Pueblo'). He has a mandate to defend the constitutional and fundamental rights of the individual and society, and to supervise the fulfillment of the obligations of the public administration and the public service.[44] He has carried out a number of investigations into persons injured by anti-personnel landmines. He has also published a general report on anti-personnel landmines. The discussion in this report is based on the one hand on the consideration that accidents caused by landmines are a violation of the right to life and the right to physical integrity, and on the other hand on the obligations of the state of Peru under an instrument of international humanitarian law, the Ottawa Convention.[45] In his first annual report of 1998 the ombudsman also condemned the hostage taking in the Japanese Ambassador's residence in Lima in 1996 as a violation of international humanitarian law.[46] In short, the Peruvian ombudsman applies international humanitarian law, but only to a limited extent.

The Colombian ombudsman ('Defensor del Pueblo') makes much more systematic reference to international humanitarian law. The Colombian Constitution states that the mandate of the ombudsman is to ensure the promotion, protection and dissemination of human rights.[47] In the Colombian context, human rights are understood as including international humanitarian law. In a 1995 decision concerning the constitutionality of Additional Protocol II to the Geneva Conventions, the Constitutional Tribunal decided that international humanitarian law is part of a normative corpus of human rights, because similar to human rights in the strict sense it is composed of rules of *ius cogens* the main purpose of which is to protect the dignity of the human person.[48]

---

44 Organic Law of the Ombudsman institution, Law No. 26520 of 8 August 1995, Art. 1.

45 Ombudsman Report 35 (Informe Defensorial 35: El Problema de las Minas Antipersonales dentro del Territorio Nacional).

46 First Annual Report to Congress, May 1998 (Primer Informe del Defensor del Pueblo al Congreso) 94. For an account of the hostage crisis see R. Panjabi, *Terror at the Emperor's Birthday Party: An Analysis of the Hostage-Taking Incident at the Japanese Embassy in Lima, Peru*,16 Dickinson Journal of International Law 1 (1997).

47 Article 282 of the Constitution.

48 Decision No. C-225/95 of 18 May 1995, para. 11 ("Para ello conviene tener en cuenta que estos convenios hacen parte, en sentido genérico, del *corpus* normativo de los derechos humanos, puesto que, tanto los tratados de derechos humanos en sentido estricto como los convenios de derecho humanitario son normas de *ius cogens* que buscan, ante todo, proteger la dignidad de la persona humana.") See also F. Kalshoven, *A Colombian View on Protocol II*, 1 Yearbook of International Humanitarian 262 (1998).

It determined that the 1949 Geneva Conventions and the 1977 Additional Protocols are among those conventions that take precedence over other rules of domestic law on the basis of Article 93 of the Constitution, and that they are part of a 'constitutional bloc' of rules which are integrated in the Constitution without formally appearing in that document.[49] This provides a solid legal basis for the ombudsman to use international humanitarian law as a standard of review in his investigations, and the ombudsman regularly makes use of this standard. Investigations into specific cases result in the adoption of resolutions by the ombudsman in which he presents his conclusions and recommendations. The ombudsman stated in his 2001 annual report that he will use these resolutions to condemn serious violations of international humanitarian law committed in non-international armed conflict.[50] In practice, he has adopted a number of resolutions which are exclusively concerned with violations of international humanitarian law. For example, in a resolution of 8 April 2002 the ombudsman discusses a case in which the Autodefensas Unidas de Colombia (AUC), a paramilitary armed group, boobytrapped the body of a member of the insurgent FARC (Revolutionary Armed Forces of Colombia).[51] As a result one civilian was killed and two others were seriously wounded when they tried to recover the body. The ombudsman recalls that rules of international humanitarian law, including the 1949 Geneva Conventions and the 1977 Additional Protocols, as well as Protocol II to the 1980 United Nations Convention on Conventional Weapons, are directly applicable in domestic Colombian law. He concludes that the act of boobytrapping constituted a violation of the prohibition of perfidy in Article 37 of Additional Protocol I, a violation of Article 7 (b) of Protocol II to the 1980 Conventional Weapons Convention, and a violation of the principle of discrimination. As of 12 December 2002, the ombudsman had adopted as many as fourteen resolutions specifically concerning international humanitarian law.

6.4.4 The application of the ombudsman concept to international organizations

6.4.4.1 Preliminary observations

As stated, the ombudsman evolved as a mechanism to ensure accountability in the domestic context. This begs the question whether the concept can be applied in the context of peace support operations which are an organ of, or closely linked to, an international organization. An international organization does not have the legislative, executive and judicial division of powers which is largely followed in most munic-

49 *Id.*, para. 12 ("el bloque de constitucionalidad está compuesto por aquellas normas y principios que, sin aparecer formalmente en el articulado del texto constitucional, son utilizados como parámetros del control de constitucionalidad de las leyes, por cuanto han sido normativamente integrados a la Constitución, por diversas vías y por mandato de la propia Constitución.")

50 Ninth Annual Report of the Ombudsman to Congress (Noveno Informe Annual del Defensor del Pueblo al Congreso de la República) 255 (2001).

51 Ombudsman Humanitarian Resolution 011 (Resolución Defensorial Humanitaria No. 011) of 8 April 2002.

ipal legal systems[52] and which pervades the structure of many national ombudsmen. It may be recalled that the first ombudsman was established by parliament as a mechanism to control the executive. The international environment in which peace support operations operate also differs from the domestic sphere in many other ways. Peace support operations involve not one authority but several international legal persons which have certain powers over national contingents in an operation. Most international organizations do not have citizens or residents with which they have a direct connection. These differences have been given as grounds for opposing proposals for the establishment of ombudsman schemes at the international level. For example, the European Parliament at one moment opposed the establishment of an ombudsman in the European Community based on the view that the existing differences between national legal systems and the Community legal system made it impossible purely and simply to transpose the institution of the ombudsman on to the Community system.[53]

Nevertheless, the concept of the ombudsman does exist at the international level. It has developed mainly as a corollary of the demand for accountability of international organizations, and in particular accountability toward individuals. Three institutions can be identified.

6.4.4.2 The World Bank Inspection Panel

The first ombudsman-like mechanism to emerge out of this debate was the World Bank Inspection Panel.[54] The Panel's creation was the result of both internal and external demands on the Bank to be more accountable in its operational work by providing the Bank's Board with an independent review mechanism. These pressures led to a number of proposed solutions to increase the Bank's accountability. One of the three main solutions proposed by Bank officials and other persons and organizations was to establish a Bank ombudsman.[55] This proposal was not put into practice, but in 1993 the Executive Directors of the Bank established an Inspection Panel (the Panel) that was heavily influenced by the ombudsman proposal.[56] The Panel has a mandate to receive complaints by groups of individuals whose rights or interests have been or are likely to be affected by an action or omission of the Bank as a result of a failure by the Bank to follow its operational policies and procedures with respect to the design, appraisal and/or implementation of a project financed by the Bank provided in all cases that such failure has had, or threatens to have, a material adverse effect. The term 'affected individuals' excludes a single individual but is very broadly interpreted

52 *Prosecutor* v. *Duško Tadić*, Decision on the Defence Motion for Interlocutory Appeal on Jurisdiction, Case No. IT-94-1-AR72, A. Ch., 2 October 1995, para. 43.

53 See report of Mr Chanterie on behalf of the Committee on the Rules of Procedure and Petitions, Doc A2 – 41/85, resolution adopted on 14 June 1985, OJ C175, 15 July 1985, at 273.

54 See D. Bradlow, *International Organizations and Private Complaints: The Case of the World Bank Inspection Panel*, 34 Virginia Journal of International Law 553 (1994).

55 D. Bradlow, *Why the World Bank Needs an Ombudsman*, Financial Times, 14 July 1993, at 13.

56 Resolution No. IBRD 93-10, "The World Bank Inspection Panel", 22 September 1993.

as including any two or more persons who share common interests or concerns.[57] The operational rules and procedures of the Bank do not include binding rules of international law. They are policy documents issued by Bank managers to staff members concerning procedures to be followed in preparing and executing projects financed by the Bank. The different Operational Policies, Bank Procedures and Operational Directives which constitute the Bank's operational rules and procedures cover a wide range of activities.[58] As a result the standard of review available to the Inspection Panel is very broad. It gives the Panel much potential to influence the development of the human rights obligations of the World Bank.[59]

The resolution establishing the Panel included a number of provisions designed to ensure the independence of the members of the Panel from the Bank's Management, by providing that they are appointed by the Executive Directors and that they may be removed from office only by decision of those Directors, for cause. Members of the Panel are ineligible for employment by the Bank following the end of their service on the Panel.

Under the procedure for handling complaints, the Inspection Panel, when it receives a complaint, must notify the Board and President of the Bank. The Bank's Management must provide the Panel with evidence that it has complied with, or intends to comply with the relevant policies and procedures. The Panel subsequently determines whether the request for inspection meets the eligibility criteria in the resolution establishing the Panel, and, based on this assessment, make a recommendation to the Executive Directors as to whether the matter should be investigated. An investigation only takes place if it is authorized by the Executive Directors. In that case, the Panel carries out an investigation and issues its findings to the Executive Directors indicating whether the Bank has seriously violated its operational rules and policies. After the inspection is completed, the Executive Directors decide on any actions to be taken.

The resolution establishing the Panel includes several provisions which relate to the transparency of the process. In case of complaints by affected parties there is an obligation to inform them of the decision of Executive Directors on a recommendation to investigate, and to inform them of the results of an investigation and the action taken in its respect. The Bank is also obliged to make a request for an inspection, the recommendation of the Panel concerning investigation and the report of the Panel and the Bank's response publicly available within a certain period of time. The

57 See Clarifications of Certain Aspects of the Resolution Establishing the Inspection Panel (R96-204), 30 September 1996, approved by the Board of Executive Directors on 17 October 1996.

58 See L. Boisson de Chazournes, *Policy Guidance and Compliance Issues: The World Bank Operational Standards*, in D. Shelton (Ed.), Commitment and Compliance: The Role of Non-Binding Norms in the International Legal System 281 (2000).

59 D. Bradlow & S. Schlemmer-Schulte, *The World Bank's New Inspection Panel: A Constructive Step in the Transformation of the International Legal Order*, 54 Zeitschrift für ausländisches öffentliches Recht und Völkerrecht 405 (1994). Operational rules and procedures which have a human rights element include Operational Directive 4.20, Indigenous Peoples, para. 6, and Operational Policy 4.20, October 1999.

annual report of the Panel to the President and Executive Directors is also publicly available.

The Panel is not empowered to take binding decisions. As with the ombudsman, its mandate does not extend to determining responsibility in the strict sense. The operational rules and procedures on which the Panel bases its findings are not obligations which result in an internationally wrongful act when they are breached.[60]

It may be noted that within the World Bank Group a second ombudsperson-type institution was established in 1998. This institution is called the Compliance Advisor/Ombudsman. The purpose of the Compliance Advisor/Ombudsman is to assist the International Finance Corporation (IFC) and the Multilateral Investment Guarantee Agency (MIGA) to address complaints of people affected by projects in a manner that is fair, objective and constructive. The mechanism has three functions, one of which is the ombudsman function, in other words responding to complaints from project-affected people.[61]

6.4.4.3 The European Union Ombudsman

A second institution for accountability in international organizations is the European Ombudsman.[62] The institution was established in the 1992 Treaty on European Union (Maastricht Treaty). This treaty inserted two new articles in the European Community Treaty, the European Coal and Steel Community Treaty[63] and the European Atomic Energy Community Treaty.[64] The new Article 21 of the EC Treaty provides that every citizen of the Union may apply to the Ombudsman established in accordance with Article 195. Article 195 provides for the establishment, mandate and powers of the ombudsman as well as for the European Parliament to lay down more detailed regulations for the ombudsman, after seeking an opinion from the Commission and with the approval of the Council acting by a qualified majority. In accordance with this provision the European Parliament adopted the European Ombudsman Statute on 9 March 1994.[65]

---

60 S. Schlemmer-Schulte, *The World Bank's Experience With Its Inspection Panel*, 58 Zeitschrift für ausländisches öffentliches Recht und Völkerrecht 353 (1998), at 387.

61 See for a discussion of this mechanism A. Rigo, *Process Integrity and Institutional Independence in International Organizations: The Inspection Panel and the Sanctions Committee of the World Bank*, in L. Boisson de Chazournes, C. Romano & R. Mackenzie (Eds.), International Organizations and International Dispute Settlement: Trends and Prospects 165 (2002).

62 See generally I. Harden, *When Europeans Complain: The Work of the European Ombudsman*, 3 Cambridge Yearbook of European Legal Studies 199 (2000); K. Heede, European Ombudsman: Redress and Control at Union Level (2000) and P. Bonnor, *The European Ombudsman: A Novel Source of Soft Law in the European Union*, 25 European Law Review 39 (2000).

63 Article 20 (d).

64 Article 107 (d).

65 Decision of the European Parliament on the Regulations and General Conditions Governing the Performance of the Ombudsman's Duties (European Ombudsman Statute), OJ L 113, 4 April 1994, at 15.

The genesis of the institution makes clear that it is a result of the increasing focus on the direct relationship between international organizations and individuals and a concomitant accountability of the former to the latter. In the nation state, the concept of citizenship is an important expression of the relationship between the state and individuals. The European Ombudsman is rooted in the concept of European citizenship[66] which expresses a similar direct relationship between the European Union and individuals. In the period directly preceding the first Intergovernmental Conference on European Political Union in 1990, the Spanish government circulated a memorandum entitled 'The Road to European Citizenship'. The Spanish concept of European citizenship called for the adoption of a catalogue of rights for citizens of the Union accompanied by the establishment of a European Ombudsman to protect those rights.[67] The Danish government supported the main gist of the idea, first in its proposals for the Intergovernmental Conference and later in a set of draft treaty articles on a European Ombudsman. The core of these draft articles is reproduced in the final treaty text of the Treaty on European Union and links the concept of citizenship and the European Ombudsman. Article 21 of the Treaty states that "Every citizen of the Union may apply to the ombudsman established in accordance with Article 195."

In contrast to the World Bank Inspection Panel, the name of the new institution refers directly to the ombudsman concept. A closer analysis of the European Ombudsman makes clear that the institution also substantively refers to the concept in the sense that it has many characteristics of a classical ombudsman.

Article 195 of the EC Treaty states the mandate of the Ombudsman. He is empowered to:

> Receive complaints from any citizen of the Union or any natural or legal person residing or having its headquarters in a Member State concerning instances of maladministration in the activities of the Community institutions or bodies, with the exception of the Court of Justice and the Court of First Instance acting in their judicial role.

The mandate demonstrates that the protection ensured by the Ombudsman actually goes beyond the European Union citizenship, because apart from citizens, persons residing in the Union are eligible to make a complaint. Heede explains that the requirement that the complainant must reside in a member state is interpreted extensively by the Ombudsman. It is not necessary that the residence of the complainant has been legalized but it is sufficient that the person is actually present in the territory of the Union.[68] The complainant is not required to have a direct and personal interest. An *actio popularis* concerning broader systemic issues is also admissible. The complaint must allow the person lodging the complaint and the object to be identified by the

66 For an analysis of European citizenship see J. Shaw, *The Interpretation of European Union Citizenship*, 61 Modern Law Review 293 (1998).

67 E. Marias, *The European Ombudsman: Competences and Relations with the Other Community Institutions and Bodies*, in E. Marias (Ed.), the European Ombudsman: Working Document 71 (1994), at 73.

68 Heede, *supra* note 62, at 117.

Ombudsman, but the person lodging the complaint may request that his complaint remain confidential toward others.[69]

The precise scope of the mandate in relation to the different Union pillars is unclear. The transfer provisions in the Treaty of Amsterdam include the Ombudsman in a provision on the Third Pillar concerning Justice and Home Affairs (Article 41 EU), but the transfer provision on the Second Pillar concerning a Common Foreign and Security Policy (Article 28) does not. Heede concludes that the mandate nevertheless includes the activities of the Community authorities under the Second and Third Pillar as well as the activities of the Union organs created under the Third Pillar.[70]

The independence of the Ombudsman is ensured through several provisions in the Maastricht Treaty and the Statute of the Ombudsman. The European Ombudsman is appointed by the European Parliament. In this sense he is different from the classical ombudsman because an organ which is subject to his jurisdiction appoints him. In contrast to the majority of national ombudsmen the European Ombudsman can receive complaints against parliament.[71] Attempts have however been made to ensure independence in other ways. The Maastricht Treaty itself provides that he shall be completely independent in the performance of his duties. The Ombudsman Statute provides that the incumbent shall be chosen from among persons who offer every guarantee of independence, and meet the conditions required for the exercise of the highest judicial office in their country or have the acknowledged competence and experience to undertake the duties of Ombudsman.[72] The Ombudsman shall give a solemn undertaking before the Court of Justice of the European Communities that he will perform his duties with complete independence and impartiality, and he is given privileges and immunities.[73]

A complaint to the European Ombudsman must allege an instance of maladministration in order to be admissible. Neither the Maastricht Treaty nor the European Ombudsman Statute defines the term 'maladministration'. In his first annual report, the Ombudsman gave a provisional definition of maladministration, including failure to respect human rights but also violation of administrative principles such as abuse of power, negligence, avoidable delay and unfairness.[74] In his 1997 annual report the Ombudsman, at the request of the European Parliament, stated that "Maladministration occurs when a public body fails to act in accordance with a rule or principle which is binding upon it."[75] According to the Ombudsman, this means that his first and most essential task must be to establish whether the body had acted law-

---

69 European Ombudsman Statute, Art. 2 (3).

70 Heede, *supra* note 62, at 23.

71 In practice this is not an important part of the mandate of the Ombudsman. The 2001 Report of the European Ombudsman notes that 7 percent of the inquiries started by the Ombudsman concerned Parliament, 2001 Report, at 271.

72 European Ombudsman Statute, Art. 6 (2).

73 *Id.*, Arts. 9 (2) and 10 (3).

74 The European Ombudsman, Report for the Year 1995, para. I.3.2.

75 The European Ombudsman, Report for the Year 1997, at 23.

fully. Other criteria are whether the body has acted in accordance with rules and principles of good administrative behavior.[76] These non-legal standards are secondary, in the sense of coming after a legality review. These rules and principles were elaborated in a Code of Good Administrative Behaviour proposed as draft recommendations by the Ombudsman to Union institutions and bodies in 1999. On 6 September 2001, the European Parliament adopted a document with the same title substantially similar to the Code proposed by the Ombudsman and called on the Ombudsman to apply it in examining whether there is maladministration.[77] The Ombudsman has stated that institutions and officials who follow the Code can be sure that they will thereby avoid instances of maladministration.[78]

Even if there is no complaint, the Ombudsman can conduct inquiries on his own initiative, according to Article 195 EC Treaty. In this case, as well as in case of complaints which meet the requirements of admissibility, the Ombudsman has a discretionary right but no obligation to start an inquiry. In case of a complaint he must find that there are 'grounds for an enquiry' (Article 195, paragraph 1, EC Treaty) or consider the enquiry 'justified'(Article 3, paragraph 1, Statute).

The Ombudsman does not have the power to take binding decisions at the outcome of investigations. The most he can do, in cases where maladministration is established and follow-up action appears necessary, is to make a draft recommendation to the institution or body concerned. The institution or body must respond with a detailed opinion within three months. If it fails to respond satisfactorily to a draft recommendation, the Ombudsman can send a report to the European Parliament. The outcome of investigations is reported in the annual, public, report submitted to the European Parliament.

The person lodging the complaint shall be informed by the Ombudsman of the outcome of the inquiries, of the opinion expressed by the institution or body concerned and of any recommendations made by the Ombudsman.[79]

It is reported that the European Ombudsman has constituted a real contribution to the accountability of the European Union.[80] This conclusion is supported by the fact that the Ombudsman institution is included in the treaty establishing a Constitution for Europe, adopted by the Intergovernmental Conference on 18 June 2004.[81] The treaty imports the existing institution into the new structure of the Union. The mandate of the Ombudsman will be to receive, examine and report on complaints about

76 *Id.*, at 25-27

77 The European Ombudsman, Report for the Year 2001, at 19. The text of the Code can be found at www.euro-ombudsman.eu.int/code/en/default.htm.

78 Letter from the European Ombudsman to the President of the European Parliament concerning the European Code of Good Administrative Behaviour, 11 March 2002.

79 European Ombudsman Statute, Art. 3 (7).

80 W. Yeng-Seng, *Le Médiateur Européen; Artisan du Développement du Droit à une Bonne Administration Communautaire*, 15 Revue Trimestrielle des Droits de l'Homme 527 (2004), at 551.

81 Provisional consolidated version of the draft treaty establishing a Constitution for Europe, Intergovernmental Conference document CIG 86/04 of 25 June 2004.

maladministration in the activities of the Union Institutions, bodies, offices or agencies, with the exception of the Court of Justice in its judicial role.[82] Article III-237 of the treaty reproduces the text of the old Article 195 of the EC Treaty without any material changes.[83] The most important difference is that the new treaty no longer leaves any doubt that the mandate of the Ombudsman extends to all the pillars of the EU.

6.4.4.4 The Kosovo Ombudsperson Institution

The UN established an ombudsman institution in Kosovo in November 2000.[84] The legal basis for the institution is Regulation 2000/38 issued by the Special Representative of the Secretary-General in Kosovo. Regulations are instruments used by the United Nations Mission in Kosovo to legislate. Regulation 2000/38 provides that the Ombudsperson shall:

> promote and protect the rights and freedoms of individuals and legal entities and ensure that all persons in Kosovo are able to exercise effectively the human rights and fundamental freedoms safeguarded by international human rights standards, in particular the European Convention on Human Rights and its Protocols and the International Covenant on Civil and Political Rights.

It appears that the establishment of the institution is closely linked to the characteristics of the operation in Kosovo. This operation is not an operation with a limited mandate and powers, but a full-fledged transitional administration of the territory. In Kosovo the UN asserts extensive administrative powers which would normally be exercised by the executive of a national government.[85] It has for example determined the applicable law in the territory, it levies taxes, and it appoints and removes judges and has established post and telecommunications services. In other words, in Kosovo the UN acts very much as any other government does in its territory. This similarity between the administrative activity of the Mission and a state coupled with the lack of a comparable regulatory regime – mainly caused by the immunity from jurisdiction of the Mission before domestic courts – was considered as necessitating the establishment of an ombudsman. The Ombudsperson stated in this regard in his first Special Report that "UNMIK acts as a surrogate state" and that "no democratic state operating under the rule of law accords itself total immunity from any administrative, civil or criminal responsibility."[86]

---

82 *Id.*, Articles I-48 and II-43.

83 *Id.*, Art. III-237.

84 See C. Waters, *Human Rights in an International Protectorate: Kosovo's Ombudsman*, 4 The International Ombudsman Yearbook 141 (2000).

85 See M. Ruffert, *The Administration of Kosovo and East-Timor by the International Community*, 50 International & Comparative Law Quarterly 613 (2001).

86 Special Report No. 1, On the Compatibility with Recognized International Standards of UNMIK Regulation No. 2000/47, 26 April 2001, at 8, para. 23. See also R. Wilde, *Accountability and International Actors in Bosnia and Herzegovina, Kosovo and East Timor*, 7 ILSA Journal of International & Comparative Law 455 (2001), at 457.

The Kosovo Ombudsperson Institution has many of the characteristics of the archetypal ombudsman. For the purpose of achieving his mandate the ombudsperson can receive and investigate complaints from any person or entity in Kosovo concerning human rights violations and actions constituting an abuse of authority by the interim civil administration or any emerging central or local institution.[87] The Ombudsperson however does not have jurisdiction to receive complaints against the international security presence in Kosovo. Regulation 2000/38 provides that "in order to deal with cases involving the international security presence, the Ombudsperson may enter into an agreement with the Commander of the Kosovo Forces".[88] No such agreement has been concluded yet.

A number of provisions in the regulation establishing the institution are designed to ensure the independence of the Ombudsperson. The regulation states that the Ombudsperson shall act independently and that no person or entity may interfere with his or her functions.[89] The Ombudsperson shall be an eminent international figure of high moral character, impartiality and integrity, and he and his staff are given privileges and immunities.[90] On the other hand, the officeholder is appointed and removed by the Special Representative of the Secretary-General, the head of the administration which the Ombudsperson supervises, without consultation with local or international partners. This provision must be seen in the light of the specific political arrangements on the ground. At the time of the drafting of the regulation there were no domestic organs. The drafters thus considered that there was no institutional choice and that only the civilian administration could appoint the ombudsman.[91]

The Ombudsperson's standard of review is whether there has been a violation of human rights and 'abuse of authority'. The interim administration in determining the applicable law in Kosovo has included a variety of international human rights instruments. These instruments bind all persons in Kosovo, including international personnel. There is no definition of 'abuse of authority' in the regulation or the rules of procedure for the Ombudsperson nor has the Ombudsperson given a definition. Waters identifies the failure to explicitly include maladministration as grounds for investigation in the regulation as a shortcoming.[92] In practice however the Ombudsperson seems to interpret the term 'abuse of authority' broadly to include many elements of maladministration as defined by, for example, the European Ombudsman.[93] The reports of the Ombudsperson make it clear that the focus is on human rights.

---

87 UNMIK regulation No. 2000/38 on the Establishment of the Ombudsperson Institution in Kosovo, 30 June 2000, UNMIK/REG/2000/38, section 3 (1).

88 *Id.*, section 3 (4).

89 *Id.*, section 2 (1).

90 *Id.*, sections 6 (1) and 13.

91 See Kosovo International Human Rights Conference, 10-11 December 1999, Conference Documents and Report 127.

92 Waters, *supra* note 84, at 145. It may be noted that a draft regulation on the Ombudsperson did include maladministration. See Kosovo International Human Rights Conference, 10-11 December 1999, Conference Documents and Report 121.

93 In his second annual report the Ombudsperson states that complaints concerning failure of administrative authorities to respond to proper requests and arbitrary or discriminatory

Of special interest is the fact that the Ombudsperson has used international humanitarian law as a standard of reference. In a Special Report on the legality of the UNMIK regulation granting UNMIK and KFOR immunity from jurisdiction in the Kosovar courts (Regulation 2000/47), the Ombudsperson focuses on the consequences of the immunity from legal process. One consequence is the lack of compensation and procedural mechanisms for obtaining compensation in respect of the taking and continuing occupation of private property of individual residents of Kosovo. It is worthwhile to cite extensively from the Ombudsperson's Report:

> Section 7 of UNMIK Regulation 2000/47, which addresses third party liability of KFOR, UNMIK or their respective personnel for, inter alia [sic], reads in pertinent part as follows: Third party claims for property loss or damage .... arising from or directly attributed to KFOR, UNMIK or their respective personnel and which do not arise from 'operational necessity' of either international presence, shall be settled by Claims Commissions established by KFOR and UNMIK, in the manner to be provided for.
>
> The Ombudsperson recalls that Article 1 of Protocol No. 1 of the European Convention on Human Rights can be considered to provide certain procedural protections that are necessary to ensure the effective protection of the right to property. The Ombudsperson also recalls that the European Court of Human Rights has found the inability of an individual to participate in fair proceedings that are determinative of his or her property rights to be a significant factor in concluding that an interference imposed an 'individual and excessive burden' on an individual so that that interference failed to strike the necessary fair balance between the relevant competing interests (Hentrich v. France judgment of 22 September 1994, Series A No. 296, pp. 20-21, paras. 43-48).
>
> Regarding the procedures envisioned under Section 7 of UNMIK Regulation 2000/47, the Ombudsperson first observes that an individual wishing to lodge a claim against KFOR or UNMIK must meet two threshold requirements in order to have the claim reviewed by the future Claims Commissions. First, he or she must establish that the matter at issue arose from or was directly attributed to KFOR, UNMIK or their respective personnel. Second, he or she must show that the matter at issue did not arise from 'operational necessity' of either international presence. The Ombudsperson observes that, whereas an individual may reasonably be expected to establish an arguable claim regarding the former criterion, with regard to the latter criterion both the individual and the respondent party or parties must necessarily have their views heard. However, neither Section 7 nor any other Section of Regulation 2000/47 envisions procedural mechanisms for the conduct of any effective inquiry into the 'operational necessity' of the contested act, whether as a threshold requirement for gaining access to the future Claims Commissions or in the context of procedures before the future Claims Commissions. As this preliminary inquiry is therefore directly decisive

---

administrative decisions were treated as complaints against abuse of authority. Second Annual Report of the Ombudsperson Institution in Kosovo, at 9.

> of the outcome of any ensuing civil proceeding, the full panoply of procedural protections afforded by Article 6 of the European Convention on Human Rights must be guaranteed (Ringeisen v. Austria judgment of 16 July 1971, Series A No. 13).

In this respect the Ombudsperson investigated whether the provision on third party liability in UNMIK Regulation 2000/47 complied with certain procedural protections provided by Article 1 of Protocol No. 1 to the European Convention on Human Rights. He determined that this was not the case because the requirement that an individual wishing to lodge a claim against KFOR or UNMIK must show that the matter did not arise from "operational necessity" of either international presence is not accompanied by a provision that the views of both parties are heard. In this context the Ombudsperson observed that:

> Going beyond consideration even of standards set forth under Article 15 of the Convention, the Ombudsperson observes that even in the event that Kosovo were to be considered in a state of armed conflict, as opposed to a state of emergency or a state of peace, the 1949 Geneva Conventions reinforce the views expressed in the preceding discussion. Article 147 of the Geneva Convention Relative to the Protection of Civilian Persons in Time of War of August 12, 1949 (Geneva Convention IV), for example, includes in its definition of 'grave breaches' of the Geneva Convention the following:
>
> ...wilful killing, torture or inhuman treatment, ... wilfully causing great suffering or serious injury to body or health,... and extensive destruction and appropriation of property, not justified by military necessity and carried out unlawfully....
>
> The Ombudsperson considers that the additional requirement, even during wartime, of 'military' necessity for the appropriation of property, implies a much stricter standard than does the 'operational' necessity provided for in Section 7 of UNMIK Regulation 2000/47. The Ombudsperson therefore considers that by permitting UNMIK and KFOR to invoke 'operational necessity' to preclude any review of allegations that their actions caused harm that could fall within the category of grave breaches of Geneva Convention IV, Section 7 of UNMIK Regulation 2000/47 fails to meet any reasonable standard of proportionality.[94]

Several conclusions can be drawn from the passages cited. First, the reference to international humanitarian law is apparently an indirect reference in the sense that international humanitarian law is used to interpret human rights. Regulation 2000/38 does not include international humanitarian law as such in the standards of review which the Ombudsman is mandated to use.

Secondly, the Ombudsperson appears to deliberately leave open the possibility that international humanitarian law does apply to the situation in Kosovo. If this is a valid conclusion, it is however unclear why the Ombudsperson has refrained

---

94 Special Report No. 1, On the Compatibility with Recognized International Standards of UNMIK Regulation No. 2000/47, 26 April 2001, at 13.

from referring to international humanitarian law in any of his other special or annual reports.

Finally, the passage cited makes clear that where possible the Ombudsperson indirectly exercises jurisdiction over KFOR, in spite of the lack of a formal basis for jurisdiction.

6.5 Proposal for an ombudsman in peace support operations

The discussion of the ombudsman concept in national and international context makes clear that the ombudsman is potentially an appropriate mechanism to ensure, or at least improve, accountability for breaches of individual rights under international humanitarian law, and that the concept has been introduced successfully at the international level. At the root of the concept is the idea that an ombudsman can be a remedial mechanism where the rights of individuals are affected by the administration. This administration can be complete, as in the case of a state or an international transitional administration, but individual rights can also be affected where administration is not complete, as in the case of peace support operations. Moreover, in the case of peace support operations there are generally few alternatives for individuals to implement the accountability of the operation. In particular in peace support operations the following statement by Wellens applies:

> The distinct, remedial role of an ombudsman within the accountability regime of international organizations becomes more important as its complementary character is so low given the limited availability of other non-legal or legal remedial opportunities and mechanisms.[95]

The cases of the World Bank Inspection Panel, the European Ombudsman and the Ombudsperson Institution in Kosovo make clear that an ombudsman at the international level must have certain indispensable characteristics to be an effective accountability mechanism. These characteristics are the same as the irreducible characteristics of the 'classical' ombudsman at the national level: independence, impartiality and fairness, credibility of the review process and confidentiality. The constituent documents of the institutions all contain provisions designed to ensure these requirements. This observation provides a basis for a proposal for an ombudsman in peace support operations. The proposal concerns the establishment of an ombudsman for UN peace support operations, and another for NATO peace support operations.

An ombudsman in peace support operations should preferably be a standing institution. This would ensure that an accountability mechanism is available at the start of an operation. In contrast, the Kosovo Ombudsperson Institution was established more than a year after the beginning of the international administration. A General Assembly resolution would be the preferred legal basis for an ombudsman for UN peace support operations. Such a resolution adopted by the UN principal organ with the widest representation would lend the institution legitimacy. However,

95 K. Wellens, Remedies Against International Organisations 181 (2002).

negotiations in the General Assembly might lead to a political compromise and therefore an ombudsman which would not have the required characteristics. The UN Secretary-General could also establish such an ombudsman in his capacity as the commander of peace support operations.[96] The legal basis for a NATO peace support operations ombudsman should be a decision by the North Atlantic Council. This is the only NATO organ institutionally capable of taking such a decision. A decision by the Secretary-General is not appropriate because he has only limited powers. He is responsible for promoting and directing the process of consultation and decision-making throughout the alliance. He may propose items for discussion and decision and has the authority to use his good offices in cases of dispute between member countries.[97]

The UN ombudsman could be appointed by the Secretary-General in consultation with the ICRC and the UN General Assembly Special Committee on Peacekeeping Operations. Consultation with the ICRC would provide input from an organization with special expertise. Consultation with troop contributing states would increase trust in these states that the ombudsman is impartial and has no hidden political agenda.

The NATO ombudsman could be appointed by the North Atlantic Council in consultation with the ICRC.

The standing character of the ombudsman would contribute to the independence of the office because the ombudsman would be free to criticize without fear that the office would be abolished or not created in a next peace support operation. Another measure to ensure independence would be to give the ombudsman privileges and immunities. There should also be a requirement that candidates for the office be of high moral character, impartiality and integrity, who possess a demonstrated commitment to respect for, and expertise in, international humanitarian law. The office should also be adequately staffed and financed.

The ombudsman's mandate should be to receive and investigate complaints from any person or entity in the host state concerning violations of international humanitarian law. Violations of international humanitarian law should include not only grave breaches of the 1949 Geneva Conventions and Additional Protocol I, but also 'common' violations. This subdivision of violations of international humanitarian law is important mainly in respect of individual criminal liability but not for accountability purposes. A 'common' violation can have great impact on the lives of individuals in the host state. International law can be defined as customary international law where conduct is attributable to the UN or NATO and additionally the treaty and customary law obligations of troop contributing states where conduct is attributable to them. Where necessary the ombudsman will need to apply international humanitarian law *mutatis mutandis*. In this way he can contribute to the development of doctrine in this field of law. The institution is particularly suitable for this task: because the ombudsman's recommendations are not binding, he can be more flexible. Secondly, application of the law will be well argued because the ombudsman depends on well-argued

96 See also Bongiorno, *supra* note 19, at 683-685.

97 NATO Handbook 220 (2001).

recommendations and the power of persuasion to gain the trust and cooperation of the complainants and respondents.

The ombudsman should have jurisdiction over the UN and NATO respectively, and over troop contributing states, each for conduct of peace support operations which is attributable to them. Jurisdiction should not be limited to the international organizations. This would provide an escape clause for the organizations which could point to troop contributing states instead of engaging in meaningful dialogue with the ombudsman. Jurisdiction over troop contributing states could be provided by including a clause in participating state agreements in which the states accept the jurisdiction. The organization should make acceptance mandatory for participation in a peace support operation.

It should be possible for individuals and legal entities to lodge a complaint with the ombudsman. This would enable non-governmental organizations to play a role to protect the rights of individuals who might be too intimidated to make a complaint themselves. Non-governmental organizations have proven that they can play an important role in exposing violations of the law by peace support operations. For this reason an entity should not have to demonstrate that it has an interest of its own. The ombudsman should have the power to maintain the confidentiality of complainants. Complainants may have a legitimate fear of persecution, intimidation or retribution by the entity or person that they complain about and it should be possible to protect the complainant.[98]

The ombudsman should have broad powers of investigation as well as access to places and documents, but there should also be a possibility for international organizations and troop contributing states to protect vital security interests. Protection of such information is particularly necessary in situations where international humanitarian law applies and disclosure of information may directly endanger the lives of members of the operation.

The ombudsman should state the outcome of an investigation in his findings. If he finds that there has been a violation of international humanitarian law, he should make recommendations to the respondent to remedy the situation. The respondent should be obliged to respond to the findings. The findings and recommendations of the ombudsman as well as the reaction of the respondent should be made public by the ombudsman. The UN ombudsman should have the obligation to present a public annual report to the UN Secretary-General. The NATO ombudsman should have the obligation to present a public annual report to the North Atlantic Council.

The specific function of the ombudsman makes the office complementary to the claims commission proposed above. For this reason the fact that a claims commission is dealing with the same matter should not make a complaint to the ombudsman inadmissible. To preserve the independence and avoid the impression that the ombudsman is concerned with formal responsibility there should be no direct relationship between the two institutions.

---

98 African Rights reported that several Somalis who tried to complain against conduct by the United Nations Operation in Somalia were intimidated. African Rights, Somalia: Human Rights Abuses by the United Nations Forces 16 (1993).

6.6 Conclusion

This chapter has proposed mechanisms for implementing the responsibility and accountability of peace support operations. It has focused in particular on mechanisms which are available to individuals. This focus is justified on the one hand by the fact that the present remedial regime is in an immature state especially for non-state claimants in comparison to states,[99] and on the other by the practical need for peace support operations to foster the support of those individuals. As Bedont argues in respect of the UN:

> The crimes committed by peacekeepers bring the UN into disrepute and reduce the trust of the local community in the mission. This lack of confidence of the local community in the peacekeeping operation can further compromise the success of the mission.[100]

To avoid such a reduction of trust it is not sufficient to acknowledge that international rules are applicable. It is also necessary to provide redress when these rules are breached. This is slowly being recognized in the UN, but NATO lags far behind.[101]

The mechanisms proposed are to a large extent based on mechanisms which, although not used in practice, are provided for in institutional instruments or institutional proposals. In other words, the basis for these mechanisms is on the table. Hopefully this will make the proposals for a permanent claims commission and an ombudsman for peace support operations more acceptable to states and the organization. On the other hand, the additional elements proposed are revolutionary. One new element is the possibility of directly invoking the breach of an international right, making the claims commission from a private law or *sui generis* mechanism into an international mechanism. Another element is the extension of a permanent claims commission's jurisdiction over troop contributing states. The organizations and their member states will have to muster considerable political will to realize these proposals, and there is a possibility that they will not be able to do so. In the case of NATO, the direction that negotiations on an out-of-area claims policy have taken is an indication. This is why this book proposes that at the very least, the organization and its member states consider dispensing with the principle that combat-related claims are inadmissible in claims settlement procedures. In respect of UN operations it may be noted that the government of the Netherlands did not adopt the recommendation by a governmental advisory committee to lobby for the establishment of a Central

---

99 Wellens, *supra* note 95, at 265.

100 Bedont, *supra* note 19.

101 Non-governmental organizations do urge the establishment of accountability mechanisms in North Atlantic Treaty Organization peace support operations. See *e.g.* Amnesty International, Kosovo: Amnesty Urges Accountability in KFOR, 6 January 2000, AI Index EUR 70/01/00; *Kritiek Amnesty op VN en KFOR*, NRC Handelsblad 14 March 2000; Amnesty International, The Apparent Lack of Accountability of International Peace-keeping Forces in Kosovo and Bosnia-Herzegovina, 1 April 2004, AI Index EUR 05/002/2004.

Claims Commission which would be able to receive claims from victims of wrongful acts by UN peace support operations.[102]

The more the idea takes root that troop contributing states cannot free themselves from their own obligations under human rights and international humanitarian law by placing troops at the disposal of an international organization, and it is accepted that monitoring mechanisms enforce these obligations, the less imperative it is that permanent claims commissions have jurisdiction over troop contributing states. At the same time, this could make the proposal more attractive to troop contributing states because if there is an independent claims commission, the chances that states would have to appear before human rights monitoring bodies would decrease.

It must be noted that the permanent claims commission and an ombudsman are complementary mechanisms. They are both necessary if accountability is to be implemented in all its components.[103] The ombudsman cannot implement responsibility in the legal sense, and the permanent claims commission is not the most appropriate mechanism for implementing accountability in the more political sense.

102 Bijlagen Handelingen II, 2001-02, 28000 V, 68.
103 Wellens, *supra* note 95, at 179.

Findings and conclusions

1 Findings

This study examined the scope and content of responsibility and accountability for breaches of international humanitarian law by peace support operations. More specifically, it examined peace support operations under the command and control of the UN and NATO. The term 'peace support operation' denotes, for the purposes of this study, the following:

> Multifunctional operations, conducted impartially, normally in support of an internationally recognized organization such as the UN or OSCE, involving military forces and diplomatic and humanitarian agencies. Peace support operations are designed to achieve a long-term political settlement or other specified conditions. They include peacekeeping and peace enforcement as well as conflict prevention, peacemaking, peacebuilding and humanitarian relief.

This definition is taken from NATO doctrine. Since international humanitarian law is principally relevant in relation to armed forces, and peacekeeping and peace enforcement are the types of peace support operations which are mainly the province of the armed forces, this study focuses mainly on these types of peace support operations. These types of operations must be distinguished, on the grounds of the principle of impartiality which is central to them, from enforcement action or war. The term 'peace support operations' gives rise to questions concerning the relation between this term and the different international operations which have been established with a peace function. Many of these questions are directly relevant to international policy and national and international military doctrine, but not to international law. From a legal perspective, and in particular from the perspective of the responsibility for breaches of international humanitarian law, the legal or institutional status, and command and control relationships in these operations are important, principally because of their consequences for the attribution of conduct of peace support operations. Although these quantities are determined separately for every peace support operation, practice in the UN and NATO demonstrates certain patterns. UN operations comprise national contingents placed at the disposal of the organization by troop contributing states. The operations are subsidiary organs of the Security Council, or, exceptionally, of the General Assembly or the Secretary-General. They are brought under UN command and control by agreement between the organization and troop contributing states, although the troop contributing states do not always respect this agreement.

NATO peace support operations are also composed of troops contributed by states, including non-member states of the organization. These operations are subsidiary organs of the organization, being established by the organization and command and control being conferred on a NATO commander who delegates it to the force commander. It is not correct to say that member states merely use NATO as a facilitating instrument in establishing peace support operations.

It only makes sense to refer to peace support operations as organs of NATO if the organization has international legal personality. Considerable confusion is caused in this respect because some writers incorrectly equate having international legal personality with being a supranational international organization. Once this confusion is dispelled, it seems that NATO does have international legal personality and has on a number of occasions been treated accordingly by states, including member states, and other international bodies.

One reason why this finding is important is that this study argues that legal personality is central to the application of the principles of international responsibility. International legal personality is the capacity to have rights and obligations under international law. International responsibility is, in a sense, the corollary of the obligations under international law which an international organization is capable of having by virtue of its international legal personality.[1] The institution of responsibility is at least in part a defense of the legal order against breaches by a subject of that legal order, as the ILC underlines in respect of state responsibility when it states that:

> Over and above the gravity or effects of individual cases, the rules and institutions of State responsibility are significant for the maintenance of respect for international law and for the achievement of the goals which States advance through law-making at the international level.[2]

Now that international organizations are also subjects of international law there is no reason to make a distinction between states and international organizations, because an internationally wrongful act of an international organization is not less detrimental, and maybe more so, to upholding the international rule of law as an internationally wrongful act of a state.

International responsibility is a component of the broader concept of international accountability. Accountability is a complex concept, which is particularly receiving attention among international lawyers in its application between international organizations and individuals. As such, the concept also has certain implications for peace support operations, in that expectations are raised for the establishment of mechanisms to implement the different components of their accountability.

State practice in respect of UN peace support operations demonstrates the application *mutatis mutandis* of article 6 of the ILC draft articles on state responsibility. The conduct of troops placed at the disposal of the UN by a state shall be considered an act of the organization if the troops are acting in the exercise of the authority of the organization at whose disposal they have been placed. The corresponding principle in the ILC draft articles was developed in part on the basis of practice concerning

1 P. Klein, La Responsabilité des Organisations Internationales dans les Ordres Juridiques Internes et en Droit des Gens 3 (1998).

2 Report of the International Law Commission on the work if its fifty-third session, 23 April – 1 June and 2 July – 10 August 2001 (A/56/10), at 213, para. 1.

conduct of organs placed at the disposal of international organizations, in particular national contingents placed at the disposal of the UN for participating in ONUC. The application of this principle is supported by a body of subsequent practice, as well as by the work of the ILC to date on the responsibility of international organizations. The command and control exercised by the UN over peace support operations is the essential element and condition for the application of this principle of attribution, because as a consequence the national contingents constituting the operations are under the organization's direction and control. It is also relevant that peace support operations have exclusively international functions and as a consequence no longer act in the exercise of elements of the governmental authority of the respective troop contributing states.

State practice in respect of UN peace support operations is inconclusive concerning the responsibility of member states for the conduct of that organization. Writers have put forward a number of different theories concerning responsibility of member states for conduct which is attributable to the organization, theories which are concerned with lifting the so-called 'organizational veil'. These theories can be distinguished according to whether they make member states responsible for conduct which breaches an obligation of the organization, or of the member states itself. Another distinction can be made according to whether member state responsibility is concurrent or secondary, that is whether it can be invoked at the same time as the responsibility of the organization itself or only after the responsibility of the organization has been invoked and the organization has failed to make reparation. The practice examined in this study at most justifies the conclusion that member state responsibility is secondary, because in those cases where international responsibility has been invoked for the conduct of UN peace support operations in breach of international humanitarian law the claims were generally addressed to the UN.

State practice in respect of UN peace support operations does not provide support for the attribution of conduct of national contingents to troop contributing states unless the troop contributing state exercises direction and control over its contingent in a particular case. The agreement in which troop contributing states transfer command and control to the UN establishes a presumption that this is not the case in that particular situation. The fact that disciplinary and penal jurisdiction lie with the troop contributing states does not constitute a form of direction and control.

This does not exclude the possibility that troop contributing states can be held internationally responsible for their own conduct, in particular the act of placing a national contingent at the disposal of the UN. The 1949 Geneva Conventions and Additional Protocol I require that states parties respect and ensure respect for these instruments. It can be argued that placing a national contingent at the disposal of the UN without adequate guarantees that the organization will respect international humanitarian law is a breach of this obligation. If in these circumstances the national contingent would breach international humanitarian law, the troop contributing state would arguably be responsible. The precise scope of the due diligence obligation placed on states parties by the obligation to ensure respect needs fleshing out by state practice. There is as yet little practice to support this theory of troop contributing responsibility for breaches of international humanitarian law, but more generally the theory that a state can be responsible for the transfer of competences to an international organization is supported by human rights case-law.

State practice concerning international responsibility in respect of NATO peace support operations is rare if not non-existent. Claims settlement procedures govern private and not international law claims. International procedures arising out of Operation Allied Force are instructive because the command and control relationships in that operation were similar to those in peace support operations. In both cases the troops involved were national troops placed at the disposal of the organization and under the command and control of a NATO commander, who was subordinate to the North Atlantic Council.

During the proceedings in the *Banković* case (ECHR) and *the Legality of the Use of Force* cases (ICJ), the applicants and respondents put forward observations concerning possible bases of attribution of conduct of troops involved in Operation Allied Force. The theories put forward in the *Legality of the Use of Force* cases are especially interesting. The European Court of Human Rights declared the application in *Banković* inadmissible without addressing the question of attribution of conduct. The Federal Republic of Yugoslavia appears to have argued in the *Use of Force* cases that the respondents used their military forces for bombing, and that the military forces are organs of the state and their acts are attributable to the state. This argument can only be made under the assumption that either NATO does not have international legal personality, or that the national troops were not effectively placed under the direction and control of the organization and acted in fact on behalf of the states. If the ICJ would accept the latter assumption, and considering that the command and control relationships in peace support operations are similar, this would argue against the organization being responsible for conduct of national contingents in peace support operations on the basis of direction and control over the contingents on an analogy with article 6 of the ILC draft articles.

Conduct which is attributed to a state, or to the UN or NATO, only leads to international responsibility if it constitutes a breach of an international obligation of the state or organization. The obligations of states under international humanitarian law are relatively clear, in contrast to the obligations of the UN and NATO. Practice points to the conclusion that it is accepted that the UN is bound by a corpus of international humanitarian law norms. From the first peace support operations, the organization assured that it would respect the principles and spirit of international humanitarian law, and it considered itself responsible for breaches of those principles as illustrated by the compensation paid pursuant to claims made in connection with ONUC. In the course of time the recognition of the scope of the obligations has developed, to the point where the UN Secretary-General, in the Bulletin on the Observance by United Nations Forces of International Humanitarian Law, has acknowledged that the UN is bound by principles and rules, instead of the principles and spirit, of international humanitarian law. It is still not clear precisely which rules the organization considers are applicable and which are not applicable.

State practice confirms that the UN is bound by international humanitarian law but it does not clarify the legal basis for this conclusion. Such a legal basis is not found in international humanitarian law treaties, to which the organization is not and cannot become a party. It can be found under certain conditions in the UN Charter. Under Article 24 read together with Article 1 (1) the Security Council is bound to act in conformity with international law, except when it is acting under Chapter VII. The only possible exception to the possibility of derogation concerns peremptory norms. If the Council derogates from international law, it should do so expressly and unambiguously. Under Article 24 read together with Article 1 (3) the organization is arguably also bound to respect international humanitarian law. Although this article does not provide for the possibility of derogation by the Security Council when it is acting under Chapter VII, a systematic reading of the Charter points to the possibility of such an exception.

The UN is also bound by international humanitarian law as general international law. International organizations are bound by the obligations under general international law which are attendant to their functions. The organizations are bound by international law because they partake of personality under this system. Their obligations are circumscribed by the principle of functionality, that is to say by the question of whether the obligations are necessary for the effective exercise of the organization's functions. The application of international humanitarian law to UN peace support operations engaged in armed conflict is necessary in the sense that the unrestrained conduct of armed conflict is unthinkable, and would destroy the element of crude reciprocity that protects personnel in peace support operations. The application of international humanitarian law is also necessary for, or at least its non-application would be greatly detrimental to, the achievement of several of the organization's purposes. The application of international humanitarian law to non-state entities is not revolutionary, its application to armed groups having been accepted. The UN and certain other international organizations have a fundamental characteristic in common with armed groups, namely that they are capable of implementing the rules. In the same way as members of armed opposition groups to which international humanitarian law applies, peace support operation personnel are under a responsible command.

State practice does not point to the recognition by NATO or its member states that the organization has obligations under international humanitarian law, although there are some signs that third parties consider it has. The attitude in the organization seems to be linked to the rejection by some of the idea that the organization has international legal personality. It seems however that the organization does have international legal personality. Under those circumstances it must also be bound by general international law as circumscribed by the principle of functionality, and consequently when it engages in armed conflict it must be bound by international humanitarian law. The application of international humanitarian law is an obligation which is 'attendant to' the organization's deployment of peace support operations, to use the words of the ICJ.[3]

In case a peace support operation becomes a party to a conflict, the regime of international armed conflicts, not the more limited regime of non-international con-

3 Reparations for Injuries Suffered in the Service of the United Nations, Advisory Opinion of 11 April 1949, 1949 ICJ Reports 174, at 180.

flicts, is applicable. The principal reason is that because international organizations such as the UN and NATO do not enjoy sovereignty, there is no question of deferring to sovereignty by limiting the applicable rules. The Secretary-General's Bulletin avoids the question by applying a uniform regime to all cases in which peace support operation personnel become combatants, following a trend to blur the distinction between international and non-international conflicts. As long as the distinction still plays a role, state practice supports the application of the regime of international conflicts to peace support operations, including in case the opponent is not a state.

In principle it seems to be accepted that the threshold of application of international humanitarian law to peace support operations is to be determined by the threshold in customary international law. State practice demonstrates that hostilities involving a peace support operation need to have a relatively high level of intensity before the operation's personnel is considered combatant. It cannot be excluded that the political desire to consider an operation as impartial as long as possible plays a role in this respect.

Most state practice does not support the application of the law of occupation to peace support operations. This might be linked to the policy consideration that applying the law of occupation would be detrimental to creating 'ownership' of a peace process among the local authorities and population. It is questionable whether this policy consideration leads to the conclusion that the law of occupation is not applicable. On the contrary, this regime seems to provide a much-needed legal framework. In addition, the Security Council can derogate from specific rules if necessary.

There is a close relationship between the limited number of instances in which international responsibility for the conduct of peace support operations has actually been invoked, and an examination of the legal consequences of the conduct. In principle prior invocation of responsibility is not necessary for legal consequences to arise. Legal consequences flow automatically from an internationally wrongful act. This is underlined in the ILC draft articles on state responsibility which state the consequences of a wrongful act in terms of general international obligations of the responsible state and not as specific rights of an injured party.[4] Without invocation of responsibility, however, it is frequently unclear whether measures taken by an author state or organization must be considered as legal consequences of an internationally wrongful act.

On the whole, state practice does not contradict the application of the provisions in the ILC draft articles on state responsibility concerning legal consequences to UN peace support operations. Exceptions are certain forms of satisfaction, specifically disciplinary or penal action against individuals. The exercise of disciplinary and penal jurisdiction by troop contributing states is a consequence of delegation by the UN, which does not have a full fledged judicial system, to the troop contributing states.

Expressions of apology by SFOR for conduct of personnel of national contingents are difficult to reconcile with arguments that NATO does not have international

---

4 D. Shelton, *Righting Wrongs: Reparations in the Articles on State Responsibility*, 96 American Journal of International Law 833 (2002), at 839.

legal personality and as a consequence cannot be internationally responsible. Apart from these instances, state practice is too scarce to base conclusions on.

The invocation of international responsibility for breaches of international (humanitarian) law by peace support operations presents a paradox. States have relatively many possibilities to invoke the international responsibility of another state or another organization. In respect of the invocation of international responsibility this is particularly the case if the state is a member of the organization and can consequently put forward claims in the organs of the organization in which it is represented. The possibilities for the invocation of responsibility have increased as a consequence of a shift from bilateralism to multilateralism in the law of responsibility. This new paradigm is expressed in the ILC draft articles, which do not only allow injured states but also states with a legal interest to invoke responsibility. Such an interest attaches to at least some rules of international humanitarian law. This is confirmed by common Article 1 of the Geneva Conventions and Additional Protocol I, which in the form of a primary rule constitutes a forerunner of the secondary rule embodied in article 48 of the ILC draft articles. Hitherto, states have hardly utilized the possibilities at their disposal for invoking international responsibility for violations of international humanitarian law by peace support operations and this is unlikely to change. Political considerations play a role when states decide whether or not to invoke responsibility. In addition, the multilateral element of international responsibility is weighted in favor of an institutional, particularly a UN, response which is unlikely in case this organization has a stake in the matter because it has established or authorized the operation concerned.

An individual on the other hand has very few effective possibilities to invoke international responsibility for a violation of international humanitarian law by a peace support operation, although it is likely that many individuals would make use of this possibility if it were available. The law of responsibility and specifically the ILC draft articles neglect the individual, although this was not the case at the beginning of the ILC project.[5] Although the individual can be said to have individual rights under international humanitarian law, this does not automatically imply that he can invoke a breach of those rights either directly under international law or indirectly under domestic law or through claims settlement mechanisms. In this respect Article 3 of the Hague Convention (IV) 1907 does not provide *lex specialis* as is sometimes asserted.

Domestic procedures (where available), claims settlement procedures created specifically for peace support operations, and human rights monitoring bodies do not effectively mitigate this lack of legal protection of the individual. This is problematic for the individuals concerned but also for peace support operations, as they risk losing much of their legitimacy, a loss which is likely to have a negative impact on the achievement of their mandate.

Although a right to a remedy for individuals under international humanitarian law has not (yet) been recognized, there is considerable logical force to establishing

5 E. Brown Weiss, *Invoking State Responsibility in the Twenty-First Century*, 96 American Journal of International Law 798 (2002).

mechanisms for individuals to invoke the responsibility and accountability of states and international organizations for breaches of international humanitarian law by peace support operations. First, this is a logical next step after the recognition that individuals are right-holders, and not mere beneficiaries, under international humanitarian law. An individual right without a remedy is likely to be illusory. Secondly, the lack of a complaint mechanism diminishes the legitimacy of the international organizations concerned as well as the operational effectiveness of peace support operations, as they require the support of the local population in their area of operations.

This study proposes the establishment of a permanent claims commission based on Article 51 of the United Nations Model Status of Forces Agreement. The commission would be able to receive claims of a private law nature as well as claims of breaches of international humanitarian law by UN peace support operations. It would be able to consider complaints against the UN and troop contributing states, depending on the entity to which the conduct complained of was attributable.

The establishment of a similar mechanism in respect of NATO peace support operations is also proposed. This proposal could be introduced in negotiations on an out-of-area claims policy for the organization. The commission would be able to receive complaints against the organization as well as against troop contributing states. If the organization continues on the other hand to organize claims settlement mechanisms on the model of the SFOR claims commissions, it is proposed that it change the policy that all combat-related claims are inadmissible, because this includes claims for alleged violations of international humanitarian law.

In addition to permanent claims commissions, this study proposes the establishment of an ombudsperson in UN and NATO peace support operations. Such an ombudsperson could achieve broader objectives of accountability than claims commissions which are only concerned with its responsibility component. An ombudsperson is also an appropriate institution for further exploring which rules of international humanitarian law can only be applied *mutatis mutandis* by international organizations, and the nature of the mutation required.

2 Main conclusions

The proposal for a mechanism enabling individuals to invoke the international responsibility of the UN and NATO under international humanitarian law implies that these organizations are responsible for their internationally wrongful acts. It has long been recognized that the UN is capable of being internationally responsible.[6] This study demonstrates that in principle NATO can also be internationally responsible. It has provided a theoretical basis for the responsibility of international organizations which is centered on their international legal personality and on the purposes of international responsibility, in particular the purpose of upholding the rule of law in the interest of the international community as a whole. The practice in respect of UN

6 *E.g.* P. de Visscher, *Observations sur le Fondement et la Mise en Oeuvre du Principe de la Responsabilité de l'Organisation des Nations Unies*, 23 Annales de Droit et de Sciences Politiques 133 (1963).

peace support operations examined demonstrates that the principles of state responsibility in the ILC draft articles on state responsibility can in most cases be applied to international organizations without any changes. On the other hand it must be recognized that the state practice examined is limited and only relates to one type of activity and that consequently its importance for the ILC's work on the responsibility of international organizations should not be overestimated. It may be noted, however, that practice relating to peace support operations has played a relatively important role in the ILC's work on the responsibility of international organizations hitherto. Partly on this basis, the ILC has until now largely followed the course of applying the principles of state responsibility to international organizations. The practice examined does not resolve the controversial question of whether member states of an international organization are responsible for the conduct of that organization, and if they are subject to which conditions, although it was established that member state responsibility is not concurrent.

The pivotal role which international legal personality plays in international law was demonstrated. The international legal personality of international organizations, that is to say their capacity to have rights and obligations under international law, is the basis for holding international organizations responsible. The international legal personality of international organizations is also central to determining their rights and obligations under international law. General international law applies to them precisely because they partake of personality under the system of international law, and its application is circumscribed by the functional nature of the personality concerned. Consequently, it is important to establish whether an international organization has international legal personality. It is insufficient to state that it "is generally recognized that organizations have such capacity, unless there is clear evidence to the contrary",[7] as the case of the NATO illustrates. The case of NATO also illustrates that the determination whether a particular international organization is an international legal person may be controversial. NATO is not unique in this respect: the legal personality of the EU and OSCE has also been disputed. The existence of two different theories on the issue, the subjective and the objective theory, complicates such a determination considerably, although it may be recalled that the subjective theory of international legal personality seems more acceptable than the objective theory. In the specific case of NATO, the lack of transparency in the organization is also relevant. Documents which could shed light on the legal character of the organization are classified. In any event, and whether the subjective or objective theory of international legal personality is taken as a point of departure, it appears that NATO has such personality. This was reaffirmed by a number of states during the oral hearings in the *Legality of the Use of Force* cases in 2004.

This study has demonstrated that international humanitarian law is applicable to UN peace support operations, as well as to NATO peace support operations. Other authors have come to many of the same conclusions on aspects of application of international humanitarian law to UN peace support operations,[8] but these

7 H. Schermers & N. Blokker, International Institutional Law 991 (2003).
8 F. Seyersted, United Nations Forces in the Law of Peace and War (1966).

conclusions are now supported by recent state practice. This includes in particular the Secretary-General's Bulletin on Observance by United Nations Forces of International Humanitarian Law. The applicability of international humanitarian law to UN peace support operations is supported not only by state practice but also by a theoretical underpinning. This underpinning must be seen from the broad perspective of the place of international organizations, and the UN in particular, in international law. The main conclusion in respect of international humanitarian law is that customary rules are applicable to peace support operations *mutatis mutandis*. This study does not include a detailed examination of the customary character of rules of international humanitarian law. Such an examination would necessarily be of limited value because custom is not static. In addition, the ICRC has done important work on the issue of determining the customary status of international humanitarian law norms in a study to be published in 2005. Moreover, international organizations are not precluded from respecting rules that are not customary international law. International humanitarian law generally encourages the voluntary acceptance of obligations.[9] In this context it is pertinent that the Secretary-General's Bulletin includes a number of norms which are clearly not customary.

This study has highlighted common Article 1 to the 1949 Geneva Conventions and Additional Protocol I. This provision plays two important roles. One role relates to the invocation of international responsibility. Common Article 1 establishes that all states parties have an interest in the respect by others of the provisions of the conventions. Consequently, all states parties are entitled to invoke a breach of those provisions. This does not make them 'injured states' in the sense of the ILC draft articles on state responsibility, however. A second role of common Article 1 is concerned with the scope of the obligations in the conventions. There is increasing state practice which accepts that the obligation to 'ensure' respect for the conventions applies between states parties and imposes an obligation to take steps to prevent or end breaches of the conventions by others. The ICJ subscribed to this interpretation of the provision in its Advisory Opinion on the *Legal Consequences of the Construction of a Wall in the Occupied Palestinian Territory*. The UN General Assembly by an overwhelming majority has acknowledged the Advisory Opinion and has called upon all member states of the UN "to comply with legal obligations as mentioned in the Advisory Opinion."[10] Acceptance of such an interpretation of common Article 1 is of tremendous importance for ensuring compliance with international humanitarian law. It is precisely such compliance and the mechanisms to ensure it which are presently at the heart of debates in the international community on international humanitarian law.

The legal position of the individual under international humanitarian law is more ambiguous than that of international organizations as referred to above, and this has important consequences for his legal protection under international humanitarian law, including against breaches of that law by peace support operations. On the one hand, it is accepted that individuals have obligations under international humanitarian law,

9 See common Article 3 of the 1949 Geneva Conventions.

10 General Assembly Tenth Special Emergency Session Resolution ES-10/18 of 20 July 2004, para. 3.

and the enforcement of these obligations has been one of the focal points of international law in recent years. Two *ad hoc* international criminal tribunals and a permanent International Criminal Court have been established to enforce these obligations. On the other hand, the rights of individuals under international humanitarian law have received much less attention, although this field of law does grant rights to individuals. It is disputed by some that this makes individuals subjects of international law, because being a subject of international law would require that rights can be enforced at the international level. This however also applies to a certain extent to international organizations, whose character as subjects of international law is not disputed even though, for example, they do not have standing before the ICJ. More importantly, this is only one dimension of the problem. It seems to be rather futile to give individuals rights without effective mechanisms to which individuals can turn to have these rights enforced, which as this study demonstrated is the case in respect of breaches of international humanitarian law by peace support operations. There is much force to Aldrich's plea for more attention for efforts to improve the ability of individual victims to enforce their rights.[11] It seems particularly appropriate to start these efforts in respect of peace support operations, as has been done in this study through proposals for establishing remedial mechanisms. The establishment of peace support operations is often justified at least in part in reference to the protection of individuals, and accepting these proposals would contribute to that objective, as well as create a best practice that states might be persuaded to follow outside the specific context of peace support operations.

This course of action is ultimately in the interest of the organizations which establish peace support operations, as has been argued throughout this study. An international organization which asserts its own responsibility and, more broadly, its accountability, also asserts its independence in decision-making in general,[12] and unity of command in peace support operations in particular. Moreover, this course of action substantially contributes to the legitimacy of these international organizations and of the activities that their member states and civil society at large expect these organizations to perform.

11 G. Aldrich, *Individuals as Subjects of International Humanitarian Law*, in J. Makarczyk (Ed.), Theory of International Law at the Threshold of the 21st Century: Essays in Honour of Krzysztof Skubiszewski 851 (1996).

12 Klein, *supra* note 1, at 626.

Table of cases

1 Permanent Court of International Justice

Appeal from a Judgment of the Hungaro-Czechoslovak Mixed Arbitral Tribunal *(The Peter Pázmány University* v. *the State of Czechoslovokia)*, Judgment of 15 December 1933, PCIJ Series A/B, No. 61.

Factory at Chorzów (*Germany* v. *Poland*), Indemnity, 1928 PCIJ Series A, No 17.

Factory at Chorzów (*Germany* v. *Poland*), Jurisdiction, 1927, PCIJ. Series A, No. 9.

Mavrommatis Palestine Concessions Case (*Greece* v. *United Kingdom*), Jurisdiction, 1924 PCIJ Series A, No. 2.

2 International Court of Justice

Legal Consequences of the Construction of a Wall in the Occupied Palestinian Territory, Advisory Opinion of 9 July 2004.

Case concerning the Arrest Warrant of 11 April 2000 (*Democratic Republic of the Congo* v. *Belgium*), Judgment of 14 February 2002, reproduced in 41 ILM 536 (2002).

LaGrand case (*Germany* v. *United States of America*), Judgment of 27 June 2001, reproduced in 40 ILM 1069 (2001).

Difference Relating to Immunity from Legal Process of a Special Rapporteur of the Commission on Human Rights, Advisory Opinion of 29 April 1999, 1999 ICJ Reports 62.

Questions of Interpretation and Application of the 1971 Montreal Convention arising from the Aerial Incident at Lockerbie (*Libya* v. *United Kingdom*; *Libya* v. *United States of America*), Preliminary Objections, Judgment of 27 February 1998, 1998 ICJ Reports 9, 115.

Gabčikovo-Nagymaros Project (*Hungary* v. *Slovakia*), Judgment of 25 September 1997, 1997 ICJ Reports 7.

Legality of the Threat or Use of Nuclear Weapons, Advisory Opinion of 8 July 1996, 1996 ICJ Reports 226.

Case concerning East Timor (*Portugal* v. *Australia*), Judgment of 30 June 1995, 1995 ICJ Reports 90.

Application of the Convention on the Prevention and Punishment of the Crime of Genocide (Provisional Measures) (*Bosnia and Herzegovina* v. *Yugoslavia (Serbia & Montenegro)*, Order of 13 September 1993, 1993 ICJ Reports 325.

Questions of Interpretation and Application of the 1971 Montreal Convention arising from the Aerial Incident at Lockerbie (*Libya* v. *United Kingdom*; *Libya* v. *United States of America*), Provisional Measures, Order of 14 April 1992, 1992 ICJ Reports 3, 114.

Military and Paramilitary Activities in and against Nicaragua (*Nicaragua* v. *United States of America*), Merits, Judgment of 27 June 1986, 1986 ICJ Reports 14.

Interpretation of the Agreement of 25 March 1951 between the WHO and Egypt, Advisory Opinion of 20 December 1980, 1980 ICJ Reports 4.

Legal Consequences for States of the Continued Presence of South Africa in Namibia (South West Africa) notwithstanding Security Council Resolution 276 (1970), Advisory Opinion of 21 June 1971, 1971 ICJ Reports 16.

Barcelona Traction, Light and Power Company, Limited (*Belgium* v. *Spain*), Judgment of 5 February 1970, 1970 ICJ Reports 3.

Certain Expenses of the United Nations (Article 17, paragraph 2 of the Charter), Advisory Opinion of 20 July 1962, 1962 ICJ Reports 151.

Effect of Awards of Compensation Made by the United Nations Administrative Tribunal, Advisory Opinion of 13 July 1954, 1954 ICJ Reports 57.

Monetary Gold Removed from Rome in 1943 (*Italy* v. *France, United Kingdom and the United States*), Judgment of 15 June 1954, 1954 ICJ Reports 32.

Reparations for Injuries Suffered in the Service of the United Nations, Advisory Opinion of 11 April 1949, 1949 ICJ Reports 174.

3 International Criminal Tribunal for the former Yugoslavia

Prosecutor v. *Mladen Naletilić and Vinko Martinović*, Judgment, Case No. IT-98-34-T, Tr. Ch. I, 31 March 2003.

Prosecutor v. *Dragan Nikolić*, Decision on Defence Motion Challenging the Exercise of Jurisdiction by the Tribunal, Case No. IT-94-2-PT, Tr. Ch. II, 9 October 2002.

Prosecutor v. *Pavle Strugar et al*, Decision on Defence Preliminary Motion Challenging Jurisdiction, Case No. IT-01-42-PT, Tr. Ch. I, 7 June 2002.

Prosecutor v. *Miroslav Kvočka, Milojica Kos, Mlado Radir, Zoran Žigić and Drogoljub Prcać*, Judgement, Case No. IT-98-30/1, Tr. Ch. I, 2 November 2001.

Prosecutor v. *Radoljub Kunarac, Radomir Kovać and Zoran Vuković*, Judgement, Case No. IT-96-23, Tr. Ch, II, 22 February 2001.

Prosecutor v. *Zejnil Delalić, Zdravko Mucić, Hazim Delić and Esad Landžo ('Čelebići Case')*, Case No. IT-96-21, Judgement, A. Ch., 20 February 2001.

Prosecutor v. *Blagoje Simić, Milan Simić, Miroslav Tadić, Stevan Todorović and Simo Zarić*, Decision on Motion for Judicial Assistance to be Provided by SFOR and Others, Case No. IT-95-9-PT, Tr. Ch. I, 18 October 2000.

Prosecutor v. *Dario Kordić & Mario Čerkez*, Decision on Joint Defence Motion to Dismiss the Amended Indictment for Lack of Jurisdiction based on Limited Jurisdictional Reach of Articles 2 and 3, Case No. IT-95-14/2-PT, Tr. Ch. III, 2 March 1999.

Prosecutor v. *Tihomir Blaskič*, Judgement on the Request of the Republic of Croatia for Review of the Decision of Trial Chamber II of 18 July 1997, Case No. IT-95-14-AR108 bis, A. Ch., 2 October 1997.

Prosecutor v. *Duško Tadić*, Opinion and Judgment ,Case No. IT-94-1, Tr. Ch. II, 7 May 1997.

Prosecutor v. *Duško Tadić*, Decision on the Defence Motion for Interlocutory Appeal on Jurisdiction, Case No. IT-94-1-AR72, A. Ch., 2 October 1995.

4 International Criminal Tribunal for Rwanda

Prosecutor v. *Alfred Musema*, Judgment and Sentence, Case No. ICTR-96-13, Tr. Ch. I, 27 January 2000.

Prosecutor v. *Georges Rutaganda*, Judgment, Case No. ICTR-96-3, Tr. Ch. I, 6 December 1999.

Prosecutor v. *Jean-Paul Akayesu*, Judgment, Case No. ICTR-96-4-T, Tr. Ch. I, 2 September 1998.

5 United Nations Human Rights Committee

Winata v. *Australia*, 16 August 2001, UN Doc. CCPR/C/72/D/930/2000, Communication No. 930/2000.

Des Fours Walderode v. *Czech Republic*, 2 November 2001, UN Doc. CCPR/C/73/D/747/1997, Communication No. 747/1997.

Paul v. *Republic of Guyana*, 21 December 2001, UN Doc. CCPR/C/73/D/728/1996, Communication No. 728/1996.

Lilian Celiberti de Casariego v. *Uruguay*, 29 July 1981, UN Doc. CCPR/C/OP/1, Communication No. 56/1979.

Sergio Euben Lopez Burgos v. *Uruguay*, 29 July 1981, UN Doc. Supp. No. 40 (A/36/40) at 176 (1981), Communication No. R.12/52.

6 European Court of Human Rights

Ilaşcu, Leşco, Ivanţoc and Petrov-Popa v. *Moldova and the Russian Federation*, Judgment of 8 July 2004 (Appl. No. 48787/99).

Öcalan v. *Turkey*, Judgment of 12 March 2003, (Appl. No. 46221/99).

Vlastimir and Borka Banković, Živana Stojanović, Mirjana Stoimenovski, Dragana Joksimović and Dragan Suković v. *Belgium, the Czech Republic, Denmark, France, Germany, Greece, Hungary, Iceland, Italy, Luxembourg, the Netherlands, Norway, Poland, Portugal, Spain, Turkey and the United Kingdom*, Decision of 12 December 2001 (Appl. No. 52207/99).

Waite & Kennedy v. *Germany*, Judgment of 18 February 1999 (Application No. 26083/94), 42 Yearbook of the European Convention on Human Rights 80 (1999).

Beer & Regan v. *Germany*, Judgment of 18 February 1999, (Application No. 28934/95 (1999) 33 EHHR 54.

Matthews v. *United Kingdom*, Judgment of 18 February 1999 (Application No. 24833/94), 42 Yearbook of the European Convention on Human Rights 78 (1999).

Drozd and Janousek v. *France and Spain*, E.C.H.R. Series A, No. 240 (1992).

7 European Commission of Human Rights

M. & Co. v. *Federal Republic of Germany*, Decision of 9 February 1990, 33 Yearbook of the European Convention on Human Rights 46 (1990).

8 Inter-American Court of Human Rights

Hernán Javier Cuaran et al v. *Colombia (Las Palmeras)*, Preliminary Objections, 4 February 2000, Series C, No. 67.

Suárez Rosero v. *Ecuador*, Reparations, Judgment of 20 January 1999, Series C, No. 44.

9 Inter-American Commission on Human Rights

Bernard Coard et al v. *United States*, Case No. 10.951, Report No. 109/99, 29 September 1999.

Armando Alejandre Jr. et al v. *Cuba*, Case No. 11.589, Report No. 86/99, 29 September 1999.

Juan Carlos Abella v. *Argentina (La Tablada)*, Case No. 11.137, Report No. 55/97, 18 November 1997.

10 Arbitration awards

Eritrea v. *Ethiopia*, Partial Award Central Front Eritrea's Claims 2, 4, 6, 7, 8 & 22, 28 April 2004.

Westland Helicopters Ltd. and Arab Industrialization Organization, United Arab Emirates, Kingdom of Saudi Arabia, State of Quatar, Arab Republic of Egypt and Arab British

Helicopters Company, International Chamber of Commerce, Court of Arbitration, 5 March 1984, 80 ILR 610 (1989).

British Claims in the Spanish Zone of Morocco Arbitration, UNRIAA vol. II, 615 (1925).

11 Domestic courts

11.1 Austria

N.K. v. *Austria*, Superior Provincial Court (Oberlandesgericht) Vienna, 26 February 1979, 77 ILR 470.

11.2 Belgium

Brussels Military Tribunal (Krijgshof), *Military Prosecutor CGKR* v. *Dirk N.*, 7 May 1998.

Belgian Military Court of Appeal (Militair Gerechtshof), *Prosecutor* v. *C.K. and B.C.*, Judgment of 17 December 1997, reported in Journal des Tribunaux 1998, 286-289.

Military Prosecutor v. *V.G.C. & R.E.*, Court Martial, reported in Rechtskundig Weekblad 1995-1996, nr. 26, 9 March 1996, at 949.

Manderlier v. *United Nations and Belgium*, Court of Appeals of Brussels, 15 September 1969, 69 ILR 139.

Manderlier v. *United Nations and Belgium*, Court of First Instance of Brussels, 11 May 1966, 81 Journal des Tribunaux No. 4553 (1966), 721, 45 ILR 446.

11.3 Canada

Abubakar Arone Rage and Dahabo Omar Samow by their Litigation Guardian Abdullahi Godah Barre v. *the Attorney General of Canada* (unreported, 6 July 1999, Ontario Superior Court of Justice, Cunningham J.).

11.4 Colombia

Constitutional Court, Colombia, Decision No. C-225/95 of 18 May 1995.

11.5 Germany

Landgericht Bonn, Case no. 1 O 361/02 of 10 December 2003.

Bundesgerichtshof, Judgment of 26 June 2003, III ZR 245/98.

Landgericht Bonn, Judgment of 26 February 1992 (1 O 446/90).

11.6 Greece

Prefecture of Voiotia v. *Federal Republic of Germany*, Case No. 137/1997, Court of First Instance of Leivadia, Greece, 30 October 1997.

11.7 Italy

Prime Minister's Office v. *Marković et al.*, Court of Cassation of Italy, 5 June 2002.

Tribunal of Livorno, Criminal Division, Sentence No. 439, 13 April 2000.

11.8 Netherlands

Association 'Udruzenja Gradana 'Zene Srebrenice' v. *the Netherlands*, Court of First Instance of the Hague, Decision of 27 November 2003, case no. 03.351.

Daniković et al. v. *the Netherlands*, Supreme Court of the Netherlands, 29 November 2002, NJ 2003, 35.

Slobodan Milosevic v. *the Netherlands*, Judgment in the interlocutory injunction proceedings, President of the District Court of the Hague, 21 August 2001, reproduced in 48 Netherlands International Law Review 357 (2001) .

11.9 Switzerland

Westland Helicopters v. *Arab Organization for Industrialization and Others*, Federal Supreme Court, 19 July 1988, 80 ILR 652.

Arab Organization for Industrialization and Others v. *Westland Helicopters*, Court of Justice of Geneva, 23 October 1987, 80 ILR 622.

11.10 United Kingdom

Maclaine Watson v. *Department of Trade and Industry* and *J.H Rayner (Mincing Lane) Ltd.* v. *Department of Trade and Industry and others*, House of Lords, 26 October 1989 [1989] 3 All ER 523.

Maclaine Watson v. *Department of Trade and Industry* and *J.H. Rayner (Mincing Lane) Ltd.* v. *Department of Trade and Industry and others*, Court of Appeal, 27 April 1989, 80 ILR 49 (1989).

J.H. Rayner (Mincing Lane) Ltd. v. *Department of Trade and Industry*, High Court, Queen's Bench Division, 24 June 1987, 77 ILR 55 (1985).

Attorney-General v. *Nissan*, House of Lords, 11 February 1969, [1969] All ER 629.

Nissan v. *Attorney-General*, Court of Appeal, Civil Division, 29 June 1967, [1967] All ER 1238.

Nissan v. *Attorney-General*, Queen's Bench Division, 17 February 1967, [1967] 2 All ER 200.

11.11 United States

Princz v. *Federal Republic of Germany*, 307 U.S. App. D.C. 102; 26 F.3d 1166 (U.S. App. D.C. 1994).

Goldstar (Panama) S.A. v. *United States*, 967 F.2d 965 (4th Cir. 1992).

Handel v. *Artukovic*, 601 F. Supp. 1421 (C.D. Cal. 1985).

Tel-Oren v. *Libyan Arab Republic*, 233 U.S. App. D.C. 384, 726 F.2d 774 (D.C. Cir. 1984.

United States v. *Wilhelm List and others (the Hostages Trial)*, United States Military Tribunal, Nuremberg, VIII Law Reports of Trials of War Criminals 55 (1949).

Bibliography

Books

Ahlquist, L. (Ed.), Co-operation, Command and Control in UN Peace-keeping Operations (1996).

Amerasinghe, C.F., Principles of the Institutional Law of International Organizations (1996).

Amerasinghe, C.F., The Law of the International Civil Service: As Applied by International Administrative Tribunals, vol. I (1988).

Barnett, M., Eyewitness to a Genocide: The United Nations and Rwanda (2002).

Benvenisti, E., The International Law of Occupation (1993).

Best, G., Humanity in Warfare: The Modern History of the International Law of Armed Conflicts (1980).

Bissonnette, P., La Satisfaction Comme Mode de Réparation en Droit International (1952).

Blokker, N. & Schermers, H., International Institutional Law: Unity Within Diversity (2003).

Boerefijn, I., The Reporting Procedure under the Covenant on Civil and Political Rights: Practice and Procedures of the Human Rights Committee (1999).

Bothe, M., Streitkräfte Internationaler Organisationen: Zugleich ein Beitrag zu völkerrechtlichen Grundfragen der Anwesenheit fremder Truppen (1968).

Bowett, D., United Nations Forces: A Legal Study of United Nations Practice (1964).

Brownlie, I., Principles of Public International Law (1998).

Brownlie, I., System of the Law of Nations, State Responsibility, Part I (1983).

Castren, E., The Present Law of War and Neutrality (1954).

Childers, E., & Urquhart, B., Renewing the United Nations System (1994).

Combacau, J., Le Pouvoir de Sanction de l'O.N.U.: Étude Théorique de la Coercition non Militaire 282 (1974).

Cot, P.P. & Pellet, A., (Eds.), La Charte des Nations Unies (1985).

David, E., Principes de Droit des Conflits Armés (1994).

Goodrich, L., Hambro, E., & Simons, A.P., (Eds.), The United Nations Charter: A Commentary (1969).

Goodrich, L., The United Nations (1960).

Eagleton, C., The Responsibility of States in International Law (1928).

Emanuelli, C., Les Actions Militaires de l'ONU et le Droit International Humanitaire (1995).

Heede, K., European Ombudsman: Redress and Control at Union Level (2000).

Hewson, M., & Sinclair, T., (Eds.), Approaches to Global Governance Theory (1999).

Higgins, R., Problems & Process: International Law and How We Use It (1994).

Higgins, R., United Nations Peacekeeping: Documents and Commentary: 1, the Middle East (1969).

Hirsch, M., The Responsibility of International Organizations Toward Third Parties: Some Basic Principles (1995).

Hoogh, A. de, Obligations Erga Omnes and International Crimes: A Theoretical Inquiry into the Implementation and Enforcement of the International Responsibility of States (1995).

Jennings, R., & Watts, A., Oppenheim's International Law, Vol 1 (1992).

Jørgensen, N.H.B., The Responsibility of States for International Crimes (2001).

Kalshoven, F., & Zegveld, L., Constraints on the Waging of War (2001).

Kelly, M., Restoring and Maintaining Order in Complex Peace Operations: The Search for a Legal Framework (1999).

Kelsen, H., The Law of the United Nations (1951).

Klein, P., La Responsabilité des Organisations Internationales dans les Ordres Juridiques Internes et en Droit des Gens (1998).

Lauterpacht, H., Oppenheim's International Law: A Treatise, Vol. 2 (1952).

Lawson, R., Het EVRM en de Europese Gemeenschappen: Bouwstenen voor een Aansprakelijkheidsregime van Internationale Organisaties (1999).

Lillich, R., & Magraw, D., (Eds.), The Iran – United States Claims Tribunal: Its Contribution to the Law of State Responsibility (1998).

Lowenthal, A., The Dominican Intervention (1972).

Magraw, D., & Lillich, R., (Eds.), The Iran – United States Claims Tribunal: Its Contribution to the Law of State Responsibility (1998).

McCoubrey, H., & Morris, J., Regional Peacekeeping in the Post-Cold War Era (2000).

McCoubrey, H., & White, N., The Blue Helmets: Legal Regulation of United Nations Military Operations (1996).

McDonald, G., Peace Enforcement: Mapping the 'Middle Ground' in Peace Operations, dissertation University of Geneva 2001 (unpublished).

Meron, T., Human Rights and Humanitarian Norms as Customary Law (1989).

Morris, J., & McCoubrey, H., Regional Peacekeeping in the Post-Cold War Era (2000).

Pellet, A., & Cot, J.P., (Eds.), La Charte des Nations Unies (1985).

Pictet, J., Le Droit Humanitaire et la Protection des Victimes de la Guerre (1973).

Pilloud, C., Sandoz, Y., Swinarski, C., & Zimmermann, B., Commentary on the Additional Protocols of 8 June 1977 to the Geneva Conventions of 12 August 1949 (1987).

Pitschas, C., Die Völkerrechtliche Verantwortlichkeit der Europäischen Gemeinschaft und ihrer Mitgliedstaaten: Zugleich ein beitrag zu den völkerrechtlichen Kompetenzen der Europäischen Gemeinschaft (2001).

Quoc Dinh, N., Daillier, P., & Pellet, A., Droit International Public (1999).

Raič, D., Statehood and the Law of Self-Determination (2002).

Reitzer, L., La Réparation comme Conséquence de l'Acte Illicite en Droit International (1938).

Rose, M., Fighting for Peace (1998).

Rosner, G., The United Nations Emergency Force (1963).

Sands, P., & Klein, P., Bowett's Law of International Institutions (2001).

Sarooshi, D., The U.N. and the Development of Collective Security: The Delegation by the Security Council of its Chapter VII Powers (1999).

Sassòli, M., & Bouvier, A., How Does Law Protect in War (1999).

Schweigman, D., The Authority of the Security Council under Chapter VII of the UN Charter: Legal Limits and the Role of the International Court of Justice (2001).

Seyersted, F., United Nations Forces in the Law of Peace and War (1966).

Shelton, Remedies in International Human Rights Law (2001).

Simma, B., (Ed.), The Charter of the United Nations: A Commentary (1995).

Simmonds, R., Legal Problems Arising from the United Nations Military Operations in the Congo (1968).

Sinclair, T., & Hewson, M., (Eds.), Approaches to Global Governance Theory (1999).

Stone, J., Legal Controls of International Conflict: A Treatise on the Dynamics of Disputes and War Law (1954).

United Nations, The United Nations and Somalia 1992-1996 (1996).

United Nations, The Blue Helmets: A Review of United Nations Peacekeeping (1996).

United Nations, The Blue Helmets: A Review of United Nations Peacekeeping (1990).

Waltzog, A., Recht der Landkriegführung (1942).

Wellens, K., Remedies Against International Organisations (2002).

Wet, E. de, The Chapter VII Powers of the United Nations Security Council (2004).

White, N.D., The Law of International Organisations (1996).

White, N.D., Keeping the Peace: The United Nations and the Maintenance of International Peace and Security (1993).

Zegveld, L., Accountability of Armed Opposition Groups in International Law (2002).

Articles and book contributions

Akande, D., *The International Court of Justice and the Security Council: Is there Room for Judicial Control of Decisions of the Political Organs of the United Nations?*, 46 International & Comparative Law Quarterly 309 (1997).

Aldrich, G., *Individuals as Subjects of International Humanitarian Law*, in J. Makarczyk (Ed.), Theory of International Law at the Threshold of the 21st Century: Essays in Honour of Krzysztof Skubiszewski 851 (1996).

Aldrich, G., *Prospects for United States Ratification of Additional Protocol I to the 1949 Geneva Conventions*, 85 American Journal of International Law 1 (1991).

Alvarez de Miranda y Torres, F., *Human Rights and their Functioning in the Institutional Strengthening of the Ombudsman*, 2 International Ombudsman Yearbook 146 (1998).

Amerasinghe, C., *Liability to Third Parties of Member States of International Organizations: Practice, Principle and Judicial Precedent*, 85 American Journal of International Law 259 (1991).

Amrallah, B., *The International Responsibility of the U.N. for the Activities Carried out by U.N. Peacekeeping Forces*, 32 Revue Egyptienne de Droit International 57 (1976).

Annan, K., *Peace-keeping in Situations of Civil War*, 26 New York University Journal of International Law & Politics 623 (1994).

Annan, K., *UN Peacekeeping Operations and Cooperation with NATO*, 41 NATO Review 3 (1993).

Arsanjani, M., *Claims against International Organizations: Quis custodiet ipsos custodes*, 7 The Yale Journal of World Public Order 131 (1981).

Bank, R., *International Efforts to Combat Torture and Inhuman Treatment: Have New Mechanisms Improved Protection?*, 8 European Journal of International Law 613 (1997).

Bederman, D., *Article 40 (2) (E) & (F) of the ILC Draft Articles on State Responsibility: Standing of Injured States under Customary International Law and Multilateral Treaties*, 92 ASIL Proc. 291 (1998).

Benvenuti, P., *The ICTY's Prosecutor and the Review of the NATO Bombing Campaign against the Federal Republic of Yugoslavia*, 12 European Journal of International Law 503 (2001).

Berdal, M., *The Security Council, Peacekeeping and Internal Conflict after the Cold War*, 7 Duke Journal of Comparative & International Law 71 (1996).

Beresford, S., & Muller, A., *The Special Court for Sierra Leone: An Initial Comment*, 14 Leiden Journal of International Law 635 (2001).

Berman, E., & Sams, K., *Regional Peacekeeping in Africa*, 3 Conflict Trends 50 (2001).

Berman, E., *The Security Council's Increasing Reliance on Burden-Sharing: Collaboration or Abrogation?*, 5 International Peacekeeping 1 (1998).

Bierzanek, R., *The Responsibility of States in Armed Conflicts*, 11 Polish Yearbook of International Law 93 (1981-1982).

Bleckmann, A., *Zur Verbindlichkeit des Algemeinen Völkerrechts für Internationale Organisationen*, 37 Zeitschrift für ausländisches öffentliches Recht und Völkerrecht 107 (1977).

Blokker, N., *Is the Authorization Authorized? Powers and Practice of the UN Security Council to Authorize the Use of Force by 'Coalitions of the Able and Willing'*, 11 European Journal of International Law 541 (2000).

Bloom, E., *Protecting Peacekeepers: The Convention on the Safety of United Nations and Associated Personnel*, 89 American Journal of International Law 621 (1995).

Boisson de Chazournes, L., *Policy Guidance and Compliance Issues: The World Bank Operational Standards*, in D. Shelton (Ed.), Commitment and Compliance: The Role of Non-Binding Norms in the International Legal System 281 (2000).

Bongiorno, C., *A Culture of Impunity: Applying International Human Rights Law to the United Nations in East Timor*, 33 Columbia Human Rights Law Review 623 (2002).

Bonnor, P., *The European Ombudsman: A Novel Source of Soft Law in the European Union*, 25 European Law Review 39 (2000).

Boot, M., *Paving the Road to Hell: The Failure of U.N. Peacekeeping*, 79 Foreign Affairs 143 (2000).

Boothby, D., Background paper, Report of an International Peace Academy Seminar on UN/NATO Relationship, New York, 11 June 1999.

Bossuyt, M., *The Development of Special Procedures of the United Nations Commission on Human Rights*, 6 Human Rights Law Journal 179 (1985).

Bothe, M., *Friedenssicherung und Kriegsrecht*, in W. Graf Vitzhum (Ed.), Völkerrecht 645 (2001).

Bothe, M., *Völkerrechtliche Eingrenzung von Gewalt – das Recht bewaffneter Konflikte (ius in bello)*, in W. Graf Vitzthum (Ed.), Völkerrecht 642 (2001).

Bothe, M., *Peacekeeping and International Humanitarian Law: Friends or Foes?*, 3 International Peacekeeping 91 (1996).

Bourloyannis-Vrailas, C., *The Convention on the Safety of United Nations and Associated Personnel*, 44 International & Comparative Law Quarterly 561 (1995).

Boutros-Ghali, B., *Beyond Peacekeeping*, 25 New York University Journal of International Law and Politics 113 (1992).

Bouvier, A., *Convention on the Safety of United Nations and Associated Personnel: Presentation and Analysis*, 35 International Review of the Red Cross 638 (1995).

Bowett, D., *The Impact of Security Council Decisions on Dispute Settlement Procedures*, 5 European Journal of International Law 1 (1994).

Brabant, K., van., *Regaining Perspective: The Debate over Quality Assurance and Accountability*, Humanitarian Exchange: The Magazine of the Humanitarian Practice Network No. 17 (2000).

Bradlow, D., & Schlemmer-Schulte, S., *The World Bank's New Inspection Panel: A Constructive Step in the Transformation of the International Legal Order*, 54 Zeitschrift für ausländisches öffentliches Recht und Völkerrecht 405 (1994).

Bradlow, D., *International Organizations and Private Complaints: The Case of the World Bank Inspection Panel*, 34 Virginia Journal of International Law 553 (1994).

Bradlow, D., *Why the World Bank Needs an Ombudsman*, Financial Times, 14 July 1993, at 13.

Bradlow, D., & Grossman, C., *Are We Being Propelled Towards a People-Centered Transnational Legal Order?*, 9 American University Journal of International Law & Policy 1 (1993).

Brölmann, C., *A Flat Earth? International Organizations in the System of International Law*, 70 Nordic Journal of International Law 319 (2001).

Brown, D., *The Role of the United Nations in Peacekeeping and Truce-monitoring: What are the Applicable Norms*, 27 Revue Belge de Droit International 559 (1994).

Brown Weiss, E., *Invoking State Responsibility in the Twenty-First Century*, 96 American Journal of International Law 798 (2002).

Bull, T., *The Original Ombudsman: Blueprint in Need of Revision or a Concept with More to Offer?*, 6 European Public Law 334 (2000).

Burger, J., *International Humanitarian Law and the Kosovo Crisis: Lessons Learned or to Be Learned*, 82 International Review of the Red Cross 129 (2000).

Butkiewicz, E., *The Premisses of International Responsibility of Inter-Governmental Organizations*, 11 Polish Yearbook of International Law 117 (1981-82).

Carlucci, G., *L'Obligation de Restitution des Biens Culturels et des Objets d'Art en Cas de Conflit Armé: Droit Coutumier et Droit Conventionnel Avant et Après la Convention de la Haye de 1954*, 104 Revue Générale de Droit International Public 289 (2000).

Carreau, D, & Stein, E., *Law and Peaceful Change in a Subsystem "Withdrawal" of France from the North Atlantic Treaty Organization*, 62 American Journal of International Law 577 (1968).

Cartledge, G., *Legal Constraints on Military Personnel Deployed on Peacekeeping Operations*, in H. Durman & T. McCormack (Eds.), The Changing Face of Conflict and the Efficacy of International Humanitarian Law 121 (1999).

Cassese, A., *Remarks on Scelle's Theory of "Role Splitting"(Dédoublement Fonctionnel) in International Law*, 1 European Journal of International Law 210 (1990).

Castillo-Suárez, A., *Hors de Logique: Contemporary Issues in International Humanitarian Law as Applied to Internal Armed Conflict*, 15 American University International Law Review 1 (1999).

Cerone, J., *Minding the Gap: Outlining KFOR Accountability in Post-Conflict Kosovo*, 12 European Journal of International Law 469 (2001).

Charney, J., *The Persistent Objector Rule and the Development of International Law*, 56 British Yearbook of International Law 1 (1985).

Cheng, B., *Introduction to Subjects of International Law*, in M. Bedjaoui (Ed.), International Law: Achievements and Prospects 23 (1991).

Chetail, V., *The Contribution of the International Court of Justice to International Humanitarian Law*, 85 International Review of the Red Cross 235 (2003).

Chinkin, C., & Sadurska, R., *The Collapse of the International Tin Council: A Case of State Responsibility?* 30 Virginia Journal of International Law 845 (1989).

Chopra, J., *Peace Maintenance: A Concept for Collective Political Authority*, 89 ASIL Proc. 280 (1995).

Ciobanu, D., *The Power of the Security Council to Organize Peace-Keeping Operations*, in A. Cassese (Ed.), United Nations Peace-Keeping: Legal Essays 15 (1978).

Cohen-Jonathan, G., *Observations: La Territorialisation de la Jurisdiction de la Cour Européenne des Droits de l'Homme*, 12 Revue Trimestrielle des Droits de l'Homme 1069 (2002).

Cohen-Jonathan, G., & Flauss, J.F., *A Propos de l'Arrêt Matthews c/ Royaume-Uni (18 février 1999)*, 35 Revue Trimestrielle de Droit Européen 637 (1999).

Colby, E., *Occupation under the Laws of War*, 25 Columbia Law Review 904 (1925).

Committee on Study of Legal Problems of the United Nations, *Should the Laws of War Apply to United Nations Enforcement Action?*, 46 ASIL Proc. 216 (1952).

Condorelli, L., *Nuclear Weapons: A Weighty Matter for the International Court of Justice*, 79 International Review of the Red Cross 9 (1997).

Condorelli, L., *Le Statut des Forces de l'ONU et le Droit International Humanitaire*, 78 Rivista di Diritto Internazionale 881 (1995).

Condorelli, L., *Imputation à l'Etat d'un Fait Internationalement Illicite*, 189 Recueil des Cours (1984-VI).

Corell, H., *Nuremberg and the Development of an International Criminal Court*, 149 Military Law Review 87 (1995).

Corten, O., & Klein, P., *Action Humanitaire et Chapitre VII: La Redéfinition du Mandat et des Moyens d'Action des Forces des Nations Unies*, 39 Annuaire Français de Droit International 105 (1994).

Cortright, D., & Lopez, G., *Are Sanctions Just? The Problematic Case of Iraq*, 52 Journal of International Affairs 33 (1999).

Cottier, M., *Attacks on Humanitarian Assistance or Peacekeeping Missions*, in O. Triffterer (Ed.), Commentary on the Rome Statute of the International Criminal Court: Observer's Notes, Article by Article 187 (1999).

Cox, K., *Beyond Self-defense: United Nations Peacekeeping Operations & the Use of Force*, 27 Denver Journal of International Law & Policy 239 (1999).

Crawford, J., *Responsibility to the International Community as a Whole*, 8 Indiana Journal of Global Legal Studies 303 (2001).

Crawford, J., Bodeau, P., & Peel, J., *The ILC's Draft Articles on State Responsibility: Toward Completion of a Second Reading*, 94 American Journal of International Law 660(2000).

Crocker, C., *The Lessons of Somalia: Not Everything Went Wrong*, 74 Foreign Affairs 2 (1995).

Czapliński, W., *UN Codification of Law of State Responsibility*, 41 Archiv des Völkerrechts 62 (2003).

Deman, C., *La Cessation de l'Acte Illicite*, 23 Revue Belge de Droit International 476 (1990).

Dewast, P., *Quelques Aspects du Statut des «Casques Bleus."*, 81 Revue Générale de Droit International Public 1007 (1977).

Dobbie, C., *A Concept for Post-Cold War Peacekeeping*, 36 Survival 121 (1994).

Dolzer, R., *The Settlement of War-Related Claims: Does International Law Recognize a Victim's Private Right of Action? Lessons after 1945*, 20 Berkeley Journal of International Law 296 (2002).

Dominicé, C., *La Satisfaction en Droit des Gens*, in Mélanges Georges Perrin 91 (1984).

Donner, M., *Völkerrechtliche und Verfassungsrechtliche Aspekte der Militärischen Absicherung der Friedensvereinbarung von Dayton*, 10 Humanitäres Völkerrecht - Informationsschriften 63 (1997).

Dorn, W., *Regional Peacekeeping Is Not the Way*, 27 Peacekeeping and International Relations 1 (1998).

Draper, G., *The Legal Limitations upon the Employment of Weapons by the United Nations Force in the Congo*, 12 International & Comparative Law Quarterly 387 (1963).

Dreist, P., *Die Task Force Harvest und die Task Force Fox – Beiträge zur StabilisierungM akedoniens*, 8 Humanitäres Völkerrecht – Informationsschriften 4 (2002).

Dreist, P., *Rechtliche Aspekte des KFOR-Einsatzes*, 43 Neue Zeitschrift für Wehrrecht 1 (2001).

Dupuy, P.M., *A General Stocktaking of the Connections between the Multilateral Dimension of Obligations and Codification of the Law of Responsibility*, 13 European Journal of International Law 1053 (2002).

Dupuy, P.M., *The Constitutional Dimension of the Charter of the United Nations Revisited*, 1 Max Planck Yearbook of United Nations Law 33 (1997).

Eagleton, C., *International Organization and the Law of Responsibility*, 76 Recueil des Cours (1950-I).

Eide, E., The Internal Security Challenge in Kosovo, paper prepared for UNA-USA/IAI Conference on 'Kosovo's Final Status'.

Elaraby, N., *United Nations Peacekeeping by Consent: A Case Study of the Withdrawal of the United Nations Emergency Force*, in J. Norton Moore (Ed.), The Arab-Israeli Conflict, Volume II: Readings 620 (1974).

Emanuelli, C., *The Protection Afforded to Humanitarian Assistance Personnel under the Convention on the Safety of United Nations and Associated Personnel*, 6 Humanitäres Völkerrecht – Informationsschriften 4 (1990).

Fassbender, B., *The United Nations Charter as Constitution of the International Community*, 36 Columbia Journal of Transnational Law 529 (1998).

Fenwick, C., *The Dominican Republic: Intervention or Collective Self-Defense*, 60 American Journal of International Law 64 (1966).

Figà-Talamanca, N., *The Role of NATO in the Peace Agreement for Bosnia and Herzegovina*, 7 European Journal of International Law 164 (1996).

Finkelstein, L., *What is Global Governance?*, 1 Global Governance 367 (1995).

Flauss, J.F., & Cohen-Jonathan, G., *A Propos de l'Arrêt Matthews c/ Royaume-Uni (18 février 1999)*, 35 Revue Trimestrielle de Droit Européen 637 (1999).

Franceschet, A., *Justice and International Organization: Two Models of Global Governance*, 8 Global Governance 19 (2002).

François, J., L'Egalité d'Application des Règles du Droit de la Guerre aux Parties à un Conflit Armé, Rapport Provisoire, Annuaire IDI 50-I (1963) 5.

François, J., Reconsidération des Principes du Droit de la Guerre, Rapport Provisoire, Annuaire IDI 47-I (1957) 323.

Freeman, A., *Responsibility of States for Unlawful Acts of their Armed Forces*, 88 Recueil des Cours (1955-II).

Fröhlich, M., *Keeping Track of UN Peace-keeping – Suez, Srebrenica, Rwanda and the Brahimi Report*, 5 Max Planck Yearbook of United Nations Law 185 (2001).

Gaja, G., *Obligations Erga Omnes, International Crimes and Jus Cogens: A Tentative Analysis of Three Related Concepts*, in J. Weiler, A. Cassese & M. Spinedi (Eds.), International Crimes of States: A Critical Analysis of the ILC's Draft Article 19 on State Responsibility 151 (1989).

Gaja, G., *A 'New' Vienna Convention on Treaties between States and International Organizations or between International Organizations: A Critical Commentary*, 63 British Yearbook of International Law 253 (1987).

Gardam, J., *The Contribution of the International Court of Justice to International Humanitarian Law*, 14 Leiden Journal of International Law 349 (2001).

Gardam, J., *Legal Restraints on Security Council Military Enforcement Action*, 17 Michigan Journal of International Law 285 (1996).

Gasiokwu, M., *ECOWAS Intervention in Liberia and Sierra Leone: A New Dimension in Regional Security System*, 24 Polish Yearbook of International Law 157 (2001).

Gasser, H.P., *Collective Economic Sanctions and International Humanitarian Law: An Enforcement Measure under the United Nations Charter and the Right of Civilians to Immunity: An Unavoidable Clash of Policy Goals*, 56 Zeitschrift fur ausländisches öffentliches Recht und Völkerrecht 871 (1996).

Gasser, H.P., *Die Anwendbarkeit des Humanitären Völkerrechts auf Militärische Operationen der Vereinten Nationen*, 4 Schweizerische Zeitschrift für Internationales und Europäisches Recht 443 (1994).

Gerven, W. van, *Of Rights, Remedies and Procedures*, 37 Common Market Law Review 501 (2000).

Gill, T., *Legal and Some Political Limitations on the Power of the UN Security Council to Exercise its Enforcement Powers under Chapter VII of the Charter*, 26 Netherlands Yearbook of International Law 33 (1995).

Glick, R., *Lip Service to the Laws of War: Humanitarian Law and United Nations Armed Forces*, 17 Michigan Journal of International Law 53 (1995).

Gordon, J., *A Peaceful, Silent, Deadly Remedy: The Ethics of Economic Sanctions*, 13 Ethics & International Affairs (1999).

Gordon, S., *Icarus Rising and Falling: The Evolution of UN Command and Control Structures*, in D. Gordon & F. Toase (Eds.), Aspects of Peacekeeping 19 (2001).

Gottehrer, D., & Hostina, M., Essential Characteristics of a Classical Ombudsman, Annex 1 to Ombudsman and Human Rights Protection Institutions in OSCE Participating States, OSCE Human Dimension Implementation Meeting October 1998, Background paper.

Goulding, M., *The Evolution of United Nations Peacekeeping*, 69 International Affairs 451 (1993).

Gowlland-Debbas, V., *Security Council Enforcement Action and Issues of State Responsibility*, 43 International & Comparative Law Quarterly 55 (1994).

Gowlland-Debbas, V., *The Relationship between the International Court of Justice and the Security Council in the Light of the Lockerbie Case*, 88 American Journal of International Law 643 (1994).

Granatstein, J., *The United Nations and the North Atlantic Treaty Organization*, in G. Schmidt (Ed.), A History of NATO – The First Fifty Years, Vol I, 29 (2001).

Grant, T., *Asil Insight: Iraq: How to Reconcile Conflicting Obligations of Occupation and Reform*, June 2003.

Gray, C., *The Choice Between Restitution and Compensation*, 10 European Journal of International Law 413 (1999).

Gray, C., *Host-state Consent and United Nations Peacekeeping in Yugoslavia*, 7 Duke Journal of Comparative & International Law 241 (1996).

Greenwood, C., *International Humanitarian Law, Revised report for the Centennial Commemoration of the First Hague Peace Conference 1899*, in F. Kalshoven (Ed.), The Centennial of the First International Peace Conference: Reports & Conclusions 161 (2000).

Greenwood, C., *International Humanitarian Law and United Nations Military Operations*, 1 Yearbook of International Humanitarian Law 3 (1998).

Greenwood, C., *Scope of Application of Humanitarian Law*, in D. Fleck (Ed.), The Handbook of Humanitarian Law in Armed Conflicts 39 (1995).

Griffin, M., *Retrenchment, Reform and Regionalization: Trends in UN Peace Support Operations*, 6 International Peacekeeping 1 (1999).

Grossman, C., & Bradlow, D., *Are We Being Propelled Towards a People-Centered Transnational Legal Order?*, 9 American University Journal of International Law & Policy 1 (1993).

Guéhenno, J.M., *On the Challenges and Achievements of Reforming UN Peace Operations*, 9 International Peacekeeping 69 (2002).

Guillaume, M., *Le Cadre Juridique de l'Action de la KFOR au Kosovo*, in C. Tomuschat (Ed.), Kosovo and the International Community 243 (2002).

Halderman, J., *Legal Basis for United Nations Armed Forces*, 56 American Journal of International Law 971 (1962).

Hampson, F., *States' Military Operations Authorized by the United Nations and International Humanitarian Law*, in L. Condorelli, A.M. La Rosa & S. Scherrer (Eds), Les Nations Unies et le Droit International Humanitaire 371 (1995).

Hampson, F., *Using International Human Rights Machinery to Enforce the International Law of Armed Conflicts*, 31 Military Law and Law of War Review 117 (1992).

Harden, I., *When Europeans Complain: The Work of the European Ombudsman*, 3 Cambridge Yearbook of European Legal Studies 199 (2000).

Hegelsom, G.J., van, *The Law of Armed Conflict and UN Peace-keeping and Peace-enforcing Operations*, 6 Hague Yearbook of International Law 45 (1993).

Henckaerts, J.M., *Study on Customary Rules of International Humanitarian Law: Purpose, Coverage and Methodology*, 81 International Review of the Red Cross 660 (1999).

Herdegen, M., *The Insolvency of International Organizations and the Legal Position of Creditors: Some Observations in the Light of the International Tin Council Crisis*, 35 Netherlands International Law Review 135 (1988).

Hey, E., *The World Bank Inspection Panel: Towards the Recognition of a New Legally Relevant Relationship in International Law*, 2 Hofstra Law & Policy Symposium 61 (1997).

Higgins, R., *Second-Generation Peacekeeping*, 89 ASIL Proc. 275 (1995).

Higgins, R., Final report, Annuaire IDI 66-I (1995) 461.

Higgins, R., Provisional report, Annuaire IDI 66-I (1995) 373.

Higgins, R., Preliminary exposé and draft questionnaire, Annuaire IDI 66-I (1995) 249.

Higgins, R., *The Place of International Law in the Settlement of Disputes by the Security Council*, 64 American Journal of International Law 1 (1970).

Hoffman, M., *Peace-enforcement Actions and Humanitarian Law: Emerging Rules for "Interventional Armed Conflict"*, 82 International Review of the Red Cross 193 (2000).

Hüber, M., *Die Fortbildung des Völkerrechts auf dem Gebiete des Prozeß- und Landkriegsrechts*, 2 Das Öffentliche Recht der Gegenwart 471 (1908).

Igarashi, M., *Post-War Compensation Cases, Japanese Courts and International Law*, 43 Japanese Annual of International Law 1 (2000).

Irmscher, T., *The Legal Framework for the Activities of the United Nations Interim Administration Mission in Kosovo: The Charter, Human Rights, and the Law of Occupation*, 44 German Yearbook of International Law 353 (2001).

Jablonsky, D., & McCallum, J., *Peace Implementation and the Concept of Induced Consent in Peace Operations*, 29 Parameters 54 (1999).

Janssens, B., *Les Règles d'Engagement pendant les Opérations des Nations Unies en Somalie*, 35 Military Law and Law of War Review 209 (1996).

Jimenez de Aréchaga, E., *International Responsibility*, in M. Sørensen (Ed.), Manual of Public International Law 532 (1968).

Johnson, M., *The Function of Legal Advisors in NATO with Regard to International Humanitarian Law*, 35 Military Law and Law of War Review 167 (1996).

Jones, M., *The Non-Contractual Liability of the EEC and the Availability of an Alternative Remedy in the National Courts*, 1 Legal Issues of European Integration 1 (1981).

Kalshoven, F., *A Colombian View on Protocol II*, 1 Yearbook of International Humanitarian 262 (1998).

Kalshoven, F., *State Responsibility for Warlike Acts of the Armed Forces: From Article 3 of the Hague Convention IV of 1907 to Article 91 of Additional Protocol I of 1977 and Beyond*, 40 International & Comparative Law Quarterly 827 (1991).

Kalshoven, F., *The Undertaking to Respect and Ensure Respect in all Circumstances: From Tiny Seed to Ripening Fruit*, 2 Yearbook of International Humanitarian Law 3 (1999).

Kelly, M., *Legitimacy and the Public Security Function*, in R. Oakley, M. Dziedzic & E.Goldberg (Eds.), Policing the New World Disorder 399 (1998).

Kirgis, F., *Security Council Governance of Postconflict Societies: A Plea for Good Faith and Informed Decision Making*, 95 American Journal of International Law 579 (2001).

Kirsch, P., *The Convention on the Safety of United Nations and Associated Personnel*, 2 International Peacekeeping 102 (1995).

Kleffner, J., *Improving Compliance with International Humanitarian Law Through the Establishment of an Individual Complaints Procedure*, 15 Leiden Journal of International Law 237 (2002).

Kleffner, J., & Zegveld, L., *Establishing an Individual Complaints Procedure for Violations of International Humanitarian Law*, 3 Yearbook of International Humanitarian Law 384 (2000).

Klein, P., *Responsabilité pour Violation Grave d'Obligations Découlant de Normes Impératives de Droit International et Droit des Nations Unies*, in P.M. Dupuy, (Ed.) Obligations Multilaterales, Droit Impératif et Responsabilité Internationale des Etats 189 (2003).

Klein, P., & Corten, O., *Action Humanitaire et Chapitre VII: La Redéfinition du Mandat et des Moyens d'Action des Forces des Nations Unies*, 39 Annuaire Français de Droit International 105 (1993).

Kondoch, B., *The Limits of Economic Sanctions under International Law: The Case of Iraq*, 7 International Peacekeeping 267 (2001).

Kovács, P., *Intervention Armée des Forces de l'OTAN au Kosovo: Fondement de l'Obligation de Respecter le Droit International Humanitaire*, 82 International Review of the Red Cross 103 (2000).

Krieger, H., *Die Verantwortlichkeit Deutschlands nach der EMRK für seine Streitkräfte im Auslandeinsatz*, 62 Zeitschrift für ausländisches öffentliches Recht und Völkerrecht 669 (2002).

Kunz, J.L., *The Laws of War*, 50 American Journal of International Law 313 (1956).

Lalande, S., *Somalia: Major Issues for Future UN Peacekeeping*, in D. Warner (Ed.), New Dimensions of Peacekeeping 69 (1995).

Lattanzi, F., *Le Accuse al Contingente Italiano in Somalia alla Luce del Diritto Internazionale*, Diritto Penale e Processo 1131 (1997).

Lawson, R., *Life after Bankovic – On the Extraterritorial Reach of the ECHR*, in F. Coomans & M. Kamminga (Eds.), The Extraterritorial Scope of Human Rights Treaties 83 (2004).

Lee, R., *United Nations Peacekeeping: Developments and Prospects*, 28 Cornell International Law Journal 619 (1995).

Letowska, E., *The Polish Ombudsman (The Commissioner for the Protection of Civil Rights)*, 39 International & Comparative Law Quarterly 206 (1990).

Levrat, B., *Le Droit International Humanitaire au Timor Oriental: Entre Théorie et Pratique*, 83 International Review of the Red Cross 77 (2001).

Levrat, N., *Les Conséquences de l'Engagement Pris par les Hautes Parties Contractantes de «Faire Respecter" les Conventions Humanitaires*, in F. Kalshoven & Y. Sandoz (Eds.), Implementation of International Humanitarian Law 263 (1989).

Lietzau, W., *International Criminal Law after Rome: Concerns from a U.S. Military Perspective*, 64 Law and Contemporary Problems 119 (2001).

Lightburn, D., *NATO and the Challenge of Multifunctional Peacekeeping*, 44 NATO Review 10 (1996).

Loon, A., van., *Kosovo Force-1: Tussen Trauma en Toekomst (II)*, 169 Militaire Spectator 656 (2000).

Lorenz, F., *The U.S. Perspective of Operation Restore Hope*, in R. Oakley, M. Dziedzic & E. Goldberg (Eds.), Policing the New World Disorder (1998).

Lüder, S., *Die Völkerrechtliche Verantwortlichkeit der Nordatlantikvertrags-Organisation bei Militärische Absicherung der Friedensvereinbarung van Dayton*, 43 Neue Zeitschrift für Wehrrecht 107 (2001).

Lupi, N., *Report by the Enquiry Commission on the Behaviour of Italian Peace-keeping Troops in Somalia*, 1 Yearbook of International Humanitarian Law 375 (1998).

Malone, D., & Wermester, K., *The Changing Nature of UN Peacekeeping*, 7 International Peacekeeping 37 (2000).

Mann, F., *The Consequences of an International Wrong in International and National Law*, 48 British Yearbook of International Law 1 (1976).

Marias, E., *The European Ombudsman: Competences and Relations with the Other Community Institutions and Bodies*, in E. Marias (Ed.), the European Ombudsman: Working Document 71 (1994).

Martenczuk, B., *The Security Council, the International Court and Judicial Review: What Lessons from Lockerbie?*, 10 European Journal of International Law 517 (1999).

Martin, F., *Application du Droit International Humanitaire par la Cour Interaméricaine des Droits de l'Homme*, 83 International Review of the Red Cross 1037 (2001).

Matheson, M., *United Nations Governance of Postconflict Societies*, 95 American Journal of International Law 76 (2001).

McCoubrey, H., & Morris, J., *Regional Peacekeeping in the Post-Cold War Era*, 6 International Peacekeeping 129 (1999).

McCoubrey, H., *The Nature of the Modern Doctrine of Military Necessity*, 30 Revue de Droit Militaire et de Droit de la Guerre 215 (1991).

McDonald, A., *Sierra Leone's Shoestring Special Court*, 84 International Review of the Red Cross 121 (2002).

Mearsheimer, J., & Evera, S., van., *The Partition that Dare not Speak its Name: When Peace Means War*, The New Republic, 5 December 1995.

Meng, W., *Internationale Organisationen im völkerrechtlichen Deliktsrecht*, 45 Zeitschrift für ausländisches öffentliches Recht und Völkerrecht 324 (1985).

Meron, T., *The Humanization of Humanitarian Law*, 94 American Journal of International Law 239 (2000).

Meron, T., *The Continuing Role of Custom in the Formation of International Humanitarian Law*, 90 American Journal of International Law 238 (1996).

Morgenstern, F., *The Convention on the Law of Treaties between States and International Organizations or between International Organizations*, in Y. Dinstein (Ed.), International Law at a Time of Perplexity: Essays in Honour of Shabtai Rosenne 435 (1988).

Moritz, G., *The Common Application of the Laws of War within the NATO-Forces*, 13 Military Law Review 1 (1961).

Morris, J., & McCoubrey, H., *Regional Peacekeeping in the Post-Cold War Era*, 6 International Peacekeeping 129 (1999).

Murphy, R., *Legal Framework of UN Forces and Issues of Command and Control of Canadian and Irish Forces*, 4 Journal of Armed Conflict Law 41 (1999).

Murphy, R., *UN Peacekeeping in Lebanon and the Use of Force*, 6 International Peacekeeping 38 (1999).

Naldi, G., *Peace-keeping Attempts by the Organisation of African Unity*, 34 International & Comparative Law Quarterly 593 (1985).

O'Brien, D., *The Search for Subsidiarity: The UN, African Regional Organizations and Humanitarian Action*, 7 International Peacekeeping 57 (2000).

O'Donnell, D., *Trends in the Application of International Humanitarian Law by United Nations Human Rights Mechanisms*, 38 International Review of the Red Cross 481 (1998).

Oosthuizen, G., *Playing the Devil's Advocate: the United Nations Security Council is Unbound by Law*, 12 Leiden Journal of International Law 549 (1999).

Oosting, M., *The National Ombudsman of the Netherlands and Human Rights*, 12 International Ombudsman Journal 1 (1994).

Orakhelashvili, A., *The Legal Basis of United Nations Peace-keeping Operations*, 43 Virginia Journal Of International Law 485 (2003).

Palmisano, G., *Les Garanties de Non-Répétition entre Codification et Réalisation Juridictionnelle du Droit: A Propos de l'Affaire Lagrand*, 106 Revue Générale de Droit International Public 753 (2002).

Palwankar, U., *Measures Available to States for Fulfilling their Obligation to Ensure Respect for International Humanitarian Law*, 76 International Review of the Red Cross 9 (1994).

Palwankar, U., *Applicability of International Humanitarian Law to United Nations Peacekeeping Forces*, 75 International Review of the Red Cross 227 (1993).

Panjabi, R., *Terror at the Emperor's Birthday Party: An Analysis of the Hostage-Taking Incident at the Japanese Embassy in Lima, Peru*, 16 Dickinson Journal of International Law 1 (1997).

Paphiti, A., *Rules of Engagement within Multinational Land Operations*, 89 Militair Rechtelijk Tijdschrift 1 (1996).

Pastor Ridruejo, J., *Les Procédures Spéciales de la Commission des Droits de l'Homme des Nations Unies*, 228 Recueil des Cours (1991-III).

Pellet, A., *L'Imputabilité d'Éventuels Actes Illicites Responsabilité de l'OTAN ou des États Membres*, in C. Tomuschat (Ed.), Kosovo and the International Community 193 (2002).

Perez Gonzalez, M., *Les Organisations Internationales et le Droit de la Responsabilité*, 92 Revue Générale de Droit International Public 63 (1988).

Pescatore, P., *Les Relations Extérieures des Communautés Européennes*, 103 Recueil des Cours (1966-II).

Prescott, J., *Claims*, in D. Fleck (Ed.), The Handbook of the Law of Visiting Forces 159 (2001).

Przetacznik, F., *La Responsabilité Internationale de l'État à Raison des Préjudices de Caractère Moral et Politique Causés à un Autre État*, 78 Revue Générale de Droit International Public 919 (1974).

Provost, R., *Starvation as a Weapon: Legal Implications of the United Nations Food Blockade against Iraq and Kuwait*, 30 Columbia Journal of Transnational Law 577 (1992).

Rawski, F., *To Waive or Not to Waive: Immunity and Accountability in U.N. Peacekeeping Operations*, 18 Connecticut Journal of International Law 103 (2002).

Reichard, M., *Some Legal Issues Concerning the EU-NATO Berlin Plus Agreements*, 73 Nordic Journal of International Law 37 (2004).

Reif, L., *Building Democratic Institutions: The Role of National Human Rights Institutions in Good Governance and Human Rights Protection*, 13 Harvard Human Rights Journal 1 (2000).

Reinisch, A., *Governance Without Accountability?*, 44 German Yearbook of International Law 270 (2002).

Reinisch, A., *Developing Human Rights and Humanitarian Law Accountability of the Security Council for the Imposition of Economic Sanctions*, 95 American Journal of International Law 851 (2001).

Reinisch, A., *Securing the Accountability of International Organizations*, 7 Global Governance 131 (2001).

Reisman, M., *The Constitutional Crisis in the United Nations*, 87 American Journal of International Law 83 (1993).

Reuter, P., *Sur Quelques Limites du Droit des Organisations Internationales*, in E. Diez, J. Monnier, J. Müller, H. Reimann and L. Wildhaber (Eds.), Festschrift für Rudolf

Bindschedler, Botschafter, Professor Dr. Iur. Zum 65. Geburtstag 8. Juli 1980, 491 (1980).

Rigo, A., *Process Integrity and Institutional Independence in International Organizations: The Inspection Panel and the Sanctions Committee of the World Bank*, in L. Boisson de Chazournes, C. Romano & R. Mackenzie (Eds.), International Organizations and International Dispute Settlement: Trends and Prospects 165 (2002).

Ritter, J.P., *La protection Diplomatique à l'Egard d'une Organisation Internationale*, 8 Annuaire Français de Droit International 427 (1962).

Roberts, A., *The Crisis in UN Peacekeeping*, 36 Survival 93 (1994).

Roberts, A., *What is a Military Occupation*, 55 British Yearbook of International Law 250 (1984).

Ruffert, M., *The Administration of Kosovo and East-Timor by the International Community*, 50 International & Comparative Law Quarterly 613 (2001).

Rüth, A., & Trilsch, M., *Case Report: Banković* v. *Belgium*, 97 American Journal of International Law 168 (2003).

Ryan, A., *The Strong Lead-nation Model in an ad hoc Coalition of the Willing: Operation Stabilise in East Timor*, 9 International Peacekeeping 23 (2002).

Ryan, S., *United Nations Peace-keeping: A Matter of Principles?*, in T. Woodhouse & O. Ramsbotham (Eds.), Peacekeeping and Conflict Resolution 27 (2000).

Ryniker, A., *Respect du Droit International Humanitaire par les Forces des Nations Unies*, 81 International Review of the Red Cross 795 (1999).

Sachariew, K., *States' Entitlement to Take Action to Enforce International Humanitarian Law*, 29 International Review of the Red Cross 177 (1989).

Sadurska, R., & Chinkin, C., *The Collapse of the International Tin Council: A Case of State Responsibility?* 30 Virginia Journal of International Law 845 (1989).

Salmon, J., *Immunités et Actes de la Fonction*, 38 Annuaire Français de Droit International 314 (1992).

Salmon, J., *De Quelques Problèmes Posés aux Tribunaux Belges par les Actions des Citoyens Belges contre l'O.N.U. en Raison des Faits Survenus sur le Territoire de la République Démocratique du Congo*, 81 Journal des Tribunaux 713 (1966).

Salmon, J., *Les Accords Spaak-U Thant du 20 Février 1965*, 11 Annuaire Français de Droit International 468 (1965).

Sams, K., & Berman, E., *Regional Peacekeeping in Africa*, 3 Conflict Trends 50 (2001).

Sassòli, M., *State Responsibility for Violations of International Humanitarian Law*, 84 International Review of the Red Cross 401 (2002).

Scelle, G., *Le Phénomène Juridique du Dédoublement Fonctionnel*, in W. Schätzel & H.J. Slochauer (Eds.), Rechtsfragen der Internationalen Organisation: Festschrift für Hans Wehberg zu seinem 70. Geburtstag 324 (1956).

Scelle, G., *Théorie et Pratique de la Fonction Exécutive en Droit International*, 55 Recueil des Cours (1936).

Schachter, O., *United Nations Law in the Gulf Conflict*, 85 American Journal of International Law 452 (1991).

Scheffer, D., *Staying the Course with the International Criminal Court*, 35 Cornell International Law Journal 47 (2002).

Scheffer, D., *Problems and Prospects for UN Peacekeeping*, 89 ASIL Proc. 285 (1995).

Schermers, H., *Liability of International Organizations*, 1 Leiden Journal of International Organizations 3 (1988).

Schindler, D., *United Nations Forces and International Humanitarian Law*, in C. Swinarski (Ed.), Etudes et Essais sur le Droit International Humanitaire et sur les Principes de la Croix-Rouge en l'Honneur de Jean Pictet 521 (1984).

Schindler, D., *The Different Types of Armed Conflicts According to the Geneva Conventions and Protocols*, 163 Recueil des Cours (1979-II).

Schlemmer-Schulte, S., *The World Bank's Experience With Its Inspection Panel*, 58 Zeitschrift für ausländisches öffentliches Recht und Völkerrecht 353 (1998).

Schlemmer-Schulte, S., & Bradlow, D., *The World Bank's New Inspection Panel: A Constructive Step in the Transformation of the International Legal Order*, 54 Zeitschrift für ausländisches öffentliches Recht und Völkerrecht 405 (1994).

Schmidl, E., *The Evolution of Peace Operations from the Nineteenth Century*, in E. Schmidl (Ed.), Peace Operations between War and Peace 4 (2000).

Schrijver, N., *Introducing Second Generation Peace-keeping: the case of Namibia*, 6 African Journal of International and Comparative Law 1 (1994).

Schrijver, N., *The Use of Economic Sanctions by the United Nations Security Council: An International Law Perspective*, in H. Post (Ed.), International Economic Law and Armed Conflict 123 (1994).

Schwarzenberger, G., *Legal Effects of Illegal War*, in K. Zemanek (Ed.), Völkerrecht und Rechtliches Weltbilt, Festschrift für Alfred Verdross 243 (1960).

Scobbie, I., *International Responsibility*, in R.J. Dupuy (Ed.), Manuel sur les Organisations Internationales 886 (1998).

Scott, S., *Legality in a Collapsed State: The Somali Experience*, 45 International & Comparative Law Quarterly 910 (1996).

Seidl-Hohenveldern, I., *Liability of Member States for Acts or Omissions of an International Organization*, in S. Schlemmer-Schulte & K-Y. Tung (Eds.), Liber Amicorum Ibrahim F.I. Shihata: International Finance and Development Law 727 (2001).

Seidl-Hohenveldern, I., *Piercing the Corporate Veil of International Organizations: The International Tin Council Case in the English Court of Appeals*, 32 German Yearbook of International Law 43 (1980).

Seyersted, F., *Objective International Personality of Intergovernmental Organizations*, 34 Nordisk Tidsskrift for International Ret 1 (1964).

Sharp, W., Jr., *Protecting the Avatars of International Peace and Security*, 7 Duke Journal of Comparative & International Law 93 (1996).

Shaw, J., *The Interpretation of European Union Citizenship*, 61 Modern Law Review 293 (1998).

Shaw, M., *The Security Council and the International Court of Justice: Judicial Drift and Judicial Function*, in A. Muller, D. Raič & H. Thuránsky (Eds.), The International Court of Justice: Its Future after Fifty Years 219 (1997).

Shelton, D., *Righting Wrongs: Reparations in the Articles on State Responsibility*, 96 American Journal of International Law 833 (2002).

Shraga, D., *UN Peacekeeping Operations: Applicability of International Humanitarian Law and Responsibility for Operations-Related Damage*, 94 American Journal of International Law 406 (2000).

Shraga, D., *The United Nations as an Actor Bound by International Humanitarian Law*, 5 International Peacekeeping 64 (1998).

Sicilianos, L.A., *The Classification of Obligations and the Multilateral Dimension of the Relations of International Responsibility*, 13 European Journal of International Law 1127 (2002).

Sicilianos, L.A., *L'Autorisation par le Conseil de Securité de Recourir à la Force: Une Tentative d'Evaluation,* 106 Revue Générale de Droit International Public 5 (2002).

Sicilianos, L.A., *Classification des Obligations et Dimension Multilatérale de la Responsabilité Internationale*, in P.M. Dupuy (Ed.), Obligations Multilaterales, Droit Impératif et Responsabilité Internationale des Etats 57 (2003).

Siekmann, R., *The Fall of Srebrenica and the Attitude of Dutchbat from an International Legal Perspective*, 1 Yearbook of International Humanitarian Law 301 (1998).

Simons, A., & Vandenberghe, B., *Der Fall der UN "Safe Area" Srebrenica und die Rolle des niederländischen Bataillons Dutchbat – Eine Zusammenfassung der niederländischen Untersuchungen*, 61 Zeitschrift für ausländisches öffentliches Recht und Völkerrecht 681 (2001).

Siordet, F., *Commentaire de l'Article 3 de la IIIe Convention de Genève*, 40 International Review of the Red Cross 644 (1958).

Slaughter, A.M., *The Accountability of Government Networks*, 8 Indiana Journal of Global Legal Studies 347 (2001).

Sorel, J.M., *La Responsabilité des Nations Unies dans les Opérations de Maintien de la Paix*, 3 International Law Forum 127 (2001).

Spieker, H, *The International Criminal Court and Non-International Armed Conflicts*, 13 Leiden Journal of International Law 395 (2000).

Spieker, H., *Changing "Peacekeeping" in the New Millennium? – The Recommendations of the Panel on United Nations Peace Operations of August 2000*, 6 International Peacekeeping 144 (2000).

Spinedi, M., *From One Codification to Another: Bilateralism and Multilateralism in the Genesis of the Law of Treaties and the Law of State Responsibility*, 13 European Journal of International Law 1099 (2002).

Stahn, C., *The Ambiguities of Security Council Resolution 1422*, 14 European Journal of International Law 85 (2003).

Stahn, C., *The United Nations Transitional Administrations in Kosovo and East Timor: A First Analysis*, 5 Max Planck Yearbook of United Nations Law 105 (2001).

Stein, E. & Carreau, D., *Law and Peaceful Change in a Subsystem: "Withdrawal" of France from the North Atlantic Treaty Organization*, 62 American Journal of International Law 577 (1968).

Stein, T., *Kosovo and the International Community. The Attribution of Possible International Wrongful Acts: Responsibility of NATO or of its Member States?*, in C. Tomuschat (Ed.), Kosovo and the International Community 181 (2002).

Stephan, P., *Legitimacy, Accountability, Authority, and Freedom in the New Global Order*, 70 University of Colorado Law Review 1555 (1999).

Stern, B., *Et Si l'On Utilisait le Concept de Préjudice Juridique? Retour sur une Notion Délaissée à l'Occasion de la Fin des Travaux de la CDI sur la Responsabilité des Etats*, 47 Annuaire Français de Droit International 3 (2002).

Suy, E., *Legal Aspects of UN Peace-keeping Operations*, 35 Netherlands International Law Review 318 (1988).

Sybesma-Knol, N., *The Indispensable Parties Rule in the East Timor Case*, in E. Denters & N. Schrijver (Eds.), Reflections on International Law from the Low Countries: In Honour of Paul de Waart 442 (1998).

Teitel, R., *Humanity's Law: Rule of Law for the New Global Politics*, 35 Cornell International Law Journal 355 (2002).

Tharoor, S., *The Changing Face of Peace-keeping and Peace-enforcement*, 19 Fordham International Law Journal 408 (1995).

Thonton, R., *The Role of Peace Support Operations Doctrine in the British Army*, 7 International Peacekeeping 41 (2000).

Thouvenin, J.M., *Le Statut des Forces de Maintien de la Paix des Nations Unies*, 3 International Law Forum 105 (2001).

Thwaites, M.J., *Negotiating a Convention on the Safety of UN Personnel*, in H. Smith (Ed.), International Peacekeeping; Building on the Cambodian Experience 169 (1994).

Tittemore, B., *Belligerents in Blue Helmets: Applying International Humanitarian Law to United Nations Peace Operations*, 33 Stanford Journal of International Law 61 (1997).

Torres Bernárdez, S., *The New Theory of "Indispensable Parties" Under the Statute of the International Court of Justice*, in K. Wellens (Ed.), International Law: Theory and Practice: Essays in Honour of Eric Suy 737 (1998).

Trilsch, M., & Rüth, A., *Case Report: Banković v. Belgium*, 97 American Journal of International Law 168 (2003).

Visscher, P., de., Rapport définitif, Les Conditions d'application des Lois de la Guerre aux Opérations Militaires des Nations Unies, Annuaire IDI 54-I (1971) 116.

Visscher, P., de., Rapport préliminaire, Les Conditions d'application des Lois de la Guerre aux Opérations Militaires des Nations Unies, Annuaire IDI 54-I (1971) 45.

Visscher, P., de., *Observations sur le Fondement et la Mise en Oeuvre du Principe de la Responsabilité de l'Organisation des Nations Unies*, 23 Annales de Droit et de Sciences Politiques 133 (1963).

Vité, S., *L'Applicabilité du Droit International de l'Occupation Militaire aux Activités des Organisations Internationales*, 86 International Review of the Red Cross 9 (2004).

Vohra, S., *Impartiality in United Nations Peace-Keeping*, 9 Leiden Journal of International Law 63 (1996).

Vradenburgh, A., *The Chapter VII Powers of the United Nations Charter: Do They "Trump" Human Rights Law?*, 14 Loyola of Los Angeles International and Comparative Law Journal 175 (1991).

Waters, C., *Human Rights in an International Protectorate: Kosovo's Ombudsman*, 4 The International Ombudsman Yearbook 141 (2000).

Weissbrodt, D., *The Role of International Organizations in the Implementation of Human Rights and Humanitarian Law in Situations of Armed Conflict*, 21 Vanderbilt Journal of Transnational Law 313 (1988).

Wermester, K., & Malone, D., *The Changing Nature of UN Peacekeeping*, 7 International Peacekeeping 37 (2000).

Weston, B.H., *Security Council Resolution 678 and Persian Gulf Decision Making: Precarious Legitimacy*, 85 American Journal of International Law 516 (1991).

Wet, E., de., *The Relationship between the Security Council and Regional Organizations during Enforcement Action under Chapter VII of the United Nations Charter*, 71 Nordic Journal of International Law 1 (2002).

Wet, E., de., *Human Rights Limitations to Economic Enforcement Measures under Article 41 of the United Nations Charter and the Iraqi Sanctions Regime*, 14 Leiden Journal of International Law 277 (2001).

Weyemberg, A., *La Notion de Conflit Armé, le Droit International Humanitaire et les Forces des Nations Unies en Somalie (A Propos de l'Arrêt de la Cour Militaire du 17 décembre 1997)*, 79 Revue de Droit Pénal et de Criminologie 177 (1999).

White, N., *Commentary on the Report of the Panel on United Nations Peace Operations (The Brahimi report)*, 6 Journal of Conflict and Security Law 127 (2001).

White, N., *The UN Charter and Peacekeeping Forces: Constitutional Issues*, in M. Pugh (Ed.), The UN, Peace and Force 43 (1997).

White, N., *Accountability and Democracy Within the United Nations: A Legal Perspective*, 13 International Relations 1 (1997).

Wickremasinghe, C., & Verdirame, G., *Responsibility and Liability for Violations of Human Rights in the Course of UN Field Operations*, in C. Scott (Ed.), Torture as Tort: Comparative Perspectives on the Development of Transnational Human Rights Litigation 465 (2001).

Wilde, R., *Accountability and International Actors in Bosnia and Herzegovina, Kosovo and East Timor*, 7 ILSA Journal of International & Comparative Law 455 (2001).

Wittich, S., *The ILC's Articles on the Responsibility of States for Internationally Wrongful Acts Adopted on Second Reading*, 15 Leiden Journal of International Law 891 (2002).

Yeng-Seng, W., *Le Médiateur Européen; Artisan du Développement du Droit à une Bonne Administration Communautaire*, 15 Revue Trimestrielle des Droits de l'Homme 527 (2004).

Zacklin, R., *United Nations Management of Legal Issues*, in J. Howard & B. Oswald (Eds.), The Rule of Law on Peace Operations 155 (2002).

Zappalà, S., *Are Some Peacekeepers Better than Others? UN Security Council Resolution 1497 (2003) and the ICC*, 1 Journal of International Criminal Justice 671 (2003).

Zegveld, L., *Remedies for Victims of Violations of International Humanitarian Law*, 85 International Review of the Red Cross 497 (2003).

Zegveld, L., *The Inter-American Commission on Human Rights and International Humanitarian Law: A comment on the Tablada Case*, 38 International Review of the Red Cross 505 (1998).

Zwanenburg, M., *The Secretary-General's Bulletin on Observance by United Nations Forces of International Humanitarian Law*, 39 Military Law and Law of War Review 14 (2000).

Index

International Humanitarian Law Series

1 Michael J. Kelly, *Restoring and Maintaining Order in Complex Peace Operations: The Search for a Legal Framework*, 1999 ISBN 90 411 1179 4

2 Helen Durham and Timothy L.H. McCormack (eds.), *The Changing Face of Conflict and the Efficacy of International Humanitarian Law*, 1999 ISBN 90 411 1180 8

3 Richard May, David Tolbert, John Hocking, Ken Roberts, Bing Bing Jia, Daryl Mundis and Gabriël Oosthuizen (eds.), *Essays on ICTY Procedure and Evidence in Honour of Gabrielle Kirk McDonald*, 2001 ISBN 90 411 1482 3

4 Elizabeth Chadwick, *Traditional Neutrality Revisited:Law, Theory and Case Studies*, 2002 ISBN 90 411 1787 3

5 Lal Chand Vohrah, Fausto Pocar, Yvonne Featherstone, Olivier Fourmy, Christine Graham, John Hocking and Nicholas Robson (eds.), *Man's Inhumanity to Man: Essays on International Law in Honour of Antonio Cassese*, 2003 ISBN 90 411 1986 8

6 Gideon Boas and William A. Schabas (eds.), *International Criminal Law Developments in the Case Law of the ICTY*, 2003 ISBN 90 411 1987 6

7 Karen Hulme, *War Torn Environment: Interpreting the Legal Threshold*, 2004 ISBN 90 04 13848 X

8 Helen Durham and Tracey Gurd (eds.), *Listening to the Silences: Women and War*, 2005 ISBN 90 04 14365 3

9 Marten Zwanenburg, *Accountability of Peace Support Operations*, 2005 ISBN 90 04 14350 5